A Short Practical Russian Grammar

И. Милославский

Краткая практическая грамматика русского языка

Москва
«Русский язык»
1988

I. Miloslavsky

A Short Practical Russian Grammar

Russky Yazyk Publishers
Moscow
1988

ББК 81.2Р—96
М—60

Translated from the Russian by *V. Korotky*
Cover designed by *A. Oreshin*

Reviewers:
Chair of Russian for Foreign Students, the Moscow Lenin Teacher Training College; Head of the Chair: Prof. *L. A. Deribas*, Cand. Sc. (Philology)
T. M. Dorofeyeva, Cand. Sc. (Philology), Senior Lecturer, the Pushkin Russian Language Institute

ISBN 5-200-00038-6

© Издательство «Русский язык» 1987, перевод на английский язык 1988

CONTENTS
Introduction

1. The subject of grammar 14
2. Words in a dictionary and in a text 14
3. How a grammar for a reader (listener) differs from that for a writer (speaker) 14
4. The scope of the facts dealt with in this grammar 15
5. How to use this grammar 16

Part I. RUSSIAN WORDS. THEIR CLASSES AND GRAMMATICAL CHARACTERISTICS

1. What words are nouns? 18

1.1. Division of nouns according to gender 18
1.2. Number as a characteristic of noun forms 19
1.3. Case as a characteristic of noun forms 19
1.4. Grammatical peculiarities of the nouns 20

2. What words are adjectives? 21

2.1. The long and short forms as characteristics of adjectives 21
2.2. Gender as a characteristic of adjectival forms 21
2.3. Number as a characteristic of adjectival forms 22
2.4. Case as a characteristic of adjectival forms 22
2.5. Grammatical peculiarities of the adjectives 22

3. What words are numerals? 22

3.1. Case as a characteristic of numerals 23

4. What words are pronouns? 23

4.1. How pronominal nouns differ from ordinary nouns 23
4.2. How pronominal adjectives differ from ordinary adjectives . . . 23
4.3. Pronominal numerals and adverbs 24
4.4. Grammatical peculiarities of the pronominal words 24

5. What words are verbs? 24

5.1. Finite and non-finite verb forms 24
5.2. The differences between perfective and imperfective verbs . . . 25
5.3. What is voice? 25
5.3.1. Do all the verbs have both voice forms? 26
5.4. What is verb mood? 26
5.5. What is tense? 27
5.6. Person in verb forms 27
5.6.1. Person in indicative mood verbs 28
5.6.2. Person in imperative mood verbs 28
5.6.3. Verbs which do not have all the persons 28
5.7. Number in verb forms 28
5.8. Gender in verb forms 29
5.9. Case and the short/long form in verbs 29
5.10. Grammatical peculiarities of the verbs 29

6. The unchangeable words 36

6.1. The adverb 36
6.2. Prepositions 36

6.3. Conjunctions 37
6.4. Particles 37
6.5. Interjections 38

Part II. "FROM THE FORM TO THE MEANING" GRAMMAR

A. DETERMINATION OF THE GRAMMATICAL CHARACTERISTICS OF A WORD

A.1. DETERMINATION OF THE GRAMMATICAL CHARACTERISTICS OF A WORD BY ITS TERMINATION

1. Grammatical characteristics of words ending in -а/-я 39
2. Grammatical characteristics of words ending in -и/-ы 43
3. Grammatical characteristics of words ending in -е 46
4. Grammatical characteristics of words ending in -у/-ю 50
5. Grammatical characteristics of words ending in -о/-ё 51
6. Grammatical characteristics of words ending in -й 55
7. Grammatical characteristics of words ending in -ь 56
8. Grammatical characteristics of words ending in -м 58
9. Grammatical characteristics of words ending in -т 62
10. Grammatical characteristics of words ending in -в 62
11. Grammatical characteristics of words ending in -л 64
12. Grammatical characteristics of words ending in -х 65
13. Grammatical characteristics of words ending in -с 66
14. Grammatical characteristics of words ending in -н 69
15. Grammatical characteristics of words ending in -к 69
16. Grammatical characteristics of words ending in -г 70
17. Grammatical characteristics of words ending in -ш 70
18. Grammatical characteristics of words ending in -б, -п, -з, -р, -д, -ж, -ч, -щ, -ф or -ц 72

A.2. DETERMINATION OF THE GRAMMATICAL CHARACTERISTICS OF A WORD BY THE PRESENCE OF OTHER WORDS IN THE SENTENCE 75

1.1. How to distinguish nouns of different numbers and cases ending in -а or -я 77
1.2. How to distinguish nouns of different numbers and cases ending in -и or -ы 78
1.3. How to distinguish nouns of different cases ending in -е after a consonant 79
1.4. How to distinguish nouns of different cases ending in -у or -ю . 79
1.5. How to distinguish nouns in the nominative and the accusative ending in -о or -ё 80
1.6. How to distinguish nouns of different numbers and cases ending in -й 80
1.7. How to distinguish nouns of different cases and numbers ending in -ь 80
1.8. How to distinguish nouns of different cases and numbers ending in -т, -в, -л, -с, -н, -к, -г, -б, -п, -з, -р, -д, -ж, -ч, -ш, -щ, -ф, -ц . . . 80
1.9. How to distinguish nouns of different cases and numbers ending in -м 81
1.10. How to distinguish nouns of different cases and numbers ending in -х 81
2.1. How to distinguish nouns ending in -и and verb forms ending in -и in the past tense plural indicative mood, in the subjunctive plural, and in the imperative singular 81
2.2. How to distinguish nouns ending in -у or -ю and verb forms ending in -у or -ю in the 1st person singular present/future tense 82
2.3. How to distinguish nouns ending in -й and imperative verb forms ending in -й 82
2.4. How to distinguish nouns ending in -ь and imperative verb forms ending in -ь 82

2.5. How to distinguish nouns ending in -л and past tense and subjunctive mood verb forms 82
3.1. How to distinguish adjectives (and participles) and nouns declined like adjectives 82
3.2. How to distinguish nouns ending in a consonant, short-form adjectives and participles, and masculine past tense and subjunctive mood verb forms 83
3.3. How to distinguish nouns ending in -а or -я and feminine short-form adjectives and participles 83
3.4. How to distinguish nouns ending in -о or -е and neuter short-form adjectives and participles, and adverbs 83
3.5. How to distinguish nouns ending in -и or -ы and short-form adjectives and participles in the plural 83

A.3. DETERMINATION OF THE GRAMMATICAL CHARACTERISTICS OF A WORD BY THE END OF THE STEM 83
1. What stems ending in a vowel may indicate 84
2. What stems ending in -к may indicate 84
3. What stems ending in -н may indicate 86
4. What stems ending in -т may indicate 88
5. What stems ending in -в may indicate 89
6. What stems ending in -х, -ц, -ч, -ш, -щ may indicate 90
7. What stems ending in -б, -д, -л, -м, -р may indicate 92

B. DERIVATION OF THE DICTIONARY FORM OF A WORD
1. The Noun
1.1. How to derive the dictionary form of a noun in the genitive singular 94
1.2. How to derive the dictionary form of a noun in the dative singular 95
1.3. How to derive the dictionary form of a noun in the accusative singular 96
1.4. How to derive the dictionary form of a noun in the instrumental singular 97
1.5. How to derive the dictionary form of a noun in the prepositional singular 98
1.6. How to derive the dictionary form of a noun in the nominative plural 99
1.7. How to derive the dictionary form of a noun in the genitive plural 101
1.8. How to derive the dictionary form of a noun in the accusative plural 103
1.9. How to derive the dictionary form of a noun in the dative, instrumental or prepositional plural 103

2. The Adjective
2.1. How to derive the dictionary form of a long-form adjective in an oblique case singular or plural 104
2.2. How to derive the dictionary form of a short-form adjective . . . 106
2.3. How to derive the dictionary form of an adjective in the comparative degree 106

3. The Verb
3.1. How to derive the dictionary form of a verb in the 1st person singular present tense (of imperfective verbs)/future tense (of perfective verbs) . . . 107
3.2. How to derive the dictionary form of verbs in the 2nd and 3rd persons singular and the 1st, 2nd and 3rd persons plural present tense (of imperfective verbs)/future tense (of perfective verbs) 113
3.3. How to derive the dictionary form of a verb in the imperative . . . 114
3.4. How to derive the dictionary form of an active or passive present participle and of an imperfective verbal adverb 114
3.5. How to derive the dictionary form of a past tense verb in the indicative mood and of a verb in the subjunctive mood 114

3.6. How to derive the dictionary forms of an active past participle and of a perfective verbal adverb 115
3.7. How to derive the dictionary form of a passive past participle . . . 116

C. DETERMINATION OF THE MEANING OF A FORM

1. The Meaning of Noun Endings

1.1. What the singular endings indicate 116
1.2. What the plural endings indicate 117
1.3. What the nominative endings indicate 118
1.4. What the genitive endings indicate 118
1.5. What the dative endings indicate 120
1.6. What the accusative endings indicate 120
1.7. What the instrumental endings indicate 121
1.8. What the prepositional endings indicate 122

2. The Meaning of Adjectival Endings

2.1. What the masculine, feminine and neuter endings indicate 122
2.2. What the singular and plural endings indicate 123
2.3. What the case endings indicate 123
2.4. What the endings of short-form adjectives indicate 123

3. The Meaning of Verb Endings

3.1. What the endings of finite present/future tense indicative mood verb forms indicate 123
3.2. What the endings of finite past tense indicative mood verb forms indicate 126
3.3. What the endings of the finite future tense indicative mood imperfective verb forms indicate 127
3.4. What the endings of finite subjunctive mood verb forms indicate . . 127
3.5. What the endings of finite imperative mood verb forms indicate . . . 127
3.6. What the endings of active participles indicate 128
3.7. What the endings of passive participles indicate 129
3.8. What -ся/-сь, in which verb forms terminate, indicates 129
3.9. What time of an action or state sentences without a finite verb form denote 130

Part III. "FROM THE MEANING TO THE FORM" GRAMMAR

A. DERIVATION OF ALL THE GRAMMATICAL FORMS FROM THE DICTIONARY FORM OF A WORD 131

1. The Noun

1.1.1. How to derive the forms of the overwhelming majority of masculine nouns which have a zero ending (i. e. which end in a consonant, -й or -ь) in the dictionary form 132
1.1.2. What deviations in the set of the endings occur in some masculine nouns 132
1.1.3. What transformations in the stems of masculine nouns occur in the forms of both numbers 136
1.1.4. What transformations in the stems of masculine nouns occur in the plural 136
1.1.5. Nouns in which prepositional and locative case forms are distinguished 137
1.2.1. How to derive the forms of the overwhelming majority of the nouns whose dictionary form ends in -а/-я 137
1.2.2. What deviations in the set of the endings occur in some nouns whose dictionary form ends in -а/-я 138
1.2.3. What transformations occur in the stems of the nouns whose dictionary form ends in -а/-я 138
1.3.1. How to derive the forms of feminine nouns whose dictionary form ends in -ь 138

1.4.1. How to derive the forms of neuter nouns whose dictionary form ends in -о/-е 141
1.4.2. What deviations in the set of the endings occur in some nouns whose dictionary form ends in -о/-е 144
1.4.3. What transformations occur in the stems of the nouns whose dictionary form ends in -о/-е 144
1.5. How to derive the forms of the nouns whose dictionary form ends in -мя 144
1.6. How to derive the forms of other nouns 145

2. The Adjective

2.1.1. How to derive the long forms of adjectives 145
2.1.2. How to derive the short forms of adjectives 145
2.2. How to derive the forms of the possessive adjectives whose dictionary form ends in -ин/-ын, -ов/-ев/-ёв or -ий 148
2.3. Nouns whose forms are derived in the same way as those of some adjectives 148
2.4. How to derive the comparative degree of an adjective 149

3. Pronouns

3.1 How to derive the forms of the pronouns я, ты, мы, вы, кто, что and себя 150
3.2. How to derive the forms of the pronouns он, она́, оно́, они́ with and without a preposition 150
3.3. How to derive the forms of the pronouns никто́, ничто́, не́кого, не́чего, друг дру́га, не́кто, не́что with and without a preposition 150
3.4. How to derive the forms of the pronouns э́тот, тот, оди́н, сам, весь, наш, ваш, мой, твой, свой, чей, ниче́й 151
3.5. How to derive the forms of the pronouns whose dictionary form ends in -ый/-ий/-ой of the type ка́ждый, вся́кий, тако́й 151

4. The Numeral

4.1. How to derive the forms of the cardinal numerals from 1 to 4 . . . 151
4.2. How to derive the forms of the cardinal numerals from 5 to 20 and also 30, 50, 60, 70 and 80 153
4.3. How to derive the forms of the cardinal numerals 40, 90, 100 and полтора́ста 153
4.4. How to derive the forms of the names of the hundreds 153
4.5. How to derive the forms of the collective numerals and of the numerals ско́лько, не́сколько, сто́лько; мно́го and немно́го 153

5. The Verb

5.1 What grammatical forms can be derived from the dictionary forms of transitive and intransitive perfective and imperfective verbs 154
5.2. What grammatical forms can be derived directly from the infinitive 156
5.2.1. How to derive finite past tense forms 156
5.2.2. How to derive subjunctive mood forms 157
5.2.3. How to derive the forms of active past participles 157
5.2.4. How to derive the forms of passive past participles 158
5.2.5. How to derive the forms of perfective verbal adverbs 158
5.3. What correlations exist between the infinitive stem and the stem of the present tense (of imperfective verbs)/future tense (of perfective verbs) . . . 159
5.3.1. What regular differences in the final consonants there are between the infinitive stem and the stem of the present tense (of imperfective verbs)/future tense (of perfective verbs) forms 159
5.3.2. What vowel—zero alternations there are in the infinitive stem and the stem of the present tense (of imperfective verbs)/future tense (of perfective verbs) forms 165
5.4. What grammatical forms can be derived from the present tense (of imperfective verbs)/future tense (of perfective verbs) stem 166

5.4.1. How to derive the finite present tense (of imperfective verbs)/future tense (of perfective verbs) forms 166
5.4.2. How to derive the finite future tense forms of imperfective verbs . 167
5.4.3. How to derive the imperative mood forms 167
5.4.4. How to derive the forms of active present participles 168
5.4.5. How to derive the forms of imperfective verbal adverbs 168
5.4.6. How to derive the forms of passive present participles 169
5.4.7. The cases when the forms of passive past participles are derived from the present/future tense stem 169
5.5. How to derive the finite passive voice verb forms 170

6. The Adverb. How to derive the comparative degree 170

B. HOW TO CHARACTERISE AN OBJECT OR PERSON, OR AN ACTION OR STATE BY MEANS OF SENTENCES CONTAINING A MINIMAL NUMBER OF WORDS

1. Sentences Characterising an Object or Person 170
1.1. How to characterise an object or person through its/his action . . 171
1.2. How to characterise an object or person through its/his features (properties) 171
1.3. How to characterise an object or person through its/his state . 172
1.4. How to report the existence (presence) or non-existence (absence) of an object 173
1.5. How to report the existence (presence) of a certain quantity of an object (objects) 174

2. Sentences Characterising an Action or State 175

C. WHAT MEANINGS CAN BE EXPRESSED BY GRAMMATICAL MEANS AND HOW THEY CAN BE EXPRESSED

1. How to express the relation between an action and reality with the help of verb moods and other means 177
1.1. How to express an action actually taking place 177
1.2. How to express a desirable action 178
1.3. How to express the possibility or impossibility of performing an action 179
1.4. How to express the necessity of performing an action 180
1.5. How to express a supposed action 182

2. How to express the participant in a communication who is the performer of a real action by means of verb person and other means 183
2.1. How to express the fact that the performer of an action is the speaker 184
2.2. How to express the fact that the performer of an action is the listener 184

3. How to express negation 184
3.1. The most usual way of expressing negation 184
3.2. How to strengthen a negation 185

4. How to express relations between the performer and the object acted upon 186
4.1. How to express the performer 186
4.2. How to express the object acted upon 187
4.2.1. How to express the object directly acted upon 187
4.2.2. How to express the object which is the "receiver" of an action . . 189
4.2.3. How to express the instrument, means or device wherewith an action is performed 190

5. How to express circumstantial characteristics by means of noun case and preposition-cum-case forms 190
5.1. How to express spatial characteristics 190
5.1.1.1. How to express the position of an object or person inside some space 190

5.1.1.2. How to express the position of an object or person outside some space 191
5.1.2.1. How to express the movement of an object away from a reference-point 193
5.1.2.2. How to express the movement of an object or person towards a reference-point 193
5.1.2.3. How to express the movement of an object or person along a route 194
5.2. How to express temporal characteristics 194
5.2.1. How to express the time of an action with respect to the moment of speaking 194
5.2.2. How to express the specific time of an action 195
5.2.2.1. How the point of time when an action occurs is usually expressed 195
5.2.2.2. How the time period when an action occurs is usually expressed 196
5.2.2.3. How to express the time during which an action occurs . . . 197
5.2.2.4. How to express an action occurring periodically 198
5.2.3. How to express the time of an action in relation to another action or event 199
5.2.3.1. How to express the time of the action which follows some event 199
5.2.3.2. How to express the time for which an action or event is planned 199
5.2.3.3. How to express the time of an action preceding another action or event 200
5.3. How to express the reason for an action or state with the help of noun preposition-cum-case forms and other means 201
5.4. How to express the purpose of an action with the help of noun preposition-cum-case forms and other means 202

6. How to modify the action or state expressed by a verb with the help of prefixes and other means 203

6.1. How to express single and repeated actions 204
6.2. How to express the result of an action 205
6.3. How to express the direction of an action in space 205
6.4. How to express the phasal characteristics of an action 207
6.5. How to express the relation between two actions 207
6.6. How to express various degrees of the intensity of an action . . . 207

7. How to modify the meaning of a person or object denoted by a noun with the help of adjectival gender forms, noun number forms and other means 208

7.1. How to express the sex of a living being 208
7.1.1. How to express the female sex of a living being 208
7.1.2. How to express the male sex of a living being 209
7.1.3. How to leave the sex characteristic of a living being unspecified 209
7.2. How to express a quantity of objects or persons 210
7.2.1. How to express a plurality of objects or persons 210
7.2.2. How to express a single object or person 211

8. How to express a feature or attribute of an object or person by means of noun case and preposition-cum-case forms 212

8.1. How to express the degrees of a quality or property 214

9. How to express in Russian the meanings expressed in other languages by grammatical means 215

9.1. How to express the definiteness or indefiniteness of an object or person 215
9.2. How to express the contrast between an action performed at a specific moment and an action performed habitually 216
9.3. How to express the sequence of actions preceding or following the moment of speaking 217

D. WHAT FORMAL RULES SHOULD BE FOLLOWED WHEN BUILDING A SENTENCE

1. What the form of a verb should be, depending on the grammatical features of the word which denotes the object characterised by the verb . . . 218

2.1. What the form of the adjectives and participles which qualify nouns should be 218
2.2. What the form of the words один, два, оба and полтора should be in combination with a noun 219
2.3. How to determine the gender of a noun from its dictionary form 219
3. What the form of a noun should be in combination with a numeral 220
4. What the form of an adjective or participle characterising an object should be 220
5. What case forms should be used after prepositions 221

E. How to Ask a Question 223

Part IV. HOW TO PRONOUNCE WHAT IS WRITTEN CORRECTLY

1. How to Pronounce Consonants

1.1. How to pronounce consonants at the end of a word and before other consonants 225
1.2. How to pronounce consonants before ь 226
1.3. How to pronounce consonant before vowels 227

2. How to pronounce Vowels

2.1. How to pronounce the vowels represented by the letters а, у, ы, и and э 227
2.2. How to pronounce the vowel represented by the letter о 227
2.3. How to pronounce the vowel represented by the letter ё 227
2.4. How to pronounce the vowel represented by the letter е 227
2.5. How to pronounce the vowel represented by the letter я 228
2.6. How to pronounce the vowel represented by the letter ю 228

3. How to Determine the Position of the Stress in a Word

3.1. How the position of the stress may shift in most nouns 229
3.2. How the position of the stress may shift in adjectives and in nouns declined like adjectives 230
3.3. How the position of the stress shifts in pronouns 231
3.4. How the position of the stress shifts in the derivation of finite verb forms 231
3.5. How the position of the stress shifts in the derivation of participles and verbal adverbs 233
3.6. The cases in which the stress shifts from a noun or numeral to the preposition 234

Part V. HOW TO WRITE DOWN WHAT ONE HEARS CORRECTLY

1. What is written as one word, what as two words and what is hyphenated 236
2. How to carry words from one line to the next 237
3. When to use capital letters 237
4. What letters represent stressed vowel sounds at the beginning of a word and after vowels and consonants, with the exception of [ж], [ш], [ч], [щ] 238
5. What letters represent unstressed vowel sounds after the soft consonants, with the exception of [ч] and [щ] 238
6. What letters represent unstressed vowel sounds after a hard consonant (with the exception of [ж], [ш], [ц]) at the beginning of a word or after a vowel 239
7. What letters represent vowel sounds after the consonants [ж], [ш], [ч], [щ], [ц] 239
8. How to represent voiceless and voiced consonants 240
9. How to represent the long sounds [щщ], [чч], [шш], [жж], the soft [ш'ш'] and some consonant clusters 241
10. How to indicate the softness of a consonant 243
11. How to indicate the sound [й] 243
12. When to write ь after ж, ш, ч, щ 244
13. How to spell adjectival endings in the genitive singular masculine and neuter 244

ABBREVIATIONS

The following abbreviations are used throughout the grammar:

acc., accusative
adj., adjective
adv., adverb
anim., animate
arch., archaic
cf., compare
coll., colloquial
comp., comparative
dat., dative
f., fem., feminine
fut., future
gen., genitive
hist., history
imper., imperative
inanim., inanimate

indic., indicative
instr., instrumental
m., masc., masculine
n., neut., neuter
nom., nominative
part., participle
pass., passive
pers., person
pop., popular
pr., preposition
prep., prepositional
pres., present
refl., reflexive
subj., subjunctive
v., verbal

INTRODUCTION

1. The subject of grammar.

The words of a language, which make up its vocabulary, are described in dictionaries. The rules in accordance with which phrases and sentences consisting of words are built constitute the *grammar* of a language. A description of these rules is also called grammar.

It is obvious that when learning a foreign language one will need not only a dictionary, which describes its vocabulary, but also a grammar book—a compendium of the rules of that language helping us to understand and build sentences and texts in the language.

2. Words in a dictionary and in a text.

A distinctive feature of Russian, as of many other inflectional languages (i. e. languages in which the words have endings) consists in the fact that not every word encountered in a text can be found in a dictionary. The problem is that words are entered in dictionaries in a definite form: nouns in the nominative case (see I, 1.3) singular (see I, 1.2), adjectives in the nominative case (see 2.4) singular (see I, 2.3) masculine (see I, 2.2), and verbs in the infinitive (see I, 5.1). However, in actual texts words may be used both in their dictionary form and in many other forms, the latter differing from the dictionary form both in form and meaning.

The part of a word which remains unchanged in all its forms is traditionally called the *stem*, whereas the part that changes in the different forms of the word is called the *inflection* or *ending*. The ending usually has a form of its own; however, there are such forms of words in which they have only the stem. When a word has other forms with endings, the form without an ending is said to have a *zero ending*.

A dictionary reflects the information contained in the *stem* of a word, whereas grammar deals with the information contained in its *ending*. The information contained in the ending may be of two types. It either only shows that the relevant words in a text *are connected* with one another or adds a certain new, additional *meaning*. Part I of this grammar deals with the forms which the Russian words entered in dictionaries possess and their meanings.

3. How a grammar for a reader (listener) differs from that for a writer (speaker).

As is known, language exists in two forms: oral and written. In oral speech we use sounds which we pronounce and hear, whereas in written speech we use letters which we write and see when we read.

Every beginner in Russian must have a clear idea of his purpose: whether he wants to learn only to read, or to speak and understand spoken Russian, or only to write. But even if he wants to learn the first, the second and the third, he will deal in each case only with one quite specific task.

In order to understand the meaning of a text *when reading*, it is not sufficient to know only the meaning of the words making up sentences, i.e. the information on the words given in a dictionary is insufficient. Besides, to get this information from a dictionary, one must obtain the form entered in the dictionary from the form he has encountered in the text; in other words, one must be able to derive the so-called *primary form* of the word. In order to understand the meaning of the text, it is also necessary to understand the *connections* between the words in the sentence and then the whole sentence itself, for which the information contained in the endings of the words making up this sentence is indispensable.

In order to express an idea, one must be able to *construct a text*. For this, it is not enough to know the dictionary forms of words denoting the relevant objects, qualities, actions, etc. One must also know in what forms these words must be used and how sentences incorporating them should be built in order to express one's idea without violating the rules that exist in the language concerned.

Parts II and III of this grammar are arranged in accordance with the differences between the *receptive* and *reproductive* goals. Part II explains how to infer the grammatical characteristics of a form, how to derive the dictionary form from the form occurring in the text, and how to infer the meanings of the endings of the words used in a text, i.e. the analysis proceeds *from the form to the meaning*. Part III deals with the rules of building such forms of a word which meet the speaker's requirements, i.e. the analysis proceeds *from the meaning to the form*. The fact that this grammar deals only with such quite specific tasks makes it *practical*.

There is a long tradition of describing Russian grammar to native speakers. The description of Russian grammar to foreigners is a relatively new endeavour; however, here, too, definite principles have been evolved and valuable observations have been made. This grammar is an attempt to combine with a practical end in view, on the one hand, the *Русская грамматика* (Moscow, 1980) and the *Грамматический словарь русского языка* by A. A. Zaliznyak (Moscow, 1987) and, on the other, the numerous investigations in grammar "from the meaning" published by teachers of Russian as a foreign language in the 1970's.

4. The scope of the facts dealt with in this grammar.

As is known, Russian dictionaries describe tens of thousands of words pertaining both to the various stylistic layers of Russian and to the numerous spheres of its use. This grammar does not claim to reflect the grammatical peculiarities of all these words; it first of all takes into account the most frequently used Russian words. Besides, grammars usually give not only information about the meanings of words in a text and the rules of building such words, but also detailed information about the phonetic system and the types of derivative words, phrases and sentences. This grammar does not contain comprehensive information about the Russian phonetic system, while all the other information is given in so far as it makes it possible to understand the word forms occurring in a text or build word forms having the required meaning. The distinctive feature of many problems discussed in this grammar consists in the fact that it often gives only a limited list of possible solutions. It is this that makes this grammar a *short* one.

When promoting such a type of speech activity as reading, it is necessary to strive to present grammatical information as comprehensively as possible, irrespective of the frequency of usage. Otherwise, the reader will encounter some "obscure" passages, particularly when dealing with specialised literature or fiction. When promoting the reproductive types of speech activity, it is not at all necessary to give all the methods or variants of formalising the relevant idea in the grammar: it is sufficient to know the simplest or the most frequently used ones. However, there are situations when the little used elements are the simplest to derive or are derived in accordance with a sufficiently often used rule. It is precisely owing to this that if the principles of practicality and brevity clash, the preference is given to practicality when the rule is complicated but covers a wide and useful range of language phenomena, and to brevity when the rule is sufficiently clear and simple but covers a not too wide and not too useful range of facts.

5. How to use this grammar.

A distinctive feature of this grammar is that in it the reader will find definite recommendations as to his actions, depending on the chosen type of speech activity in Russian. However, one should not think that it can to some degree substitute for a textbook, exercise book or—all the more—a dictionary.

If the reader knows the principal concepts of Russian grammar, he may dispense with Part I. If, on the other hand, he has no knowledge of them or his knowledge is vague, Part I may prove to be very useful, although in this case it should not be read through, but only those portions which are necessary to understand more-clearly a certain place in Part II or III.

When reading Russian texts, information should be sought in Part II to infer the possible grammatical characteristic of a word in a text, to derive the form in which this word should be looked up in a dictionary, to clarify the relations existing between this word and the other words in a sentence, and to establish what precise meaning is determined by the given grammatical characteristic of the word with the given lexical content in the sentence concerned. In this case students just learning to read Russian will find Sections A, B and C particularly useful. A Russian teacher will be able to use these sections for drilling the relevant rules.

When creating Russian texts, one should use information from Part III. Here the author of a text, who has a clear idea of what he wants to say, will learn what devices Russian places at his disposal and how the relevant words should be formalised. However, grammar will not always be able to resolve any difficulty that may arise: it will only indicate the sphere of possible resolutions, while the feasibility and appropriateness of each of the possible resolutions must be checked with a dictionary. In other words, grammar either gives a precise solution of one's problem or points to the place in a dictionary one should refer to. This last circumstance is very important, since without a "key" to a dictionary one will be practically unable to find in it the information one seeks in each specific case. It is obvious that a person who has a fairly good command of Russian will refer to a grammar comparatively rarely and only when he has encountered a specific difficulty in understanding or reproducing speech, looking for the answers to his questions in the relevant part of the grammar. On the contrary, a beginner will have to refer to a grammar constantly, often to solve problems having many solutions connected either with the recognition of a form and determining its meaning in context or with the derivation of forms which would express his idea accurately without violating the rules of building Russian sentences. Therefore, depending on his purpose and level, the student may refer to some parts of this grammar and ignore others. Like a dictionary, a practical grammar is not meant to be read through, but to be referred to when specific problems arise.

In each section the user will find references to other parts and sections, designated by relevant numbers and letters, for example: see III C, 5.2.3 or see II A.2, 3.3. The references within one and the same part or section are designated by the word "above" or "below" followed by the relevant number, for example: see above, 5.6.3.

PART I

RUSSIAN WORDS. THEIR CLASSES AND GRAMMATICAL CHARACTERISTICS

Russian words are traditionally divided into *notional*, i.e. words that can be used independently, and *syntactic*, i.e. words that are not used independently, but mainly to connect words and sentences.

Notional words are traditionally divided into the following groups generally called *parts of speech*: **nouns, adjectives, numerals, pronouns, verbs** and **adverbs**. This division is based on the following factors: (1) the most general meaning, and (2) the existence of different forms of words. The adverb differs from the other notional parts of speech in that it has no word forms, which in the case of nouns and adjectives happens very rarely and in the case of numerals and verbs never.

All *syntactic* words are unchangeable and traditionally divided into **prepositions, conjunctions** and **particles**. This division is based on what precise groups of notional words may be connected by means of the relevant syntactic words. **Interjections** constitute a special group. They are also unchangeable.

1. What words are nouns?

Words which are nouns denote objects in the broadest and most general sense of the word.

Nouns may denote specific objects (дом, го́род, у́лица, доро́га, пло́щадь, окно́, кре́сло, по́ле), qualities or properties (доброта́, белизна́, се́рость, тишина́, го́рдость), actions (бег, чте́ние, рисова́ние, убо́рка) or states (о́тдых, сон, ра́дость, согла́сие), expressed as an abstract phenomenon. As a rule, nouns have several meanings; however, they remain precisely nouns in all their meanings and possess definite grammatical characteristics.

1.1. Division of nouns according to gender.

With a few exceptions, all the nouns belong to one of *three genders*: **masculine, feminine** and **neuter**. The gender of a noun determines the form to be taken by the words connected with that noun: adjectives (see 2), pronouns (see 4.2), participles (see 5.1, 5.9), past tense verbs in the indicative mood (see 5.4, 5.5) and verbs in the subjunctive mood (see 5.4): Э́тот большо́й цвету́щий *сад* (masculine noun) был (был бы) ...; Э́та больша́я цвету́щая *я́блоня* (feminine noun) была́ (была́ бы) ...; Э́то большо́е цвету́щее *де́рево* (neuter noun) бы́ло (бы́ло бы) ... .The gender of some nouns which denote living beings conveys their sex: бык — коро́ва, бара́н — овца́, студе́нт — студе́нтка, учи́тель — учи́тельница. Some nouns denoting persons belong to the so-called *common gender*. When they denote males, they behave as masculine nouns, and when they denote females, they behave as feminine nouns: Моя дочь *такая неряха*.— Мой сын *такой неряха*.

The meaning of a noun and the outward "appearance" of its dictionary form do not always predetermine its gender (see also III C, 7.1; III D, 1; D, 2; D, 4).

1.2. Number as a characteristic of noun forms.

All the nouns, except very few, possess *two numbers*. Nouns are generally entered in dictionaries in the nominative (see 1.3) **singular**. From this form the nominative **plural** of the same noun can be derived (дом — дома, стол — столы, дерево — деревья, книга — книги, сын — сыновья, дочь — дочери). There are three exceptions to this rule:

1. Nouns whose meaning is incompatible with the idea of counting (молоко, сметана, счастье, терпение, футбол, строительство) practically do not have the plural.
2. Some nouns, among which there are those whose meaning is incompatible with the idea of counting (хлопоты, сливки, духи) and those whose meaning is not incompatible with the idea of counting (ворота, сани, часы, брюки, весы, ножницы), have only the plural form.
3. Some nouns, whose meaning may or may not be incompatible with the idea of counting (пальто, кино, такси, кенгуру, Токио, Осло), do not change—either for number or for case.

As a rule, the singular of a noun denotes *one* object, and its plural a number of objects, i.e. *more than one* object, and, vice versa, one object is denoted by a singular form and more than one by a plural form. However, this is not always so.

The singular or plural form of a noun determines the form of the words connected with that noun: adjectives (see 2.3), pronouns (see 4.2), participles (see 5.7) and the finite verb forms (see 5.7).

The plural of a noun is derived by replacing the singular ending, including the zero ending (see Introduction, 2) with the plural ending (стол — столы, стена — стены, яблоко — яблоки). When this happens, changes in the stem may occur in addition to the replacement of the ending (кусок — куски, сын — сыновья, цветок — цветы). The ending indicating the number of a noun simultaneously indicates its case (see 1.3).

1.3. Case as a characteristic of noun forms.

All the nouns, with few exceptions, change for case. Taken separately, outside a context, the different case forms of one and the same noun do not differ semantically.[1] However, depending on the word with which any given case form is connected, the latter may either reveal its subordinated or subordinating role with respect to that word or point to the nature of the relations existing between the phenomena in-

---

[1] Forms used as independent sentences and having intonational characteristics may denote either the existence or presence of an object (Дом. Улица. Фонарь. Аптека) or the command or request to make an object available (Машину! Доктора! Тишина! Огня!).

dicated by the connected words. Thus, for example, in подошёл к до́му or встре́тился с дру́гом the forms до́му and дру́гом are simply subordinated to the relevant verbs and prepositions, while in Рука́ уда́рила. Ру́ку уда́рила. Руко́й уда́рила or Сын принёс. Сы́на принёс. Сы́ну принёс the juxtaposition of the forms рука́— ру́ку— руко́й shows the contrast between the performer, the object acted upon and the instrument, while the juxtaposition of the forms сын— сы́на— сы́ну shows the contrast between the performer, the object acted upon and the "receiver" of the action.

The distinction between the cases is based on the following principle. A whole block of the case forms of different words is considered to be one and the same case when it can be placed in a specific context with one and the same meaning. Thus, for example, the block consisting of the forms of the до́му, столу́, дере́вне, по́лю type, placed in contexts of the Я подошёл к ... type, forms grammatically correct sentences.

There are *six cases*: the **nominative, genitive, dative, accusative, instrumental** and **prepositional**. The dictionary form is that of the *nominative*. There are no nouns all of whose six case forms would differ one from another in form. Thus, for example, the nominative and the accusative singular of the noun дом (дом) coincide, as do the dative and the prepositional singular of the noun жена́ (жене́), as do the genitive, the dative and the prepositional singular of the noun ло́шадь (ло́шади), etc. The forms of one and the same case of different nouns are different. Thus, for example, the dative singular of the noun жена́ is жене́; of сын, сы́ну; and of дочь, до́чери. Case markers differ depending on the number characteristic; the instrumental singular is женой, сы́ном, до́черью, whereas the instrumental plural is жёнами, сыновья́ми, дочерьми́. The ending indicating the case of the noun also indicates its number.

The case of a noun determines the form of the adjectives (see 2.4), pronouns (see 4.2) and participles (see 5.1) which agree with it.

1.4. Grammatical peculiarities of the nouns.

1. Most nouns have 12 forms (6 cases in each of the 2 numbers), some of which coincide. Some nouns have 6 forms (6 cases in one of the two numbers—singular or plural). A number of nouns have only 1 form (nouns which change neither for number nor for case).

2. The case and number of a noun are indicated simultaneously by one and the same ending.

3. The gender of a noun is not clearly expressed by its endings, but is shown consistently by its agreement, i.e. by the forms of the long-form adjectives and participles which agree with it.

4. The meanings of the number and case of a noun do not always coincide with the meaning of the real quantity and the nature of the real relations between the object denoted by that noun and actions or other objects.

5. As a rule, the dictionary form of a noun is the nominative singu-

lar. The dictionary form of a noun which exists only in the plural is the nominative plural.

2. What words are adjectives?

Adjectives are words which convey the quality of an object in the broadest and most general sense of the word. They are connected with words denoting objects in a broad sense, i.e. with nouns, and qualify them.

Adjectives may denote qualities arising from a sensual (бе́лый, кру́глый, высо́кий, бли́зкий, тёплый, вку́сный) or rational (злой, бога́тый, аккура́тный, ве́рный) perception. Adjectives may denote a quality either directly (си́ний, ле́вый, го́рдый) or through its relation to another substance, namely to an object (желе́зный, i.e. "made of iron" or "like iron", моско́вский, i.e. usually "situated in Moscow", автомоби́льный, i.e. usually "pertaining to a motor car"), an action (горе́лый, i.e. "that which has burnt", колю́чий, i.e. "that which pricks", переводно́й, i.e. "that which has been translated from another language") or a quantity (пя́тый, деся́тый, со́тый).[1]

A few adjectives which denote a quality belonging to a person, such as ма́мин and отцо́в, have certain inflexional peculiarities. They are called possessive adjectives.

In addition to the dictionary form, nearly all the adjectives have other forms. Very few adjectives have only the dictionary form. Most of them were borrowed from foreign languages: беж, бордо́, ха́ки, не́тто, люкс, а́виа and others.

Such adjectives are called unchangeable.

2.1. The long and short forms as characteristics of adjectives.

Adjectives are nearly always entered in dictionaries in the *long* form (краси́вый, у́мный, си́льный, сове́тский). Many adjectives, first of all those denoting a quality directly, also have the short form (краси́в, умён, силён). Adjectives which name a quality through its relation to an object, action or quantity generally have no short form. There are also a few adjectives which have only the short form: рад, до́лжен, etc.

The meanings of the short and long forms of one and the same adjective (out of context) do not differ, but these forms fulfil different functions in a sentence. The use of the short form is more restricted. Unlike the long form, it never combines with nouns connected with finite verb forms: Уда́рил си́льный моро́з, Си́льный моро́з and Моро́з силён; but *Уда́рил силён моро́з is impossible.

2.2. Gender as a characteristic of adjectival forms.

All long- and short-form adjectives have *three genders:* **masculine** (злой, чёрный, до́брый; зол, чёрен, добр), **feminine** (зла́я, чёрная, до́брая; зла, черна́, добра́) and **neuter** (зло́е, чёрное, до́брое; зло, черно́, добро́). The use of one of the three gender forms is determined

---

[1] Traditionally the preceding words are considered to be numerals (see 3). However, their qualities, while setting them apart from numerals, do not differ essentially from those of adjectives.

by the gender of the noun to which the adjective refers: большо́й дом, си́ний каранда́ш, го́род краси́в (masculine), больша́я стро́йка, си́няя река́, де́вушка краси́ва (feminine), большо́е собы́тие, си́нее не́бо, село́ краси́во (neuter). The *masculine* form of an adjective is its dictionary form.

2.3. Number as a characteristic of adjectival forms.

All changeable long- and short-form adjectives have *two number forms*: the **singular** (in all the three genders; see 2.2) and the **plural** (злы́е, чёрные, до́брые; злы, черны́, добры́). The use of the singular or plural form of an adjective is determined by the number of the noun (but not the quantity of the objects denoted by it!) to which the adjective refers: но́вый дом, интере́сная кни́га, большо́е окно́ (singular), но́вые дома́, интере́сные кни́ги, вку́сные сли́вки, тупы́е но́жницы, определе́ния пра́вильны, поля́ зе́лены (plural). The *singular* form of an adjective is its dictionary form.

2.4. Case as a characteristic of adjectival forms.

All the long-form adjectives change for case. Some case forms coincide and have no formal differences. The use of a case form of an adjective is determined by the case form of the noun to which it refers (*nom.* большо́й дом—*dat.* большо́му до́му, *nom.* родна́я страна́—*acc.* родну́ю страну́, *nom.* горя́чее се́рдце—*instr.* горя́чим се́рдцем), in exactly the same way as the use of a gender or number form (see 2.2 and 2.3) depends on the noun to which the adjective refers. Thus, adjectives *agree* with their head nouns. Short-form adjectives have only the nominative form. The *nominative* form of an adjective is its dictionary form.

2.5. Grammatical peculiarities of the adjectives.

1. Nearly all the adjectives have the gender, number and case forms, thus possessing 24 forms (6 cases × 3 genders in the singular + 6 cases in the plural), part of these forms having no formal distinctions. In addition, many adjectives also have 4 short forms (3 in the singular + 1 in the plural). A few adjectives are either unchangeable or have only the short form.

2. The long or short form, number, gender (in the singular) and the case (in the long form) are expressed by one and the same adjectival ending.

3. The use of the long or short form of an adjective is determined by its role in the sentence.

4. The gender, number and case of an adjective are determined by the relevant characteristics of the noun to which it refers, i.e. an adjective agrees with the noun it refers to in gender, number and case.

5. The dictionary form of an adjective is the long form (and in its absence the short form) masculine singular nominative.

3. What words are numerals?

The words called numerals denote the quantity of objects (пять, де́сять, сто два́дцать во́семь, тро́е, се́меро). Traditionally, the numerals are divided into two groups: **cardinal** (два, двáдцать, стo двáдцать три) and **collective** (двóе, трóе, сéмеро). Words of the вторóй, двенáдцатый, стo двáдцать трéтий type are considered to be adjectives. The word одúн is also an adjective, since it has the gender, number and case forms.

Cardinal numerals can be **simple** (пять, семнáдцать, сéмьдесят, двéсти) and **compound** (стo двáдцать пять, шестьсóт трúдцать четы́ре), in the declension of the latter each component part changes: стa двадцатú пятú, шестистáм трúдцати четырём.

Only the numerals двa, óба and полторá have the masculine and feminine gender forms. The other numerals do not have gender forms. Numerals do not have number forms.

3.1. Case as a characteristic of numerals.

All the numerals have case forms. Like adjectives, numerals *agree* with the noun to which they refer, i.e. they take the same case form as that noun: о пятú домáх, у двадцатú студéнтов. However, unlike the adjectives, no such agreement exists in the nominative and the accusative which is identical with the nominative: in these cases the numerals *subordinate* the noun forms, making them take the genitive singular (only the numerals двa, три, четы́ре: стo двáдцать три человéка, студéнта) or the genitive plural: двáдцать пять студéнтов.

4. What words are pronouns?

Words which do not name specific objects, phenomena, qualities, properties or quantities, but merely point to them are called pronominal words or pronouns.

Pronouns have no morphological characteristics of their own. While united by their indefinite, inconcrete meaning, all these words, depending on the specificity of their forms, are divided into **pronominal nouns** (see 1), **pronominal adjectives** (see 2), **pronominal numerals** (see 3) and **pronominal adverbs**.

4.1. How pronominal nouns differ from ordinary nouns.

The pronominal nouns include such words as я, ты, oн, онá, онó, мы, вы, онú, себя́, ктo, чтo, никтó, ничтó, ктó-нибудь, ктó-то, ктó-либо, нéкто, чтó-нибудь, чтó-то, чтó-либо, нéчто, нéкого, нéчего. All these words belong to at least one of the three genders. Except the words oн, онá and онó, they do not change for number (see 1.2). Like most nouns, these nouns change according to the same six cases. Some pronominal nouns (себя́, нéкого, нéчего) do not have the nominative form. Their dictionary form is that of the nominative and, if it does not exist, that of the genitive.

4.2. How pronominal adjectives differ from ordinary adjectives.

The pronominal adjectives include such words as мой, твой, свой, наш, ваш, какóй, чей, котóрый, такóй, э́тот, тот, э́такий, сам, сáмый, весь, вся́кий, кáждый, инóй, никакóй, ничéй, какóй-то, чéй-то, какóй-либо, чéй-либо, кое-какóй, кое-чéй. Like many other adjectives, these words do not have the short form. Like the ordinary adjectives, these words have three gender forms in the singular: masculine, feminine and neuter, two number forms: singular and plural, and six case forms; the gender, number and case of a pronominal adjective being determined by the gender, number and case of the noun to which it refers.

Thus, pronominal adjectives have 24 forms (6 cases × 3 genders in the singular + 6 cases in the plural). Some of the case forms coincide (see tables on p. 146). The dictionary form is that of the masculine nominative singular.

4.3. Pronominal numerals and adverbs.

The pronominal numerals (столько, сколько, несколько, сколько-нибудь) do not at all differ from the ordinary numerals (see 3). Like the adverbs (see 6), the pronominal adverbs, such as туда, там, здесь, так, никак, никогда, как, везде, are unchangeable words.

4.4. Grammatical peculiarities of the pronominal words.

The forms of the pronominal nouns, adjectives and numerals are derived in the same way as those of the ordinary nouns, adjectives and numerals. The pronominal adverbs have only one form, since, like the ordinary adverbs, they are unchangeable words.

5. What words are verbs?

Words which denote actions in the broadest and the most general sense of the word are verbs. Verbs are somewhat like adjectives, since they both usually characterise an object; however, adjectives give an object a static characteristic, whereas verbs give it a dynamic characteristic. Such words as сон, бег, езда, занятие, улыбка and the like must not be considered to be verbs, since their meaning is that of an object in a general sense, while an action serves merely as the basis for naming an object.

5.1. Finite and non-finite verb forms.

The dictionary form of a verb is that of the **infinitive** (читать, любить, идти, беречь, кататься and many others). The distinctive feature of an infinitive is that it merely names an action without supplying any additional information about its characteristics: its reality, time, connection with the participants, etc.

Nearly all the verbs have the form of the **verbal adverb**, i.e. the form which shows that the action they express accompanies and characterises another action (читая, любя, узнав, сделав).

All the verbs have the form of the **participle**, i.e. the form which represents the action as a characteristic of an object (читающий, читавший, любящий, любимый, сделанный, улыбающийся).

The infinitive, verbal adverb and participle are called *non-finite* verbs forms. Unlike the other verbs forms, these forms do not denote an action in connection with its performer.

All the other verb forms are called *finite* (see 5.4-5.8).

5.2. The differences between perfective and imperfective verbs.

Every verb belongs either to the **perfective** or the **imperfective** aspect. Relatively few verbs are imperfective in some of their uses and perfective in the other uses. Such verbs are called biaspectual.

When a verb is said to be *perfective*, it means the following:

1. This verb usually denotes either an action which has had a result (писа́л, писа́л, писа́л... and, finally, написа́л; реша́л, реша́л, реша́л... and, finally, реши́л; ду́мал, ду́мал, ду́мал... and, finally, приду́мал) or an action which took place on one occasion only (толкну́ть, поцелова́ть, навести́ть).

2. This verb has only the past and future tense forms (напишу́, написа́л), and neither its finite nor its participial forms have the present tense (see 5.5).

3. This verb cannot combine with words denoting unlimited duration (до́лго, всё, без конца́, etc.) or unlimited, but definite repetition (ежедне́вно, вечера́ми, ка́ждый день, по утра́м, системати́чески, etc.). Besides, its infinitive cannot combine with verbs denoting the beginning or end of an action (начина́ть, продолжа́ть, ко́нчить, etc.) and with words or phrases denoting either inexpediency (undesirability) of an action (бесполе́зно, напра́сно, не сто́ит) or a subjective negative attitude towards an action (не привы́к, разучи́лся, не нра́вится).

When a verb is said to be *imperfective*, it means the following:

1. As a rule, this verb merely denotes an action without any indication of its result or the number of repetitions (although it may indicate a repeated action).

2. The finite forms of this verb have three tenses (the present, the past and the future), and its participles, two tenses (the present and the past) (see 5.5).

3. The combinability of this verb with other words is restricted only by its meaning.

Imperfective verbs can often be formed from their perfective counterparts by means of suffixes, and perfective verbs from their imperfective counterparts by means of prefixes (see III C, 6).

Perfective and imperfective verbs are quite different lexical units, represented in a dictionary independently of each other. All the forms of an imperfective or perfective verb—the finite forms, the infinitive, the participle and the verbal adverb—have the same aspectual characteristic as the verb itself.

5.3. What is voice?

In a text each verb form—finite or participial—may belong either to the **active** or to the **passive** voice.

There are no semantic differences between verbs in the active and passive voice. The choice of the voice form determines the formal structure of the sentence; namely, the case form for the agent or performer of the action and for the object acted upon: Рабо́чие стро́ят но́вую больни́цу (active voice)—Но́вая больни́ца стро́ится рабо́чими (passive voice).

The fact that a finite verb form (see 5.1) belongs to the *passive* voice is expressed by the following. The finite verb form combines with the nominative case of a noun, the person or object denoted by this noun being not the agent or performer of the action concerned, but the object acted upon. In such cases the performer of the action is usually also expressed in the sentence; however, it does not take the form of the nominative, but generally (although not always) the instrumental case: Улица освещалась *фонарями*. Такие приказы подписываются *директором*. The passive voice is generally represented in the 3rd person (see 5.6) of the present/future tense (see 5.5), in the past tense (see 5.5) of the indicative mood (see 5.4), and also in the subjunctive mood (see 5.4). In the other finite forms the passive voice is represented very rarely.

The fact that a participle belongs to the passive voice is expressed by the following. A passive participle combines with a noun and agrees with it in gender, number and case; the person or object denoted by this noun is not the performer of the action of the participle, but represents the person or object acted upon: написанное сыном письмо, строящийся дом, любимый нами писатель, изучавшийся вопрос.

The passive voice is very rarely expressed in verbal adverbs or infinitives.

In all the cases where the above restrictions do not apply, i. e. if (1) a finite verb form never combines with a noun in the nominative; (2) the nominative of a noun related to a finite verb form or the noun with which the participle concerned agrees does not denote an object acted upon, then the verbs belong to the *active* voice (человек поёт, спящая красавица, прошедший день, учитель сказал, смеркается, мне не спится).

As a rule, sentences containing a verb in the passive voice can be transformed into sentences with the same meaning, but containing a verb in the active voice. However, far from all sentences with a verb in the active voice can be transformed into sentences with a verb in the passive voice.

5.3.1. Do all the verbs have both voice forms?

The dictionary form of a verb is that of the active voice; passive voice forms are generally not indicated in dictionaries, since their formation is more or less standard. However, far from all the verbs have the forms of both voices.

As a rule, the so-called *transitive* verbs, i. e. verbs which denote an action presupposing the presence of an object acted upon: строить (дом, планы, город); читать (книгу, роман, газету); составлять (отчёт, справку, текст), have both voice forms, although this is not always so. Verbs whose dictionary form ends in **-ся** do not have the passive voice: кататься, улыбаться, сердиться, etc.

5.4. What is verb mood?

Finite verb forms may be used in *three mood* forms: the **indicative**, the **imperative** and the **subjunctive**. The infinitive, the participle and the verbal adverb do not have mood forms.

The *indicative* mood usually denotes actions actually taking place in the present, past or future (see 5.5): читáю, идýт, сказáл, узнáете, писáла.

The *imperative* mood denotes actions which the speaker urges his listener to perform: читáй, идúте, скажú, пойдёмте, пишúте.

The *subjunctive* mood denotes actions which are supposed to take place or to have taken place: читáл бы, шли бы, сказáла бы, написáла бы.

The division of verb forms into three moods only roughly corresponds to the division of events into those actually taking place, subjectively desired, and supposed. In specific sentences such a correlation between the mood form and the nature of the action itself does not always exist (see II C, 3.4 and 3.5). At the same time both a desired action and a supposed one can be expressed not only by the forms of the respective moods (see III C, 1).

The formation of mood forms is regular. All the mood forms can be obtained from the dictionary forms of verbs, although some of the forms are rarely used in practice.

5.5 What is tense?

The verbal adverb and the infinitive do not have a tense characteristic. On the contrary, the participle and the finite verb forms in the indicative mood (only!) must have it.

The *finite forms* of *imperfective* verbs in the indicative mood may convey actions in the **past** (писáл, нёс, ходúла, считáли), **present** (пишý, несёт, хóдим, считáют) and **future** (бýду писáть, бýдет нестú, бýдем ходúть, бýдут считáть) tenses. The *participial forms* of imperfective verbs may convey actions in the **past** (писáвший, пúсанный, нёсшая, ходúвшие, считáвшие, считáвшиеся) or the **present** (пúшущий, несýщая, ходящего, считáющие, считáющиеся, считáемые) tense. The participial forms of imperfective verbs have no future tense.

The *finite forms* of *perfective* verbs in the indicative mood may denote actions in the **past** (написáл, принёс, посчитáли) and **future** (напишý, принесёт, посчитáет) tenses. The finite forms of perfective verbs in the indicative mood have no present tense. The *participial forms* of perfective verbs may convey actions only in the **past** (написáвший, напúсанный, принёсшая, принесённая, посчитáвшие, посчитáвшиеся) tense. The participial forms of perfective verbs have no present and future tenses.

The derivation of the tense forms of finite verb forms is quite regular, although some forms are rarely used in practice. Active participles are also derived in a regular way. Many forms of passive participles are not used in practice.

The past, present and future tenses roughly correspond to the division of events into those taking place before the moment of speaking, at the moment of speaking, and after the moment of speaking, respectively. However, this is not always so.

5.6 Person in verb forms.

5.6.1. Person in indicative mood verbs.

The present and future tense forms of imperfective verbs in the indicative mood and the future tense forms of perfective verbs in the indicative mood have *three persons*.

The **first person** denotes an action performed either by the speaker or by a group of people in which the speaker includes himself: люблю, знаем, иду, говорим. This form is often accompanied by the personal pronoun я or мы. However, the pronoun may be absent.

The **second person** denotes an action performed by the person(s) spoken to: знаешь, считаете, купишь, говорите. This form is often accompanied by the personal pronoun ты or вы. However, the pronoun may be absent.

The **third person** denotes an action performed neither by the speaker nor by the listener, but by person(s) or object(s) spoken about: знает, видит, работают, лежат. This form is often accompanied by the personal pronoun он, она, оно or они or by practically any noun.

In specific cases the preceding meanings of the personal forms may alter somewhat (see II C, 3.1; 3.3 and III C, 2).

5.6.2. Person in imperative mood verbs.

The imperative is usually expressed in the second person, which is completely in agreement with the meaning of a desired action: иди, скажи, встань, принесите, подумайте.

In addition (more often in colloquial speech), perfective verbs may take the form of a so-called *joint action*, in which a group which includes both the speaker and those spoken to is urged to perform an action: Пойдёмте! Споёмте.

5.6.3. Verbs which do not have all the persons.

The overwhelming majority of verbs have the first, second and third persons in the indicative mood, and the second person in the imperative. These forms are derived in the regular way.

However, there are verbs which have only the third person singular: смеркается, знобит, тошнит, думается, мечтается. Such verbs are called **impersonal**. They do not combine with nouns in the nominative, nor do they have the imperative mood and the passive voice.

5.7. Number in verb forms.

All the final verb forms and participles have the forms of the **singular** and the **plural**.

The contrast between the singular and plural forms characterises the forms of both voices in all the three moods, tenses and persons. The derivation of the forms contrasted by number is quite standard. Only the impersonal verbs have no plural (see 5.6.3). The choice of the number of a finite verb form depends on *the form of the noun* which stands in the nominative case (in the sentence): if the noun is in the singular, the verb also takes the singular, and if the noun is in the plural, the verb takes the plural, too: студент читает — студенты читают.

The number in participles follows the pattern of the adjectives (see 2.3).

5.8. Gender in verb forms.

The past tense of the indicative mood and also the subjunctive mood have no personal forms, the meaning of person being conveyed only by the pronoun. Verbs have the **masculine, feminine** or **neuter gender** depending on the gender of the noun which is in the nominative case (in the sentence).

The gender of participles follows the pattern of the adjectives (see 2.2).

The impersonal verbs (see 5.6.3) have only the neuter gender.

5.9. Case and the short/long form in verbs.

Only participles have cases and can take either the short or the long form.

The case characteristic of participles is exactly the same as that of the adjectives. Passive participles usually have either the long or the short form, the basic difference between which is the same as between the long and the short forms of adjectives (see 2.1). Active participles have only the long form.

5.10. Grammatical peculiarities of the verbs.

1. Except the impersonal verbs (see 5.6.3), all the verbs have an extremely ramified system of regularly derived forms. The number of these forms is determined, first and foremost, by two factors: the aspect of the verb (perfective verbs have no present tense) and the possibility of voice juxtaposition.

2. The finite forms and the participles have a wide variety of forms, whereas the infinitive and the verbal adverb are unchangeable forms.

3. The distinction between the various verb forms is based on the following semantic factors: (1) the relation between the action and reality, between the action and the speaker's subjective intention (3 moods); (2) the relation between the moment of the action and the moment of speaking (2 or 3 tenses); and (3) the relation between the action and the participants in the speech process (usually 3 persons).

4. Besides, various verb forms are distinguished on the basis of the following connective factors: (1) the relation of the action to the object designated by the noun connected with the action (2 voices of the finite forms and the participles); (2) the number of the noun with which the verb agrees (for all the finite forms and participles); (3) the gender of the noun with which the verb agrees (for the past tense singular of the indicative mood, the subjunctive singular, and participles singular); (4) short forms versus long forms (for participles); and (5) the case (for long-form participles).

The most typical examples of the systems of verb forms are given in the following tables (see pp. 30-35).

1. Perfective Verbs with Aspectual Juxtaposition (**постро́ить**)

Mood, Tense, Number, Person, Gender				Finite Form			Participle						Infinitive	Verbal Adverb
				Voice			Active Voice		Passive Voice					
				Active Voice	Passive Voice		Present Tense	Past Tense	Present Tense		Past Tense			
									Long-form	Short-form	Long-form	Short-form		
Indicative Mood	Present Tense	Sing.	1st pers.	—	—								постро́ить	постро́ив
			2nd pers.	—	—									
			3rd pers.	—	—									
		Pl.	1st pers.	—	—									
			2nd pers.	—	—									
			3rd pers.	—	—									
	Future Tense	Sing.	1st pers.	постро́ю	—	Masculine nom.	—	постро́ивший	—	—	постро́енный	постро́ен		
			2nd pers.	постро́ишь	—	gen.	—	постро́ившего	—	—	постро́енного	—		
			3rd pers.	постро́ит	постро́ится	dat.	—	постро́ившему	—	—	постро́енному	—		
		Pl.	1st pers.	постро́им	—	acc.	—	постро́ивший	—	—	постро́енный	—		
			2nd pers.	постро́ите	—	instr.	—	постро́ившим	—	—	постро́енным	—		
			3rd pers.	постро́ят	постро́ятся	prep.	—	постро́ившем	—	—	постро́енном	—		
						Feminine nom.	—	постро́ившая	—	—	постро́енная	постро́ена		
						gen.	—	постро́ившей	—	—	постро́енной	—		
						dat.	—	постро́ившей	—	—	постро́енной	—		
						acc.	—	постро́ившую	—	—	постро́енную	—		
						instr.	—	постро́ившей	—	—	постро́енной	—		
						prep.	—	постро́ившей	—	—	постро́енной	—		
						Neuter nom.	—	постро́ившее	—	—	постро́енное	постро́ено		
						gen.	—	постро́ившего	—	—	постро́енного	—		
						dat.	—	постро́ившему	—	—	постро́енному	—		
						acc.	—	постро́ившее	—	—	постро́енное	—		
						instr.	—	постро́ившим	—	—	постро́енным	—		
						prep.	—	постро́ившем	—	—	постро́енном	—		
	Past Tense	Sing.	masc.	постро́ил	постро́ился									
			fem.	постро́ила	постро́илась									
			neut.	постро́ило	постро́илось									
		Pl.		постро́или	постро́ились									

Continued

Mood, Tense, Number, Person, Gender			Finite Form		Plural		Participle					Infinitive	Verbal Adverb
			Voice				Active Voice		Passive Voice				
			Active Voice	Passive Voice			Present Tense	Past Tense	Present Tense		Past Tense		
									Long-form	Short-form	Long-form	Short-form		
Subjunctive mood	Sing.	masc.	постро́или бы	постро́ился бы	Plural	nom.	—	постро́ившие	—	—	постро́енные	постро́ены		
		fem.	постро́ила бы	постро́илась бы		gen.	—	постро́ивших	—	—	постро́енных	—		
		neut.	постро́ило бы	постро́илось бы		dat.	—	постро́ившим	—	—	постро́енным	—		
	Pl.		постро́или бы	постро́ились бы		acc.	—	постро́ившие	—	—	постро́енные	—		
						instr.	—	постро́ившими	—	—	постро́енными	—		
Imperative Mood	Sing.	2nd pers.	постро́й	—		prep.	—	постро́ивших	—	—	постро́енных	—		
	Pl.	2nd pers.	постро́йте	—										

2. Imperfective Verbs with Aspectual Juxtaposition (**читáть**)

Finite Form

Mood	Tense	Number	Person/Gender	Active Voice	Passive Voice
Indicative Mood	Present Tense	Sing.	1st pers.	читáю	—
			2nd pers.	читáешь	читáется
			3rd pers.	читáет	
		Pl.	1st pers.	читáем	—
			2nd pers.	читáете	
			3rd pers.	читáют	читáются
	Future Tense	Sing.	1st pers.	бýду читáть	—
			2nd pers.	бýдешь читáть	
			3rd pers.	бýдет читáть	бýдет читáться
		Pl.	1st pers.	бýдем читáть	—
			2nd pers.	бýдете читáть	
			3rd pers.	бýдут читáть	бýдут читáться
	Past Tense	Sing.	masc.	читáл	читáлся
			fem.	читáла	читáлась
			neut.	читáло	читáлось
		Pl.		читáли	читáлись
Subjunctive Mood		Sing.	masc.	читáл бы	читáлся бы
			fem.	читáла бы	читáлась бы
			neut.	читáло бы	читáлось бы
		Pl.		читáли бы	читáлись бы
Imperative Mood		Sing.		читáй	—
		Pl.		читáйте	

Participle

		Active Voice		Passive Voice			
		Present Tense	Past Tense	Present Tense		Past Tense	
				Long-form	Short-form	Long-form	Short-form
Singular Masculine	nom.	читáющий	читáвший	читáемый	читáем	читанный	читан
	gen.	читáющего	читáвшего	читáемого	—	читанного	—
	dat.	читáющему	читáвшему	читáемому	—	читанному	—
	acc.	читáющий	читáвший	читáемый	—	читанный	—
	instr.	читáющим	читáвшим	читáемым	—	читанным	—
	prep.	читáющем	читáвшем	читáемом	—	читанном	—
Singular Feminine	nom.	читáющая	читáвшая	читáемая	читáема	читанная	читана
	gen.	читáющей	читáвшей	читáемой	—	читанной	—
	dat.	читáющей	читáвшей	читáемой	—	читанной	—
	acc.	читáющую	читáвшую	читáемую	—	читанную	—
	instr.	читáющей	читáвшей	читáемой	—	читанной	—
	prep.	читáющей	читáвшей	читáемой	—	читанной	—
Singular Neuter	nom.	читáющее	читáвшее	читáемое	читáемо	читанное	читано
	gen.	читáющего	читáвшего	читáемого	—	читанного	—
	dat.	читáющему	читáвшему	читáемому	—	читанному	—
	acc.	читáющее	читáвшее	читáемое	—	читанное	—
	instr.	читáющим	читáвшим	читáемым	—	читанным	—
	prep.	читáющем	читáвшем	читáемом	—	читанном	—
Plural	nom.	читáющие	читáвшие	читáемые	читáемы	читанные	читаны
	gen.	читáющих	читáвших	читáемых	—	читанных	—
	dat.	читáющим	читáвшим	читáемым	—	читанным	—
	acc.	читáющие	читáвшие	читáемые	—	читанные	—
	instr.	читáющими	читáвшими	читáемыми	—	читанными	—
	prep.	читáющих	читáвших	читáемых	—	читанных	—

3. Perfective Verbs without Aspectual Juxtaposition (сгоре́ть)

Mood, Tense, Number, Person, Gender			Finite Form		Participle			Infinitive	Verbal Adverb
			Voice	Active Voice		Active Voice			
						Present Tense	Past Tense		
Indicative Mood	Present Tense	Sing.	1st pers.	—	Masculine	nom.	— сгоре́вший	сгоре́ть	сгоре́в
			2nd pers.	—		gen.	— сгоре́вшего		
			3rd pers.	—		dat.	— сгоре́вшему		
		Pl.	1st pers.	—		acc.	— сгоре́вший		
			2nd pers.	—			— сгоре́вшего		
			3rd pers.	—		instr.	— сгоре́вшим		
						prep.	— сгоре́вшем		
	Future Tense	Sing.	1st pers.	сгорю́	Feminine	nom.	— сгоре́вшая		
			2nd pers.	сгори́шь		gen.	— сгоре́вшей		
			3rd pers.	сгори́т		dat.	— сгоре́вшей		
		Pl.	1st pers.	сгори́м		acc.	— сгоре́вшую		
			2nd pers.	сгори́те		instr.	— сгоре́вшей		
			3rd pers.	сгоря́т		prep.	— сгоре́вшей		
	Past Tense	Sing.	masc.	сгоре́л	Neuter	nom.	— сгоре́вшее		
			fem.	сгоре́ла		gen.	— сгоре́вшего		
			neut.	сгоре́ло		dat.	— сгоре́вшему		
		Pl.		сгоре́ли		acc.	— сгоре́вшее		
						instr.	— сгоре́вшим		
						prep.	— сгоре́вшем		
Subjunctive Mood		Sing.	masc.	сгоре́л бы	Plural	nom.	— сгоре́вшие		
			fem.	сгоре́ла бы		gen.	— сгоре́вших		
			neut.	сгоре́ло бы		dat.	— сгоре́вшим		
		Pl.		сгоре́ли бы		acc.	— сгоре́вшие		
							— сгоре́вших		
						instr.	— сгоре́вшими		
						prep.	— сгоре́вших		
Imperative Mood		Sing.		сгори́					
		Pl.		сгори́те					

4. Imperfective Verbs without Aspectual Juxtaposition (спать)

Mood, Tense, Number, Person, Gender		Finite Form				Participle			Infinitive	Verbal Adverb
		Voice				Active Voice				
		Active Voice					Present Tense	Past Tense		
Indicative Mood	Present Tense	Sing.	1st pers.	сплю	Singular	Masculine	спящий	спавший	спать	—
			2nd pers.	спишь			спящего	спавшего		
			3rd pers.	спит			спящему	спавшему		
						nom.	спящий	спавший		
						gen.	спящего	спавшего		
						dat.				
						acc.				
		Pl.	1st pers.	спим			спящим	спавшим		
			2nd pers.	спите		instr.	спящем	спавшем		
			3rd pers.	спят		prep.				
	Future Tense	Sing.	1st pers.	буду спать		Feminine	спящая	спавшая		
			2nd pers.	будешь спать			спящей	спавшей		
			3rd pers.	будет спать		nom.	спящей	спавшей		
						gen.	спящую	спавшую		
						dat.	спящей	спавшей		
						acc.	спящей	спавшей		
		Pl.	1st pers.	будем спать		instr.				
			2nd pers.	будете спать		prep.				
			3rd pers.	будут спать		Neuter	спящее	спавшее		
	Past Tense	Sing.	masc.	спал			спящего	спавшего		
			fem.	спала		nom.	спящему	спавшему		
			neut.	спало		gen.	спящее	спавшее		
						dat.	спящим	спавшим		
						acc.	спящем	спавшем		
		Pl.		спали		instr.				
						prep.				

	Finite Form			Participle			Infinitive	Verbal Adverb
Mood, Tense, Number, Person, Gender	Voice		Active Voice		Active Voice			
					Present Tense	Past Tense		
Subjunctive Mood	Sing.	masc. fem. neut.	спал бы спала́ бы спа́ло бы	Plural — nom. gen. dat. acc. instr. prep.	спя́щие спя́щих спя́щим спя́щие спя́щих спя́щими спя́щих	спа́вшие спа́вших спа́вшим спа́вшие спа́вших спа́вшими спа́вших		
	Pl.		спа́ли бы					
Imperative Mood	Sing.	2nd pers.	спи					
	Pl.	2nd pers.	спи́те					

5. Impersonal Verbs (**смерка́ться**)
смерка́ется — смерка́лось — смерка́лось бы

6. The unchangeable words.

Unlike inflected words, unchangeable words function in texts in the same form in which they are entered in dictionaries.

Among the unchangeable words there are some which can be used independently, and others that can be used only when accompanied by other words or/and clauses or sentences. The former, like the notional words, such as nouns, adjectives, numerals, pronouns and verbs, are *independent*, while the latter are *dependent* or *syntactic* words.

6.1. The adverb.

Adverbs are notional unchangeable words. The difference between them and the unchangeable nouns and adjectives is as follows.

Like adjectives, adverbs denote a modifier. However, unlike the adjectives, which denote a modifier of an object, adverbs usually denote a *modifier of an action*: (бежа́ть) бы́стро, (пры́гать) высоко́, (чита́ть) вслух, (писа́ть) по-ру́сски, (разгова́ривать) гро́мко, or a *modifier of an attribute*: о́чень (краси́вый челове́к), сли́шком (гру́бый приём), давно́ (гото́вое реше́ние), хорошо́ (изве́стный факт). Like adjectives, some adverbs may also denote a modifier of an object: (бег) наперегонки́, (чте́ние) вслух, (разгово́р) по-ру́сски (cf. бежа́ть наперегонки́, чита́ть вслух, разгова́ривать по-ру́сски).

An adverb fulfils functions similar to those of a verbal adverb, but unlike the latter, an adverb conveys a modifier that is not a process.

As a rule, some other independent unchangeable words are classed as adverbs, although they do not necessarily denote a modifier of an action or attribute. Such are, for example, the words мо́жно, ну́жно, нельзя́, на́до, жаль and сле́довательно, возмо́жно, наве́рное, во-пе́рвых and a number of others.

6.2. Prepositions.

Prepositions are unchangeable words which are not used independently and denote the nature of a *subordinate* relation of an object conveyed by a noun to another object or action or quality conveyed by a noun, verb, adjective or adverb: дом *в* лесу́, обсужде́ние *среди́* колле́г, смотре́ть *на* не́бо, забежа́ть *на* мину́ту, подъе́хать *к* го́роду, ве́рный *в* дру́жбе, изве́стный *по* рабо́там, бли́зко *от* ста́нции.

An important distinctive feature of the spelling of prepositions is that many of them are written as two elements: вплоть до (исключе́ния), наряду́ с (успе́хами), незави́симо от (обстоя́тельств), примени́тельно к (усло́виям), сообра́зно с (усло́виями), соотве́тственно с (настрое́нием), соразме́рно с (уси́лиями), сравни́тельно с (про́шлым), в продолже́ние (разгово́ра), в тече́ние (го́да), по по́воду (юбиле́я), по причи́не (пожа́ра), в ка́честве (дире́ктора), смотря́ по (обстоя́тельствам), несмотря́ на (возраже́ния), исходя́ из (зако́на) and a number of others.

The meanings of prepositions are extremely varied. Sometimes a preposition may only indicate the subordination of a noun to another word, without specifying the nature of the relations between the subordinating and the subordinated word: наде́яться *на* успе́х, ве́рить *в* побе́ду, зави́сеть *от* пого́ды. However, more often than not prepositions denote specific relations between the subordinated and the subordinating word.

These relations may be as follows: spatial, connected with location or direction: идти́ *из* ле́са, пти́цы *над* поля́ми, купи́ть *в* магази́не; temporal, connected with the beginning, the end or periodicity: рабо́тать *с* утра́ *до* ве́чера, чита́ть *по* вечера́м; possession: ключи́ *от* до́ма; causal: похуде́л *от* боле́зни, не уви́дел *из-за* темноты́; final: лека́рство *от* стра́ха, ко́мната *для* о́тдыха, идти́ *за* водо́й; etc.

Many prepositions are polysemantic and therefore their meaning can generally be determined only in a context. Thus, for example, the prepositions *в* and *на* may indicate the place of an action: (жить) в Москве́, на Украи́не; the direction of an action: (е́хать) в Москву́, на Украи́ну; time: на про́шлой неде́ле, на ме́сяц; or simply the subordination of one word to another: ве́рить в (успе́х), наде́яться на (уда́чу).

6.3. Conjunctions.

Conjunctions are unchangeable words which are not used independently and express either a coordinated or a subordinated relationship between words, phrases or clauses.

Thus, like prepositions, conjunctions are used for "joining or connecting" purposes, but their range is wider, since they join not only words, but clauses as well. Also: the main function of conjunctions is not to indicate the subordinated position of a noun, but to join words belonging to the same part of speech (сове́т *да* любо́вь; молодо́й, *но* осторо́жный; пи́шет *и* перево́дит), or, occasionally, to different parts of speech (писа́ть бы́стро *и* без оши́бок; челове́к необразо́ванный, *но* с прете́нзиями). Besides, unlike prepositions, conjunctions may join clauses, establishing specific semantic relations between them. In particular, these semantic relations may be: copulative (и, а та́кже), explicative (то есть, а и́менно), temporal (когда́, с тех пор как, как то́лько), conditional (е́сли, при усло́вии что), causal (поско́льку, потому́ что) and some others.

Like prepositions, many conjunctions are polysemantic.

Like prepositions, some conjunctions are not spelt as one element (потому́ что; несмотря́ на то, что; так как; перед те́м, как, etc.).

An important feature of conjunctions is that many of them, while being one word, have their components in each part of the constructions they join. These components may be identical, in which case there may be two or more of them: и... и... и, и́ли... и́ли, и́ли, то... то... то, etc. If the components are dissimilar, there can be only two of them: е́сли... то, поско́льку... посто́льку, что каса́ется... то, хотя́ и... но, etc.

6.4. Particles.

Traditionally, the unchangeable words include particles, which do not stand out from the adverbs and the conjunctions quite clearly.

They may indicate a question (ра́зве, неуже́ли, ли), affirmation (да, так), negation (не, нет, во́все не), somebody's words (мол, де́скать, я́кобы), emphasis (же, да́же, ведь) or comparison (сло́вно, то́чно, бу́дто).

Some of the particles are also spelt as two elements: вря́д ли, как ра́з, что́ за, etc.

6.5. Interjections.

Interjections are unchangeable words which express feelings, but do not denote them: ах, увы́, ай-ай-а́й, бо́же мой, ба́тюшки, etc. Interjections include various onomatopoeic words of the тсс, мя́у, гав-га́в, etc. type.

PART II
"FROM THE FORM TO THE MEANING" GRAMMAR

A. DETERMINATION OF THE GRAMMATICAL CHARACTERISTICS OF A WORD

Depending on the terminations of words in a sentence, it is possible to make suppositions about the grammatical characteristics of these words. However, such suppositions are usually inconclusive. The form of the termination of a word only points to the area of possible searches. The grammatical characteristic of a word can be inferred conclusively only when one understands the nature of the connection between this word and the other words in the sentence and knows the lexical (dictionary) meaning of the words.

A.1. DETERMINATION OF THE GRAMMATICAL CHARACTERISTICS OF A WORD BY ITS TERMINATION

1. Grammatical characteristics of words ending in -а/-я.

-а/-я may be an ending, part of a stem, and **-я** following **-а-**, **-я-**, **-м-** or **-с-** may be part of an ending.

A word with the termination **-а** or **-я** may be:

1.1.1. A noun in the *nominative singular*: рекá, стенá, дорóга, статья́, земля́, стáнция. As a rule, it is a noun of the *feminine* or *common* (сиротá, неря́ха, грязну́ля, со́ня) gender.

A number of nouns ending in this manner belong to the *masculine* gender: пáпа, дя́дя, слугá, дéдушка or are proper names — formal or affectionate — denoting males: Пéтя, Кóля, Никита, Лукá, Илья́, Гóша, Жóра, Кузьмá, etc. All the words ending in **-мя**: и́мя, знáмя, etc. are *neuter*.

Words ending in **-ая/-яя** may be the same form: кривáя, кладовáя, столóвая, мостовáя, прихóжая, мастерскáя, кондитерская, парикмáхерская, ординáторская, дéтская, учи́тельская, родослóвная, накладнáя, произвóдная, билья́рдная, нáбережная, гости́ная, чáйная, приёмная, вáнная, вселéнная, пельмéнная, убóрная, чебурéчная, прáчечная, гóрничная, молóчная, бу́лочная, закýсочная, шашлы́чная, касáтельная, запя́тая, падýчая, передняя, преиспóдняя. Some of the preceding words may also be long-form feminine adjectives in the nominative singular (see below, 1.3.4), while the words кладовáя, мостовáя, прихóжая, парикмáхерская, гости́ная, родослóвная, нáбережная, вселéнная, убóрная, прáчечная, бу́лочная, гóрничная, касáтельная are invariably nouns.

Words whose termination is **-ая** and which denote females of the рýсская, рабóчая, слýжащая, завéдующая, нóвенькая, возлю́бленная, звеньевáя type are also the same form. In all such cases **-я** is part of the ending **-ая/-яя**.

Here also belong words with the termination **-a** following **-ин** or **-ов** of the Пу́шкина, Соколо́ва type or with the termination **-ая, -яя** of the Твардо́вская, Зи́мняя type, which denote feminine surnames.

1.1.2. A noun in the *genitive* singular: (нет) са́да, ле́са, о́блака, дня, студе́нта, сле́саря, по́ля. As a rule, it is a *masculine* or *neuter* noun.

1.1.3. A noun in the *accusative* singular: (ви́жу) студе́нта, дру́га, учи́теля, быка́, сы́на, то́каря, медве́дя. As a rule, it is a masculine noun denoting a person or animal. However, it may be the noun микро́ба, ви́руса, мертвеца́ or поко́йника, or an inanimate noun applied to a person (of the ду́ба, пня, тюфяка́ type), a proper noun (of the «Москвича́», «Запоро́жца» type) denoting a make of car, or one of the nouns used when playing cards, chess or billiards (вале́та, короля́, коня́, слона́, ша́ра).

1.1.4. A noun in the *nominative plural*: леса́, воро́та, холода́, сту́лья, о́кна, поля́, сыновья́. As a rule, it is a *masculine* or *neuter* noun.

1.1.5. A noun in the *accusative plural*: (ви́жу) леса́, воро́та, сту́лья, о́кна, поля́. As a rule, it is an inanimate noun (see also 1.1.4).

1.2.1. The **pronoun** она́ in the nominative singular.

1.2.2. The pronoun я in the nominative.

1.2.3. A pronoun in the genitive: (есть у) меня́, тебя́, себя́.

1.2.4. A pronoun in the accusative: (смотрю́ на) меня́, тебя́, себя́.

1.3.1. A *feminine* **adjective** in the nominative singular: та, э́та, на́ша, ва́ша, моя́, своя́, чья, одна́, отцо́ва, де́душкина, оле́нья, тре́тья (вещь).

As a rule, it is a pronominal adjective or a possessive adjective with the marker **-ов-/-ев-** or **-ин-/-ын-** before **-а**, or the marker **-ь-** before **-я-**.

1.3.2. A *masculine* or *neuter* adjective in the *genitive* singular: (нет) де́душкина, отцо́ва (прика́за, распоряже́ния).

It must be a possessive adjective with the marker **-ов-/-ев-** or **-ин-/-ын-** before the ending **-а**.

1.3.3. A masculine adjective in the *accusative* singular: (смотрю́ на) де́душкина, отцо́ва (вну́ка). It must be a possessive adjective with the ending **-а** after **-ов-/-ев-** or **-ин-/-ын-**. Adjectives in this form can refer only to an animate noun.

1.3.4. A *feminine* long-form adjective in the nominative singular may have the form ending in **-ая**, and also in **-яя** after **-н-**: до́брая, хоро́шая, у́мная, дре́вняя, осе́нняя (see also 1.1.1). In this case **-я** is part of the ending **-ая/-яя**.

1.3.5. A feminine *short-form* adjective in the singular if the word ends in **-а**: добра́, светла́, хороша́, and also **-я** if it is the word синя́, изли́шня, дре́вня, госпо́дня, бескра́йня, и́скрення, ...сторо́ння or . ...ле́тня.

1.4.1. A masculine or neuter **numeral** in the *nominative*: два, о́ба, полтора́ or the numeral полтора́ста, три́ста or четы́реста.

1.4.2. A numeral in the *accusative*. It is the masculine or neuter numeral два, о́ба or полтора́ combined with an inanimate noun or the word полтора́ста, три́ста or четы́реста.

1.4.3. A numeral in the *genitive, dative, instrumental* or *prepositional*. It is the numeral сорока́, девяно́ста, полу́тора, полу́тораста or ста.

1.4.4. A numeral in the *instrumental*. It is the numeral двумя́, тремя́ or четырьмя́. In this case -я is part of the ending -мя.

1.5.1. A *past* tense *feminine* singular **verb** in the indicative mood: чита́ла, шла, ду́мала. In this case the ending -а is invariably preceded by -л-.

1.5.2. A feminine singular verb in the *subjunctive* mood: чита́ла бы, шла бы, ду́мала бы. In this case the ending -а is invariably preceded by -л- and the sentence must contain the particle бы.

1.5.3. An imperfective *verbal adverb*: спеша́, чу́вствуя, зака́нчивая, крича́.

1.5.4. A feminine short-form passive *participle* in the singular: постро́ена, сжа́та, люби́ма. In this case the ending -а is invariably preceded by -н-, -т- or -м-.

1.5.5. A feminine long-form participle in the singular: чита́ющая, пи́шущая, чита́вшая, нёсшая, постро́енная, сжа́тая, люби́мая. In this case -я is part of the ending, and -ая is preceded by -щ-, -ш-, -н-, -т- or -м-. The words обвиня́емая, подсуди́мая, эвакуи́рованная, урождённая, слу́жащая and заве́дующая may be used as nouns (see also 1.1.1).

1.5.6. If -я is preceded by с, the element -ся may show that the word is a *verb* form. The element -ся may either be part of any form of a verb, including its dictionary form, or be used only in some of its forms, usually in the third person present tense (both numbers), the second person singular, the first person plural, past tense of the indicative (and the subjunctive) mood masculine singular, and the participial forms which have the marker -ш-, -вш-, -ущ-/-ющ- or -ащ-/-ящ-: улыба́ешься, улыба́ется, улыба́емся, улыба́ются, улыба́лся, улыба́ющийся, улыба́вшаяся.

Besides, the following unchangeable words terminate in -а/-я:
1.6.1. Nouns: антраша́, буржуа́, амплуа́, бра, па, комполка́. There are very few such words.
1.6.2. Adverbs: за́втра, не́хотя, исподло́бья, сле́ва, шутя́, etc.
1.6.3. Conjunctions: пока́, когда́, а.
1.6.4. Prepositions: на, за, для, спустя́, благодаря́.
1.6.5. Particles: да, пожа́луйста.
1.6.6. Interjections: ха, ха-ха́, ура́, э́врика.

The preceding can be summarised in a table (see Table No. 1).

Notes on Table No. 1

It is obvious that -а/-я is the termination of forms of widely differing frequency and importance.

First, discrimination between nouns used in different cases and numbers is the most difficult. (See A.2, 1.1.)

Second, the widely used long forms of adjectives and participles are marked by at least two final elements: -ая and -яя. In a sentence—like short-form adjectives and participles—these forms are connected with feminine nouns in the nominative singular. However, it should be borne in mind that nouns may also end in -а or -я and in rare cases in -ая or -яя. (See A.2, 3.1 and A.2, 3.3.)

Table No. 1

Termi-nation	Ending								Unchangeable Words		
	Noun		Pronoun	Adjective	Numeral	Verb		Adverb	Preposition	Conjunction
	Singular	Plural	Singular	Singular						
-а	*nom.* кáрга сиротá полчасá Соколóва (*woman*) *gen.* сáда студéнта óблака получáса Соколóва (*man*) *acc.* студéнта инженéра Соколóва	*nom.* лесá воротá *acc.* лесá воротá	*nom.* онá	*nom.* та нáша вáша мáмина отцóва *gen.* мáмина отцóва *acc.* мáмина отцóва *short form* белá	*nom.* двá трúста четыреста *acc.* двá трúста четыреста *gen., dat., instr., prep.* сорокá девянóста ста полýтора полýтора-ста	*subj., mood* игрáла бы *past tense* игрáла *v. adv.* спешá ворчá *part.* сдéлана разбúта		вчерá сполнá зáвтра	на за	покá когдá а
-я	*nom.* статья́ лúния дя́дя пóлдня ничья́ *gen.* дня́ тóкаря пóля *acc.* слéсаря тóкаря	*nom.* поля́ учителя́ *acc.* поля́ хлóпья	*nom.* я *gen.* меня́ тебя́ себя́ *acc.* меня́ тебя́ себя́	*nom.* вся чья óленья трéтья дóбрая хорóшая осéнняя *short form* синя́ излúшня	*instr.* двумя́ тремя́ четырьмя́	*v. adv.* скользя́ совершéнствуя *refl. form* катáться берегýтся берёчься мóющийся *part.* сдéланная читáвшая пúшущая		шутя́ исподлóбья нехотя́	для спустя́ благодаря́	

42

Third, the widely used feminine finite verb forms in the past tense of the indicative (and the subjunctive) mood are characterised not only by the ending -a, but also by the preceding -л-, and in the case of the subjunctive mood also by the particle бы. These verb forms are generally connected with feminine nouns in the nominative. (See A.2, 2.5.)

Fourth, possessive adjectives should be distinguished which, unlike the short and long forms of "traditional" adjectives and participles, are encountered extremely rarely.

Fifth, unchangeable nouns and interjections are used extremely rarely.

Sixth, the forms of pronouns and numerals, and also the conjunctions and the prepositions are fully lexicalised.

2. Grammatical characteristics of words ending in -и/-ы.

-и/-ы may be an ending, part of a stem and also (after -м-) part of an ending.

A word with the termination -и or -ы may be:

2.1.1. A **noun** in the *genitive singular*: (нет) яблони, лошади, станции, страны, тишины, сестры. It is usually a *feminine* noun.

2.1.2. A noun in the *dative* singular: (идти к) станции, площади, молодёжи. In this case only the ending -и occurs.

2.1.3. A noun in the *prepositional* singular: (говорить о) санатории, пути, движении, жизни. In this case only the ending -и occurs.

2.1.4. A noun in the *nominative* or *accusative plural*: люди, кони, лошади, яблони, санатории, станции, столы, часы, стены, народы, слоны. Only inanimate nouns can have this form in the accusative.

2.2.1. The **pronoun** ты in the nominative singular.

2.2.2. The pronoun мы or вы in the nominative plural.

2.2.3. The pronoun они in the nominative plural.

2.3.1. An **adjective** in the *nominative* or *accusative plural*: мои, наши, эти, чьи, оленьи, старушечьи, папины, отцовы, дедовы. In this case the adjective must be either a pronominal or possessive one. In the former case only the ending -и occurs; and in the latter, either -и or -ы.

The accusative occurs only when the noun with which the adjective agrees is an inanimate one: (читаю) свои, наши, эти, мамины, отцовы (письма).

2.3.2. A *short-form* adjective in the plural: добры, здоровы, светлы, искренни, хороши, свежи. The ending -и/-ы usually occurs only after н; after ж, ч, ш, щ only -и occurs; after the other consonants usually only -ы occurs. (See also 1.3.5.)

2.4.1. The **numeral** три or двести (the nominative or the accusative).

2.4.2. A numeral in the genitive, dative or prepositional: пяти, семи, десяти, двадцати, пятнадцати. In all such cases only the ending -и occurs.

2.5.1. A **verb** in the *imperative* singular: скажи, пиши, принеси. In this case only the ending -и occurs.

2.5.2. A verb in the *past* tense *plural* of the indicative mood: сказали, читали, были. In this case only the ending -и invariably preceded by -л- occurs.

2.5.3. A verb in the *subjunctive* plural: успели бы, решили бы, знали бы. In this case only the ending -и invariably preceded by -л- occurs, the sentence containing the particle бы.

2.5.4. A *verbal adverb*: бу́дучи, узна́вши, принёсши. In this case only the termination **-и** occurs preceded by **-уч-, -ш-** or **-вш-**.

2.5.5. A plural short-form passive *participle*: постро́ены, вы́мыты, люби́мы. In this case the ending **-ы** is invariably preceded by **-н-, -м-** or **-т-**.

Besides, some unchangeable words may also end in **-и/-ы**:

2.6.1. The nouns хо́бби, ре́гби, ле́ди, управдела́ми, ре́фери and some others. There are very few such words.

2.6.2. Adjectives: хи́нди (language), суахи́ли (language). There are very few such words.

2.6.3. Adverbs: сза́ди, впереди́, снару́жи, вблизи́, вдали́, уры́вками, некста́ти, два́жды, взаймы́, etc. There are relatively many such words. A considerable part of them are adverbs of the по-моско́вски, по-ру́сски type.

2.6.4. Conjunctions: и́ли, е́сли, что́бы, да́бы, я́кобы, е́жели (*arch*.), ли, всё-таки.

2.6.5. Prepositions: ра́ди, впереди́, среди́, посреди́, вблизи́, вопреки́, внутри́, изнутри́.

2.6.6. Particles: -таки, ли, ни, бы, неуже́ли.

2.6.7. Interjections: го́споди, ба́тюшки, фи, ахти́, хи-хи́, люли́.

2.7. If a word ends in **-ми**, it may be either a verb in the *imperative* singular (see 2.5.1) or a **noun, adjective** or **numeral** in the *instrumental*. In the latter case **-и** is part of the ending **-ами/-ями** or **-ыми/-ими**.

2.7.1. The following forms end in **-ами/-ями**: (1) nouns in the instrumental plural: города́ми, доро́гами, степя́ми, друзья́ми; (2) the pronouns на́ми and ва́ми (the instrumental plural); and (3) numerals in the instrumental: двумяста́ми, пятьюста́ми, семьюста́ми.

2.7.2. The following forms end in **-ими/-ыми**: (1) nouns in the instrumental plural: прохо́жими, пере́дними, вожа́тыми, столо́выми; (2) the pronoun и́ми (the instrumental plural); (3) long-form adjectives in the instrumental plural: мои́ми, све́жими, хоро́шими, до́брыми, молоды́ми, наро́дными; and (4) the numerals обе́ими, двои́ми and трои́ми (in the instrumental).

2.7.3. Pronominal adjectives in the instrumental plural end in **-еми**: все́ми, те́ми.

2.7.4. Nouns in the instrumental plural end in **-ьми**: дверьми́, лошадьми́, людьми́.

The preceding can be summarised in a table (see Table No. 2).

Notes on Table No. 2

It is obvious that **-и/-ы** is the termination of forms of widely differing frequency and importance.

First, discrimination between nouns used in different cases and numbers, as well as identification of the imperative verb forms are of paramount importance. (See A.2, 1.2 and 2.1.)

Second, the widely used verb forms of the past tense and of the subjunctive mood plural are marked not only by the ending **-и**, but also by the preceding **-л-** and in the case of the subjunctive mood also by the particle бы. These verb forms are connected with nouns in the nominative plural.

Third, forms of possessive adjectives should be distinguished, which, unlike the short and long forms of "traditional" adjectives, occur extremely rarely.

Fourth, unchangeable nouns, adjectives and interjections are rarely used.

Fifth, the forms of pronouns and numerals, and also the conjunctions and the prepositions are fully lexicalised.

Termi-nation	Ending									
	Noun		Pronoun		Adjective		Numeral	Verb	Unchangeable Words		
	Singular	Plural	Sing.	Plural	Plural				Adverb	Preposition	Conjunction
-и	*gen.* я́блони ло́шади *dat.* ло́шади ста́нции *prep.* ло́шади ста́нции санато́рии	*nom.* я́блони ло́шади ста́нции санато́рии *acc.* я́блони ста́нции санато́рии		*nom.* они́	*nom.* на́ши чьи ры́бьи *acc.* на́ши чьи ры́бьи *short form* хоро́ший и́скренни		*nom.* три две́сти *gen., dat., prep.* пяти́ десяти́ тридцати́ восемна́дцати *acc.* три две́сти	*imper.* пиши́ неси́ *past tense pl.* чита́ли *subj, mood pl.* чита́ли бы *v. adv.* бу́дучи сня́вши	кста́ти сза́ди	ра́ди вопреки́ внутри́	и и́ли е́сли
-ы	*gen.* страны́ сестры́	*nom.* столы́ стра́ны сте́ны часы́ *acc.* столы́ стра́ны сте́ны часы́	*nom.* ты	*nom.* мы вы	*nom.* ма́мины отцо́вы *acc.* ма́мины отцо́вы *short form* умны́ здоро́вы			*part.* постро́ены измя́ты люби́мы	два́жды взаймы́		чтобы
-ми	*instr.* города́ми доро́гами прохо́жими дверьми́			*instr.* на́ми ва́ми и́ми	*instr.* мои́ми свои́ми но́выми све́жими все́ми		*instr.* двумяста́ми пятьюста́ми двои́ми трои́ми	*imper.* возьми́			

45

3. Grammatical characteristics of words ending in -e.

-e may be an ending, part of a stem and also (after **-и-, -ы-, -о-, -е-**) part of an ending.

A word with the termination **-e** may be:

3.1.1. A **noun** in the *nominative singular*: мо́ре, по́ле, пожа́рище, горю́чее, млекопита́ющее, насеко́мое. In this case **-e** may follow a consonant, less frequently **-о-/-е-**, being in the latter case part of the ending **-ое/-ее**. All such nouns are *neuter*.

3.1.2. A noun in the *accusative* singular: see 3.1.1.

3.1.3. A noun in the *dative* singular: (подойти́ к) стене́, доро́ге, дере́вне, де́душке. As a rule, such nouns are *feminine* or they may be masculine nouns with the ending **-a** in the nominative singular.

3.1.4. A noun in the *prepositional* singular: (говори́ть о) пого́де, до́ме, семье́, хле́бе.

3.1.5. A noun in the *nominative plural*: гра́ждане, англича́не, киевля́не. Such nouns usually denote persons and have the termination **-анин/-янин** in the nominative singular. Besides, they may be nouns of the млекопита́ющие, насеко́мые type. In this case **-e** follows **-и-** or **-ы-** and is part of the ending **-ые/-ие**.

3.1.6. A noun in the *accusative* plural: бу́лочные, столо́вые, пере́дние, пиро́жные. In this case **-e** usually follows **-ы-** (occasionally **-ни-**) and is part of the ending **-ые/-ие**.

3.2.1. The **pronouns** ко мне, к тебе́, к себе́ in the *dative* singular.

3.2.2. A pronoun in the *prepositional* singular: (говори́ть) обо мне́, о тебе́, о себе́.

3.3.1. A *neuter short-form* **adjective** in the *singular*: си́не, изли́шне. There are very few such forms. (See also 1.3.5.)

3.3.2. A *neuter* **adjective** in the *nominative singular*: ва́ше, пти́чье. In this case pronominal and possessive adjectives have the ending **-e** following a consonant or **ь**.

3.3.3. A *neuter long-form* adjective in the nominative singular: до́брое, хоро́шее, я́сное, после́днее. In this case **-e** follows **-о-** or **-е-** and is part of the ending **-ое/-ее**.

3.3.4. A neuter long-form adjective in the *accusative* singular: (ви́жу) све́тлое, хоро́шее, чи́стое, осе́ннее (не́бо). In this case **-e** follows **-о-** or **-е-** and is part of the ending **-ое/-ее**.

3.3.5. A long-form adjective in the *nominative plural*: све́тлые, хоро́шие, чи́стые, осе́нние, все, те. In this case **-e** frequently follows **-и-** or **-ы-** and is part of the ending **-ые/-ие**.

3.3.6. A long-form adjective in the *accusative* plural: (ви́жу) све́тлые, хоро́шие, чи́стые, сыно́вние (глаза́). (Adjectives in this form qualify inanimate nouns.)

3.4.1. The feminine **numeral** о́бе or две in the nominative.

3.4.2. The feminine numeral о́бе or две in the accusative. In this case the quantity of inanimate objects is indicated.

3.4.3. The numeral четы́ре, дво́е or тро́е in the nominative.

3.4.4. The numeral четы́ре, дво́е or тро́е in the accusative. In this case the quantity of inanimate objects is indicated.

3.5.1. A present or future tense **verb** in the *2nd person plural* of the indicative mood: идёте, ви́дите, зна́ете, хоти́те. In this case **-e** invariably follows **-ит-** or **-ет-** and is part of the ending.

3.5.2. A verb in the *imperative* plural: иди́те, зна́йте, бро́сьте. In this case **-e** invariably follows **-т-** and is but part of the ending **-те** indicating the number. The marker **-й, -и** or **-ь** of the imperative is placed before this ending.

3.5.3. A neuter long-form *participle* in the *nominative* singular: бегу́щее, люби́мое, сде́ланное, вы́росшее. In this case **-e** follows **-о-** or **-е-** and is part of the ending **-ое/-ее**.

3.5.4. A neuter long-form participle in the *accusative* singular: (ви́жу) откры́тое (окно́). In this case **-e** follows **-о-** or **-е-** and is part of the ending **-ое/-ее**.

3.5.5. A long-form participle in the nominative *plural*: цвету́щие, ухо́женные, заро́сшие, люби́мые. In this case **-e** follows **-и-** or **-ы-** and is part of the ending **-ые/-ие**.

3.5.6. A long-form participle in the *accusative* plural: (ви́жу) цвету́щие, ухо́женные, вы́росшие, люби́мые (дере́вья). In this case **-e** follows **-и-** or **-ы-** and is part of the ending **-ые/-ие**. Participles which have this form qualify inanimate nouns.

In addition, the following unchangeable words may have the termination **-e**:

3.6.1. Nouns: протеже́, фойе́, коммюнике́, желе́, реле́, резюме́, пюре́, шоссе́, ко́фе, кафе́, варьете́. There are very few such words.

3.6.2. Adjectives: мо́рзе. There are very few such words.

3.6.3. Adjectives in the comparative degree: бли́же, добре́е, умне́е, ста́рше.

3.6.4. Adverbs: налегке́, везде́, поодино́чке, ны́не, впервы́е. The number of such words is relatively small, but they are very frequently used. Specially important among them are the words which are adverbs in the comparative degree: бли́же, лу́чше, добре́е, умне́е.

3.6.5. Conjunctions: та́кже, то́же.
3.6.6. Prepositions: пре́жде, вро́де, во́зле, по́сле, кро́ме, вне, накану́не.
3.6.7. Particles: ра́зве, же, да́же, уже́.
3.6.8. Interjections: эге́, хе-хе́.

The preceding can be summarised in a table (see Table No. 3).

Notes on Table No. 3

It is obvious that **-e** is the termination of forms of widely differing frequency and importance.

First, discrimination between nouns used in different cases is of paramount importance. (See A.2, 1.3.)

Second, the widely used adjectival and participial forms ending in **-ие/-ые** and **-ое/-ее** are marked by means of two last letters. The most difficult task is discrimination between the adjectives or participles so marked and the nouns which are in fact substantivised adjectives or participles, of the вожа́тый, пере́дняя, моро́женое type. (See A.2, 3.1.)

Third, the widely used finite verb forms in the indicative and the imperative moods are marked not only by means of **-e**, but with the help of the preceding **-т** as well. The **-те** ending verb forms in the indicative and imperative moods sometimes have absolutely identical spelling: говори́те, стучи́те.

Fourth, the almost fully lexicalised forms of pronouns and numerals, and also conjunctions and prepositions must be distinguished.

Table No. 3

Termination	Ending									Unchangeable Words			
	Noun		Pronoun	Adjective			Numeral	Verb	Adverb	Preposition	Conjunction
	Singular	Plural	Singular	Singular		Plural						
-e	*nom.* море поле млекопитающее насекомое горючее *acc.* море поле насекомое горючее *dat.* стране земле *prep.* хлебе стране окне поле	*nom.* граждане крестьяне млекопитающие насекомые булочные *acc.* булочные	*dat.* мне тебе себе *prep.* мне тебе себе	*short form neut.* излишне *nom.* наше ваше *acc.* наше ваше *nom.* доброе хорошее птичье *acc.* доброе хорошее птичье		*nom.* все те *acc.* все те *nom.* добрые хорошие *acc.* добрые хорошие *comp. degree* добрее старше	*nom.* две четыре обе двое *acc.* две четыре обе трое двое	*indic. mood pres. tense 2nd pers. pl.* идёте знаете видите ходите *imper.* идите знайте сядьте *part.* бегущее любимое бегущие любимые	везде впервые *comp. degree* ближе добрее	после кроме	также тоже
-же		*nom.* передние млекопитающие *acc.* передние			*nom.* синие карие *acc.* синие карие			*part.* бегущие			

-ые	*nom.* булочные столовые насекомые *acc.* булочные столовые	*nom.* вёрные нёжные *acc.* вёрные нёжные	*part.* любимые
-ое	*nom.* пирожное насекомое *acc.* пирожное	*nom. neut.* доброе большое *acc.* доброе большое	*part.* любимое
-ее	*nom.* горячее будущее *acc.* горячее будущее	*nom. neut.* среднее нижнее *acc.* среднее нижнее *comp. degree* добрее холоднее	*part.* бегущее *comp. degree* добрее холоднее быстрее

Fifth, short-form adjectives and plural noun forms ending in **-е** (not in **-ие** or **-ые**!) must be distinguished, the former being rarely used and the latter being limited to the words which designate people and have the termination **-анин/-янин** in the nominative singular.

Sixth, unchangeable nouns, adjectives and interjections are used extremely rarely.

4. Grammatical characteristics of words ending in -у/-ю.

-у/-ю may be an ending, part of a stem or part of an ending: **-ю** follows **-о-/-е-**, **-ь-** or **-у-/-ю-** and **-у** follows **-ом-/-ем-**.

A word with the termination **-у/-ю** may be:

4.1.1. A **noun** in the *genitive singular*: (нет) са́хару, ча́ю, мёду. As a rule, it is a masculine or neuter noun denoting a substance. Such nouns are more often used in the same form with the ending **-а/-я**. (See also 1.1.2.)

4.1.2. A noun in the *dative* singular: (подойти́ к) до́му, са́ду, кра́ю, жи́телю. Such nouns are usually *masculine* or *neuter*. In addition words of the type вожа́тому, ру́сскому, рабо́чему, заве́дующему may have this form, in which case **-у** follows **-ом-/-ем-** and is part of the ending **-ому/-ему**. (See also 4.3.1.)

4.1.3. A noun in the *accusative* singular: (ви́жу) зе́млю, сте́ну, коро́ву, ня́ню. Such nouns are *feminine*. In addition nouns of the type (ви́жу) столо́вую, пере́днюю, шашлы́чную, заве́дующую, слу́жащую may have this form, in which case **-ю** follows either **-у-** or **-ню-** and is part of the ending.

4.1.4. A noun in the *instrumental* singular: (дово́лен) ло́шадью, две́рью.

In addition, nouns in which **-ю** follows **-о-** or **-ё-** and is but a part of the ending: жено́ю, стено́ю, землёю, and also the words пере́днею and столо́вою have this form. Such nouns are more often used with the ending **-ой/-ей**. All these nouns are *feminine*.

4.1.5. A noun in the *prepositional* singular: (быть) в лесу́, шкафу́, носу́, на краю́. Such nouns are usually masculine and denote the place of an action.

4.2.1. A **pronoun** in the *dative*: (дать) кому́, чему́, ему́ (нему́).

4.2.2. A pronoun in the *instrumental*: (дово́лен) е́ю, собо́ю, мно́ю, тобо́ю. These pronouns are more often used with the ending **-ой**.

4.3.1. A masculine or neuter **adjective** in the *dative singular*: (идти́ к) ма́мину, отцо́ву (до́му). In addition, adjectives in which **-у** follows **-ом-/-ем-** and is part of the ending **-ому/-ему**: (идти́ к) большо́му, хоро́шему (до́му), and also nouns of the вожа́тому, прохо́жему type may have this form.

4.3.2. A feminine adjective in the *accusative* singular: (ви́жу) ту, э́ту, чью, ма́мину, де́дову (вещь). In addition, adjectives in which **-ю** follows **-у-** or **-ю-** and is part of the ending **-ую/-юю**: до́брую, хоро́шую, осе́ннюю, ни́жнюю, and also nouns of the ру́сскую type may have this form.

4.3.3. A feminine adjective in the *instrumental* singular if **-ю** follows **-о-** or **-е-** and is part of the ending: (дово́лен) всёю, то́ю, на́шею, хоро́шею, дру́жною (семьёй). Adjectives and nouns are more often used in the same form with the ending **-ой/-ей**.

4.4. A **numeral** in the *instrumental*: (пришёл с) пятью́, семью́, двена́дцатью (друзья́ми).

4.5.1. A *1st person singular* **verb** in the present tense of the indicative mood: я пишу́, прочита́ю, сде́лаю, уви́жу, смотрю́.

4.5.2. A masculine or neuter long-form active or passive *participle* in the *dative* singular: (подошёл к) чита́ющему, писа́вшему, на́званному (челове́ку). (See also 4.3.1.)

4.5.3. A feminine long-form participle in the *accusative* singular: (ви́жу) цвету́щую, вы́росшую, сло́манную (я́блоню).(See also 4.3.2.)

4.5.4. A feminine long-form participle in the *instrumental* singular: (знако́миться с) написа́вшею, чита́ющею (же́нщиной). (See also 4.3.3.)

In addition, the following unchangeable words may terminate in **-у/-ю**:

4.6.1. Nouns: ревю́, меню́, интервью́, какаду́. There are very few such words.
4.6.2. Adjectives: ба́нту, пушту́, зу́лу. The number of such words is very small.
4.6.3. Adverbs: впра́вду, внизу́, вверху́, вплотну́ю, вовсю́, воо́чию.
4.6.4. Conjunctions: посто́льку, поско́льку.
4.6.5. Prepositions: ме́жду, ввиду́, внизу́, сни́зу, све́рху.
4.6.6. Interjections: ау́, мя́у, ей-бо́гу, хрю-хрю́, ба́юшки-баю́.

The preceding can be summarised in a table (see Table No. 4).

Notes on Table No. 4

It is obvious that **-у/-ю** is the termination of forms of widely differing frequency and importance.

First, discrimination between nouns used in different cases is of paramount importance. (See A.2, 1.4.)

Second, the widely used adjectival and participial forms ending in **-ому/-ему, -ою/-ею** and **-ую/-юю** are marked quite clearly. The most difficult thing is to discriminate between adjectives or participles having this form and the substantivised adjectives or participles of the прохо́жему, мостову́ю, шашлы́чную type. (See A.2, 3.1.)

Third, verb forms marked fairly clearly by means of **-у/-ю** must be distinguished.

Fourth, possessive adjectives and unchangeable nouns and adjectives are very rarely used.

Fifth, the forms of pronouns and numerals and also conjunctions and prepositions are fully lexicalised.

5. Grammatical characteristics of words ending in -о/-ё.

-о/-ё may be an ending or part of a stem, and **-о** (after **-ог-/-ег-**) part of an ending.

A word with the termination **-о** or **-ё** may be:

5.1.1. A **noun** in the *nominative singular*: село́, окно́, ружьё, Бородино́. Such nouns are *neuter*.

5.1.2. A noun in the *genitive* singular: (нет) вожа́того, рабо́чего, пиро́жного. In this case **-о** follows **-ог-/-ег-** and is but part of the ending **-ого/-его**.

5.1.3. A noun in the *accusative* singular: (ви́жу) строи́тельство, Бородино́, плечо́, копьё. Such nouns are neuter. In addition animate substantivised adjectives and participles may have this form: рабо́чего,

Table No. 4

Termi-nation	Noun Singular	Pronoun Singular	Adjective Singular	Numeral	Verb	Adverb	Preposition	Conjunction
-у	*gen.* са́хару ча́йку *dat.* до́му не́бу прохо́жему *acc.* сте́ну *prep.* лесу́ шкафу́	*dat.* кому́ чему́ ему́	*dat.* ма́мину отцо́ву зелёному све́тлому ни́жнему си́нему *acc.* ма́мину отцо́ву э́ту ту	*instr.* пятью́ десятью́	*pres./fut. 1st pers. sing.* несу́ веду́ *part.* чита́ющему писа́вшему	внизу́ неподалёку	ме́жду ввиду́ све́рху	поско́льку посто́льку
-ю	*gen.* ча́ю *dat.* кра́ю сле́сарю *acc.* зе́млю *prep.* кра́ю *instr.* жено́ю землёю столо́вою лопа́дью	*instr.* его́ собо́ю мно́ю тобо́ю	*acc.* чью до́брую хоро́шую си́нюю *instr.* всею́ бы́строю		*pres./fut. 1st pers. sing.* чита́ю рису́ю *part.* чита́ющую писа́вшую	вовсю́		

вожа́того. In this case **-о** follows **-ог-/-ег-** and is but part of the ending **-ого/-его**.
 5.2.1. The **pronoun** кто or что in the *nominative*.
 5.2.2. A pronoun in the *accusative*: что, кого́, никого́, ничего́, не́кого, не́чего, (н)её.
 5.2.3. A pronoun in the *genitive*: кого́, чего́, не́кого, не́чего, никого́, ничего́, (н)её.
 5.3.1. A neuter **adjective** in the *nominative* singular: то, э́то, всё, чьё, моё, ма́мино, отцо́во (де́ло).
 5.3.2. A neuter adjective in the *accusative* singular: (See 5.3.1.)
 5.3.3. A masculine adjective in the *accusative* singular: (ви́жу) до́брого, у́много, хоро́шего (ребёнка). In this case **-о** follows **-ог-/-ег-**and is but part of the ending **-ого/-его**. Adjectives in this form invariably qualify animate nouns.
 5.3.4. A masculine or neuter adjective in the *genitive* singular: (нет) большо́го, но́вого, кра́йнего (до́ма). In this case **-о** follows **-ог-/-ег-**and is but part of the ending **-ого/-его**.
 5.3.5. A *neuter short-form* adjective in the singular: (не́бо) све́тло, я́сно.
 5.4.1. A **numeral** in the *nominative*: сто, девяно́сто, че́тверо, ско́лько, сто́лько, пя́теро. In this case only the ending **-о** occurs.
 5.4.2. A numeral in the *accusative*. (See 5.4.1.)
 5.5.1. A *neuter* singular *past* tense **verb** in the indicative mood: бы́ло, прошло́, сине́ло, стоя́ло. In this case only the ending **-о** occurs, invariably after **-л-**.
 5.5.2. A neuter singular verb in the *subjunctive* mood: бы́ло бы, прошло́ бы, сине́ло бы, стоя́ло бы. In this case only the ending **-о** occurs, invariably after **-л-** (and the sentence contains the particle бы).
 5.5.3. A *neuter* short-form passive *participle* in the singular: (пла́тье) измя́то, вы́стирано, замени́мо. In this case only the ending **-о** occurs after **-м-, -т-** or **-н-**.
 5.5.4. A masculine participle in the *accusative* singular: (ви́жу) чита́ющего, писа́вшего, нарисо́ванного (ма́льчика). (See also 5.3.3.)
 5.5.5. A masculine or neuter participle in the *genitive* singular: (а́втор) напи́санного, заверша́ющего, рассмеши́вшего (расска́за). (See also 5.3.4.)

 In addition, the following unchangeable words may terminate in **-о**:
 5.6.1. Nouns: кака́о, та́нго, фиа́ско, трюмо́, харчо́. There are very few such words.
 5.6.2. Adjectives: инди́го, маре́нго, бордо́. The number of such words is very small.
 5.6.3. Adverbs: впра́во, нале́во, тоскли́во, бы́стро, дёшево. There are very many such words.
 5.6.4. Conjunctions: но, что, то, зато́, сле́довательно, бу́дто, сло́вно.
 5.6.5. Prepositions: о, о́бо, о́коло, во, по́до, безо, и́зо, о́то, соотве́тственно, про, со, по́до, вме́сте.
 5.6.6. Particles: спаси́бо, бы́ло.
 5.6.7. Interjections: о, ого́, алло́.

 The preceding can be summarised in a table (see Table No. 5).

Table No. 5

Termination	Noun Singular	Pronoun Singular	Adjective Singular	Numeral	Verb	Unchangeable Words		
						Adverb	Preposition	Conjunction
-о	*nom.* окно́ плечо́ доми́шко *acc.* окно́ плечо́ доми́шко *gen.* горю́чего млекопита́ющего рабо́чего *acc.* вожа́того рабо́чего	*nom.* кто, никто́, не́кто что, не́что *acc.* что кого́, никого́, не́кого его́/него́ *gen.* кого́, никого́, не́кого чего́, ничего́, не́чего его́/него́	*nom.* то э́то ма́мино *acc.* то э́то ма́мино *short form* высоко́ *gen.* большо́го си́него	*nom.* сто девяно́сто ско́лько че́тверо *acc.* сто девяно́сто ско́лько че́тверо	*subj. mood* сказа́ло бы *past tense* сказа́ло *part.* ска́зано изъя́то чита́ющего	впра́во хорошо́ до́рого сме́ло	о во о́коло про относи́тель- но	но что зато́ сле́дова- тельно
-ё	*nom.* ружьё копьё *acc.* ружьё копьё	*gen.* (н)её *acc.* (н)её	*nom.* всё моё чьё *acc.* всё моё чьё					

Notes on Table No. 5

It is obvious that -o/-ё is the termination of forms of widely differing frequency and importance.

First, discrimination between nouns used in the nominative and the accusative is of paramount importance. (See A.2, 1.5.)

Second, long-form adjectives and participles are marked not only by means of -o, but also with the help of -oг-/-eг-. It is very important to discriminate between such adjectives or participles and the nouns which have the same form.

Third, there are very many adverbs and short-form passive participles which terminate in -o.

Fourth, finite neuter singular past tense verb forms in the indicative and the subjunctive moods are marked not only by means of -o, but also with the help of the preceding -л- and in the case of the subjunctive mood also the particle бы. These verb forms are usually connected with neuter nouns in the nominative.

Fifth, the forms of possessive adjectives and also those of uninflected nouns and adjectives are extremely rarely used.

Sixth, the forms of pronouns and numerals, and also conjunctions and prepositions are fully lexicalised.

6. Grammatical characteristics of words ending in -й.

-й may be part of a stem and (after -e-, -o-, -и- and -ы-) part of an ending. It cannot be an ending proper.

A word with the termination -й may be:

6.1.1. A **noun** in the *nominative singular*: герóй, санатóрий, вожáтый, рулевóй, рабóчий, двугри́венный. In this case -й may be part of the stem, as in герóй, гéний, санатóрий, or part of the ending, as in вожáтый, рулевóй, рабóчий, двугри́венный. Such nouns are usually *masculine*.

6.1.2. A noun in the *accusative* singular: санатóрий, хорéй, двугри́венный.

6.1.3. A noun in the *genitive* singular: (нет) ничьéй, рýсской, завéдующей, столóвой, Соколóвой, Петрóвой. As a rule, such words are substantivised feminine adjectives or participles or feminine surnames. In this case the ending is -ой/-ей.

6.1.4. A noun in the *dative* singular. (See 6.1.3.)

6.1.5. A noun in the *prepositional* singular. (See 6.1.3.)

6.1.6. A noun in the *instrumental* singular: (говорю́ с) рýсской, завéдующей, Соколóвой, актри́сой, певи́цей. In this case the ending is -ой/-ей.

6.1.7. A noun in the *genitive plural*: (нет) костéй, ножéй, стáнций, решéний. In this case the termination -ей is the ending, and -ий a part of the stem.

6.1.8. A noun in the *accusative* plural: (ви́жу) людéй, детéй, олéней. (See 6.1.7.)

6.2.1. The **pronoun** ей (ней) in the genitive, dative, instrumental or prepositional.

6.2.2. The pronouns мной, тобóй and собóй in the instrumental.

6.3.1. A *masculine* **adjective** in the nominative singular: большóй, тóлстый, крéпкий, мой, твой, свой. In this case -ой, -ый and -ий are invariably the endings.

6.3.2. A masculine adjective in the *accusative* singular. (See 6.3.1.) Adjectives in this form qualify inanimate nouns.

6.3.3. A feminine adjective in the *genitive, dative, instrumental* or *prepositional*: у́мной, до́брой, хоро́шей, мое́й, свое́й, твое́й. In this case -й is part of the ending -ой/-ей.

6.4.1. A **verb** in the *imperative* singular: пой, жуй, пей, чита́й.

6.4.2. A masculine long-form *participle* in the nominative singular: чита́ющий, писа́вший, сде́ланный, измя́тый. (See 6.3.1.)

6.4.3. A masculine long-form participle in the *accusative* singular. (See 6.4.2.)

6.4.4. A feminine long-form participle in the *genitive, dative, instrumental* or *prepositional*: чита́ющей, писа́вшей, сде́ланной, измя́той. (See 6.3.3.)

In addition, the following unchangeable words may terminate in -й:

6.5.1. Adverbs which usually denote the degree of a modifier: сильне́й, быстре́й.
6.5.2. The conjunction пуска́й.
6.5.3. The particles пуска́й and пожа́луй.
6.5.4. The interjections ай, гей, ой, эй.

The preceding can be summarised in a table (see Table No. 6).

Notes on Table No. 6

First, adjectives and participles in -ой, -ей, -ый and -ий, which usually duplicate the number, case and gender of the noun they qualify, are the most frequently used. It is essential to distinguish between these adjectives or participles and the substantivised adjectives or participles. (See A.2, 3.1.)

Second, it is of paramount importance to distinguish between verbs in the imperative and nouns in different numbers and cases.

Third, the forms of the relevant pronouns are fully lexicalised.

7. Grammatical characteristics of words ending in -ь.

-ь may be a written ending or part of a written ending. As is known, -ь at the end of a word does not convey any sound, but merely indicates the quality of the preceding consonant or is used simply traditionally.

A word with the termination -ь may be:

7.1.1. A **noun** in the *nominative* singular: день, лень, путь, ско́рость, оле́нь, конь.

7.1.2. A noun in the *accusative* singular: (ви́жу) степь, путь, сме́лость.

7.1.3. A noun in the *genitive plural*: (нет) я́блонь, бурь, кастрю́ль. There are not so many such forms; -ь is usually preceded by -н-, -р- or -л-.

7.1.4. A noun in the *accusative plural:* (ви́жу) нянь, герои́нь. There are not so many such forms.

7.2.1. A **numeral** in the *nominative*: пять, семь, де́вять, двена́дцать, три́дцать.

7.2.2. A numeral in the *accusative*. (See 7.2.1.)

7.3.1. A **verb** in the *infinitive*: проси́ть, хоте́ть, лета́ть, бере́чь. In this case -ь occurs only after -т- or -ч-.

7.3.2. A present or future tense verb in the *2nd person singular* of the indicative mood: чита́ешь, ду́маешь, хо́чешь, ви́дишь, слы́шишь, ку́пишь. In this case -ь invariably follows -иш- or -еш-/-ёш- and is part of the ending **-ешь/-ёшь/-ишь**.

Table No. 6

Termi-nation	Noun		Pronoun	Adjective	Verb	Unchangeable Words		
	Singular	Plural	Singular	Singular		Adverb	Conjunction	Preposition
-й	*nom.* герой санаторий вожатый рабочий рулевой *gen.* ничьей *dat.* передней горничной *acc.* санаторий двугривенный *prep.* русской Соколовой *instr.* ничьей русской передней Соколовой стеной волей	*gen.* гостей ножей дрожжей станций движений *acc.* людей детей	*gen., dat., instr.,* *prep.* ей (ней) мной тобой собой	*nom.* большой мой строгий свой толстый твой олений *acc.* большой мой строгий свой толстый твой олений *gen., dat., instr., prep.* умной моей свежей твоей своей	*imper.* стой лей читай *part.* читавший пишущий читавшей пишущей	сильней быстрей	пускай	

7.3.3. A verb in the *imperative* singular: бро́сь, встань, поста́вь, сядь, насы́пь, уда́рь.

7.3.4. A verb form ending in the marker **-сь**: бо́йтесь, боя́лась, боя́лось, боя́лись, боя́лась бы, боя́лось бы, боя́лись бы, весели́сь, взя́вшись. In such cases **-сь** follows the endings terminating in a vowel (see also 1.5.6).

In addition, the following unchangeable words may terminate in **-ь**:

7.4.1. The noun мадемуазе́ль.
7.4.2. The adverbs впредь, вьявь, вскачь, наотма́шь.
7.4.3. The conjunctions ль and лишь.
7.4.4. The preposition внутрь.
7.4.5. The particles ль, лишь, -нибудь.
7.4.6. The interjections буль-бу́ль and брысь.

The preceding can be summarised in a table (see Table No. 7).

Notes on Table No. 7.

First, it is of paramount importance to distinguish between the different case and number forms of nouns. (See A.2, 1.7.)

Second, verbs in the infinitive and the 2nd person singular present (future) tense of the indicative mood are marked not only by **-ь**, but also by the preceding **-т-** or **-ч-** in the infinitive and **-ш-** in the other forms. The imperative may have practically any consonant preceding **-ь**. (See A.2, 2.4.)

Third, the relevant forms of numerals are fully lexicalised.

8. Grammatical characteristics of words ending in -м.

-м may be an ending, part of an ending or part of a stem.

A word with the termination **-м** may be:

8.1.1. A **noun** in the *nominative singular*: дом, приём, фильм, энтузиа́зм. In this case **-м** is part of the stem. Such words are usually *masculine*.

8.1.2. A noun in the *accusative* singular: дом, приём, фильм, энтузиа́зм. (See also 8.1.1.) This is the form of inanimate nouns.

8.1.3. A noun in the *instrumental* singular: (дово́лен) го́родом, бе́регом, днём, преподава́телем, вожа́тым, лесни́чим. In this case **-м** is part of the ending **-ом/-ем/-ём** or **-ым/-им**.

8.1.4. A noun in the *prepositional* singular: (говори́ть о) вожа́том, живо́тном, подлежа́щем, лесни́чем. In this case **-м** is part of the ending **-ом/-ем**.

8.1.5. A noun in the *genitive plural*: (нет) пи́сем, телегра́мм. In this case **-м** is part of the stem.

8.1.6. A noun in the *dative* plural: (идти́ к) леса́м, поля́м, вожа́тым, лесни́чим. In this case **-м** is part of the ending **-ам/-ям** or **-ым/-им** and follows **-а-, -я-, -ы-** or **-и-**.

8.2.1. The **pronouns** (дать) нам, вам, (н)им in the *dative*.

8.2.2. The pronouns (говори́ть) с кем, чем, (н)им in the *instrumental*.

8.3.1. The *masculine* **adjective** сам in the nominative.

8.3.2. A masculine or neuter long-form adjective in the *instrumental* singular: до́брым, све́тлым, хоро́шим, си́ним, тем, всем. In this

Table No. 7

Termination	Noun		Numeral	Verb	Unchangeable Words		
	Singular	Plural			Adverb	Conjunction	Preposition
-ь	*nom.* день конь ночь стро́гость степь *acc.* день степь ночь стро́гость	*gen.* я́блонь земе́ль бурь *acc.* нянь< герои́нь	*nom.* пять де́сять двена́дцать *acc.* пять де́сять два́дцать	*infinitive* проси́ть хоте́ть лета́ть бере́чь *2nd pers. sing. pres./fut. tense indic. mood* чита́ешь пи́шешь стро́ишь *imper.* брось встань поста́вь *refl. form* боя́лась боя́лись бо́йтесь	впредь въявь вскачь наотма́шь	лишь ль	внутрь

59

case -м is part of the ending -ым/-им/-ем and follows -ы-, -и- or -е-.

8.3.3. A masculine or neuter long-form adjective in the *prepositional* singular: добром, хорошем, светлом, синем, том, всём. In this case -м is part of the ending -ом/-ем/-ём and follows -о-, -е- or -ё-.

8.3.4. A masculine *short-form* adjective in the singular: неумолим, зависим.

8.3.5. A long-form adjective in the *dative plural*: добрым, светлым, хорошим, синим, тем, всем. (See also 8.3.2.)

8.4.1. A **numeral** in the *dative*: двум, трём, четырём, двоим, троим, четверым, двумстам, трёмстам. In this case -м is part of the ending and follows -у-, -е-, -ё-, -и- or -ы-.

8.5.1. A present/future tense **verb** in the *1st person singular* of the indicative mood. Here belong only the verbs ем and дам with or without prefixes. In this case -м is the ending.

8.5.2. A present/future tense verb in the *1st person plural* of the indicative mood: читаем, пишем, хотим, просим, ведём. In this case -м is part of the ending -ем/-ём/-им and follows -и-, -е- or -ё-.

8.5.3. A masculine *short-form* passive present *participle* in the singular: любим, излечим. Not infrequently such forms look exactly like those in 8.5.2.

8.5.4. A masculine or neuter *long-form* participle in the *instrumental* singular: читающим, принёсшим, читавшим, написанным. (See also 8.3.2.)

8.5.5. A masculine or neuter long-form participle in the *prepositional* singular: читающем, принёсшем, читавшем, написанном. (See also 8.3.3.)

8.5.6. A long-form present or past participle in the *dative plural*: читающим, принёсшим, читавшим, написанным. (See also 8.3.5.)

In addition, the following unchangeable words may terminate in -м:

8.6.1. The noun мадам.
8.6.2. Adverbs: проездом, целиком, тайком.
8.6.3. Conjunctions: чем, тем, причём, впрочем, притом.
8.6.4. Prepositions: посредством, кругом, путём.
8.6.5. Interjections: гм, бум, бам.

The preceding can be summarised in a table (see Table No. 8).

Notes on Table No. 8

First, it is of paramount importance to distinguish between the different case and number forms of nouns. It should be borne in mind that in some instances -м may be part of a stem, and in others part of an ending. (See A.2, 1.9.)

Second, the most frequently used are the forms of the relevant adjectives and participles, which should be distinguished from the substantivised adjectives and participles. (See A.2, 3.1.)

Third, very frequently used are present/future tense verbs in the 1st person plural indicative mood, in which -м is usually preceded by -е-, -и- or -ё-.

Fourth, the numerals are invariably in the instrumental.

Fifth, the relevant forms of the pronouns are fully lexicalised.

Table No. 8

Termi-nation	Noun		Pronoun		Adjective			Numeral	Verb	Unchangeable Words		
	Singular	Plural	Singular	Plural	Singular		Plural			Adverb	Conjunction	Preposition
-м	*nom.* дом приём *acc.* дом приём *instr.* до́мом приёмом вожа́тым *prep.* вожа́том лесни́чем	*gen.* пи́сем телегра́мм *dat.* леса́м поля́м вожа́тым	*instr.* кем чем (н)им	*dat.* нам вам (н)им	*nom.* сам неутоми́м *instr.* до́брым хоро́шим тем *prep.* до́бром хоро́шем		*dat.* до́брым хоро́шим	*dat.* двум трём тро́йм	*1st pers. sing. pres./ fut. tense indic. mood* дам *1st pers. pl. pres./fut. tense indic. mood* чита́ем про́сим ведём *part.* люби́м зави́сим чита́ющим чита́ющем напи́санном	тайко́м цели- ко́м	притом чем	круго́м путём

9. Grammatical characteristics of words ending in -т.

-т may be either part of an ending or part of a stem. It never occurs as an ending.

A word with the termination -т may be:

9.1.1. A **noun** in the *nominative singular*: брат, совéт, полёт. In this case -т is part of the stem. Such nouns are usually *masculine*.

9.1.2. A noun in the *accusative* singular: совéт, полёт. (See also 9.1.1.) This is the form of inanimate nouns.

9.1.3. A noun in the *genitive plural*: забóт, высóт, плит, лент. In this case -т is part of the stem.

9.1.4. A noun in the *accusative* plural: стáрост. (See 9.1.3.) In this case the noun denotes an animate being.

9.2.1. The *masculine* **adjective** тот or э́тот in the *nominative* singular. In this case -т is part of the stem.

9.2.2. The masculine adjective тот or э́тот in the *accusative* singular. (See 9.2.1.)

9.2.3. A masculine *short-form* adjective in the singular: крут, великовáт, узковáт. In this case -т is part of the stem.

9.3.1. A **numeral** in the *nominative*: пятьдеся́т, сéмьдесят, вóсемьдесят. In this case -т is part of the stem.

9.3.2. A numeral in the *genitive*: двухсóт, семисóт. In this case -т is part of the stem.

9.3.3. A numeral in the *accusative*: пятьдеся́т, вóсемьдесят. (See also 9.3.1.)

9.4.1. A present/future tense **verb** in the *3rd person singular* of the indicative mood: хóчет, прóсит, ведёт, съест, создаёт. In this case -т is part of the ending -ет/-ёт/-ит and usually follows -е-, -ё-, or -и-, or -с- in the words ест, даст and also in some other words with these roots.

9.4.2. A present/future tense verb in the *3rd person plural* of the indicative mood: идýт, хотя́т, читáют, молчáт. In this case -т is part of the ending -ут/-ют or -ат/-ят.

9.4.3. A masculine *short-form* passive past *participle* in the singular: измя́т, сбит, вы́пит. In this case -т is a marker of a passive past participle.

In addition, the following unchangeable words may terminate in -т:

9.5.1. The adverb вразлёт.
9.5.2. The conjunction покáмест.
9.5.3. The preposition от.
9.5.4. The particle вот.

The preceding can be summarised in a table (see Table No. 9).

10. Grammatical characteristics of words ending in -в.

-в may be either part of an ending of part of a stem.

A word with the termination -в may be:

10.1.1. A **noun** in the *nominative singular*: лев, залúв, рукáв, удáв. In this case -в is part of the stem. Such nouns are usually *masculine*.

Table No. 9

Termination	Noun		Adjective	Numeral	Verb	Unchangeable Words	
	Singular	Plural				Adverb	Conjunction / Preposition
-т	*nom.* брат совёт полёт *acc.* совёт полёт	*gen.* плит лент конфёт *acc.* стáрост	*nom.* тот этот *acc.* тот этот *short form* крут сыт великовáт маловáт	*nom.* пятьдесят сёмьдесят *acc.* пятьдесят восемьдесят *gen.* двухсот семьсот	*1st pers. sing. pres./fut. tense* хочет просит берёт ест даст *3rd pers. pl. pres./ fut. tense* хотят идут *short part.* измят выпит	вразлёт	покáмест / от

63

10.1.2. A noun in the *accusative* singular: (вижу) рука́в, зали́в. (See also 10.1.1.) In this case the noun denotes an inanimate object.

10.1.3. A noun in the *genitive plural*: (нет) коро́в, слов, студе́нтов, домо́в. In this case **-в** may either belong to the stem (коро́в, слов) or be part of the ending **-ов** (студе́нтов, домо́в).

10.1.4. A noun in the *accusative plural*: (вижу) львов, студе́нтов, коро́в. (See also 10.1.3.) In this case the noun denotes an animate being.

10.2.1. A *masculine* **adjective** in the nominative singular: како́в, тако́в, отцо́в, чёртов. In this case **-в** is part of the stem.

10.2.2. A masculine adjective in the *accusative* singular: како́в, тако́в, отцо́в, чёртов. In this case the qualified word is an inanimate noun.(See also 10.2.1.)

10.2.3. A masculine *short-form* adjective in the singular: краси́в, сча́стлив. In this case **-в** is part of the stem.

10.3.1. A **verb** in the form of a *verbal adverb*: написа́в, присе́в, сказа́в, сняв. In this case **-в** is the marker of a verbal adverb.

In addition, the following unchangeable words terminate in **-в**:

10.4.1. The adverb напро́тив.
10.4.2. The prepositions: в, про́тив, напро́тив.

The preceding can be summarised in a table (see Table No. 10).

Table No. 10

Termi-nation	Noun		Adjective	Verb	Unchangeable Words		
	Singular	Plural			Adverb	Conjunction	Preposition
-в	*nom.* лев зали́в рука́в уда́в *acc.* зали́в рука́в	*gen.* коро́в слов львов студе́нтов домо́в *acc.* коро́в львов студе́нтов	*nom.* како́в тако́в отцо́в *acc.* како́в тако́в отцо́в *short form* краси́в сча́стлив	*v. adv.* написа́в присе́в	напро́тив		в про́тив напро́тив

11. Grammatical characteristics of words ending in -л.

-л may be either an ending or part of a stem.
A word with the termination -л may be:

11.1.1. A **noun** in the *nominative singular*: стол, стул, со́кол. In this case -л is part of the stem. Such words are usually *masculine*.

11.1.2. A noun in the *accusative* singular: (вижу) стол, стул. Such nouns usually denote inanimate objects. (See also 11.1.1.)

11.1.3. A noun in the *genitive plural*: (нет) школ, пчёл, кукол. In this case -л is part of the stem.

11.1.4. A noun in the *accusative plural*: (вижу) пчёл, кукол, кобыл. Such words are invariably animate nouns. (See also 11.1.3.)

11.2.1. A masculine *short-form* **adjective** in the singular: смел, весел. In this case -л is part of the stem.

11.3.1. A *past tense masculine* singular **verb** in the indicative mood: читал, писал, ходил, говорил. In this case -л is the ending.

11.3.2. A masculine singular verb in the *subjunctive mood*: читал бы, писал бы.

In addition, some adverbs end in -л: напова́л.

The preceding can be summarised in a table (see Table No. 11).

Table No. 11

Termi-nation	Noun		Adjective	Verb	Unchangeable Words		
	Singular	Plural			Adverb	Conjunction	Preposition
-л	*nom.* стол стул сокол *acc.* стол стул	*gen.* пчёл кукол школ *acc.* кукол пчёл	*short form* смел удал	*past tense* ходил читал *subj. mood* знал бы умел бы	напова́л		

12. Grammatical characteristics of words ending in -x.

-x may be either part of an ending or part of a stem.
A word with the termination -x may be:

12.1.1. A **noun** in the *nominative singular*: успех, цех, смех, жених. In this case -x is part of the stem. Such words are usually *masculine* nouns.

12.1.2. A noun in the *accusative* singular: (вижу) успех, цех, смех. Only inanimate nouns can have this form. (See also 12.1.1.)

12.1.3. A noun in the *genitive plural*: (нет) вожатых, старух, млекопитающих, ткачих. In this case -x may be part of the ending -их/-ых of a substantivised adjective or participle of the вожатых, млекопитающих type or part of the stem of such words as старух, ткачих.

12.1.4. A noun in the *accusative plural*: (вижу) вожатых, старух, млекопитающих, ткачих. Only animate nouns may have this form. (See also 12.1.3.)

12.1.5. A noun in the *prepositional plural*: (говорить о) цветах, полях, вожатых, млекопитающих. In this case -x is part of the ending -ах/-ях or -ых/-их.

12.2.1. The **pronoun** их in the genitive, accusative or prepositional.
12.2.2. An **adjective** in the genitive, prepositional or accusative plural: тех, э́тих, всех, кра́сных, си́них. In all such cases -х is part of the ending -их/-ых.
12.2.3. The masculine *short-form* adjective сух or тих in the singular. In this case -х is part of the stem.
12.3.1. A **numeral** in the genitive: (нет) двух, трёх, четырёх, двои́х, шестеры́х (ма́льчиков). In this case -х is part of the ending.
12.3.2. A numeral in the *accusative*: (ви́жу) двои́х, двух, трёх, пятеры́х, семеры́х (ма́льчиков). This is the form of numerals which indicate the number of animate beings. (See also 12.3.1.)
12.3.3. A numeral in the *prepositional*: (говори́ть) о двух, трёх, двои́х, трои́х, двухста́х, пятиста́х. (See also 12.3.1.)
12.4.1. A *past tense masculine* singular **verb** in the indicative mood: засо́х, ути́х. In this case -х is part of the stem.
12.4.2. A masculine singular verb in the *subjunctive mood*: засо́х бы, ути́х бы. In this case -х is part of the stem.

In addition, the following unchangeable words end in -х:

12.5.1. The adverbs на́спех, вверх, наве́рх.
12.5.2. The prepositions пове́рх and сверх.
12.5.3. The interjections ах, бах, эх.

The preceding can be summarised in a table (see Table No. 12).

13. Grammatical characteristics of words ending in -с.

-с is usually part of a stem.
A word with the termination -с may be:

13.1.1. A **noun** in the *nominative singular*: час, вопро́с, матро́с, белору́с. Such words are usually *masculine*.
13.1.2. A noun in the *accusative* singular: (ви́жу) час, вопро́с. Only inanimate nouns can have this form. (See also 13.1.1.)
13.1.3. A noun in the *genitive plural*: (нет) пьес, актри́с, чуде́с, поэте́сс.
13.1.4. A noun in the *accusative* plural: (ви́жу) актри́с, поэте́сс. Only animate nouns can have this form. (See also 13.1.3.)
13.2.1. The **pronouns** нас and вас in the genitive or the accusative.
13.3.1. A masculine short-form **adjective** in the singular: бос, лыс.
13.4.1. A *past tense* masculine singular **verb** in the indicative mood: нёс, спас.
13.4.2. A masculine singular verb in the *subjunctive* mood: нёс бы, спас бы.

In addition, the following unchangeable words end in -с:

13.5.1. The nouns мисс and ми́ссис.
13.5.2. The adjective люкс.
13.5.3. Adverbs: сейча́с, навы́нос, вразбро́с.
13.5.4. The preposition с.

The preceding can be summarised in a table (see Table No. 13).

Table No. 12

Termi-nation	Noun		Pronoun	Adjective	Numeral	Verb	Unchangeable Words		
	Singular	Plural	Plural				Adverb	Conjunction	Preposition
-х	*nom.*	*gen.*	*gen.*	*short form*	*gen.*	*past tense*	нáспех		повéрх
	успéх	старýх	их	сух	двух	засóх	ввéрх		свéрх
	цех	ткачúх	*acc.*	тих	трёх	утúх	навéрх		
	женúх	вожáтых	их	*gen.*	двойх	*subj. mood*			
	смех	млекопи-	*prep.*	тех	тройх	засóх бы			
		тáющих	их	этих	*acc.*	утúх бы			
	acc.	*acc.*		всех	двух				
	успéх	старýх		крáсных	трёх				
	цех	ткачúх		сúних	двойх				
		вожáтых		*acc.*	тройх				
		млекопи-		тех	*prep.*				
		тáющих		этих	двух				
	prep.	*prep.*		всех	трёх				
		цветáх		крáсных	двухстáх				
		поляx		сúних	трёхстáх				
		вожáтых		*prep.*	двойх				
		млекопи-		тех	тройх				
		тáющих		этих					
				всех					
				крáсных					
				сúних					

Table No. 13

Termi-nation	Noun		Pronoun	Adjective	Verb	Unchangeable Words		
	Singular	Plural				Adverb	Conjunction	Preposition
-с	*nom.* час вопрóс матрóс белорýс *асс.* час вопрóс	*gen.* пьес актрúс чудéс поэтéсс *асс.* актрúс поэтéсс	*gen.* нас вас *асс.* нас вас	*short form* бос лыс	*past tense* нёс спас *subj. mood* нёс бы спас бы	сейчáс навы́нос вразбрóс		с

Table No. 14

Termi-nation	Noun		Pronoun	Adjective	Verb	Unchangeable Words			
	Singular	Plural				Adverb	Conjunction	Preposition	Particle
-н	*nom.* сон сын кабáн тумáн *асс.* сон тумáн	*gen.* армя́н ран англичáн *асс.* армя́н англичáн	*nom.* он	*short form* намéрен хóлоден *nom.* дя́дин мáмин бáбушкин *асс.* дя́дин мáмин бáбушкин	*part.* сдéлан напúсан			взамéн	вон

14. Grammatical characteristics of words ending in -н.

-н can only be part of a stem.
A word with the termination -н may be:

14.1.1. A **noun** in the *nominative singular*: сон, сын, кабáн, тумáн. Such words are usually *masculine*.

14.1.2. A noun in the *accusative* singular: (вúжу) сон, тумáн. Only inanimate nouns can have this form. (See also 14.1.1.)

14.1.3. A noun in the *genitive plural*: (нет) армя́н, ран, англичáн.

14.1.4. A noun in the *accusative* plural: (вúжу) армя́н, англичáн. Only animate nouns can have this form.

14.2.1. The **pronoun** он in the nominative.

14.3.1. A masculine **adjective** in the nominative or accusative singular: мáмин, пáпин, бáбушкин. In this case the qualified noun denotes an inanimate object.

14.3.2. A masculine *short-form* adjective in the singular: намéрен, хóлоден.

14.4.1. A masculine past **participle** in the nominative singular: сдéлан, постро́ен.

In addition, the following unchangeable words end in **-н**:

14.5.1. The noun фрéйлейн.
14.5.2. The adjectives реглáн and модéрн.
14.5.3. The preposition взамéн.
14.5.4. The particle вон.

The preceding can be summarised in a table (see Table No. 14).

15. Grammatical characteristics of words ending in -к.

-к can only be part of a stem.
A word with the termination -к may be:

15.1.1. A **noun** in the *nominative singular*: зáвтрак, кусóк, человéк, ученúк. Such words are usually *masculine*.

15.1.2. A noun in the *accusative* singular: (вúжу) зáвтрак, кусóк. Only inanimate nouns can have this form. (See also 15.1.1.)

15.1.3. A noun in the *genitive plural*: (нет) кóшек, шáпок, трýбок.

15.1.4. A noun in the *accusative* plural: (вúжу) кóшек, тёток. Only animate nouns can have this form.

15.2.1. A masculine *short-form* **adjective** in the singular: крéпок, мя́гок, одинёшенек.

15.3.1. The **numeral** сóрок in the nominative or the accusative.

15.4.1. A *masculine* singular *past tense* **verb** in the indicative mood: испёк, промóк.

15.4.2. A masculine singular verb in the *subjunctive* mood: испёк бы, промóк бы.

In addition, the following unchangeable words end in **-к**:

15.5.1. The adjective пик.
15.5.2. The adverbs напрямúк, нáбок, как, так.
15.5.3. The conjunctions так, итáк, как.
15.5.4. The prepositions к and поперёк.

The preceding can be summarised in a table (see Table No. 15).

16. Grammatical characteristics of words ending in -г.

-г can only be part of a stem.

A word with the termination -г may be:

16.1.1. A **noun** in the *nominative singular*: бéрег, шаг, педагóг. Such words are usually *masculine*.

16.1.2. A noun in the *accusative* singular: (вижу) бéрег, шаг. Only inanimate nouns can have this form. (See also 16.1.1.)

16.1.3. A noun in the *genitive plural*: (нет) дорóг, слуг, тревóг, бродя́г.

16.1.4. A noun in the *accusative* plural: (вижу) слуг, бродя́г. Only animate nouns can have this form.

16.2.1. A masculine *short-form* **adjective** in the singular: строг, дóрог.

16.3.1. A *masculine* singular *past tense* **verb** in the indicative mood: берёг, смог.

16.3.2. A masculine singular verb in the *subjunctive* mood: берёг бы, смог бы.

16.3.3. The verb ляг in the *imperative* singular.

In addition, the following unchangeable words end in -г:

16.4.1. The adverbs вдруг and вдрызг.
16.4.2. The preposition вокрýг.

The preceding can be summarised in a table (see Table No. 16).

17. Grammatical characteristics of words terminating in -ш.

-ш can be only part of a stem.

A word with the termination -ш may be:

17.1.1. A **noun** in the *nominative singular*: камы́ш, ковш, малы́ш. Such words are usually *masculine*.

17.1.2. A noun in the *accusative* singular: (вижу) камы́ш, ковш. Only inanimate nouns can have this form. (See also 17.1.1.)

17.1.3. A noun in the *genitive plural*: (нет) крыш, афи́ш, секретáрш.

17.1.4. A noun in the *accusative* plural: (вижу) секретáрш, курьéрш. Only animate nouns can have this form.

17.2.1. The masculine **adjective** наш or ваш in the nominative singular.

17.2.2. The masculine adjective наш or ваш in the accusative singular. In this case the qualified noun denotes an inanimate object.

17.2.3. The masculine *short-form* adjective хорóш in the singular.

The preceding can be summarised in a table (see Table No. 17).

Table No. 15

Termi-nation	Noun		Adjective	Numeral	Verb	Unchangeable Words		
	Singular	Plural				Adverb	Conjunction	Preposition
-к	*nom.* кусо́к челове́к диск *acc.* кусо́к диск	*gen.* ко́шек ша́пок тру́бок *acc.* ко́шек тёток	*short form* лёгок мя́гок	*nom.* со́рок *acc.* со́рок	*past tense* тёк мок *subj. mood* тёк бы мок бы	напрями́к на́бок как	так ита́к как	к поперёк

Table No. 16

Termination	Noun		Adjective	Verb	Unchangeable Words		
	Singular	Plural			Adverb	Conjunction	Preposition
-г	*nom.* бе́рег шаг педаго́г *acc.* бе́рег шаг	*gen.* доро́г слуг трево́г бродя́г *acc.* слуг бродя́г	*short form* строг до́рог	*past tense* берёг стерёг *subj. mood* берёг бы стерёг бы *imper.* ляг	вдры́зг вдруг		вокру́г

Table No. 17

Termination	Noun		Adjective
	Singular	Plural	
-ш	*nom.* камы́ш ковш малы́ш *acc.* камы́ш ковш	*gen.* крыш афи́ш секрета́рш *acc.* секрета́рш	*nom.* наш ваш *acc.* наш ваш short form хоро́ш

18. Grammatical characteristics of words ending in -б, -п, -з, -р, -д, -ж, -ч, -щ, -ф or -ц.

All these letters can only be part of a stem.

A word with the termination **-б, -п, -з, -р, -д, -ж, -ч, -щ, -ф** or **-ц** may be:

18.1.1. A **noun** in the *nominative singular*: хлеб, при́нцип, арбу́з, мир, заво́д, бага́ж, мяч, плащ, телегра́ф, ме́сяц. Such words are usually *masculine*.

18.1.2. A noun in the *accusative* singular. (See 18.1.1.) Only inanimate nouns can have this form.

18.1.3. A noun in the *genitive plural*: (нет) рыб, антило́п, коз, сестёр, неве́жд, неве́ж, кляч, тёщ, нимф, деви́ц.

18.1.4. A noun in the *accusative* plural. (See 18.1.3.) Only animate nouns can have this form.

18.2.1. If a word ends in **-б, -п, -з, -р, -д, -ж, -ч** or **-щ**, it may be a masculine *short-form* **adjective** in the singular: груб, глуп, долговя́з, мудр, рад, свеж, горя́ч, тощ.

18.3.1. If a word ends in **-б, -п, -з** or **-р,** it may be a *masculine singular past tense* **verb** in the indicative mood: грёб, уто́п, вёз, у́мер.

18.3.2. If a word ends in **-б, -п, -з** or **-р,** it may be a masculine singular verb in the *subjunctive* mood: грёб бы, уто́п бы, вёз бы, у́мер бы.

In addition, a number of unchangeable words end in **-б, -з, -р** or **-д**:

18.4.1. Adverbs: вниз, вразре́з, напереко́р, вприщу́р, наза́д.

18.4.2. Conjunctions: чтоб, раз.

18.4.3. Prepositions: об, из, че́рез, близ, напереко́р, вслед, под, над, из-под, по-над.

The preceding can be summarised in a table (see Table No. 18).

Table No. 18

Termination	Noun Singular nom.	Noun Singular acc.	Noun Plural gen.	Noun Plural acc.	Masculine Short-Form Adjective in Singular	Verb in Past Tense or Subjunctive Mood	Unchangeable Words Adverb	Unchangeable Words Conjunction	Unchangeable Words Preposition
-б	хлеб дуб ястреб	хлеб дуб	рыб просьб судеб	рыб	груб слаб	грёб грёб бы		чтоб	об
-п	штамп принцип епископ	штамп принцип	групп ламп антилоп	антилоп	скуп глуп	утоп утоп бы			
-з	арбуз союз водолаз	арбуз союз	баз фраз коз	коз	сероглаз долговяз	вёз вёз бы	вниз вразрез	раз	из через близ
-р	мир ветер пассажир	мир ветер	гитар квартир сестёр	сестёр	мудр храбр	тёр тёр бы	наперекор вприпрыг	наперекор	
-д	завод год пешеход	завод год	звёзд ягод невежд	невежд	рад горазд		назад	над под из-под по-над	
-ж	багаж этаж ёж	багаж этаж	лож бирж невеж	невеж	свеж похож				

Continued

Termi-nation	Noun					Masculine Short-Form Adjective in Singular	Verb in Past Tense or Sub-junctive Mood	Unchangeable Words		
	Singular		Plural					Adverb	Conjunction	Preposition
	nom.	acc.	gen.	acc.						
-ч	мяч меч москвич	мяч меч	встреч тысяч кляч	кляч		горяч колюч				
-ш	плащ борщ товарищ	плащ борщ	рощ чаш тёщ	тёщ		нищ тощ				
-ф	телеграф штраф философ	телеграф штраф	строф катастроф нимф	нимф						
-ц	месяц мизинец отец	месяц мизинец	таблиц столиц девиц	девиц						

74

A.2. DETERMINATION OF THE GRAMMATICAL CHARACTERISTICS OF A WORD BY THE PRESENCE OF OTHER WORDS IN THE SENTENCE

It is obvious that the termination of a word does not always make it possible to determine conclusively to what part of speech this word belongs and what grammatical characteristics it has.

Suppose the word that interests us is a **noun**. Then the sentence may also include adjectives (or participles) in the same gender, number and case as this noun: старого дома, красивую дорогу, разбитое окно. Such a connection between words is called *agreement*. In addition, other nouns and also pronouns in an oblique case with or without a preposition may relate to this noun: дом с балконом, дорога в город, Света с ним, лекция профессора.

If the noun is in the *nominative,* the sentence may also include finite verb forms (see 1, 5.1), the noun and the finite verb form usually coinciding in number: город растёт — растут города, ученик писал — ученики писали, and in the past tense of the indicative (and subjunctive) mood in gender as well: город рос, деревня росла, виднелось село, осуществилась бы мечта.

If the noun is in an *oblique case* with or without a preposition, the sentence may include verb forms—finite, participles or verbal adverbs—too, to which the noun is *subordinated*: любить природу, надеясь на успех, читал журнал. In this case the grammatical characteristics of the nouns and the verbs do not coincide. Such a connection between the head word (the verb) and the subordinated word (the noun) is called *government*, since the form of the oblique case—with or without a preposition—of the noun is determined precisely by the verb. The same type of connection can be used to join a noun in an oblique case to an adjective: полный любви, готовый к услугам, верный в дружбе, or to another noun: домом отца, по дороге в город, из окна дома.

The noun may be connected with a numeral: четыре дома, к пяти рублям, двоих друзей, an adverb (extremely rarely): взгляд вдаль, яйца всмятку, or an infinitive: стремление понять, время любить.

Suppose the word that interests us is an **adjective**. Then the sentence may include nouns in the same gender, number and case (for this, see above). The adjective may also have nouns in an oblique case with or without a preposition related to it (for this, see above), as well as adverbs: очень умный, чрезвычайно интересного, чуть синеватому, немного зелен. In very rare cases adjectives are connected with an infinitive: готовый уйти, способного понять.

Suppose the word that interests us is a **numeral**. In this case the sentence may include nouns denoting the objects whose number is indicated by the numeral. As a rule, only collective numerals can be connected with words belonging to other parts of speech: этим троим, разделить на пятерых.

Suppose the word that interests us is a finite **verb** form. In this case the sentence may include nouns and pronouns in the nominative in the same number and, if the finite verb form is in the past tense singular of the indicative mood, in the same gender as the verb form (for this, see above). In addition, the sentence may include nouns in an oblique case (with or without a preposition) subordinated to this verb form (for this, see above).

Very frequently related to the verb form are **adverbs**: чита́л гро́мко, говори́те ясне́е, приезжа́й за́втра, or infinitives: реши́л уйти́, посове́товал купи́ть. In this case the adverb and the infinitive are subordinated to the verb form only semantically: their subordinated position in respect to the verb form does not cause any changes in their grammatical characteristics. This type of connection is called *parataxis*.

As a rule, there are no connections between a finite verb form, on the one hand, and an adjective and a cardinal numeral, on the other.

Suppose the word that interests us is a verb in the form of a **participle**. In such a case this word can have only those types of connection which an adjective has. However, the presence of subordinated nouns, adverbs and infinitives is more typical of participles than of adjectives.

Suppose the word that interests us is a verb in the form of an **infinitive**. In this case this word can have only those types of connection which finite verb forms have, with the exception of the connection with a noun or pronoun in the nominative (for this, see above). In addition, an infinitive may be subordinated to a finite verb form, a participle, a verbal adverb or a noun (for this, see above).

Suppose the word that interests us is a verb in the form of a **verbal adverb**. In this case this word can have the same types of connection which finite verb forms have, with the exception of the connection with a noun in the nominative (for this, see above). In addition, sentences with a verbal adverb usually include a finite verb form to which the verbal adverb is subordinated.

It must be noted that in Russian there are sentences with "omitted" words inferred from the preceding sentences or the situation in which communication takes place. In such cases some words may relate precisely to the ommitted ones. For example: Каки́м по́ездом он прие́хал?—Ско́рым. The adjective ско́рым does not relate to the verb, but to the ommitted word по́ездом.

Not infrequently the connection between words is expressed by means of syntactic words—**conjunctions** and **prepositions**. The conjunctions и, а, о, но, и́ли and одна́ко join words of equal rank in a sentence. The presence of one of these conjunctions in the sentence shows that there are at least two words of equal rank in it: брат *и* сестра́; чита́л, *а* не писа́л; ва́жного, *но* глу́пого; сего́дня *и́ли* за́втра.

Prepositions are another matter. They may occur only within one sentence and express the connection between a *subordinating* word and a *subordinated* one. A preposition points to the presence of a subordinated noun, pronoun or—less frequently—numeral. The subordinating word may be any part of speech. Therefore, it is very important to distinguish prepositions in a sentence, for they usually help us to establish the relations between words and to find the subordinating and the subordinated words. A preposition does not necessarily immediately precede the subordinated noun or pronoun: it may be separated from it by other words, usually long-form adjectives or long-form participles. However, in a sentence a preposition invariably *precedes* the subordinated noun or pronoun.

In a sentence some words *may not be connected* with the other words *at all*. Such words may denote those spoken to: nouns—товáрищи, Пéтя, сосéд, etc.—or adjectives—дорогóй, роднáя, etc. In writing such words are set off from the rest of the sentence by commas and, when they occur at the beginning of an utterance, they may be separated from what follows by an exclamation mark. Words conveying the speaker's attitude towards what he says may also be unconnected with the other words in the sentence. Such words may convey the speaker's certainty (навéрное, конéчно), doubt (мóжет быть, вероя́тно, надéюсь), satisfaction (к счáстью), regret (к сожалéнию), source of information (по-мóему, дýмаю) or the arbitrarily established order of the reported information and the sequence of its items (во-пéрвых, в-трéтьих, наконéц, слéдовательно). All these words are set off from the rest of the sentence by commas.

Of course, although these words are not connected with the rest of the sentence, they may be connected with other words: уважáемые товáрищи, дорогóй мой, к моемý большóму сожалéнию, по словáм крúтика, по егó глубóкому убеждéнию.

1.1. How to distinguish nouns of different numbers and cases ending in **-а** or **-я**.

Nouns ending in **-а** or **-я** may be (1) in the nominative singular, (2) in the nominative plural, (3) in the genitive singular, (4) in the accusative singular, or (5) in the accusative plural.

The adjectives (pronominal and ordinary) and participles connected with a noun help to infer its form, although not conclusively. For example, the nominative singular masculine: э́тот красúвый ю́ноша, and feminine: э́та красúвая дéвушка (or э́тот ю́ноша красúв and э́та дéвушка красúва); the nominative and the accusative plural: э́ти нóвые домá (якоря́); the genitive and the accusative singular: Нет настоя́щего дéла (коня́). Вúжу красúвого коня́. Remember that the accusative of inanimate nouns coincides with their nominative and the accusative of animate nouns coincides with their genitive. The entire structure of a sentence which has the relevant forms helps to infer the form of a noun.

A noun in the *nominative* may constitute a sentence: Ночь. Тишинá. Аптéка. Besides, it may be connected with another noun or pronoun in the nominative: Стихú и прóза. Дáша и я.

As a rule, nouns in the nominative combine with finite verb forms in the relevant number: Лесá шумя́т. Дорóга стрóится. Сестрá уéхала, finite past tense verbs (and also verbs in the subjunctive mood) agreeing with the nouns also in gender: Приéхала сестрá. Наступúло ýтро.

The nominative case is also encountered in sentences built on the pattern in which one noun is characterised by another noun in the nominative: Его жена — *учительница*, by another noun with a preposition: Братья сейчас *в отпуске*, by an infinitive: Наша задача — *выиграть* этот матч, or by an adverb: Беседа *по-французски*.

A noun in the nominative may be connected with a short-form adjective or participle: Эта задача трудна. Дорога построена.

A noun in the *genitive* may also constitute a sentence: Хлеба! Чая! Besides, it may be connected with another noun or pronoun in the genitive: Хлеба и зрелищ! Чая и ещё чего-нибудь!

The genitive case is also encountered in sentences which contain negation: Нет покоя (хлеба). Ни облачка (огня). Никакого отдыха (удовольствия). In this case the sentence may also contain (1) an adverb ending in -о: Не видно посёлка; (2) a finite verb either in the past tense neuter of the indicative mood with the negative particle не: Несчастья не произошло, or in the 3rd person singular present tense: Чужого горя не бывает, or in the subjunctive mood neuter: Не случилось бы пожара.

The genitive case may be connected with a verb in various forms: добиться успеха, коснулся вопроса, or with a noun: решения директора, ножка стола.

The genitive is also encountered after the numerals два, три, четыре, оба and полтора and nouns with the meaning of quantity: много дела, два человека, три дома.

Besides, the genitive is also encountered after prepositions (see II C, 1.4 and III D, 5).

Nouns in the *accusative* case are generally connected with verbs in various forms: увидеть сына, наградить героя. Besides, the accusative is encountered after prepositions (see II C, 1.6 and III D, 5).

Note.—For nouns declined like adjectives, see 3.1.

1.2. How to distinguish nouns of different numbers and cases ending in **-и** or **-ы**.

Nouns ending in **-и** or **-ы** may be (1) in the nominative or the accusative plural, (2) in the genitive singular, or (3) in the instrumental plural (after **м** in the endings **-ами/-ями, -ми, -ыми/-ими**).

Nouns ending in **-и** may also be in the dative or the prepositional.

For the discrimination between the forms of the nominative and the accusative (genitive), see the preceding—1.1.—section.

As a rule, nouns in the dative and the prepositional do not constitute the basis of a sentence, but are its extenders, as it were.

Nouns in the *dative* are frequently connected with some other nouns in the sentence: подарок дочери, or with adverbs ending in -о: Валерии интересно. Лидии холодно, or with verb forms when they designate the person or object involved with the action: сказать матери, посвятить любви. In addition, the dative is encountered after prepositions (see II C, 1.5 and III D, 5).

Nouns in the *prepositional* are encountered only after prepositions: говорить о матери (морали, лошади). Adjectives which agree with nouns also help to distinguish the forms of the nominative from those of the dative and the prepositional: хорош**ие** лошади, but к хорош**ей** ло́шади and о хоро́шей ло́шади. Unlike the nominative forms, the forms of the dative and the prepositional never agree either in number or in gender with finite verb forms.

As a rule, nouns in the *instrumental* plural are subordinated to verbs: броди́ть, леса́ми; however, they may also be subordinated to nouns: прогу́лка поля́ми. Not infrequently the instrumental is used with prepositions: прогу́лка с детьми́. The adjectives and participles qualifying these nouns have forms ending in **-ыми** or **-ими**: широ́кими вспа́ханными поля́ми.

1.3. How to distinguish nouns of different cases ending in **-е** after a consonant.

As a rule, nouns ending in **-е** after a consonant are in the *singular*. (The exception are some words denoting people's nationality or social status, which end in **-е** after a consonant in the nominative plural.) These nouns may be (1) in the nominative, (2) in the accusative, (3) in the dative, or (4) in the prepositional.

For contexts typical of the nominative, genitive and accusative cases, see 1.1. For contexts typical of the dative and prepositional cases, see 1.2.

Since nouns ending in **-е** in the nominative or the accusative are generally *neuter*, the adjectives and participles which qualify them, if any, end in **-ое** or **-ее**: чи́стое (хоро́шее) по́ле.

Nouns ending in **-е** in the *dative* are usually feminine, therefore the adjectives and participles which qualify them, if any, end in **-ой** or **-ей**: до́брой (лю́бящей) жене́. Masculine nouns may sometimes also end in **-е** in the dative; in this case the adjectives and participles which qualify them end in **-ому/-ему**: ста́рому (поседе́вшему) де́душке.

In the *prepositional*, nouns of any of the three genders may end in **-е**; the adjectives and participles which qualify them end in **-ом/-ем** in the masculine and neuter: о ста́ром (на́шем) дру́ге (по́ле), and, **-ой/-ей** in the feminine: о ста́рой (на́шей) дере́вне.

1.4. How to distinguish nouns of different cases ending in **-ю** or **-ю**.

Nouns ending in **-у** or **-ю** after a consonant in the singular may be (1) in the genitive, (2) in the dative, (3) in the accusative, or (4) in the prepositional.

For contexts typical of the genitive and the accusative, as distinct from the dative and the prepositional, see 1.1 and 1.2.

The adjectives and participles which qualify the relevant nouns end in **-ого** or **-его** in the genitive: нет хоро́шего (вку́сного) ча́ю, in **-ому** or **-ему** in the dative: к ста́рому (хоро́шему) прия́телю, in **-ую** or **-юю** in the accusative: но́вую (си́нюю) ю́бку, and in **-ом** or **-ем** in the prepositional: в све́тлом (весе́ннем) лесу́.

Nouns ending in **-у** in the prepositional are encountered only after the preposition в or на.

Note.—For nouns declined like adjectives, see 3.1.

1.5. How to distinguish nouns in the nominative and the accusative ending in **-o** or **-ё**.

For contexts typical of the nominative and the accusative, see 1.1. In both these cases the forms of the adjectives and participles qualifying the relevant nouns coincide. Not infrequently the case of a form—the nominative or the accusative—is inferred only from the general meaning of the sentence: Облако закрыло солнце.

Note.—Since in writing **ё** is often designated by **e**, also see 1.3.

1.6. How to distinguish nouns of different numbers and cases ending in **-й**.

Many forms of nouns declined like adjectives end in **-й** (see 3.1).

With the exception of nouns which change like adjectives, the termination **-й** of nouns may indicate (1) the nominative singular, (2) the accusative singular, (3) the instrumental singular, (4) the genitive plural, or (5) the accusative plural.

For contexts typical of the nominative, accusative and genitive cases, see 1.1.

A distinctive feature of the *instrumental* singular is the fact that **-й** is preceded by **o** or **e**, i. e. **-й** is part of the ending **-ой/-ей/-ёй**. In a sentence the instrumental is usually connected with a verb: писать ручкой, стать студенткой, увлекаться химией, although it may be subordinated to a noun: занятие литературой, стихи лесенкой, увлечение археологией. These forms may also be encountered after a preposition: Хлеб с колбасой (see II C, 1.7 and III D, 5).

The adjectives and the participles which qualify the relevant nouns have a form ending in **-ый/-ий** or **-ой** in the nominative and the accusative singular: неизвестный край, большой музей, a form ending in **-ой** or **-ей** in the instrumental singular: старой дорогой, and a form ending in **-ых** or **-их** in the genitive and the accusative plural: старых (близких) друзей.

Note.—For nouns declined like adjectives, see 3.1.

1.7. How to distinguish nouns of different cases and numbers ending in **-ь**.

Nouns ending in **-ь** may be (1) in the nominative singular, (2) in the accusative singular, (3) in the genitive plural, or (4) in the accusative plural.

For contexts typical of the nominative, genitive and accusative cases, see 1.1.

The adjectives and the participles which qualify nouns in the nominative singular end in **-ая/-яя** or **-ый/-ий/-ой**: ужасная лень and ужасный день; in the accusative singular in **-ую/-юю**: ужасную лень, or in **-ый/-ий/-ой**: ужасный день; and in the genitive and the accusative plural in **-их** or **-ых**: старых нянь.

1.8. How to distinguish nouns of different cases and numbers ending in **-т**, **-в**, **-л**, **-с**, **-н**, **-к**, **-г**, **-б**, **-п**, **-з**, **-р**, **-д**, **-ж**, **-ч**, **-ш**, **-щ**, **-ф**, **-ц**.

Nouns ending in -т, -в, -л, -с, -н, -к, -г, -б, -п, -з, -р, -д, -ж, -ч, -ш, -щ, -ф or -ц may be (1) in the nominative singular, (2) in the genitive plural, (3) in the accusative singular, or (4) in the accusative plural.

For contexts typical of nouns in the nominative, accusative and genitive cases, see 1.1.

The adjectives and the participles which qualify nouns in the nominative and the accusative singular end in **-ый/-ий/-ой**: но́вый большо́й самолёт, and in the genitive and the accusative plural in **-ых** or **-их**: но́вых доро́г, но́вых студе́нтов.

Remember that the accusative of inanimate nouns coincides with their nominative, and the accusative of animate nouns coincides with their genitive.

1.9. How to distinguish nouns of different cases and numbers ending in **-м**.

Besides the forms dealt with in 1.8, nouns ending in **-м** may be in the instrumental singular or the dative plural. For contexts typical of the instrumental and dative cases, see 1.2 and 1.6. The adjectives and the participles which qualify nouns in the instrumental singular and the dative plural end in **-им/-ым**: ста́рым дру́гом and ста́рым друзья́м.

Note.—For nouns declined like adjectives, see 3.1.

1.10. How to distinguish nouns of different cases and numbers ending in **-х**.

Besides the forms dealt with in 1.8, nouns ending in **-х** may be in the prepositional plural. For contexts typical of the prepositional, see 1.2. The adjectives and the participles which qualify nouns in the prepositional plural end in **-их/-ых**: о ста́рых друзья́х.

Note.—For nouns declined like adjectives, see 3.1.

2.1. How to distinguish nouns ending in **-и** and verb forms ending in **-и** in the past tense plural indicative mood, in the subjunctive plural, and in the imperative singular.

For contexts typical of noun forms ending in **-и**, see 1.2.

Verbs in the *past tense plural indicative* mood end in **-ли**, the sentences usually containing a noun or personal pronoun also in the plural: Вы слы́шали? Бра́тья прие́хали. However, a form under discussion may constitute a sentence by itself, especially in conversation: Чита́ли?

Subjunctive forms also end in **-ли** in the plural, the sentence invariably containing бы.

Not infrequently an *imperative* form constitutes a whole sentence: Скажи́! Принеси́!, which usually has an exclamation mark at the end. The forms under discussion are frequently accompanied by a vocative: Скажи́, Воло́дя! or some other parenthetic words which are also set off by commas in writing: Принеси́, пожа́луйста! Besides, imperatives may subordinate an adverb: Пиши́ аккура́тно!, a noun in an oblique case with or without a preposition: Сходи́ в магази́н за молоко́м!, or an infinitive: Иди́ занима́ться! Иди́ обе́дать!

Nouns in the nominative combine with an imperative extremely rarely. If they do, this always shows that the imperative is not used in the sentence in its proper meaning (see II C, 3.5).

2.2. How to distinguish nouns ending in -y or -ю and verb forms ending in -y or -ю in the 1st person singular present/future tense.

For contexts typical of noun forms ending in -y or -ю, see 1.4. Occasionally a noun ending in -y or -ю constitutes a whole sentence: Наро́ду! ('What a crowd of people!'), Ча́ю! ('Bring me/us some tea!'). In writing, such sentences have an exclamation mark at the end, which is not typical of sentences consisting of a single finite verb form ending in -y or -ю.

In sentences verb forms ending in -y or -ю are not infrequently accompanied by the pronoun я: Я иду́ (пою́). However, this is not obligatory. The forms under discussion may subordinate a noun in an oblique case with or without a preposition, an adverb: Нетерпели́во жду письма́ от сы́на из Новосиби́рска, or an infinitive: Иду́ занима́ться в библиоте́ку.

2.3. How to distinguish nouns ending in -й and imperative verb forms ending in -й.

For contexts typical of noun forms ending in -й, see 1.6. For contexts typical of imperatives, see 2.1.

2.4. How to distinguish nouns ending in -ь and imperative verb forms ending in -ь.

For contexts typical of nouns ending in -ь, see 1.7. For contexts typical of imperatives, see 2.1.

2.5. How to distinguish nouns ending in -л and past tense and subjunctive mood verb forms.

For contexts typical of nouns ending in -л, see 1.8. For contexts typical of past tense and subjunctive mood verb forms, see 2.1.

3.1. How to distinguish adjectives (and participles) and nouns declined like adjectives.

If a text contains a word with an end resembling that of an adjective, one should try to find a noun in the same gender, number and case. If the sentence has such a noun, the word concerned is an adjective; if it does not, this word is a noun. For example, the sentence Здесь продаю́т столо́вую посу́ду has the word столо́вую in the accusative singular feminine; in addition, the sentence has the word посу́ду, which is in the same gender, number and case. So the word столо́вую is an adjective. The sentence Го́сти перешли́ в столо́вую also has the word столо́вую; however, it does not include any other word with the same grammatical characteristics. So the word столо́вую is a noun.

There are cases when a noun which has the form of an adjective has a subordinated adjective: К пионе́рам пришёл но́вый вожа́тый. In such cases the noun (вожа́тый) generally follows the adjective.

3.2. How to distinguish nouns ending in a consonant, short-form adjectives and participles, and masculine past tense and subjunctive mood verb forms.

Short-form adjectives and participles are usually encountered in sentences containing a noun in the nominative, which agrees with them in gender and number: ребёнок здоро́в, больни́ца постро́ена, вы́ставка откры́та. Not infrequently the words under discussion subordinate adverbs or/and nouns in an oblique case with or without a preposition: оте́ц дово́лен успе́хами своего́ сы́на. Such sentences either lack finite verb forms altogether or have finite forms of verbs of the быть, станови́ться, каза́ться type.

For contexts typical of noun forms ending in a consonant, see 1.8. For contexts typical of past tense and subjunctive mood verb forms, see 2.1.

3.3. How to distinguish nouns ending in **-а** or **-я** and feminine short-form adjectives and participles.

For contexts typical of nouns ending in **-а** or **-я**, see 1.1. For contexts typical of short-form adjectives and participles, see 3.2.

3.4. How to distinguish nouns ending in **-о** or **-е** and neuter short-form adjectives and participles, and adverbs.

Adverbs ending in **-о** or **-е** are usually encountered in sentences containing verbs to which they are subordinated: Возьмёмся дру́жно за рабо́ту. И́скренне жела́ю вам сча́стья. Less frequently adverbs may be subordinated to adjectives and nouns: соверше́нно здоро́вый, доро́га нале́во.

For contexts typical of nouns ending in **-о** or **-е**, see 1.5. For contexts typical of short-form adjectives and participles, see 3.2.

3.5. How to distinguish nouns ending in **-и** or **-ы** and short-form adjectives and participles in the plural.

For contexts typical of nouns ending in **-и** or **-ы**, see 1.2. For contexts typical of short-form adjectives and participles, see 3.2.

A.3. DETERMINATION OF THE GRAMMATICAL CHARACTERISTICS OF A WORD BY THE END OF THE STEM

The appearance of the end of *a stem* (do not confuse it with the end of a word!) may be of some help in inferring to what part of speech the word belongs and what it means. This criterion must be applied differently to changeable and unchangeable words. In the former case the stem is that part of the word which remains if the ending is taken away, in the latter case the stem is identical with the word.

A distinctive feature of changeable words which are nouns, adjectives or numerals is the fact that their stems nearly always end in a consonant. On the contrary, verb stems may end in a vowel or a consonant.

1. What stems ending in a vowel may indicate.

1.1. Words whose stem ends in -а- (more often than not after -в-) are usually verbs: забыва́ть, уча́ствовать, критикова́ть, механизи́ровать. Exceptions to this rule are masculine nouns ending in the nominative singular in -ай: урожа́й, май, край, карава́й, трамва́й, чай, слу́чай, обы́чай, etc., and feminine nouns ending in the nominative singular in -ая: сва́я, ста́я, etc.

1.2. If the stem of a word ends in -е-, this word is usually a verb: ослабе́ть, дешеве́ть, жале́ть, горе́ть. Exceptions to this rule are masculine nouns ending in the nominative singular in -ей: воробе́й, мураве́й, солове́й, злоде́й, музе́й, хокке́й, юбиле́й, и́ней, руче́й, etc., and also feminine nouns ending in the nominative singular in -ея: швея́, бакале́я, ассамбле́я, алле́я, змея́, эпопе́я, батаре́я, оранжере́я, галере́я, лотере́я, ше́я, etc.

1.3. If the stem of a word ends in -у (more often than not after -н-), this word is usually a verb: привы́кнуть, верну́ть, тяну́ть, дуть. Exceptions to this rule are masculine nouns ending in the nominative singular in -уй: буй, поцелу́й, etc., and feminine nouns ending in the nominative singular in -уя: сбру́я, струя́, ста́туя, чешуя́.

1.4. If the stem of a word ends in -и- followed by the ending -я, -и, -е, -ю, -е or -й, this word is a noun: геоло́гия, коме́дия, компа́ния, возвраще́ние, акаде́мию, остриё, санато́рий, ге́лий. Among these words there are many formations in -ние, which are deverbative nouns: зна́ние (derived from знать), терпе́ние (from терпе́ть), лише́ние (from лиши́ть).

Note.—The form of masculine nouns in the nominative and the accusative singular coincides with that of possessive adjectives of the ры́бий, ли́сий type: cf. санато́рий (*noun*) and ли́сий (*adj.*), whereas the form of neuter nouns in the nominative and the accusative singular coincides with that of adjectives in the nominative and the accusative plural: зна́ние (*noun*) and си́ние (*adj.*).

2. What stems endings in -к may indicate.

2.1. If the stem of a word ends in -анк-/-янк- or -анок-/-янок-, this word is invariably a noun (except for the adverb спозара́нок). Words with such a stem are more often than not feminine (in which case the forms in -анок or -янок are invariably in the genitive or the accusative plural) and generally denote female persons through their various characteristics (often through their domicile, citizenship or nationality): алба́нка, молдава́нка, волжа́нка, америка́нка, испа́нка, парижа́нка, англича́нка, корея́нка, сербия́нка, египтя́нка. However, this is not always so: прима́нка, изна́нка, уша́нка, водя́нка, обезья́нка, etc.

2.2. If the stem of a word ends in -онк-/-ёнк-/-енк- or -онок-/-ёнок-/-енок-, this word is invariably a noun (except for the adverb спросо́нок).

Masculine nouns ending in the nominative singular in -онок/-ёнок/-енок and having a stem with the termination

-онк-/-ёнк-/-енк- in the other cases usually denote the young of living beings: слонёнок, поросёнок, цыплёнок, медвежо́нок, зайчо́нок, лягушо́нок. However, this is not always so: звоно́к, черено́к, ва́ленок.

Feminine nouns ending in the nominative singular in **-онка/-енка/-ёнка** and having in the genitive (and the animate nouns also in the accusative) plural a stem with the termination **-онок/-енок/-ёнок** may denote female persons (туркме́нка, рекордсме́нка, францу́женка, македо́нка, чемпио́нка), the diminutive names of objects (рубашо́нка, со́сенка, сце́нка) and the colloquial designations of various objects through their properties (тушёнка, сгущёнка) or the actions associated with them (переоце́нка, отго́нка).

2.3. If the stem of a word ends in **-очк-/-ёчк-/-ечк-** or **-очек/-ёчек**, this word is invariably a noun (not to be confused with the adverbs сто́лечко, ско́лечко, ниско́лечко, хороше́нечко, лего́нечко, тихо́нечко!) and is more often than not a diminutive and affectionate name of the relevant object (ю́бочка, тетра́дочка, поля́ночка, руба́шечка, ко́шечка, денёчек, листо́чек, слове́чко, молочко́). However, this is not always so: до́чка, одино́чка, гре́чка, уте́чка.

2.4. If the stem of a word ends in **-овк-/-евк-** or **-овок/-евок/-ёвок**, this word is feminine, ends in the nominative singular in **-овка/-ёвка/-евка** and its stem has the termination **-овок/-ёвок/-евок** in the genitive and the accusative plural. Such words usually designate various objects, phenomena or states through the actions or properties typical of them: однодне́вка, постано́вка, подгото́вка. More specific meanings may also be expressed in the same way to characterise a person or object as belonging to the female sex (листо́вка, мордо́вка, плуто́вка), as being a diminutive (це́рковка, лу́ковка, голо́вка), as being "single", "one" (ты́ковка, морко́вка), etc.

2.5. If the stem of a word ends in **-няк**, this word is usually a masculine noun and more often than not designates a person or object through a quality or property characteristic of him or it: бедня́к, горня́к, сорня́к, березня́к.

2.6. If the stem of a word ends in **-щик**, this word is usually a masculine noun and more often than not designates a person through an object, quality or action characteristically associated with him: сбо́рщик, проектиро́вщик, меховщи́к. Such words often denote members of a profession or trade; however, the stems of words of entirely different meanings may also end in this way—words denoting diminutives (пла́щик) or objects (я́щик).

2.7. If the stem of a word ends in **-чик**, this word is usually a masculine noun (except for the neuter words ли́чико and пле́чико) and generally denotes a person (докла́дчик, лётчик) or a piece of machinery (штабелеукла́дчик, автопогру́зчик) or is a diminutive name of an object (стака́нчик, магази́нчик).

2.8. If the stem of a word ends in **-ник-**, this word is a masculine or feminine noun and may denote any of a very wide range of objects, phenomena or persons: прямоуго́льник, мясни́к, суббо́тник, физкульту́рник, разгово́рник, земляни́ка, меха́ника, те́хника, черни́ка, etc.

2.9. If the stem of a word ends in **-ушк-/-юшк-**, this word is (1) a feminine or masculine noun if in the nominative singular it ends in **(-ушк-/-юшк-)а** (in the genitive and the accusative plural the stem of such words has the termination **-ушек/-юшек**): де́душка, ку́кушка; (2) a neuter noun if in the nominative singular it ends in **(-юшк-)о**: по́люшко. Such words generally have a diminutive or affectionate meaning (голо́вушка, де́душка, дя́дюшка, пого́душка, зи́мушка, до́чушка, речу́шка); however, this is not always so: поду́шка, ку́кушка, безделу́шка, опу́шка, су́шка, etc.

2.10. If the stem of a word ends in **-ск-**, this word is usually an adjective: европе́йский, сове́тский, филологи́ческий, вра́жеский, etc.

However, there are exceptions to this rule: (1) proper nouns which are either geographical names of the Смоле́нск, Минск, Ильичёвск type or surnames of the Достое́вский, Остро́вский, Маяко́вский, Шахо́вска́я type; (2) masculine common nouns ending in the nominative singular in **-ский** and denoting persons: ру́сский, шта́тский, фло́тский, со́тский, деся́тский, and also masculine nouns ending in the nominative singular in **-ск**: блеск, плеск, пуск, иск and their derivatives; (3) feminine nouns ending in the nominative singular in **-ская** and having the meaning of "a room for..." (суде́йская, корре́кторская, де́тская, учи́тельская) or "public services establishment" (конди́терская, мастерска́я, парикма́херская), or denoting persons (ру́сская) and also nouns which end in the nominative singular in **-ска**: кра́ска, вы́веска, доска́, пля́ска, etc.

The additional features of adjectives alone are such stem terminations as **-анск-/-янск-, -ическ-, -овск-/-евск-**.

2.11. If the stem of a word ends in **-истк-**, this word is a feminine noun and usually designates female persons through their occupation or convictions: атеи́стка, пиани́стка, паспорти́стка. However, this is not always so: химчи́стка, очи́стка.

2.12. If the stem of a word ends in **-оньк-/-еньк-**, this word is either a feminine or masculine noun ending in the nominative singular in **-онька/-енька** and generally having a diminutive and affectionate meaning (дереве́нька, дя́денька, я́блонька) or a masculine adjective ending in the nominative singular in **-онький/-енький** and also having a diminutive and affectionate meaning (сла́бенький, моло́денький, лёгонький). However, this meaning is not always present in nouns and adjectives: ступе́нька, ма́ленький, хоро́шенький.

3. What stems ending in -н may indicate.

3.1. If the stem of a word ends in **-анин/-янин**, this word is a noun (except the adjective ня́нин) and usually designates male persons through their domicile (южа́нин, северя́нин, калужа́нин), nationality (англича́нин, молдава́нин) or religious persuasion (христиани́н, мусульма́нин). However, this is not always so: граждани́н, крестья́нин.

3.2. If the stem of a word ends in **-атин-/-ятин-**, this word is a noun. If the same word ends in the nominative singular in **-атина/-ятина**, it is more often than not the name of the flesh of an animal: медвежа́тина, зайча́тина, козля́тина, гуся́тина. However, this is not always so: it may also be the designation of a measurement (десятина) or a word with an abstract meaning (отсебятина, кислятина).The latter words have a somewhat pejorative connotation.

3.3. If the stem of a word ends in **-овин-/-евин-** (except the words тетеревиный, совиный, свекровин), this word is a noun. As a rule, it is a feminine noun and in the nominative singular has the termination **-овина/-евина**: сердцевина, луговина, половина.

3.4. If the stem of a word ends in **-ун-**, this word is usually a masculine noun. (Exceptions are the relatively rarely used verbs дунуть, окунуть, сунуть and гарпунить, трунить, струнить and their prefixed derivatives.) In the nominative singular such nouns usually end in **-ун** and designate persons through some action associated with them: бегун, крикун. However, this is not always so: чугун, табун.

3.5. If the stem of a word ends in **-унь-**, this word is a feminine noun (the nominative singular termination of such a noun is **-унья**) and designates a female person through some quality or action associated with her: плясунья, хлопотунья, певунья.

3.6. If the stem of a word ends in **-щин-**, this word is a noun (except the word тёщин). Such nouns are usually feminine and in the nominative singular end in **-щина**: годовщина, Полтавщина, военщина.(The latter word has a disapprobatory emotional connotation.)

3.7. If the stem of a word ends in **-льн-** (preceding the ending beginning with the vowel **а, о, ы** or **у**), this word is usually an adjective: читальный, самостоятельная, волейбольная, смертельный, федеральный.

However, there are exceptions to this rule: (1) the verbs льнуть and вильнуть and their prefixed derivatives and also other verbs in **-льнуть** and their derivatives; (2) feminine nouns with the general meaning "room": умывальная, спальная, инструментальная, курительная, котельная, караульная, and the feminine nouns касательная, больная, and derivatives of these nouns, and also вольная (*hist.*), рольная, застольная, ссыльная (*hist.*), рассыльная; (3) neuter nouns with the general meaning "medicine": промывательное, полоскательное, слабительное, or "part of speech": существительное, прилагательное, числительное; (4) the masculine nouns дневальный, посыльный, ссыльный (*hist.*), рассыльный, больной. The last three words may be either nouns or adjectives.

3.8. If the stem of a word ends in **-рн-** (preceding the ending beginning with the vowel **а, о, у** or **ы**), this word is usually an adjective: аграрный, санитарный, квартирный, мирный (наверное, however, is an adverb).

However, there are exceptions to this rule: (1) verbs in **-рнуть** of the вернуть, дёрнуть type and their derivatives; (2) feminine nouns with the general meaning "room" (токарная, парная, слесарная, бойлерная, костюмерная, уборная, столярная) or "person" (дежурная) and also the noun сборная; (3) masculine nouns with the general meaning "person": пожарный, дозорный, дежурный, etc.

3.9. If the stem of a word ends in **-нн-**, this word is generally an adjective: искренний, длинный, экранный, экзаменационный. However, there are exceptions to this rule: (1) the feminine nouns ва́нна, сава́нна, анте́нна, коло́нна, то́нна, and nouns with the general meaning "room" (операцио́нная, ва́нная, бли́нная) or "person" (новорождённая, возлю́бленная, etc.); (2) masculine nouns with the general meaning "person": вое́нный, новорождённый, уполномо́ченный, пле́нный, etc.; (3) neuter nouns with the general meaning "medicine": мочего́нное, потого́нное.

Note.—Participles may end in -нн- if the adjectival endings are dropped, -нн- being the ending (or part of the ending) of the participle. The stem of the verb can be obtained only after dropping this ending too, i. e. after dropping two endings: вы́полн-енн-ый.

3.10. If the stem of a word ends in -чн- (preceding the ending beginning with the vowel **a, o, y** or **ы**), this word is usually an adjective: таба́чный, апте́чный, бло́чный, ту́чный. However, there are exceptions to this rule: (1) the verb forms зача́ть (зачнёт), нача́ть (начнёт, etc.), качну́ть and their derivatives with other prefixes; (2) feminine nouns with the general meaning of "an eating place or a shop": чебуре́чная, моло́чная, бу́лочная, соси́сочная, заку́сочная, шашлы́чная or "person": го́рничная, новобра́чная, etc.; (3) the neuter noun позвоно́чное and a number of others.

3.11. If the stem of a word ends in -вн- (preceding the ending beginning with the vowel **a, o, y** or **ы**), this word may be a feminine noun ending in the nominative singular in -вна. Such nouns denote female persons: короле́вна, царе́вна. Proper nouns are feminine patronymics: Ива́новна, Ю́рьевна, Алексе́евна.

A word with such a stem may also be a masculine adjective ending in the nominative singular in -вный or -вной: ра́вный, реакти́вный, резе́рвный, призы́вный, дневно́й, основно́й.

If a word ends in the nominative singular in -ая, this word is a feminine noun: посевна́я, родосло́вная, духо́вная (*arch.*), and if it ends in -ое, it is a neuter noun: гла́вное, заливно́е.

3.12. If the stem of a word ends in -шн-, this word is usually an adjective: роско́шный, ду́шный, успе́шный, стра́шный. Some feminine nouns which end in the nominative singular in -а/-я also have the stem ending in -шн-: мошна́, ба́шня, па́шня, ви́шня, etc.

3.13. If the stem of a word ends in -льн-, -рн- or -вн- (preceding the ending beginning with the vowel **я, е, и** or **ю**), this word is a noun which generally denotes a "room" or "building": пека́рня, пса́рня, купа́льня, чита́льня, харче́вня (*arch.*). However, this is not always so: дере́вня, пятерня́ (*coll.*), говори́льня (*iron.*), etc. Some forms of adjectives also have the same stem: да́вний, дре́вний, сыно́вний, вече́рний, доче́рний, да́льний (and also го́рний and до́льний, which can be encountered only in 19th-century poetry).

4. What stems ending in -т may indicate.

4.1. If the stem of a word ends in -ост-/-ест-, this word is a noun (except the adjectives безо́стый and девяно́стый, adjectives which end in -хво́стый of the длиннохво́стый and бесхво́стый type, and also the numeral шесть). As a rule, such words are abstract feminine nouns which denote a quality or property or a qualitative state and are derived from adjectival stems: бли́зость, ско́рость, глу́пость, теку́честь, све́жесть.

4.2. If the stem of a word ends in **-ант/-ент-**, this word is a noun. Such nouns are generally masculine and their nominative singular termination is **-ант** or **-ент**: лабора́нт, доце́нт, цеме́нт, оккупа́нт, дикта́нт. (These are usually so-called international words.)

4.3. If the stem of a word ends in **-оват-/-еват-**, this word is an adjective: кривова́тый, солонова́тый, глупова́тый. Adjectives with this suffix usually have the additional meaning of "a small degree of a quality". There are exceptions to this rule: the nouns шлакова́та and стеклова́та.

4.4. If the stem of a word ends in **-ист-**, this word is more often than not a masculine noun which ends in the nominative singular in **-ист** and denotes a person: активи́ст, специали́ст, тури́ст, арти́ст. Exceptions to this rule are the words а́ист, лист, свист (and its prefixed derivatives), etc.

A word with such a stem may also be a masculine adjective ending in the nominative singular in **-истый** and usually meaning "having a high degree of a quality or property": скали́стый, гори́стый, плечи́стый.

4.5. If the stem of a word ends in **-чат-**, this word may be a plural noun denoting not fully grown or young living beings: внуча́та, девча́та, зайча́та, волча́та.

A word with such a stem may also be a masculine adjective ending in the nominative singular in **-чатый**: ды́мчатый, бреве́нчатый, мате́рчатый.

5. What stems ending in -в may indicate.

5.1. If the stem of a word ends in **-ств-**, this word is more often than not a neuter noun ending in the nominative singular in **-ство**. Such nouns are derived from nominal or verbal stems and have an abstract meaning: бога́тство, преда́тельство, сво́йство, о́бщество, строи́тельство.

The adjective чёрствый, the verbs отождестви́ть/отожестви́ть, обожестви́ть, обобществи́ть, овеществи́ть, осуществи́ть, and the adverb сы́змальства also have stems in **-ств-**.

5.2. If the stem of a word ends in **-лив-** or **-чив-**, this word is usually an adjective (терпели́вый, трусли́вый, счастли́вый, отзы́вчивый, неусто́йчивый); it may also be a feminine noun ending in the nominative singular in **-лива** (подли́ва, оли́ва, сли́ва, тернослива) or a masculine noun ending in the nominative singular in **-лив** (черносли́в and also слив and other derivatives with this root).

5.3. If the stem of a word ends in **-ов-/-ев-**, this word is usually an adjective: кла́ссовый, образцо́вый, абрико́совый, почто́вый.

Some proper nouns have the same stem. They are geographical names ending in the nominative singular in **-ов/-ёв/-ев** or **-ово/-ёво/-ево** (Льво́в, Могилёв, Вельями́ново, Жилёво) and masculine, feminine and family surnames ending in the nominative in **-ов/-ев** (Росто́в,

Тургéнев), **-ова/-ева** (Ростóва, Тургéнева) and **-овы/-евы** (Ростóвы, Тургéневы), respectively.

The following words are also masculine nouns: words ending in the nominative singular in **-овóй/-евóй** and usually denoting people's profession or trade (рулевóй, мастеровóй and some others), the words птицелóв, рыболóв, плов, припéв, перегрéв, сев and a number of others, which end in the nominative singular in **-ов/-ев**, and, finally, compound words, whose second component is -фланговый (правофланговый) and which end in the nominative singular in **-овый**.

Words ending in the nominative singular in **-овая/-евая**: кладовáя, передовáя, столóвая, буровáя, мостовáя and a number of others, and words ending in the nominative singular in **-ова/-ева**: королéва, синевá, головá, вдовá, оснóва, корóва and some others, are nouns. They are invariably of the feminine gender.

In addition, the stems of some verb forms may also end in **-ов-/-ев-**: ревéть — ревýт, звать — зовýт, ловúть — лóвят, etc.

Note.—Many possessive adjectives end in **-ов/-ев** (отцóв, дéдов). Some of them are encountered only in set phrases: дамóклов меч, эóлова áрфа, демьянова ухá, пúррова побéда, ахиллéсова пятá, мамáево побóище.

6. What stems ending in -х, -ц, -ч, -ш, -щ may indicate.

6.1. If the stem of a word ends in **-их-**, this word is a noun. Such nouns are usually feminine and end in the nominative singular in **-иха**. As a rule, they denote female persons or animals: ткачúха, поварúха, портнúха, зайчúха, крольчúха. However, this is not always so: шумúха, облепúха, гречúха, неразберúха. Some words with such a stem are masculine: женúх, стих and a number of others.

The adjectives тúхий and лихóй (*arch. & pop.*), and adverbs of the в-трéтьих type have stems ending in **-их-**.

6.2. If the stem of a word ends in **-ец-**, this words is a noun. Such nouns are usually masculine and end in the nominative singular in **-ец**. They may either designate persons (males more often than not) through their domicile (ленингрáдец, лóндонец), nationality (украúнец, китáец), socio-political activity (комсомóлец, республикáнец) or characteristic qualities (мудрéц, конькобéжец, хитрéц), or be diminutives with an affectionate nuance (морóзец, брáтец). However, this is not always so: отéц, конéц, огурéц, дворéц, сúтец and some others.

6.3. If the stem of a word ends in **-иц-**, this word is a noun. Such nouns are usually feminine and end in the nominative singular in **-ица**. More often than not they designate female persons through their profession or occupation and the termination of their stem is **-ниц-** (ученúца, шкóльница), **-чиц-** (закáзчица, аппарáтчица) or **-щиц-** (танцóвщица, спóрщица). Here also belong nouns which have no meaning of the female sex: послóвица, гранúца, единúца, ýлица.

Compound adjectives whose second component is -лицый (of the узколúцый and желтолúцый type) and the adverb ниц also have the stem ending in **-иц-**.

6.4. If the stem of a word ends in **-вич**, this word is a noun. Such nouns are masculine and end in the nominative singular in **-вич**. They usually designate male persons through their domicile: москви́ч, пско́вич. The proper nouns are masculine patronymics: Ива́нович, Серге́евич, Алексе́евич, Ю́рьевич.

6.5. If the stem of a word ends in **-уч-/-юч-**, this word is usually an adjective: теку́чий, жгу́чий, колю́чий. However, this is not always so. Words ending in the nominative singular in **-уча** are feminine nouns: ту́ча, ку́ча, кру́ча and a number of others. Words ending in the nominative singular in **-уч** are masculine nouns: за́вуч, сургу́ч, не́уч, луч and some others.

6.6. If the stem of a word ends in **-ач-/-яч-**, this word may be a noun.

If in the nominative singular it ends in **-ача/-яча**, it belongs to the feminine gender: да́ча, недоста́ча, кля́ча, ты́сяча and words which end in -дача of the отда́ча, вы́дача and сда́ча type.

If in the nominative singular it ends in **-ач**, it belongs to the masculine gender: труба́ч, скрипа́ч, бога́ч, цирка́ч, врач. All these words denote male persons. However, this is not always so: плач.

A word with such a stem may be a masculine adjective ending in the nominative singular in **-ачий/-ячий** and having the meaning of possession: соба́чий, коша́чий, лягуша́чий, жеребя́чий, цыпля́чий. However, this is not always so: куса́чий, ходя́чий.

6.7. If the stem of a word ends in **-айш-/-ейш-**, this word is more often than not an adjective conveying the highest degree of a quality: ярча́йший, зле́йший, ближа́йший, скоре́йший. The feminine nouns ге́йша and казначе́йша have the same stem.

6.8. If the ending of a word is preceded by **ш** following a consonant, but not **-ай-/-ей-**, this word may be an active past participle (нёсший, ве́дший, чита́вший, бро́сивший) or an adjective ending in the nominative singular in **-ший** or **-шой** (мла́дший, вы́сший, хоро́ший, большо́й).

Such words include masculine nouns: усо́пший, уме́рший and a number of others; feminine nouns: пострада́вшая, потерпе́вшая, сумасше́дшая and a number of others; and neuter nouns: проше́дшее, происше́дшее and some others.

Besides, some masculine nouns may end in **-ш-** following a consonant: рева́нш, пунш, марш, ёрш and a number of others, and also feminine nouns: опеку́нша, секрета́рша, лифтёрша, юбиля́рша. The latter generally denote female persons; however, this is not always so: лапша́, за́мша.

6.9. If the stem of a word ends in **-ищ-**, this word is often a noun. Such nouns may belong to any of the three genders: feminine nouns end in the nominative singular in **-ища**, and masculine and neuter nouns in **-ище**. As a rule, these nouns denote larger or greater than usual objects or phenomena (рыби́ща, бороди́ща, ножи́ща, заво́дище, холоди́ще, дожди́ще) and are stylistically somewhat "degraded" or they denote the place of an action (водохрани́лище, сто́йбище, ле́жбище).

The adjective (and noun) нищий and verb forms derived from the infinitives of the verbs чистить, искать and свистеть by means of prefixes or without them: чищу, ищет, поищем, have the same stem.

6.10. If the ending of a word is preceded by **-ущ-/-ющ-**, this word may be an active present participle: читающий, пишущий, рисующий, колющий.

The stem of adjectives ending in the nominative singular in **-ущ-/-ющ-** may have the same appearance: грядущий, будущий, царствующий. These words also include: masculine nouns generally denoting persons: нападающий, отдыхающий, управляющий, заведующий and a number of others; feminine nouns: заведующая, отдыхающая, равнодействующая, направляющая and a number of others; and neuter nouns: подлежащее, будущее, грядущее, млекопитающее, успокаивающее and some others.

Besides, some masculine and feminine nouns may end in **-ущ-/-ющ-**: хрущ, плющ, гуща, куща, пуща.

6.11. If the ending of a word is preceded by **-ащ-/-ящ-**, this word may be an active present participle: любящий, дрожащий, косящий, смотрящий.

The stem of adjectives ending in the nominative singular in **-ащий/-ящий** may have the same appearance: звучащий, кричащий, блестящий, правящий.

These words also include: masculine nouns generally denoting persons: служащий and a number of others; feminine nouns: служащая, входящая, исходящая and a number of others; and also plural nouns: окружающие, вездесущие.

Besides, the stems of some masculine and feminine nouns may end in **-ащ-/-ящ-**: плащ, хрящ, чаща.

7. What stems ending in -б, -д, -л, -м, -р may indicate.

7.1. If the stem of a word ends in **-ьб-**, this word is invariably a feminine noun. As a rule, such words are derived from verb roots and denote an action or state: стрельба (from стрелять), борьба (from бороться), просьба (from просить).

7.2. If the stem of a word ends in **-иад-**, this word is invariably a feminine noun. Not infrequently such words designate mass sports competitions through some, often external, feature of such events: универсиада (university sports competitions), олимпиада (Olympic Games), but: альпиниада (mass mountaineering expedition).

7.3. If the stem of a word ends in -тел-, this word is a noun, except a few rarely used verbs (of the канителиться type) and the adjectives облетелый, зажелтелый, пожелтелый, оголтелый (*coll.*), осиротелый, закоптелый, прокоптелый, загустелый, запустелый, опустелый and compound adjectives whose second component is **-телый** (of the полнотелый, пустотелый or мягкотелый type). As a rule, these are masculine nouns designating persons through their profession, trade or occupation (водитель, покупатель, строитель, читатель) or denoting tools, instruments, devices or mechanisms (дви́гатель, распыли́тель, снегоочисти́тель).

7.4. If the stem of a word ends in **-изм**, this word is a noun (маркси́зм, автомати́зм, романти́зм). More often than not such words belong to the masculine gender and usually denote teachings, socio-political orientations or systems, and qualities or propensities.

7.5. If the ending of a word is preceded by **-им-** or **-ом-/-ем-**, this word may be a passive present participle: руководи́мый, гони́мый, обсужда́емый.

The stem of masculine adjectives ending in the nominative singular in **-имый/-омый/-емый** may have the same appearance: неоцени́мый, допусти́мый, невесо́мый, осяза́емый. These words also include masculine nouns: обвиня́емый, люби́мый, подсуди́мый: feminine nouns: нема́я, обвиня́емая, люби́мая, знако́мая, хрома́я; and neuter nouns: слага́емое, ископа́емое, вычита́емое, уменьша́емое, сказу́емое, мно́жимое, содержи́мое, дели́мое, насеко́мое, иско́мое.

Besides, the stem of the following words may have the same appearance: some masculine nouns ending in the nominative singular in **-им, -ем, -ом** or **-ём**: сино́ним, о́тчим, шлем, райко́м, агроно́м, металлоло́м, подъём and a number of others, and some feminine nouns ending in the nominative singular in **-има, -ома** or **-ема**: зима́, пробле́ма, теоре́ма, соло́ма, трахо́ма and a number of others.

7.6. If the stem of a word ends in **-атор**, this word is a masculine noun. Such words end in the nominative singular in **-атор**. More often than not they denote persons (консерва́тор, организа́тор, кура́тор) or pieces of machinery, devices or mechanisms (экскава́тор, генера́тор, карбюра́тор). (As a rule, these nouns are international words.)

The verb тарато́рить (*coll.*) has the stem in **-атор-**.

7.7. If the stem of a word ends in **-ионер**, this word is a noun. Such nouns belong to the masculine gender and end in the nominative singular in **-ионер**. They usually designate persons (more often than not males) through their social status or political activity (пенсионе́р, оппозиционе́р, функционе́р).

B. DERIVATION OF THE DICTIONARY FORM OF A WORD

1. The Noun

The dictionary form of a noun is the *nominative singular*. In this form a changeable noun may be a pure stem, i. e. take a zero ending (ø) (заво́д), or take as the ending: **-ь** (жи́тель), **-й** (сара́й), **-а** (коро́ва), **-я** (неде́ля), **-о** (боло́то), **-е** (со́лнце), **-ой** (часово́й), **-ый** (вожа́тый), **-ое** (живо́тное), **-ее** (млекопита́ющее), **-ая** (запята́я) or **-яя** (пере́дняя). The dictionary form of the nouns which do not change for case or number (пальто́, кино́, ко́фе, такси́, мада́м, кенгуру́, МГУ, антраша́) coincides with the form in which they occur in the sentence.

1.1. How to derive the dictionary form of a noun in the genitive singular.

The ending of a noun in the genitive singular may be: -a (заво́да), -я (жи́теля), -у (са́хару), -ю (ча́ю), -ы (коро́вы), -и (неде́ли), -ого (вожа́того), -его (рабо́чего), -ой (запято́й) or -ей (пере́дней).

1.1.1. If the genitive singular form ends in -a, then, to derive the dictionary form, this ending should simply be dropped (заво́да → заво́д) or, after dropping this ending, the ending -o should be added (боло́та → болот → боло́то) or the ending -e if the word without the ending terminates in -ц or -щ (со́лнца → солнц → со́лнце, сокро́вища → сокровищ → сокро́вище).

Frequently, when the dictionary form is derived by merely dropping the ending, there appears a stem terminating in two consonants, sometimes separated by a soft mark. In such cases, to derive the dictionary form, **o, ё** or **e** should be inserted between these consonants. For example: куска́ → куск → кусо́к, конца́ → конц → коне́ц, огонька́ → огоньк → огонёк, бойца́ → бойц → бойец → бое́ц. The vowel **e** is always inserted instead of **ь** and **й**; in all the other cases the choice between **o** and **e** is unpredictable. It should not be assumed that this procedure takes place whenever the stem terminates in two consonants; however, it is most likely when the final consonant is **к, н** or **ц**.

The dictionary form of the word за́йца is not derived according to the rule: за́яц.

1.1.2. If the genitive singular form ends in -я, then, to derive the dictionary form, this ending should be dropped and: (1) after a consonant **-ь** or **-e** should be added (чита́теля → читател → чита́тель, по́ля → пол → по́ле), (2) after **-ь- -e** or **-ё** should be added (ружья́ → ружь → ружьё), (3) after a vowel **-й** should be added (санато́рия → санатори → санато́рий).

The same rules hold good in the case of the forms in -ю (ча́ю → ча → чай).

When deriving the dictionary form by means of **ь**, the vowel **o** or **e** should often be inserted, just as in the case of simply dropping the ending described in 1.1.1 (угля́ → угль → у́голь, ремня́ → ремнь → реме́нь).

1.1.3. If the genitive singular form ends in -ы, then, to derive the dictionary form, **-ы** should be replaced with **-a**: стены́ → стена́, и́скры → и́скра.

1.1.4. If the genitive singular form ends in -и, then, to derive the dictionary form, **-и** should be replaced with **-ь, -a** or **-я**: тетра́ди → тетрад → тетра́дь, доро́ги → дорог → доро́га, ста́нции → станци → ста́нция.

If the genitive singular form ends in **-ени**, then, to derive the dictionary form, besides the replacement of **и** with **я**, **-ен-** must be dropped: и́мени → и́мя, зна́мени → зна́мя.This rule applies to ten words: пла́мя, зна́мя, пле́мя, бре́мя, вре́мя, стре́мя, се́мя, те́мя, и́мя, вы́мя (but: ле́ни → лен → лень). The dictionary forms of the words ма́тери and до́чери are derived by clipping off **-ер-**: мать, дочь.

1.1.5. If the genitive singular form ends in **-ого/-его**, then, to derive the dictionary form, **-ого** should be replaced with **-ой/-ый** or **-ое**: вожа́того → вожа́тый, часово́-

го → часово́й, пиро́жного → пиро́жное, and **-его** with **-ий** or **-ее**: рабо́чего → рабо́чий, млекопита́ющего → млекопита́ющее.

1.1.6. If the genitive singular ends in **-ой/-ей**, then, to derive the dictionary form of a common noun, **-ой** should be replaced with **-ая**, and **-ей** with **-яя**: запято́й → запята́я, пере́дней → пере́дняя. The dictionary form of a proper noun may be derived by replacing **-ой** with **-а** or **-ая/-яя** (as a rule, such proper nouns are feminine surnames of the type Соколо́вой → Соколо́в → Соколо́ва, Мали́ниной → Мали́нин → Мали́нина, Петро́вской → Петро́вск → Петро́вская).

The correlation between the genitive singular and the dictionary form is shown in the folowing table:

Genitive singular ends in:	-а	-я	-у	-ю	-ы	-и	-ого (-его)	-ой (-ей)
Dictionary form ends in:	ø -о -е	-ь -е -ё -й	ø	-ь -й	-а	-ь -а -я	-ой -ый (-ий) -ое (-ее)	-ая (-яя) -а

1.2. How to derive the dictionary form of a noun in the dative singular.

The ending of a noun in the dative singular may be: **-у** (заво́ду), **-ю** (жи́телю), **-е** (коро́ве), **-и** (тетра́ди), **-ому** (вожа́тому), **-ему** (рабо́чему), **-ой** (запято́й) or **-ей** (пере́дней).

1.2.1. If the dative singular form ends in **-у,** then, to derive the dictionary form, this ending should be simply dropped (заво́ду → заво́д) or, after dropping this ending, the ending **-о** should be added (боло́ту → болот → боло́то) or the ending **-е** if the word without the ending terminates in **ц** or **щ** (со́лнцу → солнц → со́лнце, сокро́вищу → сокро́вищ → сокро́вище).

For the cases when **о** or **е** must be inserted in the dictionary form, see 1.1.1.

1.2.2. If the dative singular form ends in **-ю,** then, to derive the dictionary form, this ending should be dropped and: (1) after a consonant **-ь** or **-е** should be added (чита́телю → читател → чита́тель, по́лю → пол → по́ле), (2) after **-ь -е** or **-ё** should be added (ружью́ → ружь → ружьё), (3) after a vowel **-й** should be added (санато́рий → санатори → санато́рий).

For the cases when **о** or **е** must be inserted in the dictionary form, see 1.1.1.

1.2.3. If the dative singular form ends in **-е,** then, to derive the dictionary form, this ending should be dropped and the ending **-а** or **-я** added (after **л, н, р, д, з, т** and **с**). (The cases when **-а** must be added are far more frequent than the cases with **-я**.) After all the other consonants the ending **-е** of the dative must always be replaced with **-а(-я)**: коро́ве → коров → коро́ва, неде́ле → недел → неде́ля, шко́ле → школ → шко́ла.

1.2.4. If the dative singular form ends in **-и**, then, to derive the dictionary form, this ending should be dropped and **-ь** should be added after a consonant (тетра́ди → тетрад → тетра́дь) and **-я** after a vowel (ста́нции → станци → ста́нция).

If the dative singular form ends in **-ени**, then, to derive the dictionary form, **-ен-** should be dropped (in addition to the replacement of **-и** with **-я**): зна́мени → зна́мен → знам → зна́мя. This rule applies only to 10 words. For this and also for the words ма́тери and до́чери, see 1.1.1.

1.2.5. If the dative singular form ends in **-ому/-ему**, then, to derive the dictionary form, **-ому** should be replaced with **-ый/-ой** or **-ое**: вожа́тому → вожат → вожа́тый, часово́му → часов → часово́й, пиро́жному → пирожн → пиро́жное, and **-ему** with **-ий** or **-ее**: рабо́чему → рабоч → рабо́чий, млекопита́ющему → млекопита́ющ → млекопита́ющее.

1.2.6. If the dative singular form ends in **-ой/-ей**, then the procedure described in 1.1.6. should be followed.

The correlation between the dative singular and the dictionary form is shown in the following table:

Dative singular ends in:	-у	-ю	-е	-и	-ому (-ему)	-ой (-ей)
Dictionary form ends in:	ø -о -е	-ь -е -ё -й	-а -я	-ь -я	-ый (-ий) -ой -ое (-ее)	-ая (-яя) -а

1.3. How to derive the dictionary form of a noun in the accusative singular.

A noun in the accusative singular may be a pure stem (i. e. may have a zero ending: заво́д) or have for its ending **-ь** (день), **-й** (сара́й), **-о** (боло́то), **-е** (со́лнце), **-ый** (двугри́венный), **-ое** (пиро́жное) or **-ее** (млекопита́ющее). It is obvious that all these endings coincide with those of the nominative singular and, consequently, the words are in the dictionary form. We shall only note here that the endings **-ый, -ий** and **-ой** of this form are extremely rare.

A noun in the accusative singular may have for its ending **-а** (челове́ка), **-я** (жи́теля), **-ого** (часово́го) or **-его** (рабо́чего). It is obvious that all these endings coincide with those of the genitive singular (see 1.1.1, 1.1.2 and 1.1.5). The dictionary form may end only in a "zero", **-й, -ый (-ой)** and **-ий**.

A noun in the accusative singular may have for its ending **-у** (коро́ву), **-ю** (неде́лю) or **-ую** (запяту́ю). To derive the dictionary form of these nouns, these endings should be replaced as follows: **-у** with **-а** (жену́ → жен → жена́), **-ю** with **-я** (зе́млю → земл → земля́), **-ую** with **-ая** (столо́вую → столов → столо́вая) and **-юю** with **-яя** (пере́днюю → передн → пере́дняя).

The correlation between the accusative singular and the dictionary form is shown in the following table:

Accusative singular ends in:	ø	-ь	-й	-о -е	-ый -ий -ой	-ое -ее	-а	-я	-ого -его	-у -ю	-ую -юю
Dictionary form ends in:	ø	-ь	-й	-о -е	-ый -ий -ой	-ое -ее	ø	-ь -й	-ой -ый -ий	-а -я	-ая -яя

1.4. How to derive the dictionary form of a noun in the instrumental singular.

A noun in the instrumental singular may end in **-ом** (заво́дом), **-ем** (жи́телем), **-ём** (днём), **-ой/-ою** (коро́вой/коро́вою, запято́й/запято́ю), **-ей/-ею** (неде́лей/неде́лею, пере́дней/пере́днею), **-ью** (сте́пью), **-ым** (вожа́тым) or **-им** (рабо́чим).

1.4.1. If the instrumental singular form ends in **-ом**, then, to derive the dictionary form, this ending should simply be dropped or, after dropping this ending, the ending **-о** should be added (заво́дом → заво́д, боло́том → болот → боло́то, яйцо́м → яйц → яйцо́, плечо́м → плеч → плечо́).

For the cases when **о** or **е** must be inserted in the dictionary form, see 1.1.1.

1.4.2. If the instrumental singular form ends in **-ем/-ём**, then, to derive the dictionary form, this ending should be dropped and: (1) **-ь** or **-е** should be added after a consonant: конём → кон → конь, по́лем → пол → по́ле; 2) **-е** or **-ё** should be added after **-ь**: здоро́вьем → здоровь → здоро́вье, ружьём → ружь → ружьё; (3) **-й** should be added after a vowel: слу́чаем → случа → слу́чай.

For the cases when **о** or **е** must be inserted in the dictionary form and when the element **-ен-** must be clipped off, see 1.1.1 and 1.1.4, respectively.

1.4.3. If the instrumental singular form ends in **-ой** or **-ою**, then, to derive the dictionary form, this ending should be dropped and **-а** or **-ая** should be added instead: доро́гой → дорог → доро́га, стено́ю → стен → стена́, столо́вой → столов → столо́вая, запято́ю → запят → запята́я, Ивано́вой → Иванов → Ивано́ва.

1.4.4. If the instrumental singular ends in **-ей** or **-ею**, then, to derive the dictionary form, this ending should be dropped and **-я** or **-яя** should be added instead: неде́лей → недел → неде́ля, дере́внею → деревн → дере́вня, пере́дней → передн → пере́дняя, and **-а** or **-ая** after ж, щ, ш, ч or ц: ту́чей → туч → ту́ча, рабо́чей → рабоч → рабо́чая.

1.4.5. If the instrumental singular form ends in **-ью**, then, to derive the dictionary form, **-ю** should simply be dropped: две́рью → дверь, лóшадью → лóшадь. The dictionary forms of the words дóчерью and мáтерью are дочь and мать, respectively.

1.4.6. If the instrumental singular form ends in **-ым** or **-им**, then, to derive the dictionary form, this ending should be dropped and **-ый/-ой** or **-ое** added instead of **-ым** (in the case of a common noun): часовы́м → часов → часовóй, двугри́венным → двугри́венн → двугри́венный, пирóжным → пирожн → пирóжное, or **-ий** or **-ее** instead of **-им**: прохóжим → прохож → прохóжий, бу́дущим → будущ → бу́дущее. In the case of a proper noun, its dictionary form is equal to its stem (as a rule, such words are Russian masculine surnames with the termination **-ин** or **-ов**): Ивáновым → Ивáнов, Ники́тиным → Ники́тин.

The correlation between the instrumental singular and the dictionary form is shown in the following table:

Instrumental singular ends in:	-ом	-ем -ём	-ой -ою	-ей -ею	-ью	-ым	-им
Dictionary form ends in:	ø -о	-ь -е -ё -й	-а -ая	-я -ая -яя	-ь	-ый -ой ø -ое	-ий -ее

1.5. How to derive the dictionary form of a noun in the prepositional singular.

A noun in the prepositional singular may have for its ending **-е** (завóде, лéсе), **-у** (лесу́), **-ю** (бою́), **-и** (санатóрии), **-ом** (часовóм), **-ем** (млекопитáющем), **-ой** (столóвой), **-ей** (перéдней) or **-ой** (Соколóвой).

1.5.1. If the prepositional singular form ends in **-е**, then, to derive the dictionary form, this ending should either simply be dropped, leaving the rest of the word as it is (завóде → завóд), or be replaced: (1) after a consonant with **-ь** (гвоздé → гвозд → гвоздь), **-а** (стенé → стен → стенá), **-я** (я́блоня → яблон → я́блоня), or **-о** (окнé → окн → окнó); (2) after a vowel with **-й** (слу́чае → случа → слу́чай); or the word should be left as it is (сóлнце → сóлнце), because the prepositional of some neuter nouns coincides with their dictionary form.

For the cases when **о** or **е** must be inserted in the dictionary form, see 1.1.1.

1.5.2. If the prepositional singular form ends in **-у**, then, to derive the dictionary form, this ending should be dropped: в лесу́ → лес, в саду́ → сад. If the prepositional singular form ends in **-ю**, then **-ю** should be replaced with **-й**: в бою́ → бо → бой, в раю́ → ра → рай.

1.5.3. If the prepositional singular form ends in **-и**, then, to derive the dictionary form, this ending should be dropped and **-ь** added after a consonant: в степи́ → степ → степь, and **-й, -я** or **-е** after a vowel: в санатóрии → санатори → санатóрий, в áрмии → арми → áрмия, в завещáнии → завещани → завещáние.

For the clipping off of **-ен-** and **-ер-** in some words, see 1.1.4.

1.5.4. If the prepositional singular form ends in **-ом**, then, to derive the dictionary form, this ending should be replaced with the ending **-ой, -ый** or **-ое**: вожа́том → вожа́т → вожа́тый, часово́м → часов → часово́й, пиро́жном → пирожн → пиро́жное.

1.5.5. If the prepositional singular form ends in **-ем**, then, to derive the dictionary form, this ending should be replaced with the ending **-ий** or **-ее**: рабо́чем → рабоч → рабо́чий, млекопита́ющем → млекопитающ → млекопита́ющее.

1.5.6. If the prepositional singular form ends in **-ой**, then, to derive the dictionary form, this ending should be dropped and **-ая** should be added (столово́й → столов → столо́вая) and in the case of a proper noun (as a rule, such words are Russian feminine surnames) **-а** should be added (Соколо́вой → Соколов → Соколо́ва) or **-ая** (Петро́вской → Петровск → Петро́вская).

1.5.7. If the prepositional singular form ends in **-ей**, then, to derive the dictionary form, this ending should be replaced with the ending **-ая** (after **ч, ж, ш, щ**) or **-яя**: рабо́чий → рабоч → рабо́чая, пере́дней → передн → пере́дняя.

The correlation between the prepositional singular and the dictionary form is shown in the following table:

Prepositional singular ends in:	-е	-у -ю	-и	-ом	-ем	-ой	-ей
Dictionary form ends in:	ø -ь -й -о -е -я -а	ø -й	-ь -й -я -е	-ый -ой -ое	-ий -ее	-ая -а	-ая -яя

1.6. How to derive the dictionary form of a noun in the nominative plural.

A noun in the nominative plural may lack the singular form, in which case the nominative plural form is the dictionary form (но́жницы, са́ни, хло́поты, воро́та, ша́хматы, etc.).

A noun in the nominative plural may have for its ending **-ы** (сады́), **-и** (те́ни), **-а** (города́), **-я** (учителя́), **-е** (крестья́не), **-ые** (часовы́е) or **-ие** (млекопита́ющие).

1.6.1. If the nominative plural form ends in **-ы**, then, to derive the dictionary form, this ending should be dropped, after which the rest of the word should be left as it is: сады́ → сад, or the ending **-а** should be added: во́лны → волн → волна́.

The dictionary forms of the nouns болга́ры, тата́ры, цветы́ and ку́ры are болга́рин, тата́рин, цвето́к and ку́рица, respectively.

If the dictionary form has a zero ending, there may appear **о** or **е** between the final stem consonant and the preceding one, **ь** being replaced with **е**: лбы → лб → лоб, львы → льв → лев.

1.6.2. If the nominative plural form ends in **-и**, then, to derive the dictionary form, this ending should be dropped, after which the rest of the word should be left as it is (оре́хи → оре́х) or the following endings should be added: (1) after a consonant: **-ь** (тетра́ди → тетрад → тетра́дь), **-а** (но́ги → ног → нога́) or **-я** (неде́ли → недел → неде́ля); (2) after a vowel: **-й** (слу́чаи → случа → слу́чай), **-я** (фами́лии → фамили → фами́лия), **-e** (зда́ния → здани → зда́ние), and in the words коле́ни, колёсики, ли́чики, пле́чики: **-o**. For the words ма́тери and до́чери, see 1.1.4.

The dictionary forms of the nouns о́чи and у́ши are о́ко and у́хо, respectively.

If the dictionary form has for its ending **-ь** or "zero", there may appear **o** or **e** between the final stem consonant and the preceding one (дни → день, куски́ → кусо́к).

1.6.3. If the nominative plural form ends in **-a**, then, to derive the dictionary form, this ending should simply be dropped or, after dropping the ending **-a**, the ending **-o** or **-e** should be added: берега́ → бе́рег, бока́ → бок, ли́ца → лиц → лицо́, блю́дца → блюдц → блю́дце.

The dictionary forms of the nouns небеса́, чудеса́, словеса́ and телеса́ (the two last words are archaic) are derived by means of an additional clipping off of **-ec-**: не́бо, чу́до, сло́во, те́ло. For the words of the знамёна type, see 1.1.4.

If the nominative plural form ends in **-ата/-ята**, then, to derive the dictionary form, this marker should be replaced with **-онок/-ёнок**: медвежа́та → медвеж → медвежо́нок, волча́та → волч → волчо́нок, теля́та → тел → телёнок, ребя́та → реб → ребёнок. The dictionary form of the words щеня́та, бесеня́та and чертеня́та is derived by replacing **-ата** with **-ок**: щено́к, бесёнок and чертёнок. The dictionary forms of the nouns господа́, суда́ and хозя́ева are господи́н, су́дно and хозя́ин, respectively.

1.6.4. If the nominative plural form ends in **-я**, then, to derive the dictionary form, this ending should be dropped, after which, if the stem of the word ends in **-ь**, it should be left as it is: князья́ → князь, or **-ь** should be added (учителя́ → учител → учи́тель) or **-e** (поля́ → пол → по́ле) or **-ё** (ру́жья → ружь → ружьё).

If the nominative plural form ends in **-ья**, then, to derive the dictionary form, quite frequently not only **-я**, but also **-ь-** must be dropped: мужья́ → муж, ли́стья → лист, бра́тья → брат, сту́лья → стул, коло́сья → ко́лос, or, after dropping **-я** and **-ь**, the ending **-o** should be added: дере́вья → дерев → де́рево, пе́рья → пер → перо́, кры́лья → крыл → крыло́, зве́нья → звен → звено́.

A number of nouns which end in the nominative plural in **-ья** have different consonants in the nominative plural stem and in the stem of the dictionary form: друзья́ → друг, кло́чья → клок, крю́чья → крю́к, су́чья → сук.

The dictionary forms of the words сыновья́, кумовья́, дядья́ and шурья́ are сын, кум, дя́дя and шу́рин, respectively.

1.6.5. If the nominative plural form ends in **-e**, then, to derive the dictionary form, this ending should be dropped and **-ин** added: армя́не → армян → армяни́н, молдава́не → молдаван → молдава́нин.

An exception to this rule is the word цыга́не, whose dictionary form is цыга́н.

1.6.6. If the nominative plural form ends in **-ые**, then, to derive the dictionary form, this ending should be replaced with the ending **-ой, -ый, -ая** or **-ое**: часовы́е → часов → часово́й, вожа́тые → вожат → вожа́тый, столо́вые → столов → столо́вая, пиро́жные → пирожн → пиро́жное.

1.6.7. If the nominative plural form ends in **-ие**, then, to derive the dictionary form, this ending should be replaced with the ending **-ий, -ой, -ая, -яя** or **-ее, -ое**: рабо́чие → рабоч → рабо́чий, слу́жащие → служащ → слу́жащая, пере́дние → передн → пере́дняя, млекопита́ющие → млекопитающ → млекопита́ющее.

Note on 1.6.6. and 1.6.7.—The noun forms mentioned here often denote persons without specifying their sex; therefore they may have one dictionary form designating a female person and another dictionary form designating a male person. Thus, рабо́чие may have the dictionary forms рабо́чий (a man) and рабо́чая (a woman).

The correlation between the nominative plural and the dictionary form is shown in the following table:

Nominative plural ends in:	-ы	-и	-а	-я	-е	-ые	-ие
Dictionary form ends in:	∅ -а -ин	∅ -ь -й -а -я -е -о	∅ -о -е -онок/-ёнок	-ь -ё -е -о ∅	-ин	-ой -ый -ая -ое	-ий -ой -ая -яя -ее -ое

The dictionary forms of the words де́ти and лю́ди are ребёнок and челове́к, respectively.

1.7. How to derive the dictionary form of a noun in the genitive plural.

The dictionary form of a noun in the genitive plural is, of course, that of the nominative singular. However, the dictionary form of a noun which exists only in the plural is the nominative plural.[1]

Since a noun in the plural often differs from the same noun in the singular not only in its ending, but also in some modifications of the stem, it is advisable to derive its dictionary form in two stages: first the form of the nominative plural should be derived and then the dictionary form (if the latter is not the nominative plural form) should be derived from this nominative plural form (see 1.6.).

A noun in the genitive plural may have for its ending **-ей, -ов/-ев/-ёв** or **-ых/-их** or it may be a pure stem. Thus, for example, the genitive plural коро́в has a zero ending and **-ов** is part of the stem; the similar form свине́й also has a zero ending and **-ей** is part of the stem.

---

[1] The words щец (diminutive of щи) and дровец (diminutive of дрова́), which are in the genitive plural, do not have any other case or number form; therefore this form is their dictionary form.

1.7.1. If the genitive plural form has for its ending **-ов/-ев/-ёв**, then, to derive the nominative plural form, **-ов** should be replaced with **-ы** (огоро́дов → огоро́ды) or **-а** (городо́в → города́) and **-ев/-ёв** either with **-и** or with **-я** (музе́ев → музе́и, краёв → края́).

To derive the dictionary form, this form must be transformed into the nominative singular form (see 1.6.1, 1.6.2, 1.6.3 and 1.6.4). The dictionary form usually has a zero ending or it ends in **-й**: огоро́дов → огоро́д → огоро́ды → огоро́д,   огурцо́в → огурц → огурцы́ → огуре́ц,   ме́сяцев → месяц → ме́сяцы → ме́сяц,   музе́ев → му́зе → музе́и → музе́й, краёв → кра → края́ → край.

1.7.2. If the genitive plural form ends in **-ей**, then, to derive the nominative plural form, this marker should be replaced either with **-и** (чертей → черт → че́рти, госте́й → гост → го́сти), or with **-я** (поле́й → пол → поля́, море́й → мор → моря́), or with **-ьи** (свине́й → свин → сви́ньи, семе́й → сем → се́мьи, стате́й → стат → статьи́), or with **-ья** (ру́жей → руж → ру́жья). To derive the dictionary form, the form thus obtained must be transformed into the nominative singular (see 1.6.2 and 1.6.4). The dictionary form derived from the forms in **-и** usually has a zero ending or **-ь**; the dictionary form derived from the forms in **-я** more often than not has **-е**, and the dictionary form derived from the forms in **-ьи** has **-я**.

1.7.3. If the genitive plural form ends in **-ий**, then, to derive the nominative plural form, this marker should be replaced with **-ии, -ьи** or **-ия, -ья**. To derive the dictionary form, the final **-и** should be replaced with **-я** and the final **-я** with **-е**: певу́ний → певу́ньи → певу́нья, уще́лий → уще́лья → уще́лье,   а́рмий → а́рмии → а́рмия,   зна́ний → зна́ния → зна́ние.

1.7.4. If the genitive plural form ends in **-ь**, then, to derive the nominative plural form, this marker should be replaced with **-и**. To derive the dictionary form, **-и** should be replaced with **-я**: неде́ль → неде́ли → неде́ля, нянь → ня́ни → ня́ня, поте́рь → поте́ри → поте́ря. Not infrequently the genitive plural form has **о** or **е** before the consonant preceding **ь**, which is absent from the other forms, including the nominative singular and plural: ку́хонь → ку́хни → ку́хня, дереве́нь → дере́вни → дере́вня.

1.7.5. If the genitive plural form ends in a consonant, then, to derive the nominative plural form, the ending **-ы** should be added (стен → сте́ны) or **-и** (ног → но́ги) or **-а** (боло́т → боло́та), and if the genitive plural form ends in **-ан/-ян** and denotes people's nationality, then **-е** should be added (англича́н → англича́не). To derive the dictionary form, this form must be transformed into the nominative singular (see 1.6.1, 1.6.2, 1.6.3 and 1.6.5). The dictionary form of nouns ending in the nominative plural in **-ы/-и** more often than not ends in **-а** (сте́ны → стена́), and the dictionary form of nouns ending in the nominative plural in **-а** ends in **-о** (боло́та → боло́то) or a consonant (глаза́ → глаз).

The genitive plural form of a number of nouns coincides with the dictionary form: солда́т, боти́нок, сапо́г, чуло́к, глаз, ва́ленок, раз, партиза́н, пого́н, челове́к, etc.

Besides, the genitive plural form ending in a consonant may have the vowel **o** or **e** between the final stem consonants, which is absent from the other forms, including the dictionary form if the latter ends in a vowel: досо́к → до́ски → доска́, вёдер → вёдра → ведро́, сестёр → сёстры → сестра́, де́нег → де́ньги, стёкол → стёкла → стекло́, etc.

The dictionary forms of the genitive plural forms яи́ц and семя́н are яйцо́ and се́мя, respectively.

1.7.6. If the genitive plural form ends in **-ых/-их**, then the nominative plural form may be derived by replacing these endings with **-ые** and **-ие**, respectively: вожа́тых → вожа́тые, млекопита́ющих → млекопита́ющие.

The correlation between the genitive plural and the nominative plural forms is shown in the following table:

Genitive plural ends in:	-ов -ев -ёв	-ей	-ий	-ь	Consonant	-ых -их
Nominative plural ends in:	-ы -и -а -я	-и -я -ья -ьи	-ии -ия -ья -ьи	-и	-ы -и -а -е	-ые -ие

1.8. How to derive the dictionary form of a noun in the accusative plural.

The accusative plural form of nouns which denote inanimate objects usually coincides with their nominative plural form. In this case the dictionary form should be derived in accordance with the rules described in 1.6.

The accusative plural form of nouns which denote living beings usually coincides with their genitive plural form. In this case the dictionary form should be derived in accordance with the rules described in 1.7.

1.9. How to derive the dictionary form of a noun in the dative, instrumental or prepositional plural.

1.9.1. If a noun in the dative, instrumental and prepositional plural ends in **-ам/-ям, -ами/-ями** and **-ах/-ях**, respectively, then, to derive the nominative plural form, these endings should be replaced with **-ы/-и** or **-а/-я**: доро́гам → доро́ги, сада́ми → сады́, мужья́ми → мужья́, хозя́евах → хозя́ева. To derive the dictionary form, this form should be transformed into the nominative singular (see 1.6.1, 1.6.2, 1.6.3 and 1.6.4).

1.9.2. If a noun in the dative, instrumental and prepositional plural ends in **-ым/-им, -ыми/-ими** and **-ых/-их**, then, to derive the nominative plural form, these endings should be replaced with **-ые/-ие**: рабо́чим → рабо́чие, слу́жащими → слу́жащие, столо́выми → столо́вые, вожа́тых → вожа́тые.

To derive the dictionary form, this form should be transformed into the nominative singular (see 1.6.6).

2. The Adjective

The dictionary form of an adjective is its *masculine nominative singular long* form. In this form a changeable adjective may have the ending **-ый, -ий** or **-ой**. Besides, the dictionary form of adjectives designating a property as belonging to a person or animal may be a pure stem terminating in the suffix **-ин** (мáмин, дя́дин), **-ов** (отцóв, дéдов) or **-ий** (ли́сий, во́лчий).

It must be noted that there are adjectives which do not change for gender, case or number: беж, хáки, а́виа, бордó and a number of others. It is obvious that their dictionary form always coincides with that in which they appear in sentences.

2.1. How to derive the dictionary form of a long-form adjective in an oblique case singular or plural.

2.1.1. To derive the dictionary form, the *feminine* **nominative** *singular* endings **-ая, -яя, -ья** and the *neuter* nominative singular endings **-ое, -ее, -ье** should be replaced with the ending **-ый/-ий** or **-ой**: дóбрая → дóбрый, вéрхняя → вéрхний, ли́сья → ли́сий, вéрное → вéрный, зáднее → зáдний, трéтье → трéтий. If the adjective has the feminine ending **-а** or the neuter ending **-о**, then, to derive the dictionary form, these endings should be dropped: бáбушкина → бáбушкин, отцóво → отцóв.

The dictionary forms of моя́, моё; твоя́, твоё; своя́, своё; чья, чьё; ничья́, ничьё; э́та, э́то; вся, всё; та, то are мой, твой, свой, чей, ничéй, э́тот, весь, тот, respectively.

2.1.2. To derive the dictionary form, the endings of the **genitive** *singular* **-ого/-его, -ьего, -ей** and **-ьей** are replaced with **-ый/-ий** or **-ой**: большóго → большóй, си́него → си́ний, дóброго → дóбрый, ли́сьего → ли́сий, си́ней → си́ний, and the ending **-а** is simply dropped: бáбушкина → бáбушкин. The ending **-ой** is usually replaced with **-ый/-ой** or is simply dropped: молодóй → молодóй, воробьи́ной → воробьи́ный, бáбушкиной → бáбушкин. The dictionary forms of моегó, моéй; твоегó, твоéй; своегó, своéй; чьегó, чьей; э́того, э́той; всегó, всей; тогó, той; нáшего, нáшей; вáшего, вáшей are мой, твой, свой, чей, э́тот, весь, тот, наш, ваш, respectively.

2.1.3. To derive the dictionary form, the **dative** *singular* endings **-ому/-ему, -ьему, -ей** and **-ьей** are replaced with **-ый/ий** or **-ой**: дóброму → дóбрый, ни́жнему → ни́жний, вторóму → вторóй, трéтьему → трéтий, си́ней → си́ний, лягушáчьей → лягушáчий. The ending **-у** is simply dropped: дéдушкину → дéдушкин. The ending **-ой** is usually either replaced with **-ый/-ой**: сéрой → сéрый, молодóй → молодóй, or is simply dropped: внýчкиной → внýчкин.

The dictionary forms of моемý, моéй; твоемý, твоéй; своемý, своéй; чьемý, чьей; э́тому, э́той; всемý, всей; томý, той; нáшему, нашей; вашему, вашей are мой, твой, свой, чей, этот, весь, тот, наш, ваш, respectively.

2.1.4. The **accusative** *singular* endings may coincide either with the nominative singular endings or with the genitive singular endings. In the former case, the words are already in the dictionary form, and in the latter the dictionary form should be derived in accordance with the rules described in 2.1.2. The accusative singular endings -ую/-юю are replaced with **-ый/-ий/-ой**: зи́мнюю → зи́мний, то́лстую → то́лстый, большу́ю → большо́й, and the ending -у is simply dropped: ба́бушкину → ба́бушкин.

The dictionary forms of мою́, твою́, свою́, чью́, э́ту, всю, на́шу, ва́шу are мой, твой, свой, чей, этот, весь, тот, наш, ваш, respectively.

2.1.5. To derive the dictionary form, the **instrumental** *singular* endings -им, -ьим, -ей/-ею and -ьей/-ьею are replaced with the ending **-ий** or **-ой**, and the endings -ым and -ой are usually replaced with **-ый** or **-ой** or are simply dropped: си́ним → си́ний, ры́бьим → ры́бий, ни́жней → ни́жний, стару́шечьей → стару́шечий, до́брым → до́брый, больши́м → большо́й, ве́рной → ве́рный, ба́бушкиным → ба́бушкин.

The dictionary forms of мои́м, мое́й; твои́м, твое́й; свои́м, свое́й; чьим, чьей; э́тим, э́той; на́шим, на́шей; ва́шим, ва́шей; всем, всей; тем, той are мой, твой, свой, чей, этот, наш, ваш, весь, тот, respectively.

2.1.6. To derive the dictionary form, the **prepositional** *singular* endings -ем, -ей, -ьем and -ьей are replaced with the ending -ий or -ой, and the endings -ом and -ой are either replaced with -ый or -ой or are simply dropped: си́нем → си́ний, ни́жней → ни́жний, медве́жьем → медве́жий, во́лчьей → во́лчий, до́бром → до́брый, то́лстой → то́лстый, отцо́вом → отцо́в, ма́миной → ма́мин.

2.1.7. To derive the dictionary form, the **nominative** *plural* endings -ые/-ие and -ьи are replaced with the ending -ый/-ий or -ой, and the nominative plural ending -ы is simply dropped: до́брые → до́брый, пере́дние → пере́дний, ли́сьи → ли́сий, больши́е → большо́й, отцо́вы → отцо́в.

The dictionary forms of мои́, твои́, свои́, чьи, э́ти, на́ши, ва́ши, все, те are мой, твой, свой, чей, этот, наш, ваш, весь, тот, respectively.

2.1.8. To derive the dictionary form, the **genitive** *plural* endings -ых/-их and -ьих, the **dative** plural endings -ым/-им and -ьим, the **instrumental** plural endings -ыми/-ими and -ьими, and the **prepositional** plural endings -ых/-их and -ьих are usually either replaced with -ый/-ий, -ой or are simply dropped: до́брых → до́брый, молоды́ми → молодо́й, стару́шечьим → стару́шечий, отцо́вых → отцо́в, ма́тушкиными → ма́тушкин.

The dictionary forms of мои́х, мои́м, мои́ми; твои́х, твои́м, твои́ми; свои́х, свои́м, свои́ми; чьих, чьим, чьи́ми; э́тих, э́тим, э́тими; на́ших, на́шим, на́шими; ва́ших, ва́шим, ва́шими; всех, всем, все́ми; тех, тем, те́ми are мой, твой, свой, чей, э́тот, наш, ваш, весь, тот, respectively.

2.1.9. The **accusative** *plural* endings may coincide either with the nominative plural endings or with the genitive plural endings. In the former case, to derive the dictionary form, the words should be transformed in accordance with the rules described in 2.1.7, while in the latter case they should be transformed in accordance with the rules described in 2.1.8.

2.2 How to derive the dictionary form of a short-form adjective.

Some adjectives (рад, гора́зд, до́лжен) and also the colloquial adjectives with the suffix **-онек/-енек** of the долго́нек, молоде́нек type do not have the long form, their dictionary form being that of the masculine singular.

2.2.1. To derive the dictionary form, the ending **-а/-я** of the feminine singular short-form adjectives, **-о/-е** of the neuter singular short-form adjectives and **-ы/-и** of the plural short-form adjectives should be replaced with the ending **-ый/-ий** or **-ой**: добра́ → до́брый, све́тлы → све́тлый, и́скренне → и́скренний, жива́ → живо́й. Exceptions to this rule are солона́, со́лоно, со́лоны → солёный; велика́, велико́, велики́ → большо́й; мала́, мало́, малы́ → ма́ленький.

2.2.2. A masculine singular short-form adjective is a pure adjectival stem. To derive its dictionary form, the ending **-ый/-ий/-ой** of the masculine nominative singular long form should be added to this stem: жив → живо́й, толст → то́лстый, тих → ти́хий, нищ → ни́щий. The ending **-ий** is added only after **к, ч, х, ж, ш** or **щ**; it is also added to the forms дре́вен (дре́вний), изли́шен (изли́шний) and и́скренен (и́скренний). The dictionary form of со́лон is солёный; of вели́к, большо́й; and of мал, ма́ленький.

Besides, in deriving the dictionary form, **-н** must also be added to the stems of some masculine singular short-form adjectives which end in **-ан, -ян** or **-ен**, whereas the **-е-** standing between the two **-н-** in **-енен**, in which some masculine singular short-form adjectives end, should be dropped. For example: отча́ян → отча́янный, воспи́тан → воспи́танный, таи́нственен → таи́нственный.

Not infrequently when deriving the dictionary form, the vowel **о** or **е/ё** (less frequently **и**), which precedes the final consonant, should either be dropped altogether or be replaced with **ь** or **й**: до́лог → до́лгий, умён → у́мный, силён → си́льный, бо́ек → бо́йкий, досто́ин → досто́йный.

2.3. How to derive the dictionary form of an adjective in the comparative degree.

Comparatives are occasionally given in dictionaries as entries. However, this is not always so. Therefore, to be able to find words in a dictionary, one must know how to derive the dictionary form of the comparative degree. For this, the final markers of the comparative degree **-ее/-ей/-е** should be replaced with **-ый/-ий** or **-ой**: добре́е → до́брый, живе́е → живо́й, су́ше → сухо́й.

When dropping the marker -e, these replacements should be made: ч is usually replaced with т or к (круче → крутой, легче → лёгкий), ж with г, д or з (строже → строгий, моложе → молодой, уже → узкий), ш with х (суше → сухой) and щ with ст or ск (проще → простой, площе → плоский). Besides, к must be added to the end of the stem of the forms ближе, гаже, глаже, жиже, короче, ниже, реже, and уже, resulting in близкий, гадкий, гладкий, жидкий, короткий, низкий, редкий and узкий, respectively.

To derive the dictionary form of выше and шире, -ок- must be added to the end of their stems (after the replacement of the consonant ш with с): высокий, широкий. The dictionary forms of the comparatives in -e слаще, глубже, позже, краше and дешевле are сладкий, глубокий, поздний, красивый and дешёвый, respectively. The dictionary forms of the comparatives in -ше раньше, старше, тоньше, горше, дольше, дальше and больше are ранний, старый, тонкий, горький, долгий, далёкий and большой, respectively. The dictionary forms of меньше, лучше and хуже have different roots: мал (маленький), хороший and плохой, respectively.

3. The Verb

The dictionary form of a verb is its *infinitive*. An infinitive may end in -ть (читать, лететь, толкнуть), less frequently in -ти (нести, идти, везти), and still less frequently in -чь (беречь, помочь, привлечь). -ть and -ти are infinitival endings, while -чь represents the graphic ending -ь and the final stem consonant which alternates with к or ч.

The infinitive of many Russian verbs ends in -ся (кататься, смеяться, бороться). This -ся is not an ending (for the "passive" meaning of -ся, see I, 5.3) and is retained in all the forms of the verb concerned. After a vowel -ся changes to -сь in all the forms (with the exception of the participles) (кататься, катался, but: катались, катаюсь). Only -ся is used in participles, both after a consonant and after a vowel: катающихся, катающаяся.

3.1. How to derive the dictionary form of a verb in the 1st person singular present tense (of imperfective verbs)/future tense (of perfective verbs).

3.1.1. A verb in the 1st person singular present/future tense ends in -у or -ю. To derive the dictionary form—the infinitive—the simple replacement of the ending -у/-ю with the infinitive ending is sometimes not enough (although it is possible with some verbs: чита-ю → чита + ть). The ends of the stems of many groups of verbs in the 1st person singular present/future tense *do not coincide* with those of the infinitives. Therefore, to derive the infinitive from the 1st person singular correctly, the character of the *two stems of the verb* must be taken into consideration and also all the changes that differentiate the present/future tense stem from the infinitive stem. These correlations between the two stems are shown in the following table:

1st person singular present/ future tense ends in:	Infinitive ends in:	Examples	Note
-аю	-ать	чита́ю — чита́ть, копа́ю — копа́ть, счита́ю — счита́ть	
	-авать	(по)даю́ — (по)дава́ть, (у)знаю́ — (у)знава́ть, (до)стаю́ — (до)става́ть	Only the verbs with these three roots, but with different prefixes.
-яю	-ять	повторя́ю — повторя́ть, гуля́ю — гуля́ть and many others	
-ею	-еть	жале́ю — жале́ть, боле́ю — боле́ть, толсте́ю — толсте́ть and many others	Exceptions: (по)бре́ю — (по)бри́ть, (по)се́ю — (по)се́ять.[1]
-ую	-овать (-евать after ж, ч, ш, щ, ц)	тре́бую — тре́бовать, рису́ю — рисова́ть, ночу́ю — ночева́ть and many others	Exception: (об)у́ю — (об)у́ть.[1]
-юю	-евать	горю́ю — горева́ть, плюю́ — плева́ть, клюю́ — клева́ть and some others	
-ну	-нуть	толкну́ — толкну́ть, кри́кну — кри́кнуть, махну́ — махну́ть and many others	Exception: (до)сти́гну — (до)сти́чь.
	-ать	жну — жать, (на)чну́ — (на)ча́ть	Only the verbs with these two roots, but with different prefixes.
	-ять	мну — мять	Only the verbs with this root, but with different prefixes.

Continued

1st person singular present/future tense ends in:	Infinitive ends in:	Examples	Note
-ну	-ть	(о)де́ну — (о)де́ть, (до)ста́ну — (до)ста́ть, (о)сты́ну — (о)сты́ть	Only the verbs with these three roots, but with different prefixes.
	-сть	(про)кляну́ — (про)кля́сть	Only the verbs with this root, but with different prefixes.
-зу	-зти/-зть	(по)ползу́ — (по)ползти́, (в)ле́зу — (в)лезть, (за)грызу́ — (за)гры́зть, (у)везу́ — (у)везти́	Only the verbs with these four roots, but with different prefixes.
-су	-сти	(в)несу́ — (в)нести́, (за)пасу́ — (за)пасти́, (по)трясу́ — (по)трясти́	Only the verbs with these three roots, but with different prefixes. Exception: сосу́ — соса́ть.[1]
-ду	-сти/-сть	(у)веду́ — (у)вести́, (за)бреду́ — (за)брести́, (со)блюду́ — (со)блюсти́, (у)паду́ — (у)пасть, (у)краду́ — (у)красть, (под)ся́ду — (под)се́сть, (с)пряду́ — (с)прясть, кладу́ — класть	Only the verbs with these eight roots, but with different prefixes. Exception: е́ду — е́хать, иду́ — идти́, бу́ду — быть.[1]
-сту	-сти	(вы́)расту — (вы́)расти	Only the verbs with this root, but with different prefixes.
-ту	-сти/-сть	(вы́)мету — (вы́)мести, (от)цвету́ — (от)цвести́, (по)плету́ — (по)плести́, гнету́ — гнести́ обрету́ — обрести́, (за)чту́ — (за)че́сть	Only the verbs with these six roots, but with different prefixes.

Continued

1st person singular present/future tense ends in:	Infinitive ends in:	Examples	Note
-бу	**-сти/-сть**	(по)гребу́ — (по)грести́, (со)скребу́ — (со)скрести́	Only the verbs with these two roots, but with different prefixes. Exception: (у)шибу́ — (у)шиби́ть.[1]
-гу	**-чь**	(за)жгу́ — (за)же́чь, (по)берегу́ — (по)бере́чь, (за)ля́гу — (за)ле́чь, (у)стерегу́ — (у)стере́чь, (об)стригу́ — (об)стри́чь, (с)могу́ — (с)мочь, (в)прягу́ — (в)прячь, пренебрегу́ — пренебре́чь	The verbs with these eight roots, but with different prefixes. Exception: лгу — лгать, бегу́ — бежа́ть.[1]
-ку	**-чь**	(за)влеку́ — (за)вле́чь, (ис)пеку́ — (ис)пе́чь, (об)реку́ — (об)ре́чь, (пере)секу́ — (пере)се́чь, (о)теку́ — (о)те́чь, (при)волоку́ — (при)воло́чь, (рас)толку́ — (рас)толо́чь	Only the verbs with these seven roots, but with different prefixes.
-ру	**-ереть**	(по)мру́ — (по)мере́ть, (за)пру́ — (за)пере́ть, (на)тру́ — (на)тере́ть	Only the verbs with these three roots, but with different prefixes. Exception: (за)беру́ — (за)бра́ть, (с)деру́ — (со)дра́ть.[1]
-олю́/ -елю́	**-олоть**	(с)колю́ — (с)коло́ть, (из)мелю́ — (из)моло́ть, (про)полю́ — (про)поло́ть	Only the verbs with these three roots, but with different prefixes.

Continued

1st person singular present/ future tense ends in:	Infinitive ends in:	Examples	Note
-ью	**-ить**	(по)бью́ — (по)би́ть, (со)вью́ — (с)вить, (по)пью́ — (по)пи́ть, (на)лью́ — (на)ли́ть, (со)шью́ — (с)шить	Only the verbs with these five roots, but with different prefixes.
-ою	**-ыть**	(с)ро́ю — (с)рыть, (с)мо́ю — (с)мыть, (по)во́ю — (по)выть, (по)но́ю — (по)ныть, (по)кро́ю — (по)кры́ть	Only the verbs with these five roots, but with different prefixes. Exception: (за)пою́ — (за)пе́ть, (по)стою́ — (по)стоя́ть, (по)крою́ — (по)крои́ть.[1]
-ию	**-ить**	(с)гнию́ — (с)гнить	Only the verbs with this root, but with different prefixes.
-му	**-ать**	(со)жму́ — (с)жать	Only the verbs with this root, but with different prefixes.
	-ять	(воз)ьму́ — (вз)ять	Only the verbs with this root, but with different prefixes.
-ву	**-ть**	(о)живу́ — (о)жи́ть, (по)плыву́ — (по)плы́ть, слыву́ — слыть	Only the verbs with these three roots, but with different prefixes. Exception: (по)рву́ — (по)рва́ть, (по)зову́ — (по)зва́ть, (за)реву́ — (за)реве́ть.[1]
-ю (after ж, ш, ч, щ — -у)	**-ить**	люблю́ — люби́ть, стро́ю — стро́ить, кошу́ — коси́ть and many others	Alternation of the final stem consonant occurs.
	-ать	кричу́ — крича́ть, пишу́ — писа́ть, машу́ — маха́ть, гоню́ — гнать, стелю́ — стлать and many others	Alternation of the final stem consonant occurs.

111

Continued

1st person singular present/future tense ends in:	Infinitive ends in:	Examples	Note
	-еть	гляжу́ — гляде́ть, хочу́ — хоте́ть, терплю́ — терпе́ть and many others	Alternation of the final stem consonant occurs.

[1] Verbs with these roots, but with different prefixes are also exceptions.

The dictionary forms of verbs whose 1st person singular forms are ем and дам (and their derivatives of the съем, возда́м type) are есть and дать, respectively.

The preceding correlations are complicated by two types of alternation: (1) the appearance of unstable vowels which distinguish the dictionary form from the form under consideration; (2) alternation of the final stem consonants.

3.1.2. The infinitive may differ from the 1st person singular present/future tense in the presence (or absence) of the vowel **o** at the end of the prefix: **o** is present at the end of the prefix ending in a consonant when the latter is followed by two consonants or the consonant +ь; in all the other cases **o** is absent from the prefix. When the dictionary form is derived from the 1st person singular present/future tense, this regularity is realised in the following way: изобью́ — изби́ть, обожгу́ — обже́чь, солью́ — слить (the vowel **o** is present in the future tense, but disappears in the infinitive); отгоню́ — отогна́ть, подберу́ — подобра́ть, обзову́ — обозва́ть (the vowel **o** is absent in the future tense, but appears in the infinitive). It is not difficult to see that such an alternation at the end of the prefix occurs only when there is an alternation of vowels in the roots (see 3.1.1).

3.1.3. If the 1st person singular ends in **-ю** (or in **-у** after a sibilant) and the infinitive ends in **-ить, -ать** or **-еть**, a replacement of the final stem consonants may take place in accordance with the following table:

Final stem consonant in the 1st person singular present/future tense	бл	пл	вл	фл	мл	ж	ш	ч	щ
Final consonant (preceding a vowel) in the infinitive stem	б	п	в	ф	м	з/д	с/х	т/к	т/ст/ск

For example: люблю́ — люби́ть, терплю́ — терпе́ть, ловлю́ — лови́ть, графлю́ — графи́ть, кормлю́ — корми́ть, ма́жу — ма́зать, е́зжу — е́здить, пишу́ — писа́ть, машу́ — маха́ть, верчу́ — верте́ть, пла́чу — пла́кать, возвращу́ — возврати́ть, грущу́ — грусти́ть, ищу́ — иска́ть.

However, such a replacement, obligatory in the case of **бл, пл, вл, фл, мл,** does not always take place in the case of **ж, ш, ч, щ**: лечу́ — лечи́ть, пищу́ — пища́ть, держу́ — держа́ть, решу́ — реши́ть.

3.2. How to derive the dictionary forms of verbs in the 2nd and 3rd persons singular and the 1st, 2nd and 3rd persons plural present tense (of imperfective verbs)/future tense (of perfective verbs).

In the 2nd person singular present/future tense a verb has the ending **-ешь** or **-ишь**; in the 3rd person singular, **-ет** or **-ит**; in the 1st person plural, **-ем** or **-им**; in the 2nd person plural, **-ете** or **-ите**; and in the 3rd person plural, **-ут/-ют** or **-ат/ят**.

To derive the dictionary form (the infinitive), these endings should be replaced with the ending of the 1st person singular **-у/-ю** and transformations should be made in accordance with the table given in 3.1. For example: зна́ешь — зна́ю — зна́ть, мнут — мну — мять, метёт — мету́ — мести́, etc.

However, in this case the final consonant in the stems of the forms under consideration may sometimes differ from the final consonant in the stem of the 1st person singular. There may be the following differences:

1. If the final stem consonant in the forms under consideration is **п, б, в, ф** or **м**, then the final consonant in the stem of the 1st person singular present tense is **пл, бл, вл, фл** or **мл**, respectively (спит — сплю, ру́бят — рублю́, ло́вим — ловлю́, графи́т — графлю́, шуми́те — шумлю́). In this case the infinitive ends in **-ить** or **-ать** preceded by **п, б, в, ф** or **м**, respectively, without **л** (спать, руби́ть, лови́ть, графи́ть, шуме́ть).

2. If the final stem consonant in the forms of the 2nd and 3rd persons singular and the 1st and 2nd persons plural is **ж** or **ч**, then the final consonant of the 1st person singular may be **г** or **к**, respectively (бережём — берегу́, бежи́шь — бегу́, печёт — пеку́, течёт — теку́). In this case the infinitive usually ends in **-чь** (бере́чь, печь, течь, but: бежа́ть). Occasionally the **ж** or **ч** at the end of the stem of the forms under consideration may also be retained at the end of the stem of the 1st person singular (ре́жут — ре́жу, ска́жет — скажу́, ска́чешь — скачу́, пла́чем — пла́чу).

3. If the final stem consonant or consonant cluster in the forms under consideration is **т, д, с, з** or **ст**, then the final consonant of the stem of the 1st person singular may be **ч, ж, ш, ж** or **щ**, respectively (пла́тит — плачу́, гляди́т — гляжу́, ко́сишь — кошу́, моро́зит — моро́жу, прости́те — прощу́). In this case the infinitive usually ends in **-ать, -ить** or **-еть** preceded by **т, д, с, з** or **ст**, respectively (плати́ть, гляде́ть, коси́ть, моро́зить, прости́ть).

The dictionary form of the verb forms ешь, ест, едим, едите, едят is есть, and the dictionary form of the verb forms дашь, даст, дадим, дадите, дадут is дать. The same correlations exist between the prefixed derivatives from the same roots.

3.3. How to derive the dictionary form of a verb in the imperative.

A verb in the imperative singular may end in **-и, -ь** or **-й**, occasionally in a consonant (скажи, гляди, сядь, встань, дай, пой, ляг). The imperative plural differs from the imperative singular by the presence of the ending **-те** (скажите, возьмите, сядьте, встаньте, дайте, пойте, лягте). To derive the dictionary form, the final **-и, -ь, -й** or **-ите, -ьте, -йте**, if any, should be replaced with **-у** or **-ю**. Then the form thus obtained should be transformed in accordance with the table given in 3.1. For example: скажи — скажу́ — сказа́ть, возьмите — возьму́ — взять, говори — говорю́ — говори́ть, etc.

In this case, however, the final consonant of the imperative stem may not coincide with the final consonant of the 1st person singular present/future tense. These discrepancies are described in 3.2.

The dictionary form of the imperative ешь is есть; and of давай, дать.

3.4. How to derive the dictionary forms of an active or passive present participle and of an imperfective verbal adverb.

An active present participle has the marker **-ущ-/-ющ-** or **-ащ-/-ящ-** preceding an adjectival ending. To derive the dictionary form of such a participle, only the part before **-ущ-/-ющ-** or **-ащ-/-ящ-** should be left, which should then be transformed as described in 3.2 and 3.1. For example: знающий → зна → знаю → знать, мету́щего → мет → мету́ → мести́, etc.

A passive present participle has the marker **-им-/-ем-/-ём-** preceding an adjectival ending. To derive the dictionary form of such a participle, only the part before **-им-/-ем-/-ём-** should be left, which should then be transformed as described in 3.2 and 3.1. For example: люби́мый → люб → люблю́ → люби́ть, чита́емую → чита → чита́ю → чита́ть, etc.

An imperfective verbal adverb ends in **-я** (or **-а** after a sibilant). To derive the dictionary form of such a verbal adverb, **-я/-а** should be dropped and what has remained should be transformed as described in 3.2 and 3.1. For example: чита́я → чита → чита́ю → чита́ть, стро́я → стро → стро́ю → стро́ить, дыша́ → дыш → дышу́ → дыша́ть, etc.

3.5. How to derive the dictionary form of a past tense verb in the indicative mood and of a verb in the subjunctive mood.

3.5.1. A masculine past tense singular form of the indicative mood and a masculine singular form of the subjunctive mood usually end in **-л**. In this case, to derive the dictionary form, **-л** should by replaced with **-ть**: чита́л → чита́ть, толкну́л → толкну́ть, рисова́л → рисова́ть. However, there are exceptions to this rule. The dictionary forms of про́клял, пал, сел, крал, прял, (за)чёл, клал with or without prefixes are derived by replacing -л with -сть: прокля́сть, пасть, сесть, зачесть, etc.

The infinitives of a number of forms which end in a consonant are derived by adding the suffix -ну- to them before the infinitive marker -ть: исчéз → исчéзнуть, поги́б → поги́бнуть.

3.5.2. A past tense masculine singular form of the indicative mood (or a subjunctive mood form) may end in -д, -с, -б, -ч, -к, -р. In such a case, the following rules apply in deriving the dictionary form. After -з -ти is added to the forms полз and вёз, and -ть to the forms лез and грыз. After -с the marker -ти is added: нёс → нести́, пас → пасти́, the dictionary form of рос being расти́. In forms ending in -б, this -б is replaced with -сти: грёб → грести́, скрёб → скрести́. In forms ending in -г or -к these final consonants are replaced with -чь: лёг → лечь, пёк → печь, -еть is added to forms ending in -р: у́мер → умере́ть, тёр → тере́ть.

The dictionary forms of вёл, брёл, блюл, мёл, цвёл, плёл, обрёл (with or without prefixes) are derived by replacing -л with -сти: вести́, забрести́, соблюсти́, мести́, отцвести́, наплести́, обрести́.

3.5.3. Feminine and neuter past tense singular and plural forms of the indicative mood (and subjunctive mood forms) end in -ла, -ло, -ли. In this case, to derive the dictionary form, these markers should first be dropped. If the remainder ends in a vowel, then the procedure described in 3.5.1 should be applied. If the remainder ends in a consonant, the procedure described in 3.5.2 should be followed.

3.6. How to derive the dictionary forms of an active past participle and of a perfective verbal adverb.

Active past participles have the marker -вш- or -ш- before an adjectival ending. If a participle has the marker -вш-, then, to derive its dictionary form, only the part before -вш- should be left, which should be transformed as described in 3.5.1: чита́вший → чита → чита́ть, се́вший → се → сесть, etc. However, if a participle has the marker -ш-, then, to derive its dictionary form, only the part before -ш- should be left, which should be transformed as described in 3.5.2: нёсший → нёс → нести́, уме́рший → у́мер → умере́ть, etc.

Exceptions to this rule are forms whose final root consonant preceding -ш- is either -т- or -д- (ве́дший, бре́дший, мётший, цве́тший, плётший, обре́тший). The dictionary forms of such participles (with or without prefixes) end in -сть- or -сти- (вести́, брести́, мести́, цвести́, плести́, обрести́).

Perfective verbal adverbs end in -в/-вши/-ши. If a verbal adverb ends in -в or -вши, its dictionary form is derived in the same way as that of an active past participle with the marker -вш- (see above): сказа́вши → сказа́ → сказа́ть, написа́в → написа → написа́ть, etc. If a verbal adverb ends in -ши-, its dictionary form is derived in the same way as that of an active past participle with the marker -ш- (see above): вы́росши → вы́рос → вы́расти, пренебре́гши → пренебрег → пренебре́чь, etc.

3.7. How to derive the dictionary form of a passive past participle.

Passive past participles have the marker **-нн-** (in the short form **-н-**) or **-т-** before the adjectival endings. If the marker of a participle is **-анн-** or **-янн-** (in the short form **-ан-** or **-ян-**), then, to derive its dictionary form, only the part preceding the marker **-нн-/-н-** should be left, to which the marker of the infinitive must be added: напи́санное → написа́ → написа́ть, посе́яно → посе́я → посе́ять, etc. If the marker of a participle is **-енн-** (in the short form **-ен-**), then, to derive its dictionary form, only the part preceding the marker **-енн-/-ен-** should be left, which should be transformed as described in 3.3: принесённый → принёс → принесу́ → принести́, заведённый → завед → заведу́ → завести́.

If the marker of a participle is **-т-**, then, to derive its dictionary form, only the part preceding the marker **-т-** should be left, and if this part ends in a vowel, the marker of the infinitive **-ть** must be added (ко́лотый → коло → коло́ть, изби́тый → изби → изби́ть); if this part ends in a consonant, it must be transformed in the same way as a masculine past tense singular form of the indicative mood ending in any consonant except л (see 3.5.2). For example: стёртый → стёр → стере́ть, за́пертый → за́пер → запере́ть, etc.

C. DETERMINATION OF THE MEANING OF A FORM

After inferring the grammatical characteristics of a word from its outward appearance, one may pass on to the next stages of the analysis.

First, one should try to make sure whether one's inference about the grammatical characteristics of the word was correct, taking into consideration the "outward" context, i.e. the other words in the sentence, and the "inward" context, i.e. the final letters of the stem.

Second, one should derive the dictionary form of the grammatical form concerned in order to be able to determine its lexical meaning from a dictionary.

Third, one should, finally, determine the meaning of the form concerned itself, taking into consideration (1) its grammatical characteristics, (2) its lexical meaning, and (3) the "outward" context.

1. The Meaning of Noun Endings

The meaning of a noun ending consists of *two* components: one is connected with *number* and the other with *case*. It is precisely for this reason that a noun form is usually characterised by number and case.

1.1. What the singular endings indicate.

When used *by itself* a **singular** form shows that it designates *one object* or *phenomenon*, or such an object or phenomenon which *is essentially uncountable*.

The *uncountable* nouns basically fall into five groups: (1) nouns denoting substances which can be measured, but cannot be counted:

вода́, желе́зо, крупа́, ма́сло, мёд, медь, молоко́, се́но, серебро́, соль, цеме́нт, чугу́н, шерсть, etc., and also the names of various kinds of meat or fish of the type свини́на, бара́нина, осетри́на, etc., and various sorts of berries: сморо́дина, черни́ка, клубни́ка, etc.; (2) nouns with a collective meaning: листва́, крестья́нство, студе́нчество, детвора́, аппарату́ра, родня́, зе́лень, ме́лочь, бельё, etc.; (3) nouns with an abstract meaning: тишина́, го́рдость, успева́емость, ги́бель, терпе́ние, смех, го́лод, жар, ску́ка, сла́ва, го́ре, etc.; (4) names of games and sport activities: футбо́л, те́ннис, лапта́, (лёгкая) атле́тика, волейбо́л, etc.; (5) geographical names: Кавка́з, Ленингра́д, Замоскворе́чье, etc.

In *context* a singular form may not only indicate one of the objects or phenomena being counted, but may have a *generalising and collective* meaning, describing a property of the whole class of objects to which the object concerned belongs: Кни́га — исто́чник зна́ния (not just one particular book, but books in general), Здесь щу́ка во́дится (not just one pike, but many fish belonging to the class named "pikes"), Студе́нт ра́зный быва́ет (not one particular student, but the totality of students, consisting of people different in various respects), Плато́н Миха́лыч го́род лю́бит (Грибоедов) (not one particular city, but cities in general, i.e city life as opposed to life in the country), etc.

The singular may denote many objects in the so-called *distributive* use of the type У нас своя́ голова́ на плеча́х, i.e. in reality not one head, but many, since each of the people concerned has his own head.

1.2. What the plural endings indicate.

When used *by itself* a **plural** form shows that it designates either *many objects* or *phenomena*, or an object or phenomenon which *is essentially uncountable*, or objects or phenomena *whose number is not clear*.

The *uncountable* nouns basically fall into five groups: (1) nouns denoting substances which can be measured, but cannot be counted: дрова́, духи́, консе́рвы, сли́вки, черни́ла, щи, стройматериа́лы, etc.; (2) nouns with a collective meaning: де́ньги, мемуа́ры, не́дра, сла́сти, фина́нсы, etc.; (3) nouns with an abstract meaning, which characterise processes or states that make themselves felt over a long period of time or involve many performers or objects acted upon: бега́, вы́боры, деба́ты, перегово́ры, про́воды, ро́ды, сбо́ры, хло́поты, etc.; (4) names of games and sport activities: ша́хматы, ша́шки, лы́жи, коньки́, пря́тки, до́чки-ма́тери, etc.; (5) geographical names: Вели́кие Лу́ки, Афи́ны, Карпа́ты, Альпы, Гимала́и, Черёмушки, etc.

Uncountable nouns in the plural may denote either types, kinds and sorts of substances: кру́пы (гре́чневая, ма́нная, овся́ная, etc.), со́ки (тома́тный, я́блочный, апельси́новый, etc.), or huge masses of a substance (снега́, пески́, хлеба́), or phenomena that make themselves felt with great intensity (бо́ли, му́ки, страда́ния).

The nouns denoting *countable* objects or phenomena whose real number is, however, unclear mainly fall into two groups: (1) nouns which usually consist (or formerly consisted) of two more or less identical parts: брю́ки, воро́та, каче́ли, но́жницы, очки́, са́ни, трусы́, штаны́, шипцы́, and some others. This group also includes часы́, весы́, кура́нты, счёты; (2) nouns denoting periods of time, ceremonies, rites or celebrations: кани́кулы, су́мерки, су́тки, имени́ны, поми́нки, по́хороны.

Context may convey a deliberate refusal to attribute any individuality to an object or phenomenon and its deliberate inclusion in a group of similar objects or phenomena. In this case the plural may denote a single object with a generic meaning: У нас в купе́ но́вые *пассажи́ры*: молода́я же́нщина. У него́ *ро́дственники* есть: брат.

1.3. What the nominative endings indicate.

1. A noun in the nominative (singular or plural) usually denotes the *performer* of an active action or the *agent* of a passive state: Ма́льчик игра́ет. Наступи́ло *у́тро*. *Ребёнок* спит.

2. If a noun in the nominative (singular or plural) combines with a verb in the passive voice, it denotes *the object acted upon:* Петербу́рг был осно́ван Петро́м I в нача́ле XVIII ве́ка. *День* сменя́ется но́чью.

Sometimes the text does not contain a clue as to whether the noun in the nominative (singular or plural) denotes an object acted upon or the performer (agent) of an action: *Мост* разво́дится (This sentence may simply imply that this is a drawbridge. Then мост denotes the *performer* of the action. However, the sentence may also imply that somebody actually draws the bridge aside or raises it. Then мост denotes the *object* acted upon.), *Бельё* стира́ется в пра́чечной, etc.

A noun in the nominative (singular or plural) used in a comparative construction after the conjunction как "like" has the same meaning of an object acted upon or of the performer of an action: Москва́, люблю́ тебя́, как сын (Ле́рмонтов). It also has the same meanings after the conjunction как "as", "in the capacity of": В го́роде он изве́стен как врач.

3. A noun in the nominative (singular or plural) may designate a *feature, quality* or *property* of an object or person: Ива́н Ива́нович — наш *дире́ктор*.

1.4. What the genitive endings indicate.

1. If a noun in the genitive (singular or plural) is the *only* word *in the sentence* or if it is accompanied only by qualifying words, it denotes an object (in the most general sense) whose presence or existence the speaker desires either for himself or for the listener or for the all the participants in the communication: Прия́тного аппети́та! Споко́йной но́чи! Хле́ба и зре́лищ! Воды́! Ча́ю!

2. If a noun in the genitive is the *only* word *in the sentence* or if it is accompanied only by qualifying words, it may denote the presence of a large number of the objects or persons it designates: Наро́ду! Цвето́в!

3. If a noun in the genitive singular is used by itself to designate the number of a day, it simply denotes the relevant *date:* тридца́того ма́я ты́сяча девятьсо́т во́семьдесят второ́го го́да.

4. If a noun in the genitive (singular or plural) *follows a preposition*, this form by itself usually has no meaning of its own. The nature of the relationship between the word concerned and the word it is connected

with is determined exclusively by the meaning of the preposition: рабо́та без о́тдыха, ко́мната для го́стя, отклоня́ться от и́стины, прие́хать из го́рода.

As a rule, nouns in the genitive combine with prepositions having the meaning of moving away (от, из, с), deprivation or absence (без, кро́ме), approaching or proximity (до, у, во́зле, о́коло, близ, по́дле), or reason (из-за, от, из, с).

The following prepositions require the genitive: без, для, до, из, ме́жду (the instrumental is also possible with basically the same meaning), от, ра́ди, с (the accusative and the instrumental which have no meaning of moving away or reason are also possible), близ, вблизи́, ввиду́, вдоль, вме́сто, вне, внутри́, внутрь, во́зле, вокру́г, впереди́, вплоть до, вро́де, всле́дствие, в ви́де, во вре́мя, вдали́ от, в де́ле, в ду́хе, в заключе́ние, в зави́симости от, в знак, во избежа́ние, во и́мя, в ка́честве, в коли́честве, в нача́ле, в кругу́, в лице́, в ме́ру, в о́бласти, в отли́чие от, в отноше́нии, в поря́дке, в продолже́ние, в ра́мках, в све́те, в си́лу, в слу́чае, в смы́сле, в сто́рону от, в результа́те, в тече́ние, в хо́де, в це́лях, в це́нтре, в честь, за исключе́нием, за счёт, из-за, изнутри́, из-под, исходя́ из, каса́тельно, кро́ме, круго́м, ми́мо, накану́не, наподо́бие, напро́тив, начина́я с, на де́ло, на предме́т, на протяже́нии, на пути́, незадо́лго до, не счита́я, о́коло, относи́тельно, по́дле, пове́рх, позади́, поми́мо, поперёк, по́сле, посреди́, посреди́не, по ли́нии, по ме́ре, по по́воду, по причи́не, по слу́чаю, посре́дством, по ча́сти, пре́жде, про́тив, путём, сбо́ку, све́рху, свы́ше, сза́ди, сни́зу, среди́, со стороны́, с тече́нием, у.

5. If a noun in the genitive of either number *without a preposition is subordinated to a noun*, it may denote part of an object, animal or person: ру́чка две́ри, крыло́ самолёта, сетча́тка гла́за, хвост соба́ки, глаза́ люби́мой; their property: дом отца́, кабине́т мини́стра, кольцо́ ба́бушки; their characteristic: челове́к большо́го ума́, де́вушка высо́кого ро́ста; the performer of an action or activity: докла́д дека́на, пода́рок му́жа, возраже́ние оппоне́нта; or an object acted upon: чте́ние письма́, реше́ние зада́чи, убо́рка помеще́ния.

The nature of the relationship between a noun in the genitive and the noun which subordinates it is easily inferred from the lexical meaning of the connected forms. However, a certain ambiguity is possible. For example, уче́ние Ломоно́сова may mean "Lomonosov's teachings" and also "Lomonosov's education".

6. If a noun in the genitive (singular or plural) *without a preposition is subordinated to a verb*, it usually denotes an object acted upon: принести́ воды́, взять хле́ба, лиши́ться поко́я, доби́ться успе́ха, купи́ть са́хара, ждать весны́.

7. A noun in the genitive singular without a preposition may denote a *date*, i. e. the exact day when the event reported in the sentence took place: Пу́шкин роди́лся шесто́го ию́ня ты́сяча семьсо́т девяно́сто девя́того го́да.

8. Occasionally a noun in the genitive (singular or plural) denotes the *performer* of an action: *Воды́* прибыва́ет. На све́те *сча́стья* нет (Пу́шкин). (See III B, 1 and III C, 4.1.)

1.5. What the dative endings indicate.

1. If a noun in the dative (singular or plural) is the *only* word *in a sentence* or if it is accompanied only by qualifying words, it usually denotes people towards whom the action is "directed" or for whom an object is intended: директору, заведующему, дорогим коллегам. This usage is typical of dedications.

2. If a noun in the dative *follows a preposition*, this form by itself usually has no meaning of its own. The nature of the relationship between the word concerned and the word it is connected with is determined exclusively by the meaning of the preposition: идти навстречу ветру, путь к звёздам, сделать вопреки просьбе, прогулка по городу.

The dative combines with prepositions denoting direction towards an object, approaching an object (к, по, вслед, навстречу, etc.).

The following prepositions require the dative: благодаря, в направлении к, в отношении к, в противовес, вопреки, вслед, к, навстречу, наперекор, по (the accusative and the prepositional are also possible with different meanings), подобно, по отношению к, по пути к, применительно, смотря по, согласно, соответственно, соразмерно, судя по.

3. If a noun in the dative *without a preposition is subordinated to a noun or a verb*, it usually denotes the receiver or beneficiary of an action: послать письмо *другу*, вред *здоровью*, преградить путь *гонке вооружений*, советы *домашним хозяйкам*.

4. If a noun in the dative *is subordinated to a verb or an adverb*, it may denote the *experiencer* of an action or state: *Мне* холодно. *Ему* некогда читать. *Сыну* исполнилось десять лет. *Вам* должно быть стыдно. (See III B, 1.)

1.6. What the accusative endings indicate.

1. If a noun in the accusative (singular or plural) is the *only* word *in the sentence* or if it is accompanied only by qualifying words, it denotes the object (in the most general sense) desired by the speaker: Машину! Ложку! Тарелку!

2. If a noun in the accusative *follows a preposition*, this form by itself has no meaning of its own. The nature of the relationship between the word concerned and the word it is connected with is determined exclusively by the meaning of the preposition: путь через болото, идти сквозь тайгу, критика невзирая на лица. Prepositions which combine with the accusative have the meaning of striving to reach an object, invading an object or spreading all over an object.

The following prepositions require the accusative: включая, в борьбе за, в направлении на, в ответ на, исключая, невзирая на, несмотря на, про, сквозь, спустя, через. The prepositions в, на, о may require either the accusative or the prepositional; за and под, the accusative or the instrumental; по, the accusative, the dative or the prepositional; с, the accusative, the genitive or the instrumental. In these cases the difference in the cases usually reflects the difference either in the meanings of the forms or in the meanings of the prepositions; доро́га в лес—direction, доро́га в лесу́—place; пры́гать на стул—direction, пры́гать на сту́ле—place; уда́риться о стол, but: говори́ть о столе́; заверну́ть за́ угол—direction, стоя́ть за угло́м—place, however, скры́ться за угло́м and скры́ться за́ угол have almost the same meaning; лезть под стол—direction, сиде́ть под я́блоней—place, however, спря́таться под я́блоню and спря́таться под я́блоней have almost the same meaning; идти́ по грибы́—purpose, идти́ по доро́ге—place; слезть с де́рева—direction, отдохну́ть с неде́лю—time; идти́ с бра́том—joint action.

3. If a noun in the accusative without a preposition *is subordinated to a verb or an adverb*, it usually denotes an *object* or *person* acted upon: чита́ть кни́гу, слу́шать учи́теля, объясни́ть пра́вило, поздра́вить юбиля́ра.

4. When the accusative combines with some verb forms, it acquires the meaning of the *experiencer* of the action: Больно́го зноби́т. Кома́нду устра́ивает ничья́. (See III B, 1.)

5. Nouns in the accusative may also be used to express time (чита́л всю ночь, рабо́тал це́лый год, приезжа́ет ка́ждую весну́) (See III C, 5.2.2.) or a measure (сто́ит рубль, пробежа́л киломе́тр, ве́сит то́нну). All these meanings are backed up by the relevant lexical meanings of the nouns.

1.7. What the instrumental endings indicate.

1. If a noun in the instumental (singular or plural) is the *only* word *in the sentence* or if it is accompanied only by qualifying words, it usually denotes an object with the help of which some action can be performed: Огнём и мечо́м, or the time or place of an action: По́здней о́сенью. Ма́йским у́тром.

2. If a noun in the instrumental *follows a preposition*, this form by itself has no meaning of its own. The nature of the relationship between the word concerned and the word it is connected with is determined exclusively by the meaning of the preposition: лете́ть над го́родом, парк пе́ред до́мом, о́тпуск в связи́ с боле́знью.

The following prepositions require the instrumental: в связи́ с, в соотве́тствии с, в сравне́нии с, вме́сте с, вслед за, конча́я, над, наравне́ с, наряду́ с, одновреме́нно с, пе́ред, по сравне́нию с, сле́дом за, согла́сно с, сообра́зно с, соразме́рно с.

The prepositions за, под and с may require not only the instrумental, but also some other cases (see 1.6). The preposition ме́жду may also be used either with the instrumental or with the genitive (see 1.4).

3. If a noun in the instrumental without a preposition *is subordinated to a verb in the active voice* (less frequently to a noun), it may denote the *object* acted upon: снабди́ть *обору́дованием*, заве́довать *ка́федрой*, горди́ться *успе́хами*, владе́ние *языка́ми*, недово́льство *собо́й*. If a noun in the instrumental without a preposition is subordinated to a verb *in the passive voice*, it may denote the *performer* of the action: *коми́ссией* при́нято реше́ние, чте́ние рома́на *а́втором*, дом стро́ится *рабо́чими*, у́лица освещена́ *фонаря́ми*.

4. A very frequent meaning of the *instrumental* is that of the instrument of action: писа́ть *карандашо́м*, прие́хать *по́ездом*, разре́зать *ножо́м*, рабо́тать *рука́ми*, уда́р *голово́й*.

5. The instrumental may *characterise* an action or state, either by merely defining it (Брат бу́дет *врачо́м*). Он здесь *практика́нтом*), or by specifying the place of the action (идти́ *по́лем*), the time of the action (прие́хал *дождли́вым ве́чером*) or the manner of the action (говори́ть *ба́сом*), or by comparing the action (свисте́ть *соловьём*, пры́гать *соро́кой*).

In a number of cases the meanings of the instrumental cannot be clearly differentiated: *Ю́ношей* он прие́хал сюда́ (the defining and the temporal meanings), плати́ть *зо́лотом* (the object and the manner of the action), *Мо́лнией* зажгло́ сара́й (the performer and the instrument of the action).

1.8. What the prepositional endings indicate.

The prepositional is encountered *only after a preposition*. The following prepositions require the prepositional: при, по вопро́су о, не говоря́ о. The prepositions в, на and о may require other cases as well (see 1.6). The preposition по may also be used with other cases (see 1.5 and 1.6).

2. The Meaning of Adjectival Endings

The meaning of an adjectival ending consists in the singular of *three* components: number, gender and case, and in the plural of *two* components: number and case.

2.1. What the masculine, feminine and neuter endings indicate.

As a rule, the masculine, feminine and neuter endings of an adjective in the singular indicate *only the subordination* of this adjective to a noun of the corresponding gender (see I, 1.1). However, this rule does not apply if adjectives qualify either the pronouns я, ты, кто (кто́-нибудь, кто́-то) and себя́ or a noun of the common gender of the type ста́роста, сирота́, неве́жа, недоу́чка, зубри́ла, пла́кса, etc. In these two cases masculine adjectives indicate male persons, while feminine adjectives indicate female persons. For example: кто тако́й (about a man), кто така́я (about a woman), ужа́сный неря́ха (about a man), ужа́сная неря́ха (about a woman), etc. It is impossible to define the class of common nouns exactly, since it has a tendency to grow at the expense of masculine nouns in view of the fact that women have begun fulfilling such social functions which were previously considered men's prerogatives. So a feminine adjective qualifying a noun denoting a person more often than not indicates that the person concerned is a woman. On the contrary, a masculine adjective qualifying a noun denoting a person does not necessarily indicate that the person concerned is a man. In such a case the question of the sex either remains unresolved or can be resolved with the help of some other elements of context (the person's name, the use of the pronoun он or она́, etc.). (See III C, 7.1.)

2.2. What the singular and plural endings indicate.

As a rule, the singular and plural endings of an adjective indicate *only the subordination* of this adjective to a noun of the corresponding number (for the difference between number as a grammatical characteristic of a noun and the idea of the number of objects, see above: 1.1. and 1.2). However, this rule does not apply if adjectives qualify indeclinable nouns of the type пальто́, такси́, ле́ди, пенсне́, etc. In this case a singular adjective usually indicates one object: но́вое пальто́, свобо́дное такси́, while a plural adjective indicates more than one object: ста́рые ле́ди, но́вые пальто́.

2.3. What the case endings indicate.

As a rule, the case endings of an adjective indicate *only the subordination* of this adjective to a noun in the relevant case, however, not infrequently it is the adjective that provides the bulk of the information on the case in which the adjective plus the noun phrase stands: большо́го до́ма — больши́е дома́. And in the cases when the noun connected with an adjective is indeclinable, the adjectival ending is the sole expression of the case characteristic of the phrase: о но́вом пальто́, но́вого пальто́, но́вые пальто́, etc.

2.4. What the endings of short-form adjectives indicate.

As a rule, the meaning of a short-form adjective denoting the property or quality of an object does not at all differ from that of the corresponding long-form adjective: Он до́брый and Он добр; Доро́га краси́вая and Доро́га краси́ва.

However, when a short-form adjective describes a concrete object through its *size* (measurements), it conveys a characteristic which makes it impossible to use that object: брю́ки длинны́, ту́фли узки́, пальто́ велико́. As a rule, the objects characterised in this way are articles of clothing and footwear.

A short-form adjective may also convey a quality which characterises an object or person at precisely *the given time*: Ребёнок здоро́в (бо́лен) (the adjectives convey the child's state at the moment of speaking).

Besides, a number of short-form adjectives do not have the corresponding long forms (see I, 2.1.), and the meanings of the adjectives ви́ден, слы́шен, жив, прав, свобо́ден and some others are not correlated with those of the corresponding long forms. (See also III D, 4.)

3. The Meaning of Verb Endings

3.1. What the endings of finite present/future tense indicative mood verb forms indicate.

The meaning of the endings of these verb forms consists of *four* components: one is connected with mood (see I, 5.4), a second with number (see I, 5.7), a third with tense (see I, 5.5) and the fourth with person (see I, 5.6).

3.1.1. The **indicative** mood shows that the action of a verb *actually* takes place: Земля́ враща́ется вокру́г Со́лнца. Студе́нты сдаю́т экза́мены.

This, however, does not mean that any sentence containing a verb in the indicative mood reports an action actually taking place. Sentences which include various conjunctions, particles, adverbs (for example, е́сли, раз, мо́жет быть, наве́рное, по моему́ мне́нию, etc.), and verbs in the indicative mood may convey a situation not actually taking place: Он, мо́жет быть, приходи́л сюда́. Е́сли вы зна́ете, то ска́жете.

Perfective verbs (see I, 5.2) in the future tense of the indicative mood, when used in the 2nd person singular or plural, may denote an action which does not actually take place, but which the speaker urges the listener to perform: Ты отведёшь соба́ку к генера́лу и спро́сишь там, ска́жешь, что я нашёл и присла́л (Чехов).

3.1.2. The **singular** or **plural** of verb forms usually reflects the number of the noun denoting the performer or the experiencer of the action of the verb. (For the meaning of the number of verb forms combining with personal pronouns or used independently, see 3.1.4.)

3.1.3. What the present tense (of imperfective verbs)/future tense (of perfective verbs) indicates.

When used *by itself* an *imperfective* **present tense** verb denotes an action taking place *at the moment of speaking.* The term "the moment of speaking" should be understood broadly enough, as including not only the moment of uttering or writing the verb form concerned, but also the time before and after it. Context, situation and common sense often prompt one precisely how "the moment of speaking" coincides with the action of the verb.

Thus, for example, in a context a present tense imperfective verb may denote an action taking place at the very moment of speaking: Что ты здесь де́лаешь?; an action taking place at the moment of speaking and also, evidently, before and after that moment: Я здесь рабо́таю; an action which probably is not taking place at the moment of speaking, but which took place within a limited period before that moment and will be taking place within a limited period after that moment: Он рабо́тает над диссерта́цией; an action taking place at the moment of speaking and at all other imaginable times: Во́лга впада́ет в Каспи́йское мо́ре; an action which may not be taking place at the moment of speaking, but which takes place habitually, as a rule: Га́зы при нагрева́нии расширя́ются, etc.

Context may transfer the meaning of sentences with present tense imperfective verbs to a plane either *before* or *after* the moment of speaking. The devices which determine the temporal plane of a sentence in such cases are either words denoting time: *В бу́дущем году́* обяза́тельно е́ду в Крым. Иду́ я *вчера́* по у́лице и вдруг ви́жу Оле́га. *В 1880 году́* Достое́вский рабо́тает над «Бра́тьями Карама́зовыми», or past tense verb forms in the principal clause of a complex sentence: *Я ду́мал,* что ты за́втра е́дешь.

A **future tense** *perfective* verb denotes an action which will actually take place *after the moment of speaking*: Наступит лето, закончатся занятия, и все дети разъедутся из города. For the meaning of a desired action denoted by such forms in the 2nd person singular or plural, see 3.1.1.

Under the impact of context this form may denote an action connected with the *moment of speaking*: Не разберёшь, сколько ему лет.

Future tense verb forms are used with the meaning of the *present* tense in sentences describing successive actions: Маленькая Таня не может играть на одном месте: то побежит куда-то за дом, то принесёт какие-то новые игрушки.

Future tense perfective verbs may denote actions which occurred in the past, *before the moment of speaking*, i.e. they have the meaning of the *past* tense (sentences with such forms often incorporate the particle бывало): Раньше он придёт, бывало, к нам, всё расскажет.

Future tense perfective verbs may also occur in sentences whose temporal relation to the period *before the moment of speaking* is determined by the use of past tense verbs in them: Бежал, бежал да как прыгнет. Слушал, слушал, а потом как закричит. In such sentences, characterised by the presence of the particle как and a colloquial flavour, the perfective verbs denote a *sudden* onset of a past action of particular intensity. (See also III C, 5.2.1.)

3.1.4. Verbs in the **1st person** denote the *author* of a communication (the original source of a communication), verbs in the **2nd person** denote the *receiver* of the communication (the person or persons for whom the communication is intended), and verbs in the **3rd person** denote the *message* of the communication (not the speaker and not the listener).

Under the impact of context and situation these meanings may change. The 1st person plural may denote *one* speaker, who avoids using the 1st person singular out of modesty: Мы придерживаемся другого мнения. The same form may represent an action in such a way that the speaker himself may be thought to take part in it, which is contrary to fact: Как мы себя чувствуем? (doctors' question with a nuance of sympathy, condescension or irony).

Verbs in the 1st person singular or plural, when used without the appropriate pronouns, may denote actions generally referring to *any person*: Что имеем не храним — потерявши плачем. Verbs in the 2nd person singular or plural may also denote actions referring to *any person*: Вечно с тобой опаздываешь. Что посеешь, то и пожнёшь. Even the personal pronouns used with such verbs may not affect this meaning: Для тебя находится уголок у окошка, и *ты видишь* сначала воду, зелёную, в белых искорках, потом одинокие нефтяные вышки, а потом уже всё это. *Обведите* взглядом строения, и вы *почувствуете*: камни всё помнят (В. Песков).

Verbs in the 2nd person plural may also denote an action performed by *one* actor, whom the speaker designates by a polite formula: Алексей Николаевич, не расскажете ли вы нам о вашем новом фильме?

Verbs in the 3rd person singular or plural may represent an action as having or lacking the performer. In the latter case the absence of the performer may either reflect some distinctive feature of the action concerned: смеркáется, хватáет (this is a feature of singular verbs only) or be the result of the speaker's conscious choice. The absence of the performer may be due either to the fact that he/it is clear from the context: Идёт! Начинáется!, or to the fact that the action, which has a general character, may refer to any performer: Цыплят по óсени считáют, or to the fact that mentioning the performer is deliberately avoided: Вопрóс обсуждáют. (See III, C, 4.)

3.2. What the endings of finite past tense indicative mood verb forms indicate.

The meaning of the endings of these verb forms consists of *four* components: one is connected with the mood (see I, 5.4), a second with number (see I, 5.7), a third with tense (see I, 5.5), and the fourth (in the singular) (see I, 5.8) with gender.

3.2.1. The **indicative mood** shows that the action of the verb *actually* took place: Пришлá веснá. Вы читáли э́ту кни́гу? (For the influence of other words in a sentence containing a verb in the indicative mood on the relationship between this sentence and reality, see 3.1.1.)

Past tense forms of the verbs начáть, кóнчить, пойти́, побежáть, поéхать, поплы́ть, полетéть, взять, взя́ться and a number of others may be used in subjectless sentences to convey an *appeal* or *injunction to perform an action*: Поéхали! Вмéсте, дру́жно взяли́сь. Пошёл спать! Such forms are characteristic of colloquial speech, the singular forms having a somewhat peremptory and impolite nuance.

3.2.2. The **singular** or the **plural** of verb forms usually reflects the number of the noun which denotes the performer of the action of the verb. (For the changes in the meaning of verbs due to the use of singular or plural pronominal nouns to denote the performer, see 3.1.4.)

3.2.3. When used *by itself*, a **past tense** *imperfective* verb denotes an action completed either *by or before the moment of speaking*. *Perfective* past tense verbs denote either simply a past action or a past action whose result is relevant at the moment of speaking. This meaning is generally called *perfect*. For example: Я пáмятник себé воздви́г нерукотвóрный (Пу́шкин). Наступи́ла веснá.

Occasionally, past tense perfective verbs denote actions which are to take place *after the moment of speaking*. This reference of the relevant action to the *future is determined* either *by the context*: Éсли зáвтра бу́дет контрóльная рабóта по математи́ке, я *поги́б*, or by the situation: Спаси́бо! До свидáния! Я *пошёл*. (In this case the speaker's departure is represented by him not as a planned action, but as an accomplished fact, which contradicts reality.)

Past tense verbs of either aspect may denote a *present* time action with strong sarcastic overtones: Боя́лся я егó, как же! (i. e. "I wasn't afraid of him at all!"), Послу́шались мы их, как бы не так (i. e. "We didn't even think for a moment of obeying them!").

3.2.4. The **masculine, feminine** or **neuter gender** of a past tense singular verb usually reflects the gender of the noun which denotes the performer of the action of the verb. If such a noun belongs to the common gender, then the feminine gender of the verb shows that the performer is a female person, while the masculine gender of the verb usually shows that the performer is a male person (also see above, 2.1).

3.3. What the endings of finite future tense indicative mood imperfective verb forms indicate.

A future tense imperfective verb form consists of a finite form of the verb быть and the infinitive of the notional verb and expresses *four* components of meaning: mood (see I, 5.4), tense (see I, 5.5), number (see I, 5.7) and person (see I, 5.6).

3.3.1. The **indicative mood** shows that the action of the verb will *actually* take place: К тебе́ я бу́ду прилета́ть (Ле́рмонтов). (For the influence of other words in a sentence containing a verb in the indicative mood on the relationship between this sentence and reality, see 3.1.1.)

3.3.2. Future tense finite verb forms in the indicative mood usually denote actions which take place *after the moment of speaking* or after some other moment clear from the situation or context.

Occasionally, future tense forms denote an action taking place *at the moment of speaking*, i. e. they have the meaning of *present* tense forms; for example, in emotionally coloured (rude) turns of phrase, typical of colloquial speech, of the type: Бу́дут вся́кие по ноча́м *беспоко́ить* (the speaker is displeased to have been disturbed by somebody at night); Ещё секрета́рши мне *бу́дут ука́зывать* (the speaker is displeased at the secretaries "bossing him around").

For the meanings of the person and number of future tense indicative mood verb forms, see 3.1.2 and 3.1.4.

3.4. What the endings of finite subjunctive mood verb forms indicate.

The meaning of the combined (-л or ø + бы) marker of these verb forms consists of *three* components: one is connected with mood (see I, 5.4), a second with number (see I, 5.7) and the third (in the singular) with gender (see I. 5.8).

A verb in the subjunctive mood usually denotes an action which is not actually taking place, but which is possible or desirable. Such an action may be desirable both from the speaker's point of view and from that of the person spoken to or the object spoken about: Пое́хал бы я сейча́с на́ море, покупа́лся бы, позагора́л. Пришёл бы *ты* сего́дня домо́й пора́ньше. Знал бы об э́том *оте́ц*, он бы о́чень обра́довался.

Besides, the subjunctive mood of verbs of speech may denote a real action: Я проси́л бы тебя́ прие́хать = Я прошу́ тебя́ прие́хать.

For the meanings of the number and gender of subjunctive mood verb forms, see 3.2.2 and 3.2.4.

3.5. What the endings of finite imperative mood verb forms indicate.

The meaning of a finite verb form in the imperative mood, which may be one word (сиди́, вста́ньте) or two words (Дава́й сде́лаем! Пусть придёт!), consists of *three* components: the first is connected with mood (see I, 5.4), a second with person (see I, 5.6) and the third with number (see I, 5.7).

3.5.1. What the imperative of verbs indicates.

When used *by itself*, a verb in the imperative denotes the action the speaker *urges* the person(s) spoken to to perform: Скажи́те! Да́йте! Принеси́! Успоко́йся!

In *context* the meaning of injunction may combine with that of *desirability*: *Мину́й* нас пу́ще всех печа́лей и ба́рский гнев, и ба́рская любо́вь (Грибоедов), *obligatoriness*: Здесь *живи́* не как хо́чешь — как тётки веля́т (Пушкин), *enforcement* (usually expressed by the use of singular forms in conjunction with the particle хоть): Хоть *умри́*, но сде́лай, and the *possibility* of an action: До́брый до́ктор Айболи́т! Он под де́ревом сиди́т. *Приходи́* к нему́ лечи́ться и коро́ва, и волчи́ца, и жучо́к, и паучо́к, и медве́дица (К. Чуковский).

In a *conditional clause* (more often with a verb in the subjunctive mood in the principal clause) an imperative form has the meaning of a *conditioning action*: Но никто́ не знал о та́йной беде́ мое́й, и, *скажи́* я о ней, никто́ бы мне не пове́рил (Пастернак).

There are contexts, however, in which imperative forms may be understood as having the meaning of either an injunction or a condition: Письмо́ само́ никуда́ не пойдёт, но в я́щик его́ *опусти́* — оно́ пробежи́т, пролети́т, проплывёт ты́сячи вёрст пути́ (Маршак). This sentence may be understood as an injunction to perform an action (опусти́!) or as a condition for other actions (е́сли опусти́ть).

When following и, возьми́, возьми́ (да) и, an imperative *singular* form denotes a *real* (unexpected and usually undesirable) action prior to the moment of speaking: Ему́ бы в сто́рону бро́ситься, а он *возьми́ да* пря́мо *и побеги́* (Тургенев). In such cases возьми́ merely stresses and singles out the action of the verb in the imperative.

As a rule, the use of the singular or the plural of a verb form depends on the number (singular or plural) of the word denoting the performer(s) whose action is characterised. The plural imperative, however, may be used with respect to one person whom the speaker addresses in the second person plural (вы): Та́ня, позвони́те, пожа́луйста, ве́чером. At the same time, the singular imperative may occasionally be used with respect to many persons: Солда́ты, слу́шай мою́ кома́нду!

The plural forms of the Пойдёмте, Споёмте type imply that the performers include both the speaker and the persons spoken to.

3.6. What the endings of active participles indicate.

Active participial forms have two endings. The endings **-ущ-/-ющ-, -ащ-/-ящ-** and **-вш-/-ш-** express **tense** and **voice** meanings, while what follows them (with the exception of **-ся**, which comes at the end of some forms) are the endings of long-form adjectives and express the relevant meanings (see above, 2).

The endings **-ущ-/-ющ-, -ащ-/-ящ-** and **-вш-/-ш-** of forms that do not end in **-ся** show that the noun with which a participle with such an ending agrees conveys the performer of the action of the participle: играющие дети, живущих людей, заросшие поля, мечтающему поэту.

The endings **-ущ-/-ющ-** and **-ащ-/-ящ-** usually show that the "qualitative" action of the participle manifests itself either *at the moment of speaking*: вижу играющих детей, or at the time expressed by the finite verb of the sentence: видел играющих детей.

The endings **-вш-/-ш-** usually show that the "qualitative" action of the participle manifests itself *before* the moment of speaking.

3.7. What the endings of passive participles indicate.

Passive participial forms have two endings. The endings **-ем-/-ом-/-им-**, **-енн-/-нн-** and **-т-** express **tense** and **voice** meanings, while the endings of the short- or long-form adjectives following them express their appropriate meanings (see above, 2).

The endings **-ем-/-ом-/-им-**, **-енн-/-нн-** and **-т-** show that the noun with which a participle with such an ending agrees is the *object* experiencing the action of the participle: выполняемые (вами) обязанности, унесённые ветром листья, измятый костюм.

The endings **-ем-/-ом-/-им-** usually show that the action of the participle relates either *to the moment of speaking*: принимаю выдвигаемые условия, or to the time expressed by the finite verb form: принимал выдвигаемые условия.

The endings **-енн-/-нн-/-т-** usually show that the action represented as a quality took place either *before the moment of speaking*: полученное письмо, купленные тетради, or before the moment of the action expressed by the finite verb form.

Not infrequently passive participles lose their tense characteristic and indicate either the ability to experience an action: изменяемые слова, or the result of such an action: сгущённое молоко.

The frequently used passive past tense short-form participles often have a *perfect* meaning (see above, 3.2.3): Материал изучен. Книга прочитана. Выставка закрыта.

3.8. What **-ся/-сь**, in which verb forms terminate, indicates.

-ся/-сь, in which verb forms terminate, may be either a suffix or an ending. In the former case, the infinitive of the form with this marker also has it, and the meaning of such a verb should be looked up in the dictionary. For example: Дети катаются на коньках — the infinitive of катаются is кататься. In the latter case, the infinitive of the form with **-ся/-сь** has no such marker. For example: Пьеса исполняется музыкантом — the infinitive of исполняется is исполнять.

Both the first and the second **-ся/-сь** are practically encountered only in 3rd person present tense forms, past tense forms, subjunctive mood forms, and active participial forms. In other verb forms — with very few exceptions — only the suffix **-ся/-сь** is encountered.

These two **-ся/-сь** can be discriminated only by taking into consideration the functions fulfilled by the nouns connected with the form concerned.

In a sentence a *finite verb form* with the **ending -ся/-сь** is usually connected with a noun in the nominative which denotes the *experiencer* of the action: Улицы освещаются. Вопрос обсуждается. Дорога ремонтируется. Such sentences frequently also have a noun in the instrumental denoting the performer of the action: Улицы освещаются *фонарями*. Вопрос обсуждается *комиссией*. Дорога ремонтируется *рабочими*.

In a sentence a finite verb form with the **suffix -ся/-сь** is usually connected with a noun in the nominative denoting the *performer* of the action: Начинаются экзамены. Дети умылись.

Not infrequently sentences are encountered in which a finite verb form ending in -ся/-сь is connected with a noun in the nominative; however, it is impossible to determine what function — the performer or the experiencer — this noun fulfils: Мост разводится. It is not clear whether the sentence implies that the bridge is (being) drawn aside (or raised) (in such a case the time of the action is usually indicated: Мост разводится с 2 до 5 часов) or that it can be drawn aside (or raised) (in such a case words clarifying this meaning are usually suplied: Мост вообще-то разводится. Этот мост разводится, а тот — нет).

In a sentence, a participle with the **ending -ся/-сь** is connected with a noun which stands for the *experiencer* of the action denoted by the participle: исполняющийся марш, освещавшуюся улицу. In such cases, the sentence frequently has a noun in the instrumental denoting the performer of the action: исполняющийся *оркестром* марш, освещавшуюся *фонарём* улицу. If the noun connected with a participle with **-ся/-сь** is the *performer* of its action, then **-ся/-сь** is a **suffix**: смеющиеся лица, проснувшийся ребёнок.

Participial forms with the suffix **-ся/-сь** can sometimes be distinguished from those with the ending **-ся/-сь** only thanks to the noun connected with them: работа, переписывавшаяся студентами — the infinitive of the verb is переписывать, so **-ся** is an ending; переписывавшийся со мной коллега из Ленинграда — the infinitive of the verb is переписываться, so **-ся** is a suffix.

3.9. What time of the action or state sentences without a finite verb form denote.

Sentences without a finite verb form denoting the time of an action or state express an action taking place *at the moment of speaking*. In this case the moment of speaking must be understood broadly enough. Sentences of the type Отец — учитель. Ребёнок послушный. Поговорить не с кем denote situations related *to the moment of speaking* and, evidently, to relatively long periods both preceding and following that moment. The absence of the formal marker relating the action to the moment of speaking is indicated in writing by a dash (—): Отец — в саду. Наша Таня — молодец.

PART III
"FROM THE MEANING TO THE FORM" GRAMMAR

A. DERIVATION OF ALL THE GRAMMATICAL FORMS FROM THE DICTIONARY FORM OF A WORD

The grammatical information given in Part II is not sufficient for those who want to have an *active* command of Russian, i. e. who want not only to be able to read and understand spoken Russian, but also *to be able to build sentences orally or in writing*.

A speaker or a writer must be able to build a sentence in such a way that, on the one hand, it should correspond to his communicative intention and, on the other, it should be understood correctly, i. e. it should be built in accordance with the rules of the Russian language; for this he must use precisely those word forms which are required by the syntax of the sentence. Thus, for example, in Russian one cannot use the dictionary form of the далёкая страна type after the words Я приехал; one must write (or say) Я приехал из далёкой страны, although the use of the dictionary form in this case would not have prevented the listener from understanding the sentence: it would have merely violated the rules of correct usage. The sentence Сын напишет отцу, for example, is of a different nature. In it, the dictionary form (сын) denotes the *performer* of the action, i. e. the person who will write, whereas the form ending in -у (отцу) denotes the "receiver" of the action, i. e. the person *to whom* the son will write. The use of the dictionary forms сын and отец in this sentence would have resulted in a violation of the rules of the Russian language and would have created ambiguity (it would not have been clear who will write to whom). The use of the forms сыну and отец would have simply created a different situation from the one conveyed in the first sentence. The sentence Сыну напишет отец means that the performer of the action is the father (отец), whereas the son (сын) is the "receiver" of the action. The dictionary form написать in this sentence is also impossible. Besides violating the rules of Russian, such a sentence would simply have failed to convey who and when will perform the action concerned and whether the action will be performed at all. The use of such forms of the verb написать as написал and написал бы would have conveyed a real action in the past and an unrealised planned action, respectively.

Thus, to be able to build a Russian sentence, one must be able *to derive the necessary forms from the dictionary form*.

This part of the present grammar gives information about what forms can be derived from the dictionary form. This information relates to written Russian and is based on «Грамматический словарь русского языка» by A. A. Zaliznyak, Moscow, 1977, in which more detailed information on the derivation of the grammatical forms of words can be found.

1. The Noun

1.1.1. How to derive the forms of the overwhelming majority of masculine nouns which have a zero ending (i. e. which end in a consonant, -й or -ь) in the dictionary form.

If in the dictionary form a noun ends in a *consonant* (including -й), it is usually *masculine*.[1] Exceptions to this rule are very few rarely used nouns of foreign origin, which end in a consonant and do not have any other grammatical forms (of the мадáм type).

If the dictionary form of a noun ends in **ь**, it may be either masculine or feminine (for this, see below, 1.3.1).

In the accusative singular and plural, *inanimate* masculine nouns have a form coincident with that of the *nominative* of the same number, while *animate* nouns have the form coincident with that of the *genitive* of the same number.

Masculine nouns the dictionary form of which ends in a consonant, -й or -ь and which have a fixed stress on the stem, i. e. have an *unstressed ending*, usually derive their other forms in the following way (see pp. 133-134).

If a noun is not stressed on the stem, but on the *ending*, the following changes occur.

In the instrumental singular **-ем** is replaced with **-ём** in nouns whose dictionary form ends in **-ь** (словáрь — словарём, конь — конём) or **-й** (соловéй — соловьём) (except **-ий** or **-ый**), and with **-ом** in nouns whose dictionary form ends in **ж, ш, ч, щ** or **ц** (богáч — богачóм, нож — ножóм, кузнéц — кузнецóм).

In the genitive plural **-ев** is replaced with **-ов** in nouns whose dictionary form ends in **-ц** (кузнецóв, молодцóв), and with **-ёв** in nouns whose dictionary form ends in **-й** (соловьёв, ручьёв), except **-ий** or **-ый**.

1.1.2. What deviations in the set of the endings occur in some masculine nouns.

1. The noun путь changes in a special way.

Singular						Plural				
Nom.	Gen.	Dat.	Acc.	Instr.	Prep.	Nom.	Gen.	Dat.	Acc.	Instr.	Prep.
путь	путú	путú	путь	путём	путú	путú	путéй	путя́м	путú	путя́ми	путя́х

---

[1] The gender of a noun manifests itself not only in the peculiarities of the derivation of its forms, but also in the peculiarities of its agreement with qualifiers and some verb forms (see I, 1.1).

Quality of final consonant of dictionary form / Grammatical characteristics	Any consonant, except г, к, х, ж, ш, щ, ч	ь	г, к, х	ж, ш, щ, ч	ц	й [1] (except -ий/-ый)	-ий [2]
Singular							
Nom.	завóд артúст	портфéль жúтель	подсóлнух внук	марш товáрищ	мéсяц принц	слýчай герóй	сценáрий
Gen.	завóда артúста	портфéля жúтеля	подсóлнуха внýка	мáрша товáрища	мéсяца прúнца	слýчая герóя	сценáрия
Dat.	завóду артúсту	портфéлю жúтелю	подсóлнуху внýку	мáршу товáрищу	мéсяцу прúнцу	слýчаю герóю	сценáрию
Acc.	завóд артúста	портфéль жúтеля	подсóлнух внýка	марш товáрища	мéсяц прúнца	слýчай герóя	сценáрий
Instr.	завóдом артúстом	портфéлем жúтелем	подсóлнухом внýком	мáршем товáрищем	мéсяцем прúнцем	слýчаем герóем	сценáрием
Prep.	завóде артúсте	портфéле жúтеле	подсóлнухе внýке	мáрше товáрище	мéсяце прúнце	слýчае герóе	сценáрии

[1] Masculine nouns whose dictionary form ends in **-ый** change like adjectives with the same ending. Some masculine nouns whose dictionary form ends in **-ий** or **-ой** change in the way shown in this table; other nouns with the same dictionary form termination change like adjectives (for this, see II A, 2.3.1).

[2] Nouns which change in accordance with this pattern and whose dictionary form ends in **-ий** do not include any commonly used animate nouns.

Continued

Quality of final consonant of dictionary form / Grammatical characteristics	Any consonant, except г, к, х, ж, ш, щ, ч	ь	г, к, х	ж, ш, щ, ч	ц	й [1] (except -ий/-ый)	-ий [2]
Plural Nom.	заво́ды артисты	портфе́ли жи́тели	подсо́лнухи вну́ки	ма́рши това́рищи	ме́сяцы при́нцы	слу́чаи геро́и	сцена́рии
Gen.	заво́дов арти́стов	портфе́лей жи́телей	подсо́лнухов вну́ков	ма́ршей това́рищей	ме́сяцев при́нцев	слу́чаев геро́ев	сцена́риев
Dat.	заво́дам арти́стам	портфе́лям жи́телям	подсо́лнухам вну́кам	ма́ршам това́рищам	ме́сяцам при́нцам	слу́чаям геро́ям	сцена́риям
Acc.	заво́ды арти́стов	портфе́ли жи́телей	подсо́лнухи вну́ков	ма́рши това́рищей	ме́сяцы при́нцев	слу́чаи геро́ев	сцена́рии
Instr.	заво́дами арти́стами	портфе́лями жи́телями	подсо́лнухами вну́ками	ма́ршами това́рищами	ме́сяцами при́нцами	слу́чаями геро́ями	сцена́риями
Prep.	заво́дах арти́стах	портфе́лях жи́телях	подсо́лнухах вну́ках	ма́ршах това́рищах	ме́сяцах при́нцах	слу́чаях геро́ях	сцена́риях

2. Nouns whose dictionary form ends in **-ин** (more often in **-анин/-янин**) and which designate people through their nationality, area of settlement or social status usually have the ending **-е** in the nominative plural (армяни́н — армя́не, южа́нин — южа́не) and a zero ending (ø) in the genitive plural (армя́н, южа́н). However, the nominative plural of тата́рин is тата́ры; of грузи́н, грузи́ны; and of господи́н, господа́.

3. Nouns whose dictionary form ends in **-онок/-ёнок** or **-оночек/-ёночек** and which denote the young of animals, and also the words маслёнок, опёнок, маслёночек and опёночек have a zero ending in the genitive plural (цыплёнок — цыпля́т, цыплёночек — цыпля́ток). The nominative plural of these nouns has the ending **-а** (цыплёнок — цыпля́та).

4. A number of nouns have in the nominative plural (and inanimate nouns also in the accusative plural) the ending **-я**, if their dictionary form ends in **-ь** or **-й** (учи́тель — учителя́, край — края́) or **-а** if they have other dictionary forms (рукава́, мастера́).

Here belong the following nouns: а́дрес — адреса́, бег — бега́, бе́рег — берега́, бок — бока́, борт — борта́, ве́ер — веера́, век — века́, ве́ксель — векселя́, ве́нзель — вензеля́, ве́чер — вечера́, во́рох — вороха́, глаз — глаза́, го́лос — голоса́, го́род — города́, дире́ктор — директора́, до́ктор — доктора́, дом — дома́, жёлоб — желоба́, жёмчуг — жемчуга́, жёрнов — жернова́, ка́тер — катера́, ки́тель — кителя́, ко́локол — колокола́, ко́рпус — корпуса́, край — края́, ку́пол — купола́, луг — луга́, ма́стер — мастера́, но́мер — номера́, обшла́г — обшлага́, о́корок — окорока́, о́круг — округа́, о́рден — ордена́, о́стров — острова́, па́рус — паруса́, па́спорт — паспорта́, пе́репел — перепела́, по́вар — повара́, по́греб — погреба́, по́езд — поезда́, по́яс — пояса́, про́вод — провода́, профе́ссор — профессора́, рог — рога́, рука́в — рукава́, снег — снега́, сорт — сорта́, стог — стога́, сто́рож — сторожа́, те́терев — тетерева́, том — тома́, то́поль — тополя́, то́рмоз — тормоза́, учи́тель — учителя́, фе́льдшер — фельдшера́, фли́гель — флигеля́, флю́гер — флюгера́, хо́лод — холода́, ху́тор — хутора́, че́реп — черепа́, шёлк — шелка́, ште́мпель — штемпеля́, я́корь — якоря́.

In some cases a word may have different plurals for its different meanings: зуб — зу́бы (teeth of man or animal) and зу́бья (teeth on a rim of a wheel, cogs), лист — листы́ (sheets of paper or iron) and ли́стья (leaves of plants), про́пуск — про́пуски (lacunas) and пропуска́ (passes permitting one to do something).

5. A number of nouns in the genitive plural (and animate nouns in the accusative plural) have a zero ending. Here belong the following nouns: болга́ры — болга́р, боти́нки — боти́нок, ва́ленки — ва́ленок, во́лосы — воло́с, во́льты — вольт, глаза́ — глаз, гла́зки — гла́зок, грузи́ны — грузи́н, зу́бки — зу́бок, осети́ны — осети́н, партиза́ны — партиза́н, пого́ны — пого́н, разы́ — раз, ро́жки — ро́жек, сапо́жки — сапо́жек, сапоги́ — сапо́г, солда́ты — солда́т, тата́ры — тата́р, ту́рки — ту́рок, туркме́ны — туркме́н, хозя́ева — хозя́ев, цыга́не — цыга́н, чулки́ — чуло́к.

Thus, the genitive plural of some of these nouns coincides with their dictionary form: глаз — глаза́ — глаз.

6. The plural forms of the nouns сосе́д and чёрт are derived irregularly: *nom.* сосе́ди, че́рти; *gen.* сосе́дей, черте́й; *dat.* сосе́дям, чертя́м; *acc.* сосе́дей, черте́й; *instr.* сосе́дями, чертя́ми; *prep.* сосе́дях, чертя́х.

7. The plural forms of the nouns челове́к and ребёнок are: *nom.* лю́ди, де́ти; *gen.* люде́й, дете́й; *dat.* лю́дям, де́тям; *acc.* люде́й, дете́й; *instr.* людьми́, детьми́; *prep.* лю́дях, де́тях. The nominative plural of цыга́н is цыга́не; of болга́рин, болга́ры; of тата́рин, тата́ры; and of хаза́рин, хаза́ры.

8. The genitive plural of год is годо́в or лет (depending on the meaning of the word). The instrumental plural of зверь is either зверя́ми or зверьми́.

9. A number of nouns following the preposition в with the meaning of "inside, within or in the conditions of something" (в шкафу́, в Крыму́, в низу́, в полку́, в году́, в бою́, в быту́) or with the meaning of "covered with a lot of something, soiled with something" (в снегу́, в поту́, в грязи́) and also following the preposition на with the meaning of "on the surface of something or within the limits of something" (на шкафу́, на лугу́, на лбу, на Дону́) or with the meaning of "prepared or made with something" (на меду́, на меху́) have the forms ending in **-у** or **-ю**.

1.1.3. What transformations in the stems of masculine nouns occur in the forms of both numbers.

If the final consonant (or the final consonant plus **-ь**) of the dictionary form is preceded by **-о-, -е-** or **-ё-**, this vowel is often dropped in all the other forms (with the exception of those externally coincident with the dictionary form). It may be dropped altogether (буго́р — бугра́, бугру́, etc., ого́нь — огни́, огне́й, etc., ве́тер — ве́тра, ве́тру, etc., коне́ц — конца́, концу́, etc.) or, if **-е-** or **-ё-** is preceded by **-л-**, then **-е-** or **-ё-** is replaced with **-ь-** (па́лец — па́льца, па́льцу, etc., лёд — льда, льду, etc., лев — львы, львов, etc.). If **-е-** or **-ё-** is preceded by a vowel, then **-е-** or **-ё-** is replaced with **-й-** (бое́ц — бойца́, бойцу́, etc., китае́ц — кита́йцы, кита́йцев, etc.).

If the dictionary form ends in **-ей**, then in all the forms, except those coincident with the dictionary form, this combination is usually replaced with **-ь** before the appropriate ending (руче́й — ручья́, ручью́, etc., мураве́й — муравьи́, муравьёв, etc.); however: музе́й — музе́я, музе́ю, etc.

In accordance with the rules described, **-я** in the word за́яц is dropped: за́йца.

1.1.4. What transformations in the stems of masculine nouns occur in the plural.

1. If the dictionary form of a noun ends in **-ин** (more often in **-анин/-янин**) and the word designates a person through his/her nationality, area of settlement or social status, then the plural forms have no **-ин** (армяни́н — армя́не, горожа́нин — горожа́не).

2. If the dictionary form of a noun ends in **-онок/-ёнок** or **-оночек/-ёночек** and the word denotes the young of an animal (and also the words маслёнок, опёнок, маслёночек, опёночек), then instead of these markers the plural forms have **-ат-/-ят-** or **-атк-/-ятк-**, respectively: цыплёнок — цыпля́та, медвежо́нок — медвежа́та, мышо́ночек — мыша́тки, цыплёночек — цыпля́тки.

3. In some nouns **-ь-** is added to the stem in the plural: лист — ли́стья (leaves of a tree), стул — сту́лья, муж — мужья́, князь — князья́, ком — ко́мья, ко́лос — коло́сья, прут — пру́тья, брат — бра́тья. In this case, other changes in the stem may occur; namely, an alternation of the final consonant: сук — су́чья, клок — кло́чья, друг — друзья́, or additional increments: сын — сыновья́. (For the peculiarities of the endings of these nouns, see 1.1.2.)

4. The plural of цветок is цветы́; of хозя́ин, хозя́ева; of су́дно, суда́; of челове́к, лю́ди; and of ребёнок, де́ти.

1.1.5. Nouns in which prepositional and locative case forms are distinguished.

A number of inanimate masculine nouns preceded by the preposition в or на do not take the usual prepositional form with the ending -е (на столе́, в дневнике́), but a special form with the ending **-у/-ю**. These nouns are: ад (в аду́), бе́рег (на берегу́), бой (в бою́), бок (в боку́), бред (в бреду́), быт (в быту́), вал (на валу́), ве́тер (на ветру́), глаз (в глазу́), год (в году́), горб (на горбу́), гроб (в гробу́), долг (в долгу́), дом (на дому́ in the phrase рабо́та на дому́), край (в краю́), лес (в лесу́), лёд (во льду́), лоб (во лбу́), луг (на лугу́), мел (в мелу́), нос (в носу́), плен (в плену́), плот (на плоту́), пол (на полу́), полк (в полку́), порт (в порту́), пост (на посту́), пруд (на пруду́ and в пруду́), пух (в пуху́), рай (в раю́), ров (во рву́), рот (во рту́), ряд (в ряду́), but: в ря́де слу́чаев, сад (в саду́), снег (на снегу́), сук (на суку́), таз (в тазу́), тыл (в тылу́), у́гол (в углу́), шкаф (в шкафу́). Some nouns have two forms after the preposition в or на, distinguished to a greater or lesser extent only stylistically: на балу́ and на ба́ле, в ды́ме and в дыму́, в поту́ and в по́те, and a number of others. (See also above, 1.1.2.)

1.2.1. How to derive the forms of the overwhelming majority of the nouns whose dictionary form ends in **-а/-я**.

If the dictionary form of a noun ends in **-а** or **-я** [1] and the word does not denote a person of the male sex (ю́ноша, де́душка, дя́дя, Пе́тя) or a person of either sex (ста́роста, неве́жа, со́ня), then this noun is *feminine*.[2]

In the accusative inanimate nouns whose dictionary form ends in **-а** or **-я** have only in the *plural* a form coincident with that of the nomina-

---

[1] Feminine nouns whose dictionary form ends in **-ая** or **-яя** change in the same way as adjectives with the same endings (see below, 2,3).

[2] The gender of a noun manifests itself not only in the peculiarities of the derivation of its forms, but also in the peculiarities of its agreement with qualifiers and some verb forms (see I, 1.1).

tive plural, and animate nouns have a form coincident with the genitive plural.

Nouns whose dictionary form ends in -a/-я and whose stress is fixed on the stem, i. e. which have an unstressed ending, usually derive their other forms in the following way (see pp. 139-140).

If a noun is not stressed on the stem, but on the ending, the following changes take place. In the instrumental singular -ей is replaced with -ой after ж, ш, ч, щ and ц (межа́ — межо́й, душа́ — душо́й, пыльца́ — пыльцо́й), and with -ёй after all the consonants, except ж, ш, ч, щ and ц (заря́ — зарёй, простыня́ — простынёй) and also after vowels which do not follow -и- (змея́ — змеёй).

1.2.2. What deviations in the set of the endings occur in some nouns whose dictionary form ends in -а/-я.

1. Nouns whose dictionary form ends in -ья have in the genitive plural the stressed ending -ей (свинья́ — свине́й, статья́ — стате́й) or the unstressed -ий (го́стья — го́стий, певу́нья — певу́ний).
2. A number of nouns have the ending -ей in the genitive plural (свече́й, доле́й, схо́дней).
3. Contrary to the rule, -ь is absent from the genitive plural of some nouns whose dictionary form ends in -ня: ба́шня — ба́шен, пе́сня — пе́сен, спа́льня — спа́лен.
4. The neuter noun дитя́ has the following forms:

Nom.	Gen.	Dat.	Acc.	Instr.	Prep.
дитя́	дитя́ти	дитя́ти	дитя́	дитя́тею	о дитя́ти

1.2.3. What transformations occur in the stems of the nouns whose dictionary form ends in -а/-я.

If the last consonant before the final -а or -я of the dictionary form is preceded by another consonant (including й) or ь, then the vowel -е-, -ё- or -о- usually appears between the last two consonants in the genitive plural. In this case after ж, ч, ш and щ there appears -о- when stressed (кишка́ — кишо́к) and -е- when unstressed (ба́шня — ба́шен); after г, к, х there appears -о- (ку́кла — ку́кол, ку́хня — ку́хонь); instead of -ь- there appears -е- when unstressed (тюрьма́ — тю́рем, шпи́лька — шпи́лек, сва́дьбы — сва́деб, спа́льня — спа́лен) and -ё- when stressed (серьга́ — серёг); instead of -й- there appears -е- (бо́йня — бо́ен, ча́йка — ча́ек); however, this alternation does not occur in some nouns (война́ — войн). In other cases, the appearance of -о- or -е- is unpredictable, although -к-, generally not after ж, ч, ш or щ, is preceded by -о- when unstressed, and -н- is usually preceded by -е- (ска́зка — ска́зок, доска́ — досо́к, пе́сня — пе́сен, царе́вна — царе́вен, сосна́ — со́сен).

1.3.1. How to derive the forms of feminine nouns whose dictionary form ends in -ь.

Quality of final vowel and consonant of dictionary form	Any consonant, except г, к, х, ж, ш, ч, щ, ц before -а	Consonant (except й and ь) before -я	г, к, х before -а	ж, ш, ч, щ before -а	-ца	Vowel (except и) before -я [1]	-ия [1]
Grammatical characteristics							
Singular Nom.	ка́рта коро́ва	неде́ля ня́ня	кни́га соба́ка	ту́ча тёща	у́лица волчи́ца	ста́туя фе́я	ли́ния
Gen.	ка́рты коро́вы	неде́ли ня́ни	кни́ги соба́ки	ту́чи тёщи	у́лицы волчи́цы	ста́туи фе́и	ли́нии
Dat.	ка́рте коро́ве	неде́ле ня́не	кни́ге соба́ке	ту́че тёще	у́лице волчи́це	ста́туе фе́е	ли́нии
Acc.	ка́рту коро́ву	неде́лю ня́ню	кни́гу соба́ку	ту́чу тёщу	у́лицу волчи́цу	ста́тую фе́ю	ли́нию
Instr.	ка́ртой коро́вой	неде́лей ня́ней	кни́гой соба́кой	ту́чей тёщей	у́лицей волчи́цей	ста́туей фе́ей	ли́нией
Prep.	ка́рте коро́ве	неде́ле ня́не	кни́ге соба́ке	ту́че тёще	у́лице волчи́це	ста́туе фе́е	ли́нии

[1] The number of animate nouns with such a termination is very insignificant; most of them are proper feminine names of the Мари́я, Ли́дия type.

Continued

Grammatical characteristics / Quality of final vowel and consonant of dictionary form		Any consonant, except г, к, х, ж, ш, ч, щ, ц before -а	Consonant (except й and ь) before -я	г, к, х before -а	ж, ш, ч, щ before -а	-ца	Vowel (except и) before -я [1]	-ия [1]
Plural	Nom.	ка́рты коро́вы	неде́ли ня́ни	кни́ги соба́ки	ту́чи тёщи	у́лицы волчи́цы	ста́туи фе́и	ли́нии
	Gen.	карт коро́в	неде́ль нянь	книг соба́к	туч тёщ	у́лиц волчи́ц	ста́туй фей	ли́ний
	Dat.	ка́ртам коро́вам	неде́лям ня́ням	кни́гам соба́кам	ту́чам тёщам	у́лицам волчи́цам	ста́туям фе́ям	ли́ниям
	Acc.	ка́рты коро́в	неде́ли нянь	кни́ги соба́к	ту́чи тёщ	у́лицы волчи́ц	ста́туи фей	ли́нии
	Instr.	ка́ртами коро́вами	неде́лями ня́нями	кни́гами соба́ками	ту́чами тёщами	у́лицами волчи́цами	ста́туями фе́ями	ли́ниями
	Prep.	ка́ртах коро́вах	неде́лях ня́нях	кни́гах соба́ках	ту́чах тёщах	у́лицах волчи́цах	ста́туях фе́ях	ли́ниях

If the dictionary form of a *feminine* noun ends in **-ь**, then its forms are derived in the following way:

Singular						
Nom.	*Gen.*	*Dat.*	*Acc.*	*Instr.*	*Prep.*	
тетра́дь мышь	тетра́ди мы́ши	тетра́ди мы́ши	тетра́дь мышь	тетра́дью мы́шью	тетра́ди мы́ши	
Plural						
Nom.	*Gen.*	*Dat.*	*Acc.*	*Instr.*	*Prep.*	
тетра́ди мы́ши	тетра́дей мыше́й	тетра́дям мыша́м	тетра́ди мыше́й	тетра́дями мыша́ми	тетра́дях мыша́х	

Like the other feminine nouns, nouns whose dictionary form ends in **-ь** have, in the accusative plural only, a form which coincides with that of the nominative in the case of inanimate nouns and with that of the genitive in the case of animate nouns. The vowel **о** preceding the final stem consonant may disappear before the ending **-и** in the singular and in all the forms of the plural (ложь — лжи, це́рковь — це́ркви).

The noun це́рковь may either take the regular endings or have the forms церква́м, церква́ми, церква́х as variants.

The plural endings of the noun гроздь are irregular: гро́здья, гро́здьев, гро́здьям, гро́здья, гро́здьями, гро́здьях.

1.4.1. How to derive the forms of neuter nouns whose dictionary form ends in **-о/-е**.

If the dictionary form of a noun ends in **-о** or **-е**, this noun is usually *neuter*.[1]

Inanimate nouns whose dictionary form ends in **-о** or **-е** have in the accusative plural a form which coincides with that of the nominative plural and animate nouns have a form which coincides with that of the genitive plural.

There are a few unchangeable words among the nouns whose dictionary form ends in **-о** or **-е**, such as пальто́, кино́ and кафе́.

The grammatical forms of the overwhelming majority of nouns whose dictionary form ends in **-о** or **-е** and which have a fixed stress on the stem, i. e. which have *unstressed endings*, are derived in the following way:

---

[1] The gender of a noun manifests itself not only in the peculiarities of the derivation of its forms, but also in the peculiarities of its agreement with qualifiers and some verb forms (see I, 1.1).

Quality of final vowel and consonant of dictionary form / Grammatical characteristics	Any consonant, except г, к, х, ж, ш, ч, щ, ц, before -о	Consonant, except ж, ч, ш, щ, ц before -е	г, к, х before -о [2]	ж, ч, ш, щ before -е	-це [2]	-не [2]
Singular						
Nom.	болóто чáдо [1]	гóре	блáго	жилúще чудóвище	сóлнце	здáние
Gen.	болóта чáда	гóря	блáга	жилúща чудóвища	сóлнца	здáния
Dat.	болóту чáду	гóрю	блáгу	жилúщу чудóвищу	сóлнцу	здáнию
Acc.	болóто чáдо	гóре	блáго	жилúще чудóвище	сóлнце	здáние
Instr.	болóтом чáдом	гóрем	блáгом	жилúщем чудóвищем	сóлнцем	здáнием
Prep.	болóте чáде	гóре	блáге	жилúще чудóвище	сóлнце	здáнии

[1] The only word.
[2] Only inanimate nouns.

	Quality of final vowel and consonant of dictionary form	Any consonant, except г, к, х, ж, ш, ч, ш, ц, before -о	Consonant, except ж, ч, ш, щ, ц before -е	г, к, х before -о [2]	ж, ч, ш, щ before -е	-це [2]	-ие [2]
Plural	Nom.	болóта чáда	—	блáга	жилúща чудóвища	сóлнца	здáния
	Gen.	болóт чад	—	благ	жилúщ чудóвищ	солнц	здáний
	Dat.	болóтам чáдам	—	блáгам	жилúщам чудóвищам	сóлнцам	здáниям
	Acc.	болóта чад	—	блáга	жилúща чудóвищ	сóлнца	здáния
	Instr.	болóтами чáдами	—	блáгами	жилúщами чудóвищами	сóлнцами	здáниями
	Prep.	болóтах чáдах	—	блáгах	жилúщах чудóвищах	сóлнцах	здáниях

If a noun is not stressed on the stem, but on the *ending*, then the following changes take place. In the nominative (and the accusative identical with the nominative) -це is replaced with -цо (ружьецо́, пальтецо́). The genitive plural takes the ending -ей (поле́й, уше́й, море́й). The rarely used words остриё, житиё and бытиё follow a special declension pattern.

1.4.2. What deviations in the set of the endings occur in some nouns whose dictionary form ends in -о/-е.

1. A number of nouns in the nominative plural (and inanimate nouns also in the accusative plural) have the ending -и (я́блоко — я́блоки, плечо́ — пле́чи, очко́ — очки́).

2. A number of nouns have the ending -ов/-ев or -ёв in the genitive plural (облако́в, боло́тцев, остриёв).

3. The noun коле́но has irregular plural endings: коле́ни, коле́ней, коле́ням, коле́ни, коле́нями, коле́нях.

1.4.3. What transformations occur in the stems of the nouns whose dictionary form ends in -о/-е.

1. If the final stem consonant is preceded by another consonant (including й) or ь, then in the genitive plural there usually appears -е- or -о- between the final two consonants (кре́сло — кре́сел, окно́ — о́кон, письмо́ — пи́сем, блю́дце — блю́дец, се́рдце — серде́ц, however, яйцо́ — яи́ц).

2. Some nouns end in the plural in -ья, -ьев, -ьям, -ья, -ьями, -ьях (де́рево — дере́вья — дере́вьев, крыло́ — кры́лья — кры́льев, звено́ — зве́нья — зве́ньев, перо́ — пе́рья — пе́рьев).

3. The plural forms of the following nouns are derived irregularly: не́бо (небеса́, небе́с), чу́до (чудеса́, чуде́с), су́дно (судо́в), о́ко (о́чи, оче́й), у́хо (у́ши, уше́й).

1.5. How to derive the forms of the nouns whose dictionary form ends in -мя.

All the nouns whose dictionary form ends in -мя are *neuter* and inanimate. Their grammatical forms are derived in the following way:

Singular						
Nom.	Gen.	Dat.	Acc.	Instr.	Prep.	
зна́мя и́мя се́мя	зна́мени и́мени се́мени	зна́мени и́мени се́мени	зна́мя и́мя се́мя	зна́менем и́менем се́менем	зна́мени и́мени се́мени	

Plural						
знамёна имена́ семена́	знамён имён семя́н	знамёнам имена́м семена́м	знамёна имена́ семена́	знамёнами имена́ми семена́ми	знамёнах имена́х семена́х	

The genitive plural forms of the nouns сéмя and стрéмя are семя́н and стремя́н, respectively.

1.6. How to derive the forms of other nouns.

Nouns whose dictionary form ends in **-ой/-ый/-ий, -ая/-яя** or **-ое/-ее** change in the same way as adjectives with the same endings (see below, 2.1.1).

Nouns whose dictionary form ends in **-у** (рагу́, паспарту́) or **-э** (ало́э, кано́э) and also a number of other nouns of foreign origin may take no endings at all.

2. The Adjective

2.1.1. How to derive the long forms of adjectives.

Depending on the number, gender, case and animateness/inanimateness of the nouns which adjectives qualify, long-form adjectives change in the following way (see p. 146).

2.1.2. How to derive the short forms of adjectives.

Not all the dictionary forms of adjectives give short forms (see I, 2.1). To derive the short form, the ending of the dictionary form **-ый, -ий** or **-ой** should be dropped and the following endings added: ø (**ь**) for the masculine gender, **-а/-я** for the feminine gender, **-о/-е** for the neuter gender, and **-ы/-и** for the plural (see p. 147).

If the final stem consonant is preceded by another consonant (including **й**) or by **ь**, then there usually appears the vowel **-е-, -о-** or, less frequently (under stress), **-ё-** in the masculine short form: удо́бный — удо́бен, у́мный — умён, смешно́й — смешо́н, мя́гкий — мя́гок, до́лгий — до́лог. **-е** more often appears before **н**; and **-о-**, before **к**. However, there are adjectives with a termination in two consonants in whose forms no vowel appears: ры́хлый — рыхл, до́брый — добр, го́рдый — горд. The **-й** and **-ь-** of the dictionary forms of the type under discussion are transformed in the masculine short form in a special way: го́рький — го́рек, бо́йкий — бо́ек, дово́льный — дово́лен, споко́йный — споко́ен.

The masculine short form of some adjectives whose dictionary form ends in **-нный** or **-нний** is derived by dropping the last three letters of the dictionary form: самоуве́ренный — самоуве́рен, вы́спренний — вы́спрен. In this case the other short forms may either preserve the **-нн-** of the dictionary form: самоуве́ренный — самоуве́рен — самоуве́ренна — самоуве́ренно — самоуве́ренны, or drop one **-н-**: подве́рженный — подве́ржен — подве́ржена — подве́ржено — подве́ржены.

The short forms of the following adjectives are derived irregularly: большо́й — вели́к — велика́ — велико́ — велики́, ма́ленький — мал — мала́ — мало́ — малы́, солёный — со́лон — солона́ — со́лоно — со́лоны, досто́йный — досто́ин — досто́йна — досто́йно — досто́йны.

Grammatical characteristics		Quality of final vowel and consonant of dictionary form	-ый not after -ц	-ий not after a vowel and ж, ш, ч, ш, ц, г, к, х	-ий after г, к, х	-ий after ж, ш, ч, ш		-ый after ц	-ий after a vowel	-ой not after ж, ш, ч, ш, г, к, х	-ой after г, к, х	-ой after ж, ш, ч, ш
						without -ся	with -ся					
Singular	Neuter	Nom. masc.	новый	синий	тихий	свежий	вьющийся	купый	длинношеий	живой	сухой	большой
		neut.	новое	синее	тихое	свежее	вьющееся	купее	длинношеее	живое	сухое	большое
	Masculine	Gen.	нового	синего	тихого	свежего	вьющегося	купего	длинношеего	живого	сухого	большого
		Dat.	новому	синему	тихому	свежему	вьющемуся	купему	длинношеему	живому	сухому	большому
		Acc. m. inanim.	новый	синий	тихий	свежий	вьющийся	купый	длинношеий	живой	сухой	большой
		m. anim.	нового	синего	тихого	свежего	вьющегося	купего	длинношеего	живого	сухого	большого
		Instr.	новым	синим	тихим	свежим	вьющимся	купым	длинношеим	живым	сухим	большим
		Prep.	новом	синем	тихом	свежем	вьющемся	купем	длинношеем	живом	сухом	большом
	Feminine	Nom.	новая	синяя	тихая	свежая	вьющаяся	купая	длинношея	живая	сухая	большая
		Gen., Dat., Prep.	новой	синей	тихой	свежей	вьющейся	купей	длинношеей	живой	сухой	большой
		Acc.	новую	синюю	тихую	свежую	вьющуюся	купую	длинношеюю	живую	сухую	большую
		Instr.	новой	синей	тихой	свежей	вьющейся	купей	длинношеей	живой	сухой	большой
			новою	синею	тихою	свежею	вьющеюся	купею	длинношеею	живою	сухою	большою
Plural		Nom. Gen., Prep. inanim.	новые	синие	тихие	свежие	вьющиеся	купые	длинношеие	живые	сухие	большие
		Gen., Prep.	новых	синих	тихих	свежих	вьющихся	купых	длинношеих	живых	сухих	больших
		Dat.	новым	синим	тихим	свежим	вьющимся	купым	длинношеим	живым	сухим	большим
		Acc. anim.	новые	синие	тихие	свежие	вьющиеся	купые	длинношеие	живые	сухие	большие
			новых	синих	тихих	свежих	вьющихся	купых	длинношеих	живых	сухих	больших
		Instr.	новыми	синими	тихими	свежими	вьющимися	купыми	длинношеими	живыми	сухими	большими

Dictionary form ends in:	-ый/-ой not after ж, ш, ч, щ, ц	-ий not after г, к, х, ж, ш, ч, щ	-ий/-ой after г, к, х	-ий after ж, ш, ч, щ	-ый after ц	-ий after a vowel
Short forms	бе́лый живо́й	си́ний разносторо́нний	одино́кий сухо́й	живу́чий све́жий	ку́цый	длинноше́ий
Masculine	бел жив	синь разносторо́нен	одино́к сух	живу́ч свеж	куц	длинноше́й
Feminine	бела́ жива́	синя́ разносторо́ння	одино́ка суха́	живу́ча свежа́	ку́ца	длинноше́я
Neuter	бе́ло жи́во	си́не разносторо́нне	одино́ко су́хо	живу́че све́жо	ку́це	длинноше́е
Plural	бе́лы жи́вы	си́ни разносторо́нни	одино́ки су́хи	живу́чи све́жи	ку́цы	длинноше́и

2.2. How to derive the forms of the possessive adjectives whose dictionary form ends in **-ин/-ын, -ов/-ев/-ёв** or **-ий**.

Grammatical characteristics		Dictionary form ends in: **-ин/-ын**		**-ий** [1]	
Singular	Masculine	Nom. masc.	дя́дин	ку́рицын	ли́сий	тре́тий
		neut.	дя́дино	ку́рицыно	ли́сье	тре́тье
		Gen.	дя́диного	ку́рицыного	ли́сьего	тре́тьего
		Dat.	дя́диному	ку́рицыну	ли́сьему	тре́тьему
		Acc. m. inanim.	дя́дин	ку́рицын	ли́сий	тре́тий
		m. anim.	дя́диного	ку́рицыного	ли́сьего	тре́тьего
		neut.	дя́дино	ку́рицыно	ли́сье	тре́тье
		Instr.	дя́диным	ку́рицыным	ли́сьим	тре́тьим
		Prep.	дя́дином	ку́рицыном	ли́сьем	тре́тьем
	Feminine	Nom.	дя́дина	ку́рицына	ли́сья	тре́тья
		Gen., Dat., Prep.	дя́диной	ку́рицыной	ли́сьей	тре́тьей
		Acc.	дя́дину	ку́рицыну	ли́сью	тре́тью
		Instr.	дя́диной	ку́рицыной	ли́сьей	тре́тьей
Plural		Nom.	дя́дины	ку́рицыны	ли́сьи	тре́тьи
		Gen., Prep.	дя́диных	ку́рицыных	ли́сьих	тре́тьих
		Dat.	дя́диным	ку́рицыным	ли́сьим	тре́тьим
		Acc. inanim.	дя́дины	ку́рицыны	ли́сьи	тре́тьи
		anim.	дя́диных	ку́рицыных	ли́сьих	тре́тьих
		Instr.	дя́диными	ку́рицыными	ли́сьими	тре́тьими

[1] Only adjectives denoting possession and also тре́тий. Do not confuse with adjectives of the си́ний, отцо́вский, ры́жий type.

2.3. Nouns whose forms are derived in the same way as those of some adjectives.

The forms of nouns whose dictionary form ends in **-ий** (зо́дчий, ко́рмчий, лесни́чий, ле́ший, etc.), **-ый** (вожа́тый, новобра́чный, подсуди́мый, провожа́тый, etc.), **-ой** (вестово́й, портно́й, связно́й, etc.), **-ая** (вселе́нная, го́рничная, гости́ная, заку́сочная, запята́я, кладова́я, коте́льная, мостова́я, на́бережная, новобра́чная, парикма́херская, пра́чечная, родосло́вная, столо́вая, etc.)**, -ое** (жарко́е, насеко́мое, пиро́жное, прида́ное, сказу́емое, числи́тельное, etc.) or **-ее** (подлежа́щее, etc.) are derived in the same way as those of the adjectives discussed in 2.1.1. Unlike an adjective, each noun can belong only to *one* of the three genders and has the forms of only one gender, being either animate or inanimate. Nouns whose dictionary form ends in **-ие/-ые** follow the same declension pattern as the adjectives;

however, they have only the plural form and either the animate or inanimate accusative form.

The forms of nouns designating Russian and Slavonic surnames, whose dictionary form terminates in the suffix **-ин/-ын** or **-ов/-ев/-ёв** and a zero ending, are derived in a special way.

Number, Gender Case	Singular				Plural	
	Masculine		Feminine			
Nom.	Попо́в	Ре́пин	Попо́ва	Ре́пина	Попо́вы	Ре́пины
Gen.	Попо́ва	Ре́пина	Попо́вой	Ре́пиной	Попо́вых	Ре́пиных
Dat.	Попо́ву	Ре́пину	Попо́вой	Ре́пиной	Попо́вым	Ре́пиным
Acc.	Попо́ва	Ре́пина	Попо́ву	Ре́пину	Попо́вых	Ре́пиных
Instr.	Попо́вым	Ре́пиным	Попо́вой	Ре́пиной	Попо́выми	Ре́пиными
Prep.	Попо́ве	Ре́пине	Попо́вой	Ре́пиной	Попо́вых	Ре́пиных

Unlike the forms of nouns designating surnames, the forms of nouns the dictionary forms of which have the same termination and which are geographical names (Каля́зин, Псков, Ки́ев) are derived in the same way as those of ordinary nouns (see above, 1.1.1). The forms of the surnames of representatives of non-Slavic nations (Да́рвин, Ви́рхов, Ча́плин) are derived in the same way as those of ordinary nouns.

The forms of the inanimate feminine noun ничья́ are derived in the same way as those of the adjective ли́стья. The forms of the inanimate neuter noun тре́тье are derived in the same way as those of the neuter adjective тре́тье.

2.4. How to derive the comparative degree of an adjective.

Many adjectives denoting a quality or property which can exist in a greater or lesser degree have the comparative degree. If the adjective stem does not end in **г, к, х**, then the comparative degree is derived by adding **-ee** to the stem: до́брый — добре́е, све́тлый — светле́е, я́сный — ясне́е. The following adjectives are exceptions to this rule: бога́тый — бога́че, большо́й — бо́льше, густо́й — гу́ще, дешё́вый — деше́вле, круто́й — кру́че, ма́ленький — ме́ньше, молодо́й — моло́же, плохо́й — ху́же, просто́й — про́ще, твёрдый — твёрже, то́лстый — то́лще, хоро́ший — лу́чше, ча́стый — ча́ще, чи́стый — чи́ще.

If the adjective stem ends in **г, к, х**, then the comparative degree is derived by adding **-e** to the stem, **г** being replaced with **ж, к** with **ч** and **х** with **ш**: стро́гий — стро́же, жа́ркий — жа́рче, сухо́й — су́ше. There are exceptions to this rule, too: бли́зкий — бли́же, высо́кий — вы́ше, гла́дкий — гла́же, глубо́кий — глу́бже, жи́дкий — жи́же, коро́ткий — коро́че, ни́зкий — ни́же, пло́ский — пло́ще, ре́дкий — ре́же, сла́дкий — сла́ще, у́зкий — у́же, широ́кий — ши́ре, and also далё́кий — да́льше, до́лгий — до́льше, то́нкий — то́ньше.

3. Pronouns

3.1. How to derive the forms of the pronouns я, ты, мы, вы, кто, что and себя.

The derivation of the forms of the pronouns я, ты, мы, вы, кто, что and себя is shown in the following table:

Case	Pronouns						
	я	ты	мы	вы	кто	что	себя
Nom.	я	ты	мы	вы	кто	что	—
Gen.	меня	тебя	нас	вас	кого	чего	себя
Dat.	мне	тебе	нам	вам	кому	чему	себе
Acc.	меня	тебя	нас	вас	кого	что	себя
Instr.	мной (мною)	тобой (тобою)	нами	вами	кем	чем	собой (собою)
Prep.	мне	тебе	нас	вас	ком	чём	себе

3.2. How to derive the forms of the pronouns он, она, оно, они with or without a preposition.

The derivation of the forms of the pronouns он, она, оно, они depends on whether these forms follow a preposition or are used without a preposition (in the former case all the forms begin with **н**: от него).These forms are shown in the following table:

Nom.	*always without pr.*	он оно	она	они
Gen.	without pr.	его	её	их
	with pr.	от него	от неё	от них
Dat.	without. pr.	ему	ей	им
	with pr.	к нему	к ней	к ним
Acc.	without pr.	его	её	их
	with pr.	про него	про неё	про них
Instr.	without pr.	им	ей/ею	ими
	with. pr.	с ним	с ней/с нею	с ними
Prep.	*always with pr.*	о нём	о ней	о них

3.3. How to derive the forms of the pronouns никто, ничто, некого, нечего, друг друга, некто, нечто with or without a preposition.

The derivation of the forms of the pronouns никто, ничто, некого and нечего depends on whether these forms follow a preposition or are used without a preposition. These forms are shown in the following table (see p. 151).

The pronoun некто has only the nominative, and нечто only the nominative and the accusative which is identical with the nominative.

Case							
Nom.	always without pr.	никто́	ничто́	—	—	—	
Gen.	without pr.	никого́	ничего́	не́кого	не́чего	друг дру́га	
	with pr.	ни от кого́	ни от чего́	не́ от кого	не́ от чего	друг от дру́га	
Dat.	without pr.	никому́	ничему́	не́кому	не́чему	друг дру́гу	
	with pr.	ни к кому́	ни к чему́	не́ к кому	не́ к чему	друг к дру́гу	
Acc.	without pr.	никого́	ничто́	не́кого	—	друг дру́га	
	with pr.	ни про кого́	ни про что́	не́ про кого	не́ про что	друг про дру́га	
Instr.	without pr.	нике́м	ниче́м	не́кем	не́чем	друг дру́гом	
	with pr.	ни с ке́м	ни с чем	не́ с кем	не́ с чем	друг с дру́гом	
Prep.	always with pr.	ни о ко́м	ни о чём	не́ о ком	не́ о чем	друг о дру́ге	

3.4. How to derive the forms of the pronouns э́тот, тот, оди́н, сам, весь, наш, ваш, мой, твой, свой, чей, ниче́й.

The derivation of the forms of the pronouns э́тот, тот, оди́н, сам, весь, наш, ваш, мой, твой, свой, чей, ниче́й is shown in the following table (see p. 152).

3.5. How to derive the forms of the pronouns whose dictionary form ends in **-ый/-ий/-ой** of the type ка́ждый, вся́кий, тако́й.

The grammatical forms of the pronouns whose dictionary form ends in **-ый/-ий/-ой** of the type ка́ждый, вся́кий, тако́й are derived in the same way as those of adjectives with the same endings in the dictionary form. An exception is the word не́кий and the rarely used word нико́й. The genitive (and the animate accusative), dative and prepositional singular masculine and neuter forms of the pronoun не́кий are derived irregularly: не́коего, не́коему, не́коем.

4. The Numeral

4.1. How to derive the forms of the cardinal numerals from 1 to 4.

The grammatical forms of the numeral оди́н are derived in the same way as those of the pronoun оди́н (see 3.4).

The numeral полтора́ in the nominative and the inanimate accusative which is identical with it has the form полтора́ in the masculine and the neuter; in the nominative feminine it has the form полторы́; its other forms are полу́тора.

The derivation of the forms of the cardinal numerals два, о́ба, три, четы́ре is shown in the following table:

Case \ Gender	Masculine Neuter	Feminine	Masculine Neuter	Feminine	Masculine, Feminine Neuter	
Nom.	два	две	о́ба	о́бе	три	четы́ре
Gen., Prep.	двух	двух	обо́их	обе́их	трёх	четырёх
Dat.	двум	двум	обо́им	обе́им	трём	четырём
Acc. inanim.	два	две	о́ба	о́бе	три	четы́ре
anim.	двух	двух	обо́их	обе́их	трёх	четырёх
Instr.	двумя́	двумя́	обо́ими	обе́ими	тремя́	четырьмя́

Grammatical characteristics		Pronoun	э́тот	тот	оди́н	сам	весь	наш ваш	мой твой свой	чей ниче́й
Singular	Masculine & Neuter	Nom. masc.	э́тот	тот	оди́н	сам	весь	наш	мой	чей
		neut.	э́то	то	одно́	само́	всё	на́ше	моё	чьё
		Gen.	э́того	того́	одного́	самого́	всего́	на́шего	моего́	чьего́
		Dat.	э́тому	тому́	одному́	самому́	всему́	на́шему	моему́	чьему́
		Acc. m.inanim.	э́тот	тот	оди́н	сам	весь	наш	мой	чей
		m.anim.	э́того	того́	одного́	самого́	всего́	на́шего	моего́	чьего́
		neut.	э́то	то	одно́	само́	всё	на́ше	моё	чьё
		Instr.	э́тим	тем	одни́м	сами́м	всем	на́шим	мои́м	чьим
		Prep.	э́том	том	одно́м	само́м	всём	на́шем	моём	чьём
	Feminine	Nom.	э́та	та	одна́	сама́	вся	на́ша	моя́	чья
		Gen., Dat., Prep.	э́той	той	одно́й	само́й	всей	на́шей	мое́й	чьей
		Acc.	э́ту	ту	одну́	саму́ (само́е)	всю	на́шу	мою́	чью
		Instr.	э́той	той	одно́й	само́й	всей	на́шей	мое́й	чьей
Plural		Nom.	э́ти	те	одни́	са́ми	все	на́ши	мои́	чьи
		Gen., Prep.	э́тих	тех	одни́х	сами́х	всех	на́ших	мои́х	чьих
		Dat.	э́тим	тем	одни́м	сами́м	всем	на́шим	мои́м	чьим
		Acc. inanim.	э́ти	те	одни́	са́ми	все	на́ши	мои́	чьи
		anim.	э́тих	тех	одни́х	сами́х	всех	на́ших	мои́х	чьих
		Instr.	э́тими	те́ми	одни́ми	сами́ми	все́ми	на́шими	мои́ми	чьи́ми

4.2. How to derive the forms of the cardinal numerals from 5 to 20 and also 30, 50, 60, 70 and 80.

The grammatical forms of the cardinal numerals from 5 to 20 and also 30, 50, 60, 70 and 80 are derived in the following way:

Case	Numeral			
	5, 6, 7, 9, 10, 11, 12, 13, 14, 15, 16, 17, 18, 19, 20, 30	50, 60, 70	8	80
Nom., Acc.	пять, десять, одиннадцать тридцать	пятьдесят	восемь	восемьдесят
Gen., Dat., Prep.	пяти, десяти, одиннадцати, тридцати	пятидесяти	восьми	восьмидесяти
Instr.	пятью, десятью, одиннадцатью, тридцатью	пятьюдесятью	восемью /восьмью	восемьюдесятью/ восьмьюдесятью

4.3. How to derive the forms of the cardinal numerals 40, 90, 100 and полтора́ста.

In addition to the nominative singular (the dictionary form) and the accusative which is identical with it, the cardinal numerals со́рок, девяно́сто, сто and полтора́ста have only one form for all the other cases: сорока́, девяно́ста, ста, полу́тораста.

4.4. How to derive the forms of the names of the hundreds.

The derivation of the forms of the numerals denoting the hundreds is shown in the following table:

Nom., Acc.	две́сти	три́ста	четы́реста	пятьсо́т	восемьсо́т
Gen.	двухсо́т	трёхсо́т	четырёхсо́т	пятисо́т	восьмисо́т
Dat.	двумста́м	трёмста́м	четырёмста́м	пятиста́м	восьмиста́м
Instr.	двумяста́ми	тремяста́ми	четырьмяста́ми	пятьюста́ми	восемьюста́ми/восьмьюста́ми
Prep.	двухста́х	трёхста́х	четырёхста́х	пятиста́х	восьмиста́х

The forms of шестьсо́т, семьсо́т and девятьсо́т are derived in the same way as those of пятьсо́т.

4.5. How to derive the forms of the collective numerals and of the numerals ско́лько, не́сколько, сто́лько; мно́го and немно́го.

The derivation of the forms of the collective numerals is shown in the following table:

Nom.	Gen., Prep.	Dat.	Acc.		Instr.
			Inanim.	Anim.	
дво́е	двои́х	двои́м	дво́е	двои́х	двои́ми
че́тверо	четверы́х	четверы́м	че́тверо	четверы́х	четверы́ми
ско́лько	ско́льких	ско́льким	ско́лько	ско́льких	ско́лькими

The forms of тро́е are derived in the same way as those of дво́е; the forms of пя́теро, ше́стеро, се́меро, во́сьмеро, де́вятеро, де́сятеро in the same way as those of че́тверо; and the forms of не́сколько, сто́лько, мно́го, немно́го in the same way as those of ско́лько.

5. The Verb

5.1. What grammatical forms can be derived from the dictionary form of transitive and intransitive perfective and imperfective verbs.

As a rule, the dictionary form of a verb is its *infinitive*.

A distinctive feature of verbs is the set of forms they possess. The number of the forms depends on two factors: first, whether the verb concerned is perfective or imperfective and, second, whether it is transitive or intransitive (for these categories, see I, 5.2 and 5.3).

Transitive imperfective verbs have the largest number of forms. They have the following forms: active and passive finite present tense forms (of different persons and numbers), active and passive finite future tense forms (of different persons and numbers), active and passive finite past tense forms (of different genders and numbers), active imperative forms (of different persons and numbers), active and passive finite forms of the subjunctive mood (of different numbers and, in the singular, different genders as well), active and passive present participles (of different numbers and, in the singular, different genders as well), active and passive past participles (of different numbers and, in the singular, genders as well), and verbal adverbs.

If a verb is *perfective* and *transitive*, it lacks passive finite forms, all the finite present tense forms and all the present participles.

If a verb is *imperfective* and *intransitive* it lacks all the passive finite and participial forms.

If a verb is *perfective* and *intransitive*, it lacks all the passive finite and participial forms and also all the finite present tense forms and all the present participles.

This is represented in the following table:

Verbs	Grammatical Forms													
	Finite Form									Participle				Verbal Adverb
	Indicative Mood						Imper. Mood	Subj. Mood		Present Tense		Past Tense		
	Present Tense		Fut. Tense		Past Tense									
	active	pass.	active	pass.	active	pass.	active	active	pass.	active	pass.	active	pass.	
Transitive imperfective	+	+	+	+	+	+	+	+	+	+	+	+	+	+
Transitive perfective	−	−	+	−	+	−	+	+	−	−	−	+	+	+
Intransitive imperfective	+	−	+	−	+	−	+	+	−	+	−	+	−	+
Intransitive perfective	−	−	+	−	+	−	+	+	−	−	−	+	−	+

Note.— Theoretically, passive forms are also possible in the imperative mood and in verbal adverbs. However, such forms are extremely rarely used. Also possible are finite passive forms of perfective verbs. However, they are also used extremely rarely.

The above rules are not without exceptions. There is a group of so-called *impersonal* verbs, which denote the state of nature or the psychic or physical state of people: рассвета́ть, моро́зить, смерка́ться, зноби́ть, тошни́ть, etc. Besides the infinitive, these verbs have only the forms of the 3rd person singular, present and future tenses, and the forms of the neuter past tense and the subjunctive mood. All these forms are active only.

Some transitive imperfective verbs have no passive participles. (See also I, 5.10.)

5.2. What grammatical forms can be derived directly from the infinitive.

The following forms can be derived from the *infinitive*: the finite forms of the past tense and the subjunctive mood, active past participles, and from a number of verbs also passive past participles and verbal adverbs. All the other forms, and for a number of verbs also passive past participles (and for some verbs active past participles as well), can be derived only from *present tense* forms (for imperfective verbs) or from future tense forms (for perfective verbs).

5.2.1. How to derive finite past tense forms.

Finite past tense forms are derived by dropping the infinitive marker **-ть** and replacing it with the past tense marker **-л-** plus an ending, which depends on the number, and, in the singular, the gender of the head noun. For the plural forms this ending is **-и** and for the singular forms ø (zero ending) for the masculine gender, **-а** for the feminine gender, and **-о** for the neuter gender:

чита́ть → чита́ + л (masculine)
чита́ + л + а (feminine)
чита́ + л + о (neuter)
чита́ + л + и (plural)

For some verbs this general rule of derivation of the past tense from the infinitive stem is complicated by additional transformations.

1. If the infinitive of a verb ends in **-нуть** and the verb itself is not a semelfactive one, then, to derive the finite past tense form, **-ну-** is dropped, after which the transformations described above are performed. For example: вя́нуть → вя → вял, вя́ла, вя́ло, вя́ли. If the suffix **-ну-** is preceded by a consonant, the masculine singular form ends in that consonant (**-л-** is not added): поги́бнуть → поги́б, however: поги́бла, поги́бло, поги́бли; отве́ргнуть → отве́рг, however: отве́ргла, отве́ргло, отве́ргли.

2. Some verbs have duplicate masculine singular forms, with or without **-ну-** (стыл/сты́нул, вял/вя́нул, ги́бнул/гиб).

3. If the infinitive of a verb ends in **-сть, -зть, -сти, -зти** or **-чь**, then the finite past tense form is derived from the 1st person present tense for imperfective verbs or from the 1st person future tense for perfective verbs.

If the present tense stem ends in **з, с, б, г** or **к**, then this stem is the past tense form of the masculine singular: грызть — грызу́ — грыз, везти́ — везу́ — вёз, нести́ — несу́ — нёс, грести́ — гребу́ — грёб, бере́чь — берегу́ — берёг, толо́чь — толку́ — толо́к. (In this case the **о** in the root becomes stressed.) The feminine and the neuter forms and also the plural forms of these verbs are derived by means of **-л-** and the appropriate endings: грёб — гребла́ — гребло́ — гребли́, вёз — везла́ — везло́ — везли́.

However, if the present tense stem of verbs with the preceding infinitives ends in **д, т** or **н**, then **д, т** or **н** is replaced with **-л-** and this gives the masculine singular past tense form: брести́ — бреду́ — брёл, мести́ — мету́ — мёл, клясть — кляну́ — клял. (**-ё** appears before **-л-** in the verb уче́сть: уче́сть — учту́ — учёл, which is dropped in the other genders and the plural.) The feminine and neuter forms and also the plural forms of these verbs are derived by adding the appropriate endings: брёл — брела́ — брело́ — брели́, учёл — учла́ — учло́ — учли́.

Exceptions to this rule are the forms derived from the infinitives сесть (and its prefixed derivatives): сел, се́ла, се́ло, се́ли, and расти́ (and its prefixed derivatives): рос, росла́, росло́, росли́.

4. If the infinitive of a verb ends in **-ереть** (умере́ть, отпере́ть, вы́тереть, etc.), then the finite past tense forms are derived by dropping **-еть** and adding **-ла, -ло** or **-ли** for the feminine singular, the neuter singular and the plural, respectively: умере́ть — у́мер, умерла́, у́мерло, у́мерли.

5. The finite past tense forms of the following verbs are derived irregularly: the verbs есть (and its prefixed derivatives) — ел, е́ла, е́ло, е́ли — and идти́ (and its prefixed derivatives of the пойти́, уйти́, etc. type): шёл, шла, шло, шли, and also verbs with various prefixes + **-шибить** (with or wihout **-ся**) of the type ошиби́ться → оши́бся, оши́блась, оши́блось, оши́блись.

5.2.2. How to derive subjunctive mood forms.

Subjunctive mood forms are derived in the same way as past tense forms plus the particle бы. In a sentence the particle бы more often than not follows the verb; however, it may also take another position.

5.2.3. How to derive the forms of active past participles.

Active past participles are derived from the finite masculine singular *past* tense form (for the derivation of this form from the infinitive, see 5.2.1). If the finite masculine past tense form ends in -л, then the -л is replaced with **-вший**: чита́л — чита́вший, хоте́л — хоте́вший, купи́л — купи́вший. However, if the finite past tense form does not end in -л-, then **-ший** is added to this form: у́мер — уме́рший, поги́б — поги́бший, пёк — пёкший.

An exception to this rule is the derivation of active past participles from verbs whose infinitive ends in **-сти**: вести́, цвести́, плести́, брести́, мести́, блюсти́. The active past participles of these verbs (and of their prefixed derivatives) are derived by replacing the *present* tense ending with **-ший**: вести́ — веду́ — ве́дший, цвести́ — цвету́ —

цве́тший, плести́ — плету́ — плётший, брести́ — бреду́ — бре́дший.

Like adjectives, active past participles have singular and plural forms and, in the singular, masculine, feminine and neuter forms; in both numbers and in all the three genders they have six case forms (see above, 2.1.1). Active past participles have no short forms.

5.2.4. How to derive the forms of passive past participles.

Passive past participles are derived *only from transitive* (mainly perfective) verbs, either from the dictionary form (i. e. the infinitive) or from finite verb forms.

If the infinitive of a verb ends in **-ать** or **-ять**, then, to derive its passive past participle, **-ть** should be replaced with **-нный**: прочита́ть → прочита → прочи́танный, осмея́ть → осмея → осме́янный. Exceptions to this rule are participles derived from the verbs мять — мя́тый, жать — жа́тый (and their prefixed derivatives) and also participles derived from prefixed verbs ending in **-чать** of the нача́ть → на́чатый type, in **-ять** of the взять → взя́тый type, and in **-нять** of the приня́ть → при́нятый type, and also from распя́ть → распя́тый.

If the infinitive of a verb ends in **-нуть, -олоть** or **-ороть**, then, to derive a passive past participle, the **-ь** of the infinitive should be replaced with **-ый**: тро́нуть → тронут → тро́нутый, коло́ть → колот → ко́лотый. The passive past participles of the verbs пере́ть, тере́ть, простере́ть, бить, вить, лить, пить, шить, крыть, мыть, рыть, дуть, обу́ть, греть, петь, брить (and their prefixed derivatives) are also derived by replacing **-ь** with **-ый**: мыть → мы́тый. In this case the vowel е preceding т in the derivatives of -переть and -тереть should be dropped: тере́ть → терет → тёрт → тёртый.

The passive past participles of all the other verbs are derived from the 1st or 3rd person singular *present* tense of imperfective verbs (and *future* tense of perfective verbs) (see below, 5.4.7).

Like adjectives, passive past participles have singular and plural forms, and in the singular, masculine, feminine and neuter forms; in both numbers and in all the three genders they have six case forms (see above, 2.1.1).

Passive past participles ending in **-енный, -анный** or **-янный** have *short* forms. To derive them, **-ный** should be dropped, which gives the masculine singular form; or **-ный** should be replaced with **-а**, which gives the feminine singular form; or **-ный** should be replaced with **-о**, which gives the neuter singular form; or, finally, **-ный** should be replaced with **-ы**, which gives the plural form: постро́енный → постро́ен, постро́ена, постро́ено, постро́ены; засе́янный → засе́ян, засе́яна, засе́яно, засе́яны. The short forms of passive past participles ending in **-тый** are derived by dropping **-ый**, i. e. in the same way as are the short forms of ordinary adjectives (see above, 2.1.2): вы́мытый → вы́мыт, вы́мыта, вы́мыто, вы́мыты.

5.2.5. How to derive the forms of perfective verbal adverbs.

Perfective verbal adverbs are derived from active past participles (for whose derivation from the infinitive, see 5.2.3) by the replacement of **-ший** with **-ши**, and of **-шийся** with **-шись**: подня́вшийся → подня́вшись, испёкший → испёкши. If a participle ends in **-вший**, the verbal adverb can be formed by dropping the final **-ший**: уви́девший → уви́дев (and уви́девши), сня́вший → сняв (and сня́вши).

The perfective verbal adverbs of some verbs can also be derived from the future tense stem: привести́ → приведу́ → приведя́ (see 5.4).

5.3. What correlations exist between the infinitive stem and the stem of the present tense (of imperfective verbs)/future tense (of perfective verbs).

Only some of the verb forms can be derived from the dictionary form, i. e. the infinitive (see 5.2). As a rule, the present tense forms (of imperfective verbs) or the future tense forms (of perfective verbs) cannot be derived from the infinitive. In their turn, all the verb forms which cannot be derived from the infinitive can be derived from the 1st or 3rd person singular present/future tense, i. e. from the present/future tense stem of the verb. Thus, the knowledge of the 1st and 3rd persons singular present/future tense is as indispensable in the derivation of all the verb forms as the knowledge of the infinitive.

The possible correlations between the infinitive stem and the stem of the 1st and 3rd persons singular present/future tense are given in the following table, using which you can derive the present/future tense stem from the dictionary form of a verb.

Infinitive ends in:	Singular present/future tense ends in:		Example	Note
	1st pers.	3rd pers.		
-ать	-аю	-ает	чита́ть — чита́ю — чита́ет	
-ать	-ю -у (after ж, ш, ч, щ, ц)	-ит	дыша́ть — дышу́ — ды́шит спать — сплю — спит	Regular alternation of consonant occurs in 1st person.(See 5.3.1.)
-ать	-ю -у (after ж, ш, ч, щ, ц)	-ет	писа́ть — пишу́ — пи́шет	Regular alternation of consonants occurs in all the persons. (See 5.3.1)

159

Continued

Infinitive ends in:	Singular present/future tense ends in:		Example	Note
	1st pers.	3rd pers.		
-овать	**-ую**	**-ует**	уча́ствовать — уча́ствую — уча́ствует	
-евать (after ж, ш, ч, щ, ц)	**-ую**	**-ует**	танцева́ть — танцу́ю — танцу́ет	
-евать (not after ж, ш, ч, щ, ц)	**-юю**	**-юет**	воева́ть — вою́ю — вою́ет	
-ять	**-яю**	**-яет**	стреля́ть — стреля́ю — стреля́ет	
-ять	**-ю**	**-ит**	стоя́ть — стою́ — стои́т	
-авать	**-аю**	**-аёт**	дава́ть — даю́ — даёт	The verb дава́ть and its prefixed derivatives and also verbs in **-знавать, -ставать.**
-ать	**-у**	**-ёт**	соса́ть — сосу́ — сосёт	Only this verb and its prefixed derivatives.
-ать	**-ну**	**-нёт**	жать — жну — жнёт нача́ть — начну́ — начнёт	The verb жать and its derivatives and also prefixed verbs with **-чать** in the root.
-ать	**-му**	**-мёт**	жать — жму — жмёт	The verb жать and its derivatives.
-ать	**-ану**	**-анет**	стать — ста́ну — ста́нет	The verb стать and its derivatives.
-ать	**-м**	**-ст**	дать — дам — даст	The verbs дать and созда́ть and their derivatives.

Continued

Infinitive ends in:	Singular present/future tense ends in:		Example	Note
	1st pers.	3rd pers.		
éхать	éду	éдут	éхать — éду — éдет	Only the verb éхать and its derivatives.
-ять	-ьму	-ьмёт	взять — возьму́ — возьмёт	Prefixed verbs with -ять.
-нять	-му	-мет	приня́ть — приму́ — при́мет обня́ть — обниму́ — обни́мет	Prefixed verbs with -нять
-ять	-ну	-нет	застря́ть — застря́ну — застря́нет	The verb распя́ть and derivatives with -стря́ть.
-еть	-ею	-еет	холодéть — холодéю — холодéет	
-еть	-ю -у (after ж, ш, ч, щ, ц)	-ит	вертéть — верчу́ — вéртит	Regular alternation occurs in the 1st person. (See 5.3.1.)
-ереть	-ру	-рёт	умерéть — умру́ — умрёт	Root vowel e alternates with zero.
-веть	-ву	-вёт	ревéть — реву́ — ревёт	The verb ревéть and its prefixed derivatives.

Continued

Infinitive ends in:	Singular present/future tense ends in:		Example	Note
	1st pers.	3rd pers.		
-еть	-ену	-енет	деть — дéну — дéнет	The verb деть and its prefixed derivatives.
-еть	-ою	-ёт	петь — пою́ — поёт	The verb петь and its prefixed derivatives.
-еть	-у	-ет	хотéть — хочу́ — хóчет	Only the verb хотéть and its prefixed derivatives.
-ить	-ю -у (after ж, ш, ч, щ, ц)	-ит	люби́ть — люблю́ лю́бит носи́ть — ношу́ — нóсит	Regular alternation of consonants occurs in the 1st person. (See 5.3.1.)
-ить	-ью	-ьёт	пить — пью — пьёт	The verbs бить, вить, лить, пить, шить and their prefixed derivatives.
-ить	-ию	-иёт	гнить — гнию́ — гниёт	The verb почи́ть, гнить and their prefixed derivatives.
-ить	-ею	-еет	брить — брéю — брéет	The verb брить and its prefixed derivatives.
-ить	-иву	-ивёт	жить — живу́ — живёт	The verb жить and its prefixed derivatives.
-ить	-у	-ёт	сшиби́ть — сшибу́ — сшибёт	Prefixed derivatives of -шиби́ть.

Continued

Infinitive ends in:	Singular present/future tense ends in:		Example	Note
	1st pers.	3rd pers.		
-нуть	-ну	-нёт	толкну́ть — толкну́ — толкнёт	
-уть	-ую	-ует	дуть — ду́ю — ду́ет	The verbs обу́ть, разу́ть, дуть and the prefixed derivatives of дуть.
-ыть	-ою	-оет	выть — во́ю — во́ет	The verbs выть, крыть, мыть, ныть, рыть and their prefixed derivatives.
-ыть	-ыну	-ынет	стыть — сты́ну — сты́нет	The verb стыть and its prefixed derivatives.
-ыть	-ыву	-ывёт	плыть — плыву́ — плывёт	The verbs слыть and плыть and their prefixed derivatives.
-ыть	-уду	-удет	быть — бу́ду — бу́дет	The verb быть and its prefixed derivatives.
-оть	-ю	-ет	коло́ть — колю́ — ко́лет поро́ть — порю́ — по́рет	Verbs whose infinitives end in **-олоть** and **-ороть** and their prefixed derivatives.
-зти	-зу	-зёт	ползти́ — ползу́ — ползёт	
-зть	-зу	-зёт	грызть — грызу́ — грызёт	
-сти	-су	-сёт	нести́ — несу́ — несёт	

Continued

Infinitive ends in:	Singular present/future tense ends in:		Example	Note
	1st pers.	3rd pers.		
-сти	-ду	-дёт	брести́ — бреду́ — бредёт	
-сть	-ту	-тёт	уче́сть — учту́ — учтёт	
-сти	-ту	-тёт	мести́ — мету́ — метёт	
-сти	-сту	-стёт	расти́ — расту́ — растёт	
-сти	-бу	-бёт	грести́ — гребу́ — гребёт	
-сть	-ну	-нёт	клясть — кляну́ — клянёт	Only this verb and its prefixed derivatives.
-есть	-яду	-ядет	сесть — ся́ду — ся́дет	Only this verb and its prefixed derivatives.
-сть	-м	-ст	есть — ем — ест	Only this verb and its prefixed derivatives.
-дти -ти	-ду -ду	-дёт -дёт	идти́ — иду́ — идёт зайти́ — зайду́ — зайдёт	The verb идти́ and its prefixed derivatives with -йти́ in the root.
-чь	-гу	-жёт	бере́чь — берегу́ — бережёт	
-чь	-ку	-чёт	воло́чь — волоку́ — волочёт	

5.3.1. What regular differences in the final consonants there are between the infinitive stem and the stem of the present tense (of imperfective verbs)/future tense (of perfective verbs) forms.

-ать — -ю/-у (after ж, ш, ч, щ, ц), -ит — another consonant only in the 1st person singular: спать — сплю — спит

-ать — -ю/-у (after ж, ш, ч, щ, ц), -ет — another consonant in all the present/future tense forms: писа́ть — пишу́ — пи́шет

-еть — -ю/-у (after ж, ш, ч, щ, ц), -ит — another consonant only in the 1st person singular: ви́деть — ви́жу — ви́дит

-ить — -ю/-у (after ж, ш, ч, щ, ц), -ит—another consonant only in the 1st person singular: носи́ть — ношу́ — но́сит

The correlation between the final consonant of the infinitive stem and the final consonant of the present/future tense stem is given in the following table:

Final consonant of infinitive stem	Final consonant of present/future tense stem	Example
б	бл	люби́ть — люблю́ — лю́бит
п	пл	терпе́ть — терплю́ — те́рпит
в	вл	лови́ть — ловлю́ — ло́вит
ф	фл	разграфи́ть — разграфлю́ — разграфи́т
м	мл	корми́ть — кормлю́ — ко́рмит
з	ж	ре́зать — ре́жу — ре́жет
с	ш	писа́ть — пишу́ — пи́шет
д	ж	ви́деть — ви́жу — ви́дит
т	ч ог щ	крути́ть — кручу́ — кру́тит
		возврати́ть — возвращу́ — возврати́т
ст	щ	пусти́ть — пущу́ — пу́стит
к	ч	скака́ть — скачу́ — ска́чет
х	ш	маха́ть — машу́ — ма́шет
ск	щ	иска́ть — ищу́ — и́щет

(For the peculiarities of the alternation of the final stem consonants of the verbs бе́гать, лгать and хоте́ть, see 5.4.1.)

5.3.2. What vowel—zero alternations there are in the infinitive stem and the stem of the present tense (of imperfective verbs)/future tense (of perfective verbs) forms.

1. The infinitives and the present/future tense forms of a small group of verbs are distinguished by the presence/absence of the middle vowel.

Thus, the infinitive has a vowel which is absent in the present/future tense of verbs whose infinitive ends in **-чь** (жечь — жгу — жжёт), in **-ереть** (тере́ть — тру — трёт, умере́ть — умру́ — умрёт), in **-ить** (бить — бью — бьёт, лить — лью — льёт, вить — вью — вьёт, пить — пью — пьёт, шить — шью — шьёт), in **-ять** (мять — мну — мнёт), in **-ать** (жать — жну — жнёт, жать — жму — жмёт) and in **-сть** (проче́сть — прочту́ — прочтёт) (see the table in 5.3). The same alternations of a vowel with zero exist in the prefixed derivatives of these verbs.

2. The infinitive has no vowel which occurs in the present/future tense of the verbs гнать — гоню́ — го́нит, брать — беру́ — берёт, драть — деру́ — дерёт, звать — зову́ — зовёт, стлать — сте-

165

лю́ — сте́лет. The same alternations of a vowel with zero exist in the prefixed derivatives of these verbs.

If the preceding verb roots have a vowel, then their prefixed derivatives have the prefix в-, над-, об-, от-, под-, пред-, с-, вз- (вс- before a voiceless consonant), воз- (вос- before a voiceless consonant), из-(ис- before a voiceless consonant), низ- (нис- before a voiceless consonant) or раз- (рас- before a voiceless consonant). However, if the preceding verb roots have no vowel, then their prefixed derivatives have the prefix во-, надо-, обо-, ото-, подо-, предо-, со-, взо-, низо- or разо-.

For example: обжёчь — обожгу́ — обожжёт, растере́ть — разотру́ — разотрёт, сбить — собью́ — собьёт, подмя́ть — подомну́ — подомнёт, отозва́ть — отзову́ — отзовёт, подогна́ть — подгоню́ — подго́нит, содра́ть — сдеру́ — сдерёт, разостла́ть — расстелю́ — рассте́лет. There are some exceptions to this rule: избра́ть — изберу́ — изберёт, изгна́ть — изгоню́ — изго́нит, созва́ть — созову́ — созовёт.

5.4. What grammatical forms can be derived from the present tense (of imperfective verbs)/future tense (of perfective verbs) stem?

The following forms can be derived from the present tense stem: all the finite present tense (of imperfective verbs) and future tense (of perfective verbs) forms, some finite past tense forms (see 5.2.1), imperative mood forms, active present participles, imperfective verbal adverbs and passive present participles. The passive past participles of some verbs and the active past participles of other verbs are also derived from the present tense stem.

5.4.1. How to derive the finite present tense (of imperfective verbs)/future tense (of perfective verbs) forms.

If the 3rd person singular ends in **-ет**, then such verbs are traditionally called Conjugation I verbs. If the same form ends in **-ит**, then such verbs are called Conjugation II verbs.

The present/future tense endings of Conjugation I and II verbs are given in the following table:

Number & Person	Type of Conjugation	Conjugation I		Conjugation II
		Unstressed	Stressed	
Singular	1st person 2nd person 3rd person	-ю/-у -ешь -ет	-ю/-у -ёшь -ёт	-ю/-у -ишь -ит
Plural	1st person 2nd person 3rd person	-ем -ете -ют/-ут	-ём -ёте -ют/-ут	-им -ите -ят/-ат

To derive the necessary finite form from the dictionary form (i. e. from the infinitive), one should refer to the table giving the correlation between the infinitive stem and the present/future tense stem (see 5.3).

If the 1st and 3rd person singular stems coincide, then the same stem occurs in all the other forms.

If these stems are different, then the other forms have the same stem as the 3rd person: люби́ть — люблю́ — лю́бит → люблю́, лю́бишь, лю́бит, лю́бим, лю́бите, лю́бят. Exceptions are the following verbs which have the 1st person singular stem in the 3rd person plural: лгать — лгу — лжёт → лгу, лжёшь, лжёт, лжём, лжёте, лгут; мочь — могу́ — мо́жет → могу́, мо́жешь, мо́жет, мо́жем, мо́жете, мо́гут.

The appropriate forms of these two verbs are derived in a special way: хоте́ть — хочу́, хо́чешь, хо́чет, хоти́м, хоти́те, хотя́т and бежа́ть — бегу́, бежи́шь, бежи́т, бежи́м, бежи́те, бегу́т.

5.4.2. How to derive the finite future tense forms of imperfective verbs.

The future tense forms of imperfective verbs are derived with the help of the finite forms of the verb быть plus the infinitive of the main verb: бу́ду рабо́тать, бу́дешь рабо́тать, бу́дет рабо́тать, бу́дем рабо́тать, бу́дете рабо́тать, бу́дут рабо́тать.

5.4.3. How to derive the imperative mood forms.

The imperative mood forms are derived from the *3rd person plural* present tense (of imperfective verbs) or future tense (of perfective verbs) stem (for the derivation of this form, see 5.4.1.).

Exceptions to this rule are the verb дава́ть and its prefixed derivatives and the prefixed verbs ending in **-знавать** or **-ставать**. The imperative forms of these verbs are derived from the *infinitive* stem: дава́й, отдава́й, познава́й, отстава́й.

If the present/future tense stem ends in a *vowel*, the imperative singular ends in **-й**: стоя́ть — (стою́ — стои́т) — стоя́т → сто → стой, рисова́ть — (рису́ю — рису́ет) — рису́ют → рису → рису́й.

Exceptions to this rule are some verbs whose infinitive ends in **-ить** and which have a vowel in the termination of the present/future tense stem. The imperative singular of these verbs ends in **-и**: пои́ть — (пою́ — по́ит) — поя́т → пой; вы́кроить — (вы́крою — вы́кроит) — вы́кроят → вы́крои; дои́ть — (дою́ — до́ит) — доя́т → дой; таи́ть — (таю́ — таи́т) — тая́т → тай; гнои́ть — (гною́ — гнои́т) — гноя́т → гной. However: стро́ить — (стро́ю — стро́ит) — стро́ят → строй.

If the present tense stem ends in **-ь**, then the imperative singular is derived by replacing **-ь** with **-ей**: бить — (бью — бьёт) — бьют → бей; лить — (лью — льёт) — льют → лей; шить — (шью — шьёт) — шьют → шей.

If the present tense stem ends in a *consonant*, the imperative singular ends either in **-и** or in **-ь, -и** occurring in the following cases: (1) if the verb begins with the prefix **вы-**: вы́нести — (вы́несу — вы́несет) — вы́несут → вы́неси; вы́бросить — (вы́брошу — вы́бросит

— вы́бросят → вы́броси; (2) if the verb stem ends in two consonants or a consonant + ь + a consonant: толкну́ть — (толкну́ — толкнёт) —толкну́т → толкни́; кольну́т — (кольну́ — кольнёт) — кольну́т → кольни́, пусти́ть — (пущу́ — пу́стит) — пу́стят → пусти́; (3) if the verb stem ends in -щ: треща́ть — (трещу́ — трещи́т) — треща́т → трещи́; (4) if the 1st person singular present tense of imperfective verbs (future tense of perfective verbs) is stressed on the ending: бере́чь — (берегу́ — бережёт) — берегу́т → береги́.

In the other cases the ending is -ь: ки́нуть — (ки́ну — ки́нет) — ки́нут → кинь; бро́сить — (бро́шу — бро́сит) — бро́сят → брось.

The imperative of the verb е́хать (and its prefixed derivatives) is поезжа́й.

To derive the plural form, the marker -те should be added to the singular form: чита́й — чита́йте, неси́ — неси́те, брось — бро́сьте.

The forms of the so-called imperative of joint action (see I, 5.6.2) are usually derived from perfective verbs and the verbs идти́, бежа́ть, лете́ть, плыть, лезть, ползти́ (and their prefixed derivatives). These forms are derived by adding the ending -те to the 1st person plural non-past tense: пойдёмте.

The 3rd person of the imperative is usually derived by adding the particle пусть to the 3rd person of the indicative mood: чита́ет — пусть чита́ет, напи́шут — пусть напи́шут.

5.4.4. How to derive the forms of active present participles.

Active present participles are derived *only from imperfective* verbs by replacing the final -т of the 3rd person plural present tense with -щий: вести́ — веду́ — веду́т — веду́щий; говори́ть — говорю́ — говоря́т — говоря́щий; слу́шать — слу́шаю — слу́шают — слу́шающий.

These participles change for gender, number and case like adjectives (see above, 2.1.1). They have no short forms.

5.4.5. How to derive the forms of imperfective verbal adverbs.

Imperfective verbal adverbs are derived from the 3rd person plural present tense stem of *imperfective* verbs by adding the marker -я or -а (after ж, ш, ч, щ): люби́ть — люблю́ — лю́бят — любя́; нести́ — несу́ — несу́т — неся́; спеши́ть — спешу́ — спеша́т — спеша́.

The verb дава́ть (and its prefixed derivatives) and the verbs ending in -знавать or -ставать are exceptions to this rule; their verbal adverbs are not derived from the present tense stem, but from the *infinitive* stem by adding the same markers -я/-а: дава́ть — дава́я, познава́ть — познава́я, достава́ть — достава́я.

The following groups of verbs do not derive imperfective verbal adverbs: (1) verbs whose infinitive ends in **-нуть** and the 1st person present tense in **-ну** (of the гну́ть — гну type); (2) verbs whose infinitive ends in **-чь** and the 1st person present tense in **-гу** or **-ку** (of the бере́чь — берегу́, печь — пеку́ type); (3) the verbs мере́ть, тере́ть, бить, вить, лить, пить, шить, мять, жать, деть, стать, стыть.

5.4.6. How to derive the forms of passive present participles.

Passive present participles are derived *only from transitive imperfective* verbs either from finite present tense forms or from the dictionary form (i. e. the infinitive).

The passive present participles of a number of transitive imperfective verbs are derived by adding **-ый** to the 1st person plural present tense (**-ём** following a consonant being replaced with **-ом**): диктова́ть — (дикту́ю) — дикту́ем — дикту́емый, храни́ть — (храню́) — храни́м — храни́мый, вести́ — (веду́) — ведём — ведо́мый. These participles change for gender, number and case; like adjectives, they have short forms (see above, 2.1.1 and 2.1.2).

The verb дава́ть (and its prefixed derivatives) and also the verbs ending in **-знавать** or **-ставать** are exceptions to this rule; their passive present participles are not derived from the present tense stem, but from the *infinitive* stem by adding the marker **-ем** (+ adjectival endings): дава́ть — дава́емый, создава́ть — создава́емый, познава́ть — познава́емый, достава́ть — достава́емый.

In practice passive present participles are not derived from all the verbs, but only from the following groups: (1) from verbs whose infinitive ends in **-ать, -ять** or **-еть** and the 1st person singular present tense in **-аю, -яю** or **-ею** if the **-ю** in these endings is unstressed: чита́ть — чита́ю — чита́ем — чита́емый, теря́ть — теря́ю — теря́ем — теря́емый; (2) from verbs whose infinitive ends in **-овать** or **-евать** and the 1st person singular present tense in **-ую** or **-юю** if the **-ю** in these endings is unstressed: тре́бовать — тре́бую — тре́буем — тре́буемый, малева́ть — малю́ю — малю́ем — малю́емый; (3) from verbs whose infinitive ends in **-ать** or **-ять** and the 1st person singular present tense in an unstressed **-у** or **-ю**: се́ять — се́ю — се́ем — се́емый, колеба́ть — коле́блю — коле́блем — коле́блемый.

5.4.7. The cases when passive past participles are derived from the present/future tense stem.

As a rule, passive past participles are derived from the infinitive stem (see 5.2.4.). However, in some cases passive past participles are derived from the present tense stem.

1. When the correlation between the infinitive and the present tense forms is of the **-ить**—(**-у/-ю**), **-ит** type and of the **-еть**—(**-у/-ю**), **-ит** type. In this case passive past participles are derived by adding **-енный/-ённый** to the 1st person singular present tense (of imperfective verbs) or future tense (of perfective verbs) stem: утра́тить — утра́чу — (утра́тит) — утра́ченный, оби́деть — оби́жу — (оби́дит) — оби́женный.

2. From verbs whose infinitive ends in **-зти, -сти, -зть** or **-сть** and also **-чь**. In this case passive past participles are derived by adding **-енный/-ённый** to the 3rd person singular present/future tense stem: подмести́ — (подмету́) — подметёт — подметённый, испе́чь — (испеку́) — испечёт — испечённый.

5.5. How to derive the finite passive voice verb forms.

In theory finite passive voice verb forms can be derived *only from transitive* imperfective verbs. In practice the only forms used are the 3rd person present tense forms, past tense forms and subjunctive mood forms. To derive the passive voice, **-ся** is added to the active voice forms after a consonant (счита́лся, исполня́ется) and **-сь** after a vowel (счита́лось, исполня́лось).

6. The Adverb. How to derive the comparative degree.

The comparative degree can be derived only from those adverbs which denote a feature that may exist in a greater or lesser degree. The comparative degree of adverbs coincides with that of the adjectives with the same root: чи́стый — чи́ще and чи́сто — чи́ще, я́сный — ясне́е and я́сно — ясне́е. (See above, 2.4.)

B. HOW TO CHARACTERISE AN OBJECT OR PERSON, OR AN ACTION OR STATE BY MEANS OF SENTENCES CONTAINING A MINIMAL NUMBER OF WORDS

In practice a speaker's (or writer's) most frequent task is to characterise an object or person, or an action or state from different points of view. For example, he has to report either the action performed by an object, or the nature of an action, or the state of the environment, etc. In such cases he has to build the appropriate sentences.

The number of formal types of sentences which convey such communicative intentions of the speaker is limited. However, each type allows more or less numerous variants with different lexical content. Thus, for example, if we want to report the action of an object, we can build an endless number of sentences of just one type: Лес шуми́т. Пти́цы пою́т. Де́ти игра́ют. Со́лнце све́тит. Мы гуля́ли. Я рабо́тал, etc. The distinctive feature of the preceding sentence patterns, capable of characterising an object, action or state, lies in the fact that all these patterns represent *minimal* sentences. The speaker (or writer) cannot express his intention in shorter sentences, but he can always make his sentences longer, adding to the minimal sentence—a kind of skeleton—other words, naming, for example, some additional participants in the situation, or giving various characteristics to these participants, or describing the various circumstances in which the situation concerned develops, etc. (for the ability of various parts of speech to extend in this way, see II, A.2). Thus, the number of sentences built on one pattern is almost endless.

1. Sentences Characterising an Object or Person

The most frequent task is to characterise a certain object or person from different angles: whether the object is present or absent, what it does or is doing, in what state it is, what features characterise it, in what quantity it is represented, etc. There are various possibilities to achieve it.

1.1. How to characterise an object or person through its/his action.

To denote the *action* or *state* of an object or person, sentences are used built on the pattern "A noun (pronoun) in the nominative + a finite verb form": Лес шуми́т. Мы гуля́ли. Студе́нты занима́ются. There are practically no restrictions on the replacement of the words denoting the object or person or of the verb. Sentences of this type can be expanded practically endlessly by words having various *circumstantial* meanings: Гру́стно шуми́т лес. Мы *ча́сто* гуля́ли *в па́рке*. Студе́нты занима́ются *в лингафо́нном кабине́те*. Various *object* extenders are also possible, which are primarily determined by the properties of the verb. Nouns may be accompanied by various *qualifiers:* Мы ча́сто гуля́ли в э́том *ста́ром* па́рке. Гру́стно шуми́т *зи́мний* лес. *Иностра́нные* студе́нты занима́ются в лингафо́нном кабине́те.

1.2. How to characterise an object or person through its/his features (properties).

1.2.1. To characterise an object or person through its/his *feature*, first of all, sentences built on the "A noun in the nominative + a noun in the nominative" pattern can be used: Мой оте́ц — учи́тель, Гага́рин — пе́рвый космона́вт. The place of both the first and the second parts of the sentence may be taken by practically any noun.

In the past and future tenses of the indicative mood and also in the subjunctive and imperative moods, sentences of this type include the appropriate forms of the verb быть. Not infrequently sentences of this type include so-called semi-auxiliary verbs: стать, станови́ться, де́латься, сде́латься, получи́ться, получа́ться, каза́ться, показа́ться, счита́ться, оказа́ться, ока́зываться, оста́ться, остава́ться, быва́ть, вы́йти, выходи́ть, предста́виться, представля́ться, яви́ться, явля́ться.

As a rule, past and future tense forms of the indicative mood and also subjunctive and imperative mood forms are used with the *instrumental* of the noun characterising the performer: Мой оте́ц был *учи́телем*. Де́ти всегда́ бу́дут *детьми́*.

In sentences with semi-auxiliary verbs, the instrumental of the noun characterising the performer is regularly used: Он явля́ется *руководи́телем* э́того предприя́тия. Незнако́мец оказа́лся *врачо́м*. Such sentences may be extended by various adjuncts, modifiers and qualifiers: Мой оте́ц в э́то вре́мя был учи́телем в се́льской шко́ле.

<small>Sometimes the relations conveyed by sentences of this type may also be expressed by sentences with a finite verb form: Оте́ц — учи́тель and Оте́ц учи́тельствует. Избы́точный вес — ли́шняя нагру́зка на се́рдце и сосу́ды and Избы́точный вес изли́шне нагружа́ет се́рдце и сосу́ды.</small>

Secondly, to characterise an object or person through its/his feature or property, sentences built on the "A noun in the nominative + an adjective (long- or short-form) in the nominative" pattern are used: Ребёнок послу́шный (послу́шен).

In the past and future tenses of the indicative mood and also in the other moods, sentences of this type include the appropriate forms of the verb быть. Such sentences may be extended by the addition of various adjuncts, modifiers and qualifiers (Ребёнок у них всегда́ о́чень послу́шный); short-form adjectives may be extended by preposition-cum-case noun forms and infinitives: Я был гото́в на всё. Ты винова́т пе́ред не́ю. Short-form adjectives which denote the presence or absence of a feature or quality (прису́щ, сво́йствен, характе́рен, чужд, ро́дствен) are always used with the appropriate nouns: Осторо́жность сво́йственна э́тому челове́ку. Мой труд любо́му труду́ ро́дствен (Маяко́вский). (Also see below, D, 4.)

1.2.2. A feature of an object cannot always be conveyed with the help of a noun or adjective form. To convey a feature characterising an object or person precisely *at the given moment*, sentences built on the "A noun in the nominative + a noun in an oblique case (or an adverb)" pattern are used: Оте́ц до́ма. Студе́нты в аудито́рии. There are practically no restrictions on the replacement of the component words. In the past and future tenses of the indicative mood and in the other moods the appropriate forms of the verb быть are used. Such sentences may be extended by various adjuncts, modifiers and qualifiers: Студе́нты на́шей гру́ппы сейча́с в пя́той аудито́рии на ле́кции по анти́чной литерату́ре.

1.2.3. To express a feature of an object which *results from an action*, sentences built on the "A noun in the nominative + a short-form passive participle" pattern are used: Стол накры́т. Дом постро́ен. In the past and future tenses of the indicative mood and also in the other moods the appropriate forms of the verb быть are used: Здесь бу́дет постро́ен дом. In sentences of this type semi-auxiliary verbs of the оказа́ться or быва́ть type may be used: Всё у них оказа́лось решено́ зара́нее. Such sentences may be extended by various adjuncts, modifiers and qualifiers: Ещё в про́шлом году́ на ме́сте ста́рого пустыря́ был постро́ен но́вый стадио́н. While characterising an object or person through a feature that results from an action, sentences of this type leave a possibility to indicate the performer whose activity has led to the appearance of the given feature in the object concerned: Стол накры́т официа́нтом. Реше́ние при́нято реда́кцией (for the possibilities to denote an action without denoting the performer, see below, C, 4.1).

1.3. How to characterise an object or person through its/his state.

To express the state of an object or person, sentences built on the same patterns as those used to express an action (see 1.1) or a feature (see 1.2) are employed: Ребёнок спит. Оте́ц бо́лен.

The state of the *environment* or *surroundings* and also *man's psychic or physical state* may be expressed with the help of sentences built on the pattern "A finite 3rd person singular present/future tense or a singular neuter past tense (or subjunctive mood) verb form": Вечере́ет. Моро́зит. Похолода́ло. Зноби́т. Тошни́т. Потепле́ло бы.

When the state of nature is implied, the experiencer of the state is expressed together with the place: *На у́лице* моро́зит.

The experiencer of such a state who is a person is usually expressed either by the *accusative* case: *Большо́го* зноби́т. Вдруг *его́* осени́ло, or by the combination of the preposition *у* and the *genitive:* У меня в глазах потемнело.

In such sentences *impersonal* verbs are usually used (see also above, A, 5.1., and below, C, 4.1).

1.4. How to report the existence (presence) or non-existence (absence) of an object.

1.4.1. The *existence* or *presence* of an object, person or action represented as an object is expressed by sentences consisting of a noun in the nominative. This pattern can only be used to report the state of nature or the surroundings (Зима. Дождь.), an event or situation abstracted from the performer (Весна. Всюду жизнь), an object—a person or thing (Дом. Улица. Фонарь. Одинокий прохожий), or somebody's activity or state (Шёпот. Стыд и позор).

To convey the experiencer or possessor of an "object" of this type, sentences built on the pattern "The preposition у + a noun (pronoun) in the genitive + a noun in the nominative" may be used: У больного грипп. У него неприятности.

In the past and future tenses of the indicative mood and in the other moods sentences of this type include the appropriate forms of the verb быть: Была жара. Пусть будет чудо. У сына был грипп.

The existence of an object can also be expressed by means of the patterns described in 1.1 (Озеро находится за шоссе. У меня есть эта книга) and 1.2 (Деревня рядом. Аэропорт далеко.).

1.4.2. The *non-existence* or *absence* of an object is conveyed by sentences built on the "Нет + a noun in the genitive" pattern: Нет времени. Нет грибов. The word нет cannot be replaced with any other word, while there are no restrictions on the replacement of the noun. In the past and future tenses of the indicative mood and also in the subjunctive mood не is used instead of нет and only two forms of the verb быть: the 3rd person singular for the future tense and the neuter singular for the past tense (and the subjunctive mood): Завтра у меня *не будет* времени. Вчера у меня *не было* времени. Только *бы не было* дождя! In sentences of this type semi-auxiliary verbs of the бывать, стать, оказаться, оказываться type can also be used. The person who does not have the object concerned is usually expressed by the genitive preceded by the preposition у: *У директора* нет (не будет, не было) возражений. Sentences of this type can be extended by various circumstantial extenders: *В лесу* нет грибов. *Сегодня* приёма нет. Его нет *в аудитории.*

The absence of an object may also be conveyed by means of sentences with verbs expressing presence, being or appearing, built on the pattern "A noun in the genitive + the negative particle не + a verb in the 3rd person singular present/future tense or in the neuter singular past tense (the subjunctive mood)": Чужого горя не бывает. Препятствий не существует. Жалоб не поступало. (See also below, C, 3.)

1.4.3. The non-existence or absence of even *one* object out of the expected plurality is expressed by sentences built on the "Ни + a noun in the genitive" pattern: Ни слова. Only nouns denoting single phenomena perceived by eye or ear can be used in such sentences without any extenders: Ни зву́ка. Ни души́. The number of such nouns becomes fairly large when extenders are present: У них ни рубля́. От Све́ты ни письма́, ни звонка́. От вас ни пи́сем, ни телегра́мм.

In such sentences the future tense is denoted by means of one form of the verb быть—бу́дет (3rd person singular)—with the particle не: За́втра здесь *не бу́дет* ни души́. In the past tense (and in the subjunctive mood) also only one form—the neuter singular—is used: Вчера́ здесь *не́ было* ни души́. *Не́ было бы* там ни души́! Вокру́г *не́ было* ни де́рева.

Instead of the forms of the verb быть semi-auxiliary verbs of the быва́ть, ока́зываться/оказа́ться, etc. type can be used (also only two forms): В до́ме не оказа́лось ни души́. (Also see below, C, 3.)

1.4.4. The *complete absence* or *non-existence* of an object may be conveyed by sentences of the Ничего́ ли́шнего. Никого́ родны́х type. In the case of ничего́ the second word can be replaced practically with any adjective in the genitive singular; and in the case of никого́, with a noun (more often with one following the adjectival pattern of declension) in the genitive singular or plural. In the future tense only the 3rd person singular of the verb быть with the negative particle не is used, and in the past tense (or the subjunctive mood) only the neuter singular. The person characterised by the absence of an object is usually conveyed by the *genitive* preceded by the preposition у: *У меня́* ничего́ но́вого. *У них* не бу́дет ничего́ ли́шнего. *У него́* не́ было никого́ бли́зких.

The complete absence or non-existence of an object may also be conveyed by sentences of the Никако́й наде́жды. Ни одно́й/еди́ной оши́бки type. Their first component is the word никако́го, ни одного́, ни еди́ного or ни мале́йшего; the second component may be replaced with practically any noun. In the past tense of the indicative mood and also in the subjunctive mood only one form of the verb быть—the singular neuter—preceded by the particle не is used: У нас *не́ было* никаки́х наде́жд. In the future tense only one form—the 3rd person singular—is used: У меня́ *не бу́дет* ни одно́й оши́бки.The person who does not have the object concerned is usually conveyed by the *genitive* with the preposition у: У на́шей футбо́льной *кома́нды* никаки́х наде́жд на побе́ду. Various circumstantial extenders can be used in sentences of this type: На не́бе—ни еди́ного о́блачка (cf. На не́бе—ни о́блачка). Тепе́рь у нас—никаки́х пробле́м. (See also below, C, 3 and C, 4.)

1.5. How to report the existence (presence) of *a certain quantity of an object* (objects).

The relations between an object or person and the *quantity* in which it/he exists are expressed by sentences built on the pattern "A quantitative adverb (numeral) or a noun with a quantitative meaning + a noun in the genitive": Мно́го цвето́в. Ма́сса госте́й. (Also see below, D, 3.)

The possessor of the objects or features characterised quantitatively is usually conveyed by the *dative* (*Мне* два́дцать лет) or by the *genitive* preceded by the preposition у (*У неё* тала́нтов ви́димо-неви́димо). Besides the above components, such sentences may have various circumstantial extenders: В ко́мнате мно́го цвето́в. Сейча́с шесть часо́в. На у́лице два́дцать два гра́дуса тепла́. До ста́нции пятна́дцать мину́т хо́да.

The existence of objects (or states represented as objects) in very large numbers may also be conveyed by sentence built on the "A noun in the genitive (more often in the plural)" pattern: Наро́ду! Цвето́в! Such sentences are pronounced with a special intonation and are used only in colloquial Russian. They have vivid emotional nuances. For the past and future tenses (and also for the subjunctive mood) only two forms of the verb быть are used (see above, 1.4). The possessor of the object concerned is usually conveyed by the *genitive* with the preposition y: Цвето́в у неё. Sentences of this kind are often extended by objects and adverbial modifiers: Разгово́ров там вчера́ о тебе́ бы́ло! (See also below, C, 4.1.)

2. Sentences Characterising an Action or State

2.1. To characterise an *action* or *state* through another action or state, the pattern of the "An infinitive + a copula + an infinitive" type may be used: Хоте́ть зна́чит мочь. Толсте́ть зна́чит старе́ть. There are practically no restrictions on the replacement of the infinitives. The following words and phrases are used as copulas: (1) э́то; (2) э́то есть, э́то и есть; (3) есть, и есть; (4) зна́чит, э́то зна́чит, э́то и зна́чит.

2.2. When a *qualitative characteristic* of an action or state is to be given, three sentence patterns may be used.

The first is "A noun in the nominative + an adverb or noun". Sentences of the Труд — э́то удово́льствие. Ложь — э́то непрости́тельно type express relations between an action or state represented through an object and its qualitative characteristic. The first place (of a noun) is taken by words denoting an action, an activity or a whole situation; and the second, by words with an evaluative meaning and also the adverb навсегда́ or надо́лго.

The second pattern is "An infinitive + an adverb or a noun in an oblique case": Учи́ться легко́. Кури́ть вре́дно. Sentences built on this pattern usually convey relations between an action represented abstractly, or a state represented as a process, and its qualitative characteristic. The place of the infinitive may be taken by practically any verb; and the place of the word with a qualitative characteristic, either by an adverb in -**o** of the type легко́, тру́дно, ве́село, ску́чно, далеко́, бли́зко, поле́зно, вре́дно or by the comparative degree of an adverb (Рабо́тать здесь интере́снее и ле́гче) or by a noun in an oblique case (Реши́ть э́тот вопро́с — в на́ших интере́сах).

The third pattern is "An infinitive + a noun in the nominative": Учи́ться — ваш долг. Рабо́тать здесь — удово́льствие. Sentences built on this pattern may be used to express relations between an action or state represented as a process and its characterisation represented as a quality, ability for something or an evaluation. The place of the infinitive can be taken by practically any verb; and the place of the word with the qualifying characteristic, by a noun of the type неле́пость, глу́пость, стыд, оши́бка, заблужде́ние, удово́льствие, ра́дость, го́ре, сча́стье, до́блесть or a noun of the type де́ло, зада́ча, долг, труд, уде́л, судьба́, цель, обя́занности, мечта́ with an attribute: Стать врачо́м — моя́ мечта́. Учи́ться — ва́ша гла́вная зада́ча.

2.3. To convey the existence (presence) of a *state*, sentences may be used which consist of an adverb of the хо́лодно, гру́стно, etc. type.

To convey the *state of the environment* (with no performer implied), sentences consisting of one word may be used (Ти́хо. Шу́мно. Моро́зно. Краси́во. Лю́дно, etc.); likewise, to convey the *experiencer's* psychic or physical *state*, the following words may be used in the sentences: жаль, жа́лко, бо́льно, прия́тно, легко́, тру́дно, доса́дно, стра́шно, оби́дно, сты́дно, нело́вко, смешно́, интере́сно, зама́нчиво, любопы́тно, изве́стно, неизве́стно, etc.

States either with or without an experiencer may be expressed by the words далеко́, бли́зко, хорошо́, пло́хо, тяжело́, горячо́, хо́лодно, тепло́, жа́рко, прекра́сно, жу́тко, ве́село, трево́жно, гру́стно, уны́ло, одино́ко, споко́йно, пра́зднично, светло́, темно́, ую́тно, свобо́дно, etc.

To express the future tense, only the 3rd person singular of the verb быть is used, and to express the past tense (the subjunctive mood) also only one form is used: the neuter singular. The experiencer of the state concerned is usually conveyed by a noun or pronoun in the *dative* (*Нам* бу́дет ве́село. *Ему́* бы́ло ве́село. *Де́тям* ску́чно) or by the genitive case with the preposition у (*У них* всегда́ ве́село. *У вас* так ую́тно! (Also see below, C, 4.1.)

The presence of a state as a *result of an action* can be conveyed by sentences consisting of neuter singular short-form passive participles of the Решено́. Закры́то type. The only position can be taken by such words as заплачено, ко́нчено, наку́рено, откры́то, закры́то, за́нято, за́перто.

To express the future tense, the 3rd person singular is used; and to express the past tense (and the subjunctive mood), the neuter singular.

The performer is either absent or is expressed by the *instrumental*: *дире́ктором* прика́зано, or the *genitive* with the preposition у: *У нас* за всё запла́чено. Various extenders—objects and adverbial modifiers—are possible: У нас давно́ уже́ бы́ло решено́ в э́тот день встре́титься. (Also see below, C, 4.1.)

2.4. To convey the *impossibility of carrying out an action or assuming a state* owing to the lack of the necessary participants (persons or objects) or circumstances, sentences built on the pattern "The adverb не́куда (не́откуда, не́зачем, etc.) or the pronoun не́кого or не́чего in any case + an infinitive" can be used: Не́зачем спо́рить. Не́кому писа́ть. Не́где спать. Не́ о чем говори́ть. The first component is a negative pronominal word (adverb or pronominal noun); the second component can be replaced by practically any infinitive. The case of the pronominal noun (invariably an oblique case!) depends on the infinitive: Не́ о чем поговори́ть. Не́ с кем поговори́ть. Не́ у кого спроси́ть. Не́ за что благодари́ть, etc. To express the future tense, only the 3rd person singular is used: Не́кому *бу́дет* писа́ть; and to express the past tense (and the subjunctive mood), only the neuter singular: Не́кому *бы́ло* писа́ть.

The use of semi-auxiliary verbs of the стать, станови́ться, оказа́ться, ока́зываться type is possible: Не́ о чем ста́ло говори́ть. To convey the performer, the *dative* case is used: *Мне* не́кому писа́ть.

Нам не́ о чем ста́ло говори́ть. Such sentences may include various circumstantial extenders: Здесь мне не́ с кем посове́товаться. Вчера́ ему́ бы́ло не́зачем туда́ е́хать. (Also see below, C, 3.)

C. WHAT MEANINGS CAN BE EXPRESSED BY GRAMMATICAL MEANS AND HOW THEY CAN BE EXPRESSED.

In actual practice a speaker or a writer does not only have to build a sentence with a minimal number of words, which will characterise an object or person, or an action or state from various points of view (see above, B). As a rule, he has the task of *completing* in one way or another *the information* contained in a sentence with a minimal number of words. Then there arises the need to express the relations *between the performer and the object* acted upon, clearly stating who or what the performer of an action (or the experiencer of a state) is, who or what the person or object acted upon is, who or what the beneficiary of the action is, with the help of what person, method, device or instrument the action was accomplished, the property of whom or what the given object is, etc.

Not infrequently there arises the need to express the relations between an action (state) and the *circumstances* in which it takes place. In other words, the need to express spatial (где? куда́? отку́да?), temporal (когда́?), final (заче́м?), causal (почему́?) and qualitative (как?) characteristics. None of these relations has a universal means of expression. The latter vary, depending on many circumstances: the speaker's exact intention and the qualities of the words denoting both the actions or states themselves and the participants in, and the circumstances of, the events described.

In addition, the speaker or the writer usually has to express the *relation between an action* (or state) *and reality*: whether it actually takes place or is only *possible, desirable* or *supposed*.

With the help of grammatical means the speaker can also express other characteristics of an action or state: its time, the relation between it and the participants in the communicative act, its result, repetition, etc. The speaker also uses grammatical means to convey additional characteristics of an object or person in order to indicate either the number of the objects or persons or the sex of the persons or animals. Grammatical means can also denote the degree of a quality characterising an object or person, or an action or state.

1. How to express the relation between an action and reality with the help of verb moods and other means.

1.1. How to express an action actually taking place.

To express the fact that an action takes place, took place or will take place *in reality*, a verb in the *indicative* mood and in the appropriate tense and finite form should be used.

1.2. How to express a desirable action.

To express an action which is not taking place in reality, but is *desirable*, one of several options should be used.

1.2.1. If the speaker wants to say that he wants to perform an action *himself*, he should use either the construction "Я хочу́ + an infinitive": Я хочу́ подня́ться в го́ры. Я жить хочу́, чтоб мы́слить и страда́ть (Пу́шкин), or the construction "Мне хо́чется + an infinitive": Мне хо́чется спать (прочита́ть, знать). These two constructions are almost synonymous; however, the construction "Мне хо́чется..." (more frequently used in the colloquial language) tends to represent the speaker as the experiencer of a state rather than the performer of an action.

1.2.2. If, on the other hand, the speaker wants his *interlocutor(s)* to perform an action, then:

(1) He may use the construction "Я хочу́, что́бы ты (вы) + a verb form in the past tense of the appropriate number of the indicative mood which expresses the desired action": Я хочу́, что́бы ты ушёл (прие́хал, сказа́л, поду́мал), or: Я хочу́, что́бы вы реши́ли (зна́ли, прочита́ли).

(2) He may use the appropriate number of the imperative mood verb form which expresses the desired action: Напиши́те! Говори́! Принеси́! Стара́йтесь! Учи́тесь!, etc. In this case it must be borne in mind that the singular is used when the speaker addresses his interlocutor in the second person singular (ты) (the form of address employed when speaking to children, relatives and friends): Воло́дя, *запиши́* мой а́дрес. If the speaker addresses his interlocutor in the second person plural (вы), only the plural form is used: Влади́мир Никола́евич, *запиши́те* мой а́дрес.

(3) If the speaker wants to express the same meaning as a command or strict injunction, he may use the infinitive: Встать! Молча́ть! Рабо́тать! However, the use of such sentences is limited to specific situations and would be considered rude by the interlocutor.

(4) If the speaker wants some object to be brought or given to him, his wish can be conveyed by a construction of the type: "Да́й(те)/принеси́(те) + a noun in the accusative (genitive)": да́йте таре́лку, да́йте молока́, принеси́те хле́ба, and occasionally by a noun alone: Коня́! Ча́ю! Ру́чку! Таре́лку! The use of a noun alone is possible only in specific situations when this manner of expressing the speaker's wish would not be considered rude or tactless by his interlocutor. In all the other cases the full construction is recommended.

(5) If the speaker wants to ask (to advise) his interlocutor to perform an action, he may also use the subjunctive mood: Сходи́л бы ты к врачу́. Помо́г бы ты ба́бушке. In such sentences the speaker's wish is conveyed in a more tactful and less categoric form than in the preceding forms. These sentences are typical of colloquial speech.

1.2.3. If the speaker wants an action to be performed not by himself or his interlocutor(s), but *by some other people* (or objects), he should use either the preceding construction "Я хочу́, что́бы..." (Я хочу́, что́бы мой сын учи́лся на физи́ческом факульте́те. Я хочу́, чтобы песни звучали...) or a construction consisting of "пусть + the form of the 3rd person of the appropriate number present tense indicative mood": Пусть всегда будет солнце. Пусть не стареют наши мамы. Пусть Олег переведёт эту статью.

In colloquial speech the same meaning may be conveyed by the subjunctive mood of a verb which agrees with the word denoting the performer of the desired action or the experiencer of the desired state: Только бы дети были здоровы! Только бы он позвонил!

If in this case what is desired is that a person, object or phenomenon *should not exist*, then the noun conveying the undesirable person, object or phenomenon takes the *genitive* and the verb быть (with the negative particle не) takes the neuter gender: Не было бы дождя! Не было бы неприятностей!

1.2.4. If the speaker wants an action to happen in which *he will take part together with his interlocutor(s)*, he may use (1) either a construction of the Я хочу, чтобы мы сходили на эту выставку type; (2) or the 1st person plural non-past tense verb: Пойдём! Споём! Встанем!; (3) or a construction of the Давай сделаем (скажем, пойдём) type, if he addresses one person, or Давайте сделаем (споём, решим), if he addresses a number of persons or one person whom he usually addresses in the second person plural (вы).

1.2.5. If the person who wants an action to take place *is not the speaker himself but another person* (ты, он), constructions (in the appropriate tense and person!) of the following types should be used: either "Он (она) хочет, чтобы..." or "Ему (ей, нам, тебе, вам) хочется, чтобы... + the word denoting the person or object from whom/which the desired action is expected + the verb form denoting the desired action (in the appropriate number of the past tense indicative mood)": Отец хотел, чтобы сын стал врачом. Таня хочет, чтобы вы пришли сегодня к нам. Народы хотят, чтобы на земле всегда был мир.

1.3. How to express the possibility or impossibility of performing an action.

1.3.1. If the speaker wants to say that the possibility of an action is entirely *in the performer's competence or* (moral and physical) *power*, he should use a construction with the verb мочь in the appropriate mood, tense, number, person and gender + the infinitive of the verb denoting the possible action: Народы могут защитить мир. Ты мог пригласить друзей.

1.3.2. If, however, the speaker wants to say that the possibility of an action *depends on the* (moral and physical) *circumstances*, he should use a construction with можно—"The dative of the noun or pronoun denoting the performer of the action + можно + the infinitive of the verb denoting the possible or permitted action": Больному можно гулять. Вам можно уйти. Not infrequently constructions with мочь and можно are synonymous. This happens when owing to the circumstances the possibility of an action is not specified as external or internal with respect to the performer.

In colloquial speech, particularly in questions, the performer of the action is frequently dropped: Мо́жно здесь пройти́? Мо́жно сюда́ сесть? Occasionally the word мо́жно is also dropped: Где взять бума́гу и ру́чку? Когда́ вам позвони́ть? Куда́ обраща́ться при несча́стном слу́чае? Как пройти́ на Кра́сную пло́щадь?

1.3.3. If it is important to indicate that an action is possible *despite the unfavourable circumstances*, the construction "The dative of the noun or pronoun denoting the performer + the verb уда́ться (perfective) or удава́ться (imperfective) + the infinitive of the verb denoting the possible action" is used: Мне удало́сь уе́хать во́время. Несмотря́ на плоху́ю пого́ду, нам удало́сь загоре́ть.

If the unfavourable circumstance is time shortage a construction with the verb успе́ть + the infinitive of the verb denoting the possible action is used: Я успе́л прие́хать до отхо́да по́езда. Де́ти успева́ют верну́ться домо́й к прихо́ду отца́.

1.3.4. If the speaker wants to stress that the possibility of an action depends *on the will of other people* or on the existing social conventions, a construction with the verb разреши́ть (perfective) or разреша́ть (imperfective) + the infinitive of the verb denoting the permitted action is used. In this case the person who permits the action to take place is either designated by the nominative of a noun or pronoun or omitted altogether. The person who is permitted to perform the action (the performer of the permitted action) is designated by the *dative* of a noun or pronoun: Врачи́ разреши́ли *больно́му* гуля́ть.— *Больно́му* разреши́ли гуля́ть. Роди́тели разреша́ют *свои́м де́тям* е́хать на пляж.— *Де́тям* разреша́ют е́хать на пляж.

1.3.5. As the *antonyms* of the constructions with the verbs мочь, удава́ться/уда́ться, успева́ть/успе́ть, разреша́ть/разреши́ть the same constructions only with the negative particle не are used. In addition, the verb запреща́ть/запрети́ть may always be used instead of не разреша́ть. These constructions with не are used only to convey the failure to perform an action owing to some circumstances (moral or physical): Я не мог (не успе́л) тебе́ позвони́ть. Мне не удало́сь попа́сть на э́тот спекта́кль. Де́тям запрети́ли е́хать на пляж.

1.3.6. The construction with the word нельзя́ is the *antonym* of the construction with мо́жно; formally it does not differ from the construction with мо́жно in any other respects: Больно́му мо́жно встава́ть.— Больно́му нельзя́ встава́ть; Вам мо́жно уходи́ть.— Вам нельзя́ уходи́ть. This construction is also used to express the *impossibility* of performing an action.

If the constructions with мо́жно and нельзя́ are to be used with respect to the past, the verb быть should be employed in the singular neuter past tense *after* the word мо́жно or нельзя́ (Больно́му мо́жно *бы́ло* гуля́ть). If these constructions are to be used with respect to the future, the 3rd person singular of the verb быть should be used also *after* the word мо́жно or нельзя́ (Больно́му мо́жно *бу́дет* гуля́ть).

1.4. How to express the necessity of performing an action.

1.4.1. If the *necessity of performing an action* without any specification of the reason for it is to be expressed, a construction with the word до́лжен should be used: "A noun or pronoun in the nominative, which denotes the performer of the action concerned + the word до́лжен (должна́, должно́, должны́) + the infinitive of the verb denoting the action to be performed": Студе́нты должны́ хорошо́ учи́ться. Ка́ждый челове́к до́лжен труди́ться.

The word до́лжен may also be used as part of a passive construction in which the noun or pronoun in the nominative does not denote the performer, but the *experiencer* of the action and where instead of the infinitive of the appropriate verb the infinitive of the verb быть + the passive short-form participle of the appropriate verb is used: Ученики́ должны́ вы́полнить э́то зада́ние.—Зада́ние должно́ быть вы́полнено; Мы должны́ реши́ть э́ту зада́чу.—Э́та зада́ча должна́ быть решена́. The performer of the action may not be mentioned in this passive construction; however, if he/it is mentioned, he/it is usually conveyed by the *instrumental* case: Письмо́ должно́ быть отпра́влено *секретарём*.

All the preceding examples convey actions without any indication of the time when they take place. If the situation concerned relates only to a period before the moment of speaking, then the past tense of the verb быть in the appropriate gender and number should be added to the sentence (after the word до́лжен): Они́ должны́ бы́ли уе́хать. Зада́ча должна́ была́ быть решена́. If this situation relates only to a period after the moment of speaking, then the future tense of the verb быть in the appropriate person and number should be introduced into the sentence, which is an active construction: Ученики́ должны́ вы́полнить зада́ние.—Ученики́ должны́ бу́дут вы́полнить зада́ние. (The passive construction with the word до́лжен is not used to express an action occurring *after the moment of speaking*.)

1.4.2. To express the necessity of performing an action, the construction "The dative of a noun or pronoun which conveys the performer of the action + the word ну́жно (необходи́мо, на́до) + the infinitive of the verb denoting the action to be performed" is used: Мне ну́жно уе́хать. Де́тям на́до занима́ться. In this case the action is related to time in the same way as in the constructions with мо́жно, нельзя́ (see above): Мне ну́жно бу́дет за́втра уе́хать. Мне ну́жно бы́ло вчера́ уе́хать. There is no passive construction with ну́жно.

1.4.3. If the speaker wants to say that he must acquire some object (in the broadest sense of the word), then instead of the infinitive this construction includes the nominative of the noun or pronoun denoting the object to be acquired and the short form of the adjective ну́жен (нужна́, ну́жно, нужны́), which agrees with the noun or pronoun in gender and number: Ему́ нужна́ ва́ша по́мощь. Больно́му ну́жен све́жий во́здух. Студе́нтам нужны́ э́ти словари́.

1.4.4. If it is necessary to express the necessity of performing an action *out of moral considerations*, this construction with the word обя́зан should be used: "The nominative of the noun or pronoun denoting the performer of the action concerned + обя́зан (обя́зана, обя́зано, обя́заны) + the infinitive of the verb denoting the action to be performed": Душа́ обя́зана труди́ться (Заболо́цкий). Он обя́зан сдать э́тот экза́мен до января́. Вы обя́заны э́то сде́лать. There is no passive construction with the word обязан. The action expressed by means of this construction is related to time in the same way as in the construction with должен (see above): Он обязан был сдать этот экзамен до января. Она обязана *будет* сдать этот экзамен в сентябре.

1.4.5. If it is necessary to express the necessity of performing an action *contrary to the performer's wishes* and through force of circumstances (moral or physical), then the construction with the word вынужден is used, its usage being the same as that of the construction with the word обязан: Мы вынуждены это сделать. Директор был вынужден так поступить. Они будут вынуждены уйти.

Constructions with such forms of impersonal verbs as придётся, приходится, пришлось, приходилось are used for the same purpose. In the latter case the performer is denoted by a noun or pronoun in the dative: *Посетителю (посетителям)* придётся подождать. *Отцу (родителям)* пришлось отказаться от поездки.

1.4.6. In colloquial (emotional) speech the 2nd person singular imperative verb form is used to denote a necessary action which is extremely disagreeable to the performer. As a rule, this construction is used when the text conveys (or implies) a contrast between people who refuse to carry out their responsibilities and those who do carry them out: *Муж* читает журнал, а *я* готовь ужин. Он мне забыл сказать, а *я* отвечай.

1.4.7. If it is necessary to express not merely the necessity, but also the *advisability* of performing an action, a construction with such verb forms as следует, стоит, стоило is used. In this case (as in the case of the construction with приходится/придётся, приходилось/пришлось) the performer of the action is conveyed by a noun or pronoun in the *dative*; and the necessary (advisable) action itself, by the infinitive of the appropriate verb: Вам следует посоветоваться с врачом. Тебе стоит посмотреть этот фильм. Both these constructions are more often used when the speaker wants to recommend that his interlocutor should adopt a certain course of action. In this case the construction with следует has a somewhat more categoric meaning, stressing primarily the necessity of performing the action, whereas the construction with стоит mainly stresses the advisability of the action. It is precisely because of this that in the latter construction the performer of the action is often unmentioned and the object acted upon is denoted by the accusative case: *Этот фильм* стоило посмотреть. *Эту выставку* стоит посетить. Thus such sentences acquire an evaluative meaning: фильм хороший, интересный.

1.5. How to express a supposed action.

A *supposed* action may be either *desirable* (see 1.2) or *possible* (see 1.3), but not carried out and therefore existing in speech as a hypothetical proposition: what may happen if another event should happen.

1.5.1. If an event is perceived by the speaker as a mere condition for another event (taking or not taking place), then to denote the first event, a verb in the *indicative mood* is used in the appropriate tense, person, gender and number; this verb standing in the clause introduced by the conjunction если: Если ты придёшь после двенадцати, то я буду тебя ждать. Если солнце зашло за тучу, возможен дождь.

1.5.2. However, if it is known quite well that an event has not taken place or that it simply cannot take place, then to convey the situation, verbs in the *subjunctive mood* are used both in the clause introduced by the conjunction éсли and in the principal clause: Éсли бы я знал об э́том, я бы пришёл. Éсли бы студе́нт подгото́вился к экза́мену, он бы успе́шно сдал его́.

In colloquial speech, sentences are common in which the condition for an action (i. e. éсли бы + a subjunctive mood verb form) is expressed by means of the *imperative* singular (in this case the performer is invariably expressed by the nominative case): Позвони́ *он* на час ра́ньше, мы бы ему́ всё сказа́ли (= Éсли бы он позвони́л на час ра́ньше, ...); Знай *они́* об э́том, они́ бы то́же пришли́ (= Éсли бы они́ зна́ли об э́том, ...).

1.5.3. If the speaker wants to express a *supposition* or *apprehension* that an action may not take place, then, to convey the situation, these constructions may be used: (1) with the word до́лжен and the negative particle не (не до́лжен): Он не до́лжен опозда́ть. Де́ти не должны́ замёрзнуть. (Such sentences convey a supposition that the undesirable action will not happen.); (2) with the word мочь (in the appropriate finite forms) and the negative particle не *before the infinitive* of the verb denoting the supposed action: Она́ мо́жет не зако́нчить перево́д к пя́тнице. Он мо́жет не сдать экза́мен. Они́ мо́гут не успе́ть.

1.5.4. If the speaker *is not sure* that an action is taking (was taking, will be taking) place in reality, he can use so-called *parenthetic* words in the sentence (i. e. words not connected with the other words in the sentence), such as возмо́жно, вероя́тно, мо́жет быть, ка́жется, допу́стим, предполо́жим, etc.: Он, возмо́жно, пришёл. Сестра́, мо́жет быть, уе́дет.

When the speaker knows about an event only because somebody told him about it or when he knows about it through his own supposition, then his statement will also contain parenthetic words giving the source of information: говоря́т, по-мо́ему, по слова́м, по мне́нию, etc.: Ивано́в, говоря́т, то́же прису́тствовал там. По-мо́ему, Петро́в успе́шно сдаёт экза́мен.

2. How to express the participant in a communication who is the performer of a real action by means of verb person and other means.

The participants in a communication invariably include a speaker (or speakers), a listener (or listeners), and a subject (or subjects) spoken about.

If the performer of a real action *is neither the speaker nor the listener*, then in the indicative mood the *3rd person* non-past or past tense verb form denoting this action is used. The choice of the number of this verb form and also the choice of the gender of the past tense form depends on the gender and number of the noun denoting the performer: Студе́нт чита́ет. Студе́нты чита́ют. Идёт снег. Шёл снег. Пришла́ весна́. Начали́сь кани́кулы.

If the action is expressed by a *passive* verb form, either finite or participial, then the performer is usually expressed by the *instrumental* of a noun or pronoun, and the verb form agrees in number (if it is in the non-past tense) or in number and gender (if it is in the past tense) with the nominative of the noun or pronoun denoting the object acted upon: Спра́вка подпи́сывается врачо́м.— Спра́вки подпи́сываются врачо́м. У́лица освещена́ (освеща́лась) фонаря́ми. У́лицы освещены́ (освеща́лись) фонаря́ми.

2.1. How to express the fact that the performer of an action is the speaker.

To convey a situation in which the *speaker* is *himself* the performer of an action, the personal pronoun я (to denote one person) or мы (to denote more than one person or to denote the author of a scientific paper, monograph, etc., who refers to himself in the plural out of modesty) + the finite 1st person verb form is used—in the appropriate number in the case of a non-past tense form: Мы предлага́ем сле́дующий вариа́нт, and in the gender corresponding with the performer's sex in the case of a past tense form: Я вас люби́л (Пу́шкин); И я люби́ла вас (Пу́шкин). In the case of a non-past tense form the pronoun may be omitted: Люблю́ лови́ть ры́бу. Ду́маю о тебе́.

However, if the action is expressed by a *passive* verb form, either finite or participial, then the performer of the action is usually conveyed by the *instrumental* form мной (for the singular) or на́ми (for the plural) and the verb form agrees in gender and number with the nominative of the noun or pronoun denoting the object acted upon: Прика́з подпи́сан мной ли́чно. На́ми иссле́довались э́ти да́нные. На́ми полу́чены сле́дующие результа́ты.

2.2. How to express the fact that the performer of an action is the listener.

To convey a situation in which the performer of an action is the *listener*, the personal pronoun ты (to denote one person) or вы (to denote more than one person or one person whom the speaker addresses in the 2nd person plural as a sign of special respect) is used + the finite 2nd person verb form in the appropriate number in the case of a non-past tense form and in the appropriate gender corresponding with the performer's sex in the case of a past tense form: Ты зна́ешь э́того челове́ка? Серге́й Ива́нович, вы пришли́ во́время. Вы сдаёте экза́мен? In the case of a non-past tense form the pronoun may be omitted: Принесёшь слова́рь за́втра. Дойдёте до угла́ и уви́дите апте́ку.

However, if the action is expressed by a *passive* verb form, either finite or participial, then the performer of the action is usually conveyed by the *instrumental* form тобо́й (for the singular) or ва́ми (for the plural) and the verb form agrees in gender and number with the nominative of the noun or pronoun which denotes the object acted upon: Тобо́й не учтены́ ва́жные обстоя́тельства. Каки́е пробле́мы Ва́ми изуча́ются? Каки́е результа́ты ва́ми полу́чены?

3. How to express negation.

3.1. The most usual way of expressing negation.

If an action or state, an object or person, a feature or quality, or a condition or circumstance is to be negated, the negative particle не should be used: Не тебя́ так пы́лко я люблю́ (Ле́рмонтов); Любо́вь ещё, быть мо́жет, в душе́ мое́й уга́сла не совсе́м (Пу́шкин). In such cases the sentence frequently includes the word or phrase contrasted with the negated one. Such a contrast is often conveyed by the conjunction а: Э́то был не он, а его́ брат. Он не спал, а про́сто лежа́л. Э́то рабо́та не отли́чная, а посре́дственная. Он жил не в це́нтре, а на окра́ине.

When the speaker does not want to negate the action itself, but its *result*, a *perfective* verb is used: Он не реши́л э́ту зада́чу. Мы не сде́лали э́ту рабо́ту. If such sentences have an *imperfective* verb, then they negate the action *itself*: Он не реша́л э́ту зада́чу. Sentences with a perfective verb do not negate the action itself, leaving it for the listener or the reader to decide whether the action ever began at all or not (see also above, B, 1.4 and B, 2.4).

3.2. How to strengthen a negation.

If an *action* or *state* is negated categorically, then in addition to the negative particle не the emphasising constructions discussed in B, 1.4 may be used before the verb denoting the relevant action or state: Он не чита́л книг.— Он не чита́л *никаки́х* книг.— Он не чита́л *ни одно́й* кни́ги. In cases when an action involving a number of participants or connected with a number of similar circumstances is negated, the words denoting these participants or circumstances are preceded by ни: Он не чита́л *ни* газе́т, *ни* журна́лов. Не говори́ об э́том *ни* ученика́м, *ни* учителя́м. Она́ не звони́ла *ни* вчера́, *ни* сего́дня.

If all the possible *participants* in an action or state are negated, then in addition to the negative particle не the verb is preceded by the appropriate forms of the *negative pronoun* никто́ or ничто́: Никто́ не спал (i. e. Все не спа́ли); but only: Никто́ не приходи́л. Никто́ не звони́л. Ничего́ не случи́лось. Никого́ (ничего́) не нашли́. Не говори́ никому́ ничего́. Не удивля́йся ничему́.

When the verb requires a preposition with the appropriate case form, the preposition is placed between ни and the relevant pronoun: Не спра́шивай ни о чём. Не обраща́йся ни к кому́ (see III, A, 3).

However, if all the possible *circumstances* of the action or state are negated, then in addition to the negative particle не the relevant verb is preceded by a *negative adverb* of the нигде́, никуда́, ниоткуда, никогда́ type: Никогда́ не спра́шивай меня́ об э́том. Сего́дня он никуда́ не ходи́л. По́мощь ниотку́да не приходи́ла.

The same rules of the use of words with ни also characterise the cases when not the action itself, but its *possibility* or *advisability* is negated, which is conveyed by words of the type нельзя́, невозмо́жно, не́зачем, не́ к чему, не на́до, не ну́жно, не сто́ит, не к лицу́, не к ме́сту followed by the infinitive of the verb denoting the relevant action or state: Никому́ не ну́жно ра́но встава́ть. Никуда́ не сто́ит обраща́ться.

After the words negating the advisability or desirability of an action of the type не́зачем, не́ к чему, не на́до, не ну́жно, не сто́ит, не сле́дует, не к лицу́, не к ме́сту and also after the words conveying a subjective negative attitude towards an action of the type не привы́к, не нра́вится, не люблю́, не сове́тую, не рекоменду́ю *only imperfective* infinitives are used.

4. How to express relations between the performer and the object acted upon.

4.1. How to express the performer.

In Section B cases were considered of expressing the performer and his/its action, state or feature in sentences containing a minimal number of words. However, not infrequently the speaker has to build sentences reporting an action or state and to find the necessary grammatical form to convey the performer of the action or the experiencer of the state.

4.1.1. The most common means of expressing the performer of an action is the *nominative* case of a noun (or pronoun), which usually combines with verbs in the *active* voice: *Де́ти* расту́т. *Пти́цы* запе́ли. *Мы* у́чимся. *Он* писа́л.

4.1.2. The nominative case is not the only form of expressing the performer of an action. In Russian there are words which express states, such as хо́лодно, ве́село, тяжело́, мо́жно, нельзя́, на́до, ну́жно. In sentences with such words, the performer is expressed by the *dative* case: *Больно́му* мо́жно гуля́ть. *Де́тям* ну́жно учи́ться. *Мне* на́до рабо́тать. *Нам* бы́ло ве́село. *Ей* тяжело́ подня́ть э́ту су́мку.

4.1.3. The performer may also be expressed by the *dative* in sentences with *impersonal* verbs, i. e. verbs used only in the 3rd person non-past tense or in the neuter past tense (see above, A, 5.1): *Вам* сле́дует поду́мать. *Студе́нту* не удало́сь реши́ть зада́чу. *На э́тот раз чемпио́ну* не повезло́.

4.1.4. If an impersonal verb denotes a disagreeable physical state of man: тошни́т, зноби́т, лихора́дит (the same meanings may be expressed by personal verbs used impersonally, of the type трясёт, шата́ет, etc.), then the performer in such sentences is conveyed by the *accusative* case: *Больно́го* лихора́дит. *Ребёнка* зноби́т. *Меня́ всего́* трясёт, etc.

4.1.5. If a sentence conveys the absence of an object or phenomenon by means of the word нет or the negative particle не, then the noun denoting the absent object or phenomenon (i. e. the performer) is in the *genitive*: cf. Ви́ктор до́ма and *Ви́ктора* нет до́ма; Ви́ктор бу́дет до́ма and *Ви́ктора* не бу́дет до́ма (also see above, В. 1.4).

4.1.6. If the verb is in a finite or participial form of the *passive* voice, then the performer is usually absent altogether. However, if the performer must be indicated, he is expressed by the *instrumental* form: Спекта́кль ста́вится *молоды́м режиссёром Петро́вым*. Петербу́рг был осно́ван *Петро́м Пе́рвым*. In other words, there is a transformation formula: "The nominative (the performer) + a verb in the active voice + the accusative (the object acted upon)"→"The nominative (the object acted upon) + a verb in the passive voice + the instrumental (the performer)": Молодо́й режиссёр Орло́в ста́вит коме́дию Молье́ра.— Коме́дия Молье́ра ста́вится молоды́м режиссёром Орло́вым.

However, such a transformation does not always proceed in this way. For example: Ба́лки де́ржат кры́шу.— Кры́ша де́ржится *на ба́лках*. (In this case the performer and the place of action are not differentiated.)

In passive constructions the performer is sometimes conveyed by the *dative* (as in the case of impersonal verbs): Я представля́ю э́то так.→ *Мне* э́то представля́ется так. The dative also conveys the performer with verbs which have only the passive voice: Ему́ присни́лся сон (cf. Он ви́дит сон).

4.1.7. When the performer is characterised as the *possessor* of an object or feature, it is denoted by the *genitive* with the preposition у: *У дете́й* (был, бу́дет) пра́здник. *У сы́на* (была́, бу́дет) анги́на. *У него́* (бы́ло, бу́дет) хоро́шее настрое́ние.

4.1.8. If the noun denotes a phenomenon which is the result of the performer's activity, the performer is conveyed by the *genitive*: докла́д *дека́на* (cf. дека́н докла́дывает), объясне́ние *учи́теля* (cf. учи́тель объясня́ет), реше́ние *министе́рства* (cf. министе́рство реши́ло). In this case the meaning of the performer who has created a certain phenomenon does not differ from that of the possessor of an object.

4.1.9. If the speaker feels it important only to report the action, but finds it unnecessary to indicate the performer, he may use sentences with the verb in the finite 3rd person plural non-past tense form: Здесь обе́дают.

In the construction with the verb form (finite or participial) in the passive voice the subject is often also unmentioned: Вопро́с обсужда́ется. Реше́ние при́нято.

4.2. How to express the object acted upon.

4.2.1. How to express the object directly acted upon.

4.2.1.1. The most common means of expressing the object of an action is the *accusative* of a noun, which is usually used with so-called *transitive* verbs in the active voice: Я чита́ю *кни́гу*. Писа́тель пи́шет *истори́ческий рома́н*. В до́ме вы́мыли *о́кна*.

4.2.1.2. If such a verb is preceded by the negative particle не, then in the literary language the *genitive* is preferred to denote the direct object: Я не чита́л *э́той кни́ги*. Мы не смотре́ли *э́той карти́ны*. Я не слы́шал *э́того*. In colloquial speech the use of не before the verb may not influence the form of the direct object.

4.2.1.3. After such verbs as боя́ться, добива́ться/доби́ться, дожида́ться/дожда́ться, достига́ть/дости́гнуть, жа́ждать, ждать/подожда́ть, жела́ть/пожела́ть, заслу́живать/заслужи́ть, избега́ть/избе́гнуть, иска́ть, каса́ться/косну́ться, лиша́ть/лиши́ть, лиша́ться/лиши́ться, опаса́ться, остерега́ться, пуга́ться/испуга́ться, слу́шаться/послу́шаться, страши́ться, стесня́ться, стыди́ться/постыди́ться, тре́бовать/потре́бовать (and also after verbs with the prefix **на-** with the meaning of "a large quantity of", of the накупи́ть, начита́ться type, which are a feature of colloquial speech) the direct object is conveyed by the *genitive*: Накупи́л *игру́шек* де́тям. Начита́лся *фантасти́ческих рома́нов*.

4.2.1.4. After many commonly used verbs, such as взять, посла́ть, принести́, купи́ть, дать, съесть, вы́пить, nouns denoting substances and also plural nouns may be used with the meaning of a direct object either in the *accusative* or in the *genitive*: возьми́ соль and возьми́ со́ли, пошли́ де́ньги and пошли́ де́нег, купи́ хлеб and купи́ хле́ба, принести́ спи́чки and принести́ спи́чек. There are no clear distinctions in meaning connected with the genitive or the accusative here; therefore, to avoid infringement of the accepted norms of usage, it is recommended that in these cases, too, the accusative should be used to denote the direct object of the verb.

4.2.1.5. After such verbs as адресова́ть, аккомпани́ровать, аплоди́ровать, благоприя́тствовать, ве́рить/пове́рить, возража́ть/возрази́ть, вреди́ть/повреди́ть, доверя́ться/дове́риться, досажда́ть/досади́ть, зави́довать, изменя́ть/измени́ть, кла́няться, лгать, льстить, надое́сть/надоеда́ть, наску́чить, пере́чить, повинова́ться, подверга́ться/подве́ргнуться, поддава́ться/подда́ться, подлежа́ть, подми́гивать/подмигну́ть, подпева́ть, подчиня́ться/подчини́ться, поклоня́ться/поклони́ться, покоря́ться/покори́ться, покрови́тельствовать, помога́ть/помо́чь, предше́ствовать, препя́тствовать, принадлежа́ть, прислу́живать, присяга́ть, проти́виться, противоде́йствовать, противоре́чить, ра́доваться, симпатизи́ровать, соотве́тствовать, сопу́тствовать, сочу́вствовать, спосо́бствовать, угожда́ть/угоди́ть, угрожа́ть, удивля́ться/удиви́ться, уступа́ть/уступи́ть the object acted upon (sometimes: acted against) is conveyed by the *dative* case.

4.2.1.6. After such verbs as боле́ть, ве́дать, владе́ть, воспо́льзоваться, восторга́ться, восхища́ться, горди́ться, дорожи́ть, заболе́ть, заве́довать, занима́ться, злоупотребля́ть, интересова́ться, кома́ндовать, любова́ться, маха́ть, называ́ться, наслажда́ться/наслади́ться, облада́ть, овладе́ть, пленя́ться/плени́ться, по́льзоваться, распоряжа́ться, руководи́ть, руково́дствоваться, тяготи́ться, увлека́ться/увле́чься, управля́ть, хвали́ться, хва́статься the object acted upon is expressed by the *instrumental* case.

4.2.1.7. If the verb is a finite form in the *passive* voice or a *short-form* passive participle, then the object experiencing the action of this verb is expressed by the nominative: *Зда́ние* стро́ится (постро́ено). *Спекта́кль* ста́вится (поста́влен).

If the verb is a *long-form* passive participle, then the gender, number and case of this participle are determined by the relevant characteristics of the subordinating noun: Ви́жу *стро́ящееся здание*. Он написа́л о неда́вно *поста́вленном спекта́кле*.

4.2.1.8. The object acted upon may be expressed by a phrase consisting of a preposition and a noun or pronoun case form. The most commonly used phrases are:

в + *acc.* (ве́рить, преврати́ться, вмеша́ться)
на + *acc.* (влия́ть, реаги́ровать, смотре́ть, наде́яться)
от + *gen.* (зави́сеть, отлича́ться)

за + *instr.* (наблюда́ть, следи́ть)
над + *instr.* (рабо́тать, труди́ться, смея́ться)
с + *instr.* (согласи́ться, мири́ться)
в + *prep.* (сомнева́ться, ошиба́ться)
о + *prep.* (свиде́тельствовать)

4.2.1.9. After verbal nouns derived from *transitive* verbs the object experiencing their action, which they represent substantivally, is usually conveyed by the *genitive* case: чте́ние *кни́ги*, пра́вка *ру́кописи*, постано́вка *экспериме́нта*. In other words, there is a general regularity: "a verb + an object in the accusative" → "a verbal noun + an object in the genitive": чита́ю кни́гу → чте́ние кни́ги. However, there are quite a few exceptions to this rule. Thus, for example, люби́ть дете́й → любо́вь к де́тям; ненави́деть фаши́зм → не́нависть к фаши́зму. At the same time some transformations made "in accordance with the rule" may result in undesirable ambiguity: ожида́ть дру́га → ожида́ние дру́га (it is not clear whether the friend is the performer or the experiencer of the action; cf. the similar ожида́ние пра́здника). Therefore, to avoid mistakes in expressing the object of a verbal noun you should consult a dictionary.

More often than not verbal nouns derived from *intransitive* verbs "inherit" the form of the expression of the object acted upon which characterises the verbs they are derived from. However, this is not always so. Therefore in this case, too, you should consult a dictionary.

4.2.1.10. If it is necessary to avoid straightforward mention of the object acted upon, it may be removed from the text. For example: Ма́льчик чита́ет кни́гу.— Ма́льчик чита́ет; Он ве́рит в успе́х.— Он ве́рит. However, this is not always possible: there are verbs which require an object acted upon. Such sentences as Реше́ние зави́сит от мини́стерства. Тако́е поведе́ние свиде́тельствует о нео́пытности. Э́то повлия́ет на кли́мат cannot be shortened at the expense of the words denoting the object of their actions.

4.2.1.11. There are many cases when the meaning of the direct object of one and the same verb or verbal noun can be expressed differently. For example: наблюда́ть движе́ние плане́т and наблюда́ть за движе́нием плане́т; боро́ться с врага́ми and боро́ться про́тив враго́в; знать мне́ние оппоне́нта and знать о мне́нии оппоне́нта. In such cases the difference in the form of expression is not accompanied by the difference in the meaning.

4.2.2. How to express the object which is the "receiver" of an action.

The object which is the *receiver* of an action takes the *dative*: сказа́ть *студе́нтам*, подари́ть *сы́ну*, посла́ть *колле́гам*.

With verbs of movement, when the meanings of the receiver of an action and the object acted upon are not distinguished, this meaning is expressed by the preposition к and the dative: идти́ *к друзья́м*, пое́хать *к роди́телям*.

The choice of the form expressing the meaning of the receiver of an action is influenced also by what kind of thing the direct object of the action is. Thus, for example, if the direct object is an *inanimate* thing, then after the verb послáть or отпрáвить the receiver of the action is conveyed by the *dative* (послáть дéньги *друзья́м*, отпрáвить посы́лку *внýку*). If, however, the direct object is an *animate* being, then the receiver of the action is conveyed by a phrase consisting of the preposition к and the *dative* case (отпрáвить детéй *к рóдственникам*).

As a rule, on letters and documents addressed to a specific person the receiver (addressee) is denoted by the *dative: Дирéктору* завóда Петрóву. *Стáршему инспéктору Си́доровой. Декáну* физи́ческого факультéта *профéссору Гáлкину*.

However, if such letters and documents are not addressed to a person but to an organisation (which is a plurality of persons), such an addressee is denoted by the preposition в followed by the *accusative*: *В* дирéкцию завóда. *В* деканáт физи́ческого факультéта. (See also 5.1.2.2.)

4.2.3. How to express the instrument, means or device wherewith an action is performed.

4.2.3.1. The object with the help of which an action is performed is usually denoted by the *instrumental* case: писáть *карандашóм* и́ли *черни́лами*, сообщи́ть *письмóм* и́ли *телегрáммой*, лечи́ть *голодáнием*.

4.2.3.2. The names of the means of transport (conveyances) are used in the *prepositional* with the preposition на: éхать *на автóбусе*, прилетéть *на самолёте*, достáвить *на оленях*.

4.2.3.3. The names of the means of communication (of the рáдио, телефóн, телеви́дение type) are used in the *dative* with the preposition по: передáть *по телефóну*, показáть *по пéрвой прогрáмме телеви́дения*, смотрéть *по телеви́зору*, получи́ть *по пóчте*.

4.2.3.4. The names of languages are used in the *prepositional* with the preposition на: говори́ть *на немéцком языкé*, писáть *на рýсском языкé*. However: говори́ть по-немéцки, писáть по-рýсски.

4.2.3.5. When used after the verbs найти́, отпрáвить, передáть, послáть, разыскáть, сообщи́ть, узнáть, a phrase consisting of the *accusative* case and the preposition чéрез denotes the intermediary (a person or organisation) with whose help an action is performed: передáть *чéрез знакóмых*, сообщи́ть *чéрез газéту*.

4.2.3.6. Phrases consisting of the prepositions с пóмощью, при пóмощи, посрéдством, путём and the *genitive* are typical of academic writing.

5. How to express circumstantial characteristics by means of noun case and preposition-cum-case forms.

5.1. How to express spatial characteristics.

5.1.1.1. How to express the position of an object or person inside some space.

The *position* of an object or person *inside* some space is usually indicated by means of the preposition в and the *prepositional* of a noun or the preposition на and the *prepositional* of a noun.

The use of the preposition в or на primarily depends on what kind of noun denotes the space: учи́ться в университе́те, в институ́те, but на (физи́ческом) факульте́те, на ку́рсах; рабо́тать в институ́те, в акаде́мии, в консервато́рии, в учрежде́нии, в магази́не, в пра́чечной, but на заво́де, на фа́брике, на предприя́тии, на вокза́ле, на по́чте; отдыха́ть в санато́рии, в до́ме о́тдыха, в Подмоско́вье, but на куро́рте, на взмо́рье, на ро́дине; находи́ться в отъе́зде, в командиро́вке, but на рабо́те, на охо́те, на прогу́лке, на уро́ке, на собра́нии; жить в Казахста́не, but на Украи́не; в Евро́пе, but на Ура́ле; в гора́х, but на Кавка́зе.

With the names of cities or towns a construction with the preposition в is used: в Москве́, в Ленингра́де, в Пари́же, в Каи́ре, etc.

When the noun concerned also has the form in -у different from the prepositional form (see above, A, 1.1.5), the first form is used to indicate the position in space: находи́ться в саду́, в лесу́, в шкафу́, в Крыму́, на углу́, на мосту́, на берегу́, на Дону́, на краю́.

If the reference-point is a noun denoting a person, then, to indicate the position of an object, the construction "the preposition у + the genitive case" is used: cf. быть у сосе́да, but быть в ко́мнате сосе́да; находи́ться у дека́на, but находи́ться в декана́те.

5.1.1.2. How to express the position of an object or person outside some space.

Of course, an object or person may not only be inside some space, but also take a different position with respect to the spatial reference-point.

In this case the position of the object with respect to the reference-point may be designated either *sufficiently accurately* or in a general, non-specific way.

1. To denote the position of something *on the surface* of something else, the preposition на followed by the *prepositional* of the noun designating the spatial reference-point is used: (лежи́т) на столе́, на крова́ти, на шкафу́; (нахо́дится) на голове́, на земле́, на пове́рхности, на не́бе, на стене́, на потолке́, etc.

2. When the spatial reference-point is *below* the surface of an object, this position is indicated by the preposition под followed by the *instrumental* of the noun designating the reference-point: под де́ревом, под дождём, под столо́м, под сне́гом, под ли́стьями, etc.

3. However, when the spatial reference-point is *above* the surface of an object, this position is indicated by the preposition над followed by the *instrumental* of the noun designating the reference-point: (стоя́ть) над реко́й, над про́пастью, над бе́здной.

4. The specific position *in front of (the facade of)* the reference-point may be indicated by the preposition перед followed by the *instrumental*: (стоя́ть) пе́ред до́мом, пе́ред о́кнами, пе́ред учи́телем.

5. The specific position *at the back of (behind)* the reference-point may be indicated by the preposition за followed by the *instrumental*: за до́мом, за овра́гом, за дере́вней, за доро́гой, or by the preposition позади́ or сза́ди, followed by the *genitive*: находи́ться позади́ (сза́ди)

до́ма, магази́на, библиоте́ки, це́ркви. The latter method of indicating the position of an object is generally used with regard to reference-points which have three-dimentional measurements, of the дом, шкаф, челове́к type.

6. The position of a number of objects *along the edge* of an elongated reference-point is indicated by the preposition вдоль, followed by the *genitive*: (расти́) вдоль доро́ги, забо́ра, овра́га.

7. To denote the *exact distance* between two objects (with the help of measurement units), sentences of this type are used: Дере́вня располо́жена в шести́десяти киломе́трах к ю́гу от Москвы́. Some parts of such sentences can be used independently: Го́род нахо́дится в двух часа́х езды́ от Ленингра́да. Мы живём к за́паду (на за́пад) от грани́цы.

8. To indicate a person's position *at his place of work*, a construction consisting of the preposition за and the *instrumental* is frequently used: учени́к сиди́т за па́ртой, продаве́ц стои́т за прила́вком, учёный рабо́тает за столо́м, шофёр — за рулём. (However, we usually say рабо́чий стои́т у станка́.) In some of the above cases the replacement of за with у would change the meaning and indicate the person's position *near* the reference-point (see below).

9. The *general, non-specific, approximate* position of an object with respect to the reference-point may be indicated by the constructions "вне, за преде́лами, далеко́ от, недалеко́ от, вблизи́ от, близ + the *genitive* case": Институ́т нахо́дится вне Москвы́, за преде́лами городско́й черты́, далеко́ от це́нтра, недалеко́ от желе́зной доро́ги, вблизи́ от аэропо́рта, близ лесно́го масси́ва. The most common method of indicating the approximate position of something near a city is the use of the preposition под with the *instrumental*: Мой друг живёт под Москво́й (Ленингра́дом, Ки́евом, Оде́ссой), подо Льво́вом.

10. The non-specific (general, approximate) position of an object (*but not a person*, see 5.1.1.1) with regard to a reference-point is usually indicated by the preposition у followed by the *genitive*: Встре́тимся у теа́тра. Де́ти игра́ли у до́ма (ле́са, реки́, ручья́, овра́га).

The position of an object (or person) *near* some other object (or person) may be indicated by the preposition о́коло followed by the *genitive*: сиде́ть о́коло до́ма and сиде́ть о́коло ба́бушки.

11. The position of an object *within a stretch of distance* separating two different reference-points is indicated by means of the preposition ме́жду and *two instrumental case forms*: Кали́нин располо́жен ме́жду Москво́й и Ленингра́дом.

However, if an object is situated within a stretch of distance separating two *identical* reference-points, its position is indicated by means of the preposition ме́жду followed either by the *genitive plural* or the *instrumental plural*: сиде́ть ме́жду (двух) сту́льев and сиде́ть ме́жду (двумя́) сту́льями. There is no difference between the meanings of the genitive and the instrumental in this case.

12. The position of an object *surrounded by many reference-points* is indicated either by the preposition среди́ + the *genitive plural* or by

the preposition мéжду + the *instrumental plural*: деревня среди лесов и болот; жить среди людей (между людьми); между домами, деревьями.

5.1.2.1. How to express the movement of an object away from a reference-point.

1. If an object is *outside* the limits of the reference-point, then to express its *movement away from the reference-point*, the prepositon от followed by the *genitive* is used: идти от дома (дороги, станции). When the reference-point is indicated *inexactly, approximately*, a construction of the "со стороны + the genitive" type may be used: идти со стороны леса, поля, города. The perfective and imperfective verbs denoting the movement in this case are usually those with the prefix **от-**: отъехать от города, отойти от дома, отплыть от берега.

2. If an object is *within the limits of* the reference-point, then to denote its movement away from the reference-point, a construction either with the preposition из followed by the *genitive* or with the preposition с followed by the *genitive* is used: идти из школы (университета, магазина); ехать с работы (Украины, выставки). In this case the following regularity exists: the use of the preposition в to indicate the position of an object *within* a space (see above, 5.1.1.1) predetermines the use of the preposition из to denote its movement *out of* that space, whereas the use of the preposition на to indicate the position of an object *within* a space predetermines the use of the preposition с to denote its movement *out of* that space: учиться в школе — идти из школы; работать на заводе — ехать с завода; отдыхать в Крыму — плыть из Крыма; жить на Сахалине — лететь с Сахалина.

To denote movement out of the limits of the reference-point, verbs of motion with the prefixes **вы-, у-** and **от-** are frequently used: выехал из дома, вылетел с аэродрома, уехали из Москвы, ушёл с завода, отошёл от дома.

3. If an object is somewhere above, then its *downward* movement is usually indicated by means of the preposition с followed by the *genitive*: упасть с горы (крыши, неба). In such cases verbs with the prefix **с-** are frequently used: съехать с горы, сбежать с лестницы.

4. When movement proceeds from an unobserved point *on the left or right* or *from behind* the reference-point, such a situation is indicated by means of the preposition из-за followed by the *genitive*: выскочить из-за угла (дома, леса). When the unobserved point is *below* the reference-point, movement from there is denoted by means of the preposition из-под followed by the *genitive*: вылезти из-под стола (кровати, одеяла). In both these cases verbs with the prefix **вы-** are frequently used.

5.1.2.2. How to express the movement of an object or person towards a reference-point.

1. To indicate movement *into* a reference-point, constructions either with the preposition в + the *accusative* (ехать в город, в лес) or with the preposition на + the *accusative* (ехать на стадион, на Кавказ) are

used. The choice of the preposition in this case is determined by the same conditions as when indicating the position within an object (see 5.1.1.1).

Thus, in this case the main role in indicating the direction of the movement is played not by the preposition, but by the verb and the case form of the subordinated word: éхать в гóрод, на рабóту, в Москву́, на Кавкáз, etc.

2. To indicate movement *towards* an object or person, the construction with the preposition к followed by the *dative* is more often used: идти́ к до́му, к дире́ктору, к доро́ге, к сестре́. Less frequently this meaning is expressed by the construction по направле́нию к + the *dative*, в направле́нии к + the *dative* or в направле́нии + the *genitive*: идти́ по направле́нию к ле́су (в направле́нии к ле́су, в направле́нии ле́са).

If the reference-point towards which the movement proceeds is an object, then all the above constructions are synonymous. However, if the reference-point is a noun denoting a *person*, then the construction with the preposition к is used to convey movement the purpose of which is to contact the person concerned: идти́ к врачу́, к сосе́дке, к това́рищу, etc. All the other constructions merely indicate the reference-point towards which the movement proceeds.

5.1.2.3. How to express the movement of an object or person along a route.

1. To convey the movement of a person or object, not only the beginning or end of the movement can be used as the reference-point, but also the objects making up the route of the movement. The most common and general method of indicating the *route of movement* is the construction consisting of the preposition по and the *dative*: идти́ по ле́су (по́ полю, по доро́ге, по боло́ту, etc.). Less frequently, when a rectilinear movement is meant, this meaning may be conveyed by the prepositionless *instrumental* case: éхать ле́сом (по́лем, бе́регом).

2. To denote an *object* to be overcome while moving along a route, the preposition че́рез followed by the *accusative* is generally used: идти́ че́рез лес (по́ле, боло́то).

3. To denote the objects not situated along the route, but *close to* it, the construction with the preposition ми́мо followed by the *genitive* is used: éхать ми́мо ле́са (по́ля, боло́та, дере́вни).

4. When the route is indicated more specifically with regard to other objects, constructions with the prepositions вдоль, о́коло, посреди́, ме́жду, пе́ред, позади́, под, над are used in accordance with the rules described in 5.1.1.2.

5.2. How to express temporal characteristics.

5.2.1. How to express the time of an action with respect to the moment of speaking.

1. To express an action *preceding the moment of speaking*, a **past** tense verb should be used: Я чита́л э́ту кни́гу. Он приходи́л сюда́.

2. To express an action *following the moment of speaking*, a **future** tense verb should be used: Я скажу́ об э́том. Он бу́дет учи́ться в университе́те.

3. To express an action taking place *at the moment of speaking* or a *habitual* action (which may not be taking place at the moment of speaking), a **present** tense verb should be used: Мой друг живёт в Ки́еве. Она́ хорошо́ пла́вает. Бра́тья ча́сто встреча́ются.

The relation to the moment of speaking may also be expressed by lexical markers of the за́втра, в про́шлом году́, че́рез год type.

In sentences which have no finite verb form (of the type Де́ти в саду́. Мой оте́ц — учи́тель. Пойти́ не́куда, etc.) the relation of the action *to the moment of speaking* is indicated by the very absence of the finite verb form. The relation of such actions or states *to the past* (before the moment of speaking) or *the future* (after the moment of speaking) is expressed by the appropriate form of the verb быть: Де́ти бы́ли в саду́.— Де́ти бу́дут в саду́; Оте́ц был учи́телем.— Оте́ц бу́дет учи́телем; Пойти́ бы́ло не́куда.— Пойти́ бу́дет не́куда.

5.2.2. How to express the specific time of an action.

The time of an action may be indicated sufficiently accurately as a *moment* of time or somewhat vaguely as a *period* of time. The character of such an indication does not depend primarily on the governing word, but rather on the choice of the lexical means which are markers of the time when the action takes place (took place or will take place).

5.2.2.1. How the point of time when an action occurs is usually expressed.

More often than not, to express the *point of time* when an action occurs, constructions are used which consist of (1) the preposition в and the *accusative* of the noun denoting the time of the action; (2) the preposition в and the *prepositional* of the noun denoting the time of the action; (3) the preposition на and the *prepositional* of the noun denoting the time of the action.

1. The construction "в + the accusative" is used when the time of the action is designated *by hours* (прийти́ в оди́ннадцать часо́в, ждать в семь часо́в утра́) or *days of the week* (верну́ться в сре́ду, встре́титься в четве́рг). This construction can also be used when the time markers are the words по́лдень, по́лночь, су́мерки, пра́здник, or such words as мину́та, у́тро, день, ве́чер, час, ночь, весна́, ле́то, зима́, о́сень (these words must be accompanied by an attribute with or without agreement: в *тот* день чита́л, в *про́шлую* весну́ вы́шла за́муж, в *нена́стное* у́тро вспо́мнил, в мину́ту *отча́яния* реши́л, в день *рожде́ния* объяви́л).

The words век and год denote time in the same construction when accompanied by an attribute without agreement (произошло́ в век *Пу́шкина*, в век *ко́смоса*, в год *споко́йного со́лнца*) or an attribute with agreement which is a pronoun (в *наш* век, в *тот* год).

2. The construction "в + the prepositional" is used when the time of the action is indicated *by months* (случи́лось в апре́ле, ию́не, октя-

бре́), or *years* (роди́лся в ты́сяча девятьсо́т три́дцать восьмо́м году́), or by the words коне́ц, нача́ло and середи́на (в конце́ ле́та, в середи́не дня).

The words век and год denote time in the same construction when accompanied by attributes expressing quite specific (в девятна́дцатом ве́ке, в семна́дцатом году́) or relatively specific (в про́шлом ве́ке, в бу́дущем году́, в э́том году́) time.

3. The construction "на + the prepositional" is used when the time of the action is indicated by the word неде́ля, which is usually accompanied by an attribute with agreement: встре́титься на про́шлой (э́той, бу́дущей) неде́ле.

Besides, this construction is also used when the time of the action is indicated by the words рассве́т, заря́, восхо́д, зака́т, переме́на, кани́кулы (встать на заре́, на рассве́те, на восхо́де; уви́деться на переме́не, на кани́кулах) and also by the words рубе́ж, ста́дия, эта́п, исхо́д. In the last case an attribute with agreement (обнару́жить на ра́нней ста́дии, обсуди́ть на да́нном эта́пе) or without agreement (жить на рубеже́ двух веко́в, поня́ть на исхо́де жи́зни) must be used.

4. When the time of the action is indicated by a *date*, the *genitive* without a preposition is used: Война́ око́нчилась *девя́того ма́я ты́сяча девятьсо́т со́рок пя́того го́да*. Пу́шкин роди́лся *шесто́го ию́ня*. Прилете́л два́дцать *второ́го*. In such cases the words indicating the year and the month take the genitive without a preposition: девя́того ма́я ты́сяча девятьсо́т со́рок пя́того го́да (however: в ты́сяча девятьсо́т со́рок пя́том году́ or в ма́е ты́сяча девятьсо́т со́рок пя́того го́да).

5. When the time of the action is indicated by the word у́тро, день, ве́чер, ночь, весна́, о́сень, зима́ or ле́то, the *instrumental* without a preposition is used (ждал у́тром, днём, ве́чером; прие́хал весно́й, про́шлым ле́том, ны́нешней зимо́й).

5.2.2.2. How the time period when an action occurs is usually expressed.

1. The most frequently used construction conveying the *period of time* during which an action occurs is "во вре́мя + the *genitive* of a noun denoting the time period": во вре́мя пое́здки узна́ть, во вре́мя о́тпуска познако́миться. In this construction the time markers are usually nouns which denote various actions, states or events occurring over a period of time: во вре́мя подгото́вки (строи́тельства, заня́тий, обе́да, боле́зни, конце́рта, мете́ли, etc.).

Sometimes instead of the preposition во вре́мя the following prepositions can be used followed by the genitive: в тече́ние (э́той неде́ли), в хо́де (строи́тельства), в проце́ссе (обсужде́ния), в продолже́ние (диску́ссии), на протяже́нии (про́шлого го́да). However, unlike the preposition во вре́мя all the above prepositions combine with a limited number of nouns.

2. If the time period when an action occurs is indicated by a verbal noun with the meaning of a *process*, the construction consisting of the preposition при + the *prepositional* of a noun may be used: при под-

гото́вке, при нагрева́нии, при осмо́тре, при за́пуске, при транспорти́ровке. The same construction may also be used when the time of the action is indicated through the performer (при ста́ром дире́кторе) or the name of a social and economic system (при капитали́зме, феодали́зме) or a state system (при Сове́тской вла́сти). In the last case the nouns usually have attributes with or without agreement (при наро́дном прави́тельстве).

3. If the time period is expressed by words denoting a *meal* or a *dish*, the construction with the preposition за + the *instrumental* is frequently used: за ча́ем, за обе́дом, за у́жином, за ко́фе (обсужда́ли).

4. If the time period is indicated *by a part of a 24-hour* day (день, ночь) or by a season, then the construction with the preposition среди́ + the *genitive* case is used: среди́ но́чи, зимы́, ле́та (see also above, 5.2.2.1, for the possibility of the instrumental in this case).

5. If the time period is indicated *by a person's age* or *occupation*, the time of the action may be expressed by the *instrumental* without a preposition: Ребёнком он ча́сто боле́л. Я был здесь ещё студе́нтом.

6. When the marker of the time of the action is a noun denoting a *time period*, either the construction в + the *prepositional* is used: в де́тстве, в ю́ности, в ста́рости, в дре́вности, or the construction в + the *accusative*: в го́ды (цари́зма), в эпо́ху (феодали́зма) (see also 5.2.2.1).

7. To convey a *specific* period of action confined between two points indicated by minutes, hours, days of the week, months, years or centuries, the construction consisting of the preposition с + the *genitive* and the preposition до + the *genitive* of a noun is used: с девяти́ часо́в утра́ до шести́ часо́в ве́чера, с понеде́льника до среды́, с февраля́ до апре́ля. In the case of days and months the second part of the construction may be replaced with the preposition по + the *accusative*: с ма́я по октя́брь, со вто́рника по пя́тницу.

5.2.2.3. How to express the time during which an action occurs.

1. As a rule, the *duration* of an action which has not achieved a result is expressed by the *accusative* of the appropriate noun or numeral without a preposition: ждать (реша́ть, чита́ть, стро́ить) одну́ мину́ту (пять часо́в), два дня, всю суббо́ту, три неде́ли, ме́сяц, кварта́л, год, пять лет, etc. Semantically these forms are contrasted with some forms in the same case, but with the preposition в; cf. ждать в два часа́ (when precisely?) and ждать два часа́ (for how long?). However, this contrast between the moment of an action and its duration may be annulled when the construction with the preposition в тече́ние is used; cf. these practically synonymous phrases: ждал неде́лю and ждал в тече́ние неде́ли, рабо́тал два ме́сяца and рабо́тал в тече́ние двух ме́сяцев, жил неде́лю and жил в тече́ние неде́ли. (See also 5.2.2.2.)

As the time markers in all such cases the names of such units of time as мину́та, час, неде́ля, ме́сяц, год and век are used, and also зима́, ле́то, о́сень, весна́, ночь, день, ве́чер, у́тро, the names of the days of the week and words implying duration in time: доро́га, жизнь, уро́к, война́. In the latter case the words designating time are accompanied by attributes with agreement, usually the pronoun весь or це́лый: рабо́тать це́лую зи́му (всё у́тро, весь понеде́льник, всю жизнь, всю войну́, це́лый уро́к).

2. When a non-resultative action continues a definite period of time and ceases on the expiration of that period, the construction consisting of the preposition на + the *accusative* is used: прие́хать (верну́ться, пригласи́ть, взять) на мину́ту (два часа́, три дня, пять лет). This construction is generally used after verbs denoting movement, verbs denoting an action occurring over a limited period of time (взять, дать, лечь, закры́ть, включи́ть, etc.) and nouns of the type путёвка, план, о́тпуск, командиро́вка, переры́в, разгово́р, любо́вь, etc. As nouns denoting a period of time, the names of parts of a 24-hour day, days of the week, months and seasons are used in this construction: прие́хать на понеде́льник, откры́ть на две мину́ты, любо́вь на всю жизнь.

3. The duration of an action achieving a result is usually expressed by the construction consisting of the preposition за + the *accusative*: реши́ть (постро́ить, сде́лать, вы́полнить) за три мину́ты (за два часа́, за́ год, за́ зиму, за сре́ду). This construction is generally used when the time markers are words having a purely temporal meaning (час, день, ме́сяц, год, понеде́льник, семе́стр) or words also implying duration in time of the type уро́к, кани́кулы, жизнь, переры́в, etc.

4. The duration of an action which has achieved a result may also be conveyed by the construction consisting of the preposition в + the *accusative*: реши́ть (постро́ить, прочита́ть, сде́лать, вы́полнить) в три мину́ты, в два часа́, в год, в пять лет, в кани́кулы, в переры́в.

However, in some cases the meanings of duration and the moment of action are indistinguishable. Thus, for example, сде́лать в два часа́ or прочита́ть в кани́кулы may denote actions performed at the indicated time or lasting over the entire indicated period (see also 5.2.2.2). Therefore, to convey the duration of an action achieving a result, the construction with the preposition за should be preferred.

5. To indicate the specific duration of an action from one moment to the next, the construction consisting of the preposition с + the *genitive* and the preposition до + the *genitive* or the preposition по + the *accusative* is used (for this, see 5.2.2.2): с десяти́ до двена́дцати часо́в, с сентября́ по ноя́брь, с ты́сяча девятьсо́т се́мьдесят девя́того по ты́сяча девятьсо́т во́семьдесят пя́тый.

5.2.2.4. How to express an action occurring periodically.

1. To express the time of an action occurring not just once, but at definite periods, systematically, the *instrumental* plural of the nouns ве́чер, ночь, год, ме́сяц, век, час, неде́ля is used: чита́ть вечера́ми, ноча́ми, часа́ми; не писа́л пи́сем месяца́ми, года́ми. Some of these nouns are never used without an attribute: це́лыми дня́ми рабо́тал.

The construction with the preposition по + the *dative* plural of the nouns ночь, у́тро, ве́чер and also of the nouns denoting the days of the week has the same meaning: писа́ть по ноча́м, по среда́м.

2. To express a long period during which an action occurs more or less periodically, the construction consisting of the preposition в and the *accusative* is used: занима́ться три дня в неде́лю, встреча́ться не́сколько раз в год.

3. The time of a repeated action may be indicated with the help of the pronoun ка́ждый in constructions of the type: ка́ждую о́сень приезжа́ть, ка́ждый день выступа́ть, ка́ждую неде́лю писа́ть, etc. In sentences with these constructions only *imperfective* verbs can be used.

5.2.3. How to express the time of an action in relation to another action or event.

5.2.3.1. How to express the time of an action which follows some event.

1. To indicate the time of an action or event *following another event*, the construction consisting of the preposition по́сле and the *genitive* of the appropriate noun is used: прие́хать (встре́титься, рабо́тать, чита́ть) по́сле пра́здника (обе́да, двух часо́в, заня́тий). Sometimes constructions consisting of the preposition по оконча́нии, по истече́нии or по заверше́нии and the genitive are used with the same meaning. However, these prepositions combine with a limited number of nouns denoting events from which time is counted and occur mainly in the literary language.

2. To convey a situation in which an action or event begins immediately after another action or event, the construction consisting of the preposition с and the *genitive* is used: рабо́тать (занима́ться, чита́ть) с утра́ (понеде́льника, де́тства, ма́я).

3. To express a *specific* period of time separating one event from another, the construction consisting of the preposition че́рез + the *accusative* of the appropriate noun or numeral is used: прийти́ (нача́ть, узна́ть) че́рез (час, день, ме́сяц, три го́да) по́сле откры́тия. If the event serving as the reference-point from which time is counted is the moment of speaking, only the construction consisting of the preposition че́рез + the *accusative* is used: уе́хать (ко́нчить, реши́ть) че́рез (не́сколько секу́нд, два дня, пять лет).

The construction consisting of the preposition спустя́ + the *accusative* of the appropriate noun or numeral has the same meaning: Он прие́хал спустя́ год по́сле сва́дьбы. Only a limited number of nouns can be used in this construction.

5.2.3.2. How to express the time for which an action or event is planned.

To express the time for which an action or event *is planned*, the construction consisting of the preposition на + the *accusative* of a noun or numeral is used: назна́чить на два́дцать тре́тье ию́ня, отложи́ть на о́сень, заказа́ть на вто́рник, заплани́ровать на коне́ц го́да, наме́-

тить на кани́кулы, биле́т на два́дцать второ́е число́, про́пуск на второ́е ию́ня, тало́н на октя́брь. This construction usually occurs after the verbs назнача́ть/назна́чить, откла́дывать/отложи́ть, зака́зывать/заказа́ть, плани́ровать/заплани́ровать, намеча́ть/наме́тить and also after the nouns биле́т, про́пуск, тало́н, etc. The verb перенести́ (with the meaning "to put off", "to postpone") is also used with the construction на + the *accusative*, the "cancelled" time being indicated by the construction с + the *genitive*: перенести́ с понеде́льника на сре́ду (с о́сени на весну́, с три́дцать пе́рвого ма́я на два́дцать тре́тье ию́ня). The verbs пригласи́ть and вы́звать can be used either with the construction на + the *accusative* or with the construction в + the *accusative*: пригласи́ть в сре́ду (на сре́ду), вы́звать в два часа́ (на два часа́).

5.2.3.3. How to express the time of an action preceding another action or event.

1. To express the time of an action *preceding* another action or event, the construction consisting of the preposition до + the *genitive* of the appropriate noun or numeral is used: прие́хать (нача́ть, сде́лать, реши́ть) до обе́да (двух часо́в, октября́, зимы́, конца́ сезо́на, экза́менов). To indicate additionally over what period of time preceding the other event the action takes place, the construction "the preposition за + the *accusative*" should be used before the construction with до: прие́хать (узна́ть, сде́лать) за неде́лю (ме́сяц, два дня, три часа́, пять лет) до экза́мена, до конца́ спекта́кля.

2. To show that an action precedes some event, the construction "the preposition пе́ред + the *instrumental* of the noun denoting this event" is used: встре́титься пе́ред ле́кцией (экза́меном, обе́дом, соревнова́ниями). As a rule, words denoting parts of a 24-hour day, days of the week and months are not used in this construction.

The construction with the preposition накану́не + the *genitive* has the same meaning. However, the range of the nouns denoting events and used in this construction is limited to words usually designating major happenings (or holidays or festivities): накану́не Но́вого го́да (пра́здника, револю́ции, съе́зда).

3. To express the period of time which elapsed after the event concerned prior to the moment of speaking, the construction consisting of the word наза́д and the *accusative* of a noun or numeral denoting a time period is used: верну́ться (прие́хать, уйти́, сказа́ть) час (год, неде́лю, два дня) наза́д or тому́ наза́д. This construction is not used with future tense forms and is antonymous to the construction with the preposition че́рез indicating the time separating from the subsequent action cf. пришёл час наза́д and пришёл че́рез час (see above, 5.2.3.1).

4. To convey a situation in which an action preceding a time period also proceeds during this period, the construction consisting of the preposition по + the *accusative* is used. In this case the reference-point is usually the number of the day or the name of a month: рабо́тать (отдыха́ть, отсу́тствовать) по второ́е ма́я (по октя́брь).

5. To express the time the arrival of which signifies the completion of an action, the construction consisting of the preposition к + the *dative* is used: приéхать (сдéлать, закóнчить, вы́полнить, предстáвить) к прáзднику (Нóвому гóду, обéду, восемнáдцатому сентября́, отъéзду, свáдьбе).

5.3. How to express the reason for an action or state with the help of noun preposition-cum-case forms and other means.

When the reason for an action is to be conveyed, the best way is to use a complex sentence whose principal clause reports an event and the subordinate clause introduced by the conjunction потому́ что, поско́льку, и́бо or так как gives the reason for this event: Мы поéхали на э́тот концéрт, потому́ что óчень лю́бим му́зыку Бáха. Unlike the conjunction потому́ что, used in all the speech styles, the conjunctions так как and и́бо are encountered in the literary language and also in academic and official writing: Веснóй растéния развивáлись плóхо, так как в пóчве не хватáло влáги, whereas the conjunction поско́льку is more common in colloquial speech.

The reason for an action or state may be conveyed by preposition-cum-case constructions, the use of each construction depending on how this reason is regarded from the point of view of desirable or undesirable consequences.

5.3.1. To convey the reason leading to *undesirable* consequences, the construction consisting of the preposition из-за + the *genitive* of the noun or pronoun denoting the reason is used: Он не сдал экзáмен из-за болéзни (опоздáния). In colloquial speech, the construction из-за тебя́ (негó, неё, вас, них) is encountered, used when the interlocutor's (interlocutors') or some other person's (persons') behaviour is regarded as the source of undesirable consequences: Вéчно из-за тебя́ каки́е-нибудь недоразумéния. Тепéрь из-за них мы опоздáем.

5.3.2. To express the reason leading to *desirable* or neutral consequences, the construction consisting of the preposition благодаря́ + the *dative* of the noun or pronoun denoting the reason is used: Повы́сить урожáйность благодаря́ сортовы́м семенáм. Благодаря́ своéй общи́тельности он бы́стро познакóмился со всéми сотру́дниками. (In a sense, this construction and that with из-за are antonymous.)

5.3.3. If the reason is conveyed by nouns denoting *internal* or *external circumstances* that cause a change in or the discontinuation of existence, the construction consisting of the preposition от + the *genitive* of a noun is used: заплáкать от оби́ды, закричáть от рáдости, умерéть от рáка, поги́бнуть от хóлода.

5.3.4. When the reason for an action is either a person's quality or trait of character or state (по бéдности, по скрóмности, по болéзни) or some moral, legal or organisational circumstances (по дóлгу, по обя́занности, по инициати́ве, по предложéнию, по прикáзу, по закóну, по прóсьбе, по рекомендáции), the construction consisting of the preposition по + the *dative* of a noun is used.

5.3.5. In official, business and academic writing, to express reason, the construction consisting of the preposition в связи́ с + the *instrumental* is frequently used (various applications and requests usually begin with this: в связи́ с боле́знью (оконча́нием сро́ка обуче́ния, поступле́нием на рабо́ту), and also the construction with the preposition в результа́те or всле́дствие + the *genitive*: В результа́те (всле́дствие) несча́стного слу́чая поги́бли два челове́ка. В результа́те (всле́дствие) при́нятых мер пожа́р прекрати́лся. Unlike the construction with the preposition в связи́, the construction with the prepositions в результа́те or всле́дствие combines with a limited number of nouns denoting the reason for an action or state.

5.4. How to express the purpose of an action with the help of noun preposition-cum-case forms and other means.

5.4.1. The most common method of expressing the *purpose of an action* is a construction consisting of the conjunction что́бы and the verb denoting the purpose of the action: я пришёл, что́бы узна́ть; я говорю́, что́бы ты знал. If in this case the performer of the main action is at the same time the experiencer of the action or state which is the purpose, then the purpose is expressed by an *infinitive*: Мы занима́лись физкульту́рой, что́бы укрепи́ть здоро́вье. However, if the performer of the main action and the experiencer of the action or state which is the purpose do not coincide, the purpose is expressed by a *past* tense verb agreeing in number and gender with the noun or pronoun denoting the experiencer of the action or state which is the purpose: Я пишу́ об э́том, что́бы *вы* не *трево́жились* напра́сно. In the literary and official language, the conjunction что́бы is frequently augmented by the words для того́ (что́бы) or с тем (что́бы): Я заявля́ю об э́том для того́ (с тем), что́бы все зна́ли...

5.4.2. After verbs of volitional impact of the type убеди́ть, проси́ть, заста́вить, умоля́ть, посла́ть, напра́вить, звать the performer of their actions and the experiencer of the purpose of these actions usually do not coincide. Although after these verbs the purpose is expressed by an infinitive, the experiencer of the purpose of the action in such cases is usually conveyed by the *accusative* of a noun or pronoun: Я убежда́л *бра́та* прие́хать. Мы про́сим *вас* не серди́ться. Оте́ц посла́л *сы́на* в го́род учи́ться. Thus, on the one hand, sentences of the type Мы проси́ли его́ не волнова́ться and Мы проси́ли его́, что́бы он не волнова́лся are synonymous. On the other hand, the experiencer of the action which is the purpose may not be mentioned at all, since he/it is clear from the general meaning of the sentence: Я посла́л его́ в магази́н купи́ть (что́бы он купи́л) молоко́.

If the verb conveying the purpose of an action is preceded by the negative particle не, then the purpose of the action can be expressed only by means of the conjunction что́бы: спешу́, что́бы не опозда́ть; ухожу́, что́бы не беспоко́ить, etc.

5.4.3. If the purpose of an action is denoted by an *abstract* noun, then the construction consisting of the preposition для + the *genitive* of the appropriate noun is used. This construction is generally used after words denoting "use" or "acquisition": испо́льзовать для улучше́ния, тре́буется для подгото́вки, поле́зен для здоро́вья.

To convey the purpose of an *object*, the construction with the preposition для is used: ко́мната для о́тдыха, площа́дка для игр. If the purpose consists in the destruction or removal of an object or phenomenon, then the construction with the preposition от + the *genitive* of a noun is used: лека́рство от любви́, сре́дство от комаро́в.

5.4.4. If an object or action is intended for a *person*, the construction with the preposition для is used, too: купи́ть для до́чери, лека́рство для отца́, пода́рок для первокла́ссника. This meaning may also be expressed by the *dative*: пода́рок сы́ну, купи́ть первокла́сснику (see also C, 4.2.2).

5.4.5. If the purpose of a verb of movement in space is the acquisition of an object, the construction consisting of the preposition за + the *instrumental* is used: пойти́ (посла́ть, отпра́виться) за газе́той (за хле́бом, за сигаре́тами, за гриба́ми).

5.4.6. If the purpose is an object or phenomenon the acquisition or attainment of which requires an expenditure of another object, the construction consisting of the preposition на + the *accusative* of the noun denoting the purpose is used: материа́л на пла́тье, де́ньги на прое́зд, лице́нзия на отстре́л, вре́мя на обду́мывание, ассигнова́ть на строи́тельство.

5.4.7. In journalese, purpose may be expressed by the construction consisting of the preposition ра́ди or во имя + the *genitive*, the prepositions ра́ди and во и́мя combining with a limited number of words, mainly with abstract nouns: ра́ди (во и́мя) сча́стья (сла́вы, ми́ра, и́стины, добра́, справедли́вости, etc.).

In the literary and official language, purpose is also expressed by the construction with the preposition с це́лью, в це́лях, в интере́сах or во избежа́ние + the *genitive* of a noun. However, these prepositions also combine with a limited number of verbs and nouns denoting the purpose of an action.

6. How to modify the action or state expressed by a verb with the help of prefixes and other means.

Not infrequently, the speaker has to specify certain characteristics of the action spoken of in the sentence. For example, he has to specify whether the action was resultative or not, whether it was performed once or several times, how it is characterised with respect to its impact, its phase or in relation to another action or state.

To a certain extent both lexical and grammatical means may take part in the expression of these intentions of the speaker. A situation often arises when he knows a prefixless verb (for example, лете́ть, стро́ить, писа́ть) and his task is to express some additional characteristics inherent in the action or state denoted by the verb concerned. In some cases the speaker can use only some lexical markers with the appropriate meaning for his purpose, in other cases he can use both lexical means and prefixes, whereas in still other cases he should use prefixes alone. The use of each of these means depends on the meaning of the verb. The following recommendations should be regarded only as a *theoretical possibility*, which may not always materialise in practice. Therefore, when one intends to express one's meaning with the help of a prefixed verb, one should check the feasibility of such expression with a dictionary — either a monolingual Russian dictionary or a bilingual one. A knowledge of the prefixes which can express the intended meaning enables the speaker or writer to "find his bearings" in the dictionary. The absence in the latter of a theoretically constructed prefixed verb or its unexpected meaning should be construed as incorrectness of the theoretically constructed verb.

The range of meanings conveyed by verb prefixes is not limited to the list that follows. However, the other meanings are still more "sophisticated" as regards the number of the prefixes which convey them and the ability of these prefixes to combine with verbs. Therefore, the simplest and, as a rule, safest way to express various characteristics of an action is the choice of the appropriate lexical means (except the expression of a resultative meaning!). At the same time a sufficiently high degree of mastery of Russian presupposes the ability to find the appropriate prefixed verb in order to denote a definite type of action. In this in addition to monolingual and bilingual dictionaries, so-called word-family building dictionaries may provide help. In such dictionaries the entries are primary words arranged alphabetically, each entry being followed by all its derivatives. Thus, the entry читать is followed by the words читатель, читательница, читка, чтец, прочитать, почитать, зачитать, etc. On finding the necessary verb and its prefixed derivatives in such a dictionary, one should consult a monolingual dictionary to see whether the meaning of the prefixed verb concerned corresponds to one's intention. In this the following book may prove very useful: Тихонов А. Н. Гнездовой словообразовательный словарь русского языка. М., 1985.

6.1. How to express single and repeated actions.

If the speaker has to show how many times an action takes place (took place, will take place), he may use either perfective or imperfective verbs for this purpose: perfective verbs usually convey actions *taking place on one occasion only* (Я прочитал это письмо. Он навестил больного. Мы поцеловались), while imperfective verbs convey actions that *take place on more than one occasion* (Я звонил ей. Она навещала больного. Они целовались).

However, the imperfective verbs in the preceding sentences do not really express repetition of the actions and may be understood by the listener differently: Она навещала больного—did she do it only yesterday or did she do it regularly? Therefore, to express the fact that the action concerned took place only once or on more than one occasion, lexical means should be used to specify the meaning of the imperfective verb, such as один раз, два раза, дважды, etc.: Я дважды читал это письмо. Я несколько раз звонил ей.— Я звонил ей только один раз. Она один раз навещала больного.

In theory verbs of either aspect equally easily combine with the preceding markers of repetition/non-repetition, but to avoid deviation from the accepted usage, it is preferable to combine the lexical markers of non-repetition with perfective verbs and markers of repetition with imperfective verbs.

If the markers of repetition are words or phrases denoting an unlimited but regular repetition of an action (ежеднéвно, кáждый мéсяц, регуля́рно, по четвергáм, по чётным чи́слам, etc.), then such an action can be conveyed only by an *imperfective* verb (see also I, 5.2. for the definition of aspect).

6.2. How to express the result of an action.

If the speaker wants to convey an action which has ceased (is to cease) because it has achieved a result, a *perfective* verb should be used: Я реши́л э́ту задáчу. Онá написáла письмó. Мы изучи́ли э́тот раздéл.

It should not be thought, however, that the use of imperfective verbs in the preceding sentences would be a clear indication of a non-resultative action. Sentences of the type Я решáл э́ту задáчу. Онá писáла письмó. Мы изучáли э́тот раздéл do not at all state that their actions were without a result; they merely state that their actions were real. As to their outcome, this remains formally unexpressed, although it may be clear from the situation in which communication proceeds. Therefore, if the speaker wants to say that the action in question has remained without a result, he may use the construction consisting of an imperfective verb + the conjunction но + the negative particle не + a perfective verb: читáл, но не прочитáл (до концá); решáл, но не реши́л (потому́ что не хвати́ло врéмени); писáл, но (ещё) не написáл (всё, что хотéл).

Unlike the other characteristics of actions denoted by verbs, a result is never indicated by lexical markers. Words of the успéшно, плодотвóрно, интенси́вно, насто́йчиво, etc. type point to the character of an action which presupposes a result, but does not predetermine it. Preposition-cum-case phrases and words of the до концá, мнóго, послéдовательно, чáсто, etc. type also point to the character and limits of an action which presuppose a result, but they do not name it. Thus, the perfective aspect practically remains the sole means of expressing a resultative action.

It should be noted that although perfective verbs denoting a resultative action are derived from their imperfective counterparts with the help of various prefixes: писáть — **на**писáть, стрóить — **по**стрóить, стирáть — **вы́**стирать, дéлать — **с**дéлать, and also by replacing the suffix **-а-/-я-** with the element **-и-**: решáть — реши́ть, умоля́ть — умоли́ть, these formal means of deriving perfective verbs with a resultative meaning from their imperfective counterparts cannot be regarded as "rules", since prefixal derivation of verbs also involves a change in their lexical meaning (and not only in their aspect!): стрóить — **до**стрóить, **за**стрóить, **пере**стрóить, **на**стрóить, etc. Therefore, one should look for the necessary verb with the meaning of a result in a dictionary. (For the restrictions on the combinability of perfective verbs, see I, 5.2.)

6.3. How to express the direction of an action in space.

The direction in which an object moves is shown with the help of the preposition-cum-case form of the noun or pronoun towards which the movement proceeds (see 5.1.2.1 and 5.1.2.2).However, the verb denoting movement may also include an indication of the direction of such a movement: лете́ть "towards some place"—прилете́ть "to some place"—отлете́ть "from some place"—слете́ть "downwards"—взлете́ть "upwards", "to take off", etc.

6.3.1. *Approaching,* coming into contact with something may be denoted by the prefixes **при-** and **под- (подо-)**: **при**е́хать, **подо**дви́нуть, **при**винти́ть, **под**лете́ть. In such cases the prefix does not only denote the direction of the movement, but also the fact that the object to which the direction pointed has been reached. As a rule, the object towards which the movement proceeds is denoted by the preposition **к** and the *dative* of the appropriate noun or pronoun: пододви́нуть стул *к столу́.*

6.3.2. *Moving away,* separation from something may be denoted by the prefixes **от- (ото-)** and **у-**: **ото**дви́нуть, **от**винти́ть, **у**лете́ть (**от**лете́ть), **от**плы́ть (**у**плы́ть). As a rule, the object from which something moves away is denoted by the preposition **от** and the *genitive* of the appropriate noun or pronoun: отодви́нуть стул *от стола́.*

6.3.3. Movement up *to a certain point* in space may be indicated by the prefix **до-**: **до**е́хать, **до**вести́, **до**мча́ться. In this case the object which is the reference-point is denoted by the preposition **до** and the *genitive* of the appropriate noun or pronoun: доехать *до па́рка.*

6.3.4. An action directed *outwards* is usually indicated by the prefix **вы-** (and, rarely, by **из-**): **вы́**ехать, **вы́**плыть, **вы́**йти, **вы́**гнать (**из**гна́ть). In this case the vacated space is usually indicated with the help of the preposition **из** and the *genitive* of the appropriate noun or pronoun: вы́ехать *из па́рка.*

6.3.5. An action directed *inwards,* into an object is usually denoted by the prefix **в- (во-)**: **въ**е́хать, **в**вести́, **в**ста́вить, **в**су́нуть, **в**лить, **в**ойти́. The space into which the action intrudes is generally denoted by means of the preposition **в** and the *accusative* of the appropriate noun or pronoun: въе́хать *в парк.*

6.3.6. An action directed *downwards,* under an object is usually denoted by the prefix **под- (подо-)**: **под**ле́зть, **под**су́нуть, **под**стла́ть. The space above the reference-point where the action occurs is generally denoted by the preposition **под** and the *accusative* of the appropriate noun or pronoun: подле́зть *под стол.*

6.3.7. An action directed *upwards* is usually denoted by the prefix **вз- (вс-)** (and, less frequently, by **под-**): **вз**лете́ть, **вс**пры́гнуть (**под**пры́гнуть), **вс**плыть. The space below the reference-point where the action occurs is generally denoted by the preposition **над** and the *instrumental* of the appropriate noun or pronoun: взлете́ть *над по́лем.*

6.3.8. An action directed *past* an object is usually denoted by the prefix **про-**: **про**плы́ть, **про**скака́ть, **про**е́хать. The reference-point, which in this case is not involved with the action, may be denoted either by the preposition **ми́мо** and the *genitive*: прое́хать *ми́мо дере́вни* or by the prepositionless *accusative* of the appropriate noun or pronoun: прое́хать *дере́вню.*

6.3.9. An action directed *through* an object is usually denoted by the prefix **про-**: **про**йти́, **про**е́хать, **про**толкну́ть, **про**ползти́. The space which has thus been overcome is usually denoted by the preposition че́рез and the *accusative* of the appropriate noun or pronoun: пройти́ *че́рез парк*.

6.4. How to express the phasal characteristics of an action.

With regard to time, an action may be characterised not only with reference to the moment of speaking, i.e. as occurring before, at or after the moment of speaking (the past, the present or the future); it may also be characterised by itself, by its own phase (i.e. the initial or final phase of the action) or by its duration.

6.4.1. The beginning of an action may be denoted by the prefixes **за-, воз- (вз-)** and **по-**: **за**пе́ть, **вз**волнова́ться, **по**плы́ть. This meaning may be also conveyed by the verb нача́ть + the infinitive of the verb expressing the appropriate action. In this case only imperfective verbs can be used.

6.4.2. The *end*, the cessation of an action (not necessarily owing to the achievement of the final result) may be denoted by the prefix **от-**: **от**греме́ть, **от**говори́ть. The same meaning may also be conveyed by means of the verb ко́нчить, прекрати́ть or переста́ть + the infinitive of the verb denoting the appropriate action. In this case, too, only imperfective verbs may be used.

6.4.3. Encompassing by an action of a *limited time period* may be denoted by the prefix **по-** or **про-**: **по**сиде́ть (**про**сиде́ть), **по**говори́ть (**про**говори́ть), **по**писа́ть, **по**лежа́ть. More specifically the time period may be denoted by lexical means: пять мину́т, два часа́, сто лет, etc. (See also above, 5.2.2.)

6.4.4. Bringing the action up to a *definite moment* of time is usually denoted by the prefix **до-**: **до**сиде́ть, **до**рабо́тать, **до**жи́ть. In this case the moment which is the temporal limit is generally denoted by the preposition до and the *genitive* of the appropriate noun or pronoun: дожи́л *до ста* лет. (See also above, 5.2.3.)

6.5. How to express the relation between two actions.

6.5.1. A *repeated* action may be denoted by the prefix **пере-**: **пере**де́лать, **пере**чита́ть, **пере**ши́ть, **пере**стро́ить. For verbs with international roots this meaning may be conveyed by the prefix **ре-**: **ре**милитаризи́ровать, **ре**конструи́ровать.

6.5.2. An *additionally* performed action may be denoted by means of the prefixes **до-, под- (подо-), при-**: **до**плати́ть, **под**вари́ть, **при**купи́ть.

6.5.3. *Cancellation* of an action may be conveyed by the prefixes **раз- (рас-)** and **от-**: **раз**люби́ть, **от**кле́ить, **раз**ду́мать. The same meaning can be expressed lexically by the phrase бо́льше не.

6.6. How to express various degrees of the intensity of an action.

6.6.1. The intensity, thoroughness of an action may be expressed by the prefixes **из- (ис-), на-, рас-** and a number of others, and the unpredictability of its form of expression makes it similar to the meaning of result: суши́ть — вы́сушить — иссуши́ть, гла́дить — отгла́дить — нагла́дить, толсте́ть — потолсте́ть — растолсте́ть. This meaning can also be expressed by the addition to the verb with a resultative meaning of adverbs of the о́чень, тща́тельно, си́льно, etc. type.

6.6.2. The excessive intensity (or duration) of an action leading to an undesirable result may be expressed by means of the prefix **пере-**: **пере**гре́ть, **пере**стара́ться, **пере**лежа́ть.

6.6.3. The slight (not corresponding to the idea of the norm) intensity of an action may be expressed by means of the prefixes **по-, под- (подо-), при-**: **по**отста́ть, **под**бодри́ть, **при**глуши́ть, and also **полу-** and **недо-**: **полу**откры́ть, **недо**вы́полнить.

6.6.4. The plurality of the objects acted upon may be expressed by means of the prefixes **из-, о- (обо-), пере-, на-**: **изъ**е́здить (всю страну́), **о**бе́гать (все вокза́лы), **пере**глота́ть (все табле́тки), **на**собира́ть (мно́го материа́ла).

7. How to modify the meaning of a person or object denoted by a noun with the help of adjectival gender forms, noun number forms and other means.

7.1. How to express the sex of a living being.

7.1.1. How to express the female sex of a living being.

7.1.1.1. The female sex of a living being may be expressed by the appropriate *word*: ку́рица — пету́х, коро́ва — бык, у́тка — се́лезень.

7.1.1.2. The female sex of a person may be expressed by the *endings* of the feminine variant of the adjectival (ру́сска**я**, заве́дующа**я**) or mixed declension (Петро́в**а**, Петро́в**ой**).

7.1.1.3. Words denoting living beings of the female sex can be derived from masculine nouns with the help of *suffixes*: студе́нт — студе́нтка, учи́тель — учи́тельница, геро́й — геро́иня, актёр — актри́са, юбиля́р — юбиля́рша, сто́рож — сторожи́ха, бегу́н — бегу́нья. The number of such suffixes is fairly large. The rules determining their choice for each specific masculine noun are very inconsistent. Some masculine nouns denoting living beings either give no feminine derivatives at all or such derivatives have a stylistic nuance not always intended by the speaker or writer. That is why, knowing the masculine noun denoting a living being and wanting to derive its feminine counterpart by means of a suffix, one should always check one's supposition with a dictionary.

An exception is the derivation of nouns denoting female beings from masculine nouns with the suffix **-тель** or **-ун**. In the former case the female sex is expressed by the suffix **-ниц(а)**: люби́тель — люби́тельница, чита́тель — чита́тельница, учи́тель — учи́тельница; in the latter, it is expressed by the suffix **-j(а)**: бегу́н — бегу́нья, колду́н — колду́нья.

7.1.1.4. For nouns of the *common* gender the female sex may be expressed with the help of feminine *attributes* of these nouns (adjectives —

ordinary and pronominal—and participles), which agree with them. This is possible for the following nouns of the common gender: бедня́га, белору́чка, бродя́га, брюзга́, бу́ка, всезна́йка, вы́скочка, грязну́ля, егоза́, забия́ка, зади́ра, зазна́йка, за́йка, замара́шка, замухры́шка, зану́да, запева́ла, заправи́ла, зева́ка, злю́ка, зубри́ла, кале́ка, капризу́ля, копу́ша, кривля́ка, ла́комка, левша́, лежебо́ка, лома́ка, малю́тка, меня́ла, мя́мля, неве́жа, неве́жда, невиди́мка, недотёпа, недотро́га, недоу́чка, непосе́да, неря́ха, обжо́ра, одино́чка, пла́кса, подли́за, попроша́йка, простофи́ля, пустоме́ля, рази́ня, размазня́, растрёпа, растя́па, ро́хля, самоу́чка, свято́ша, сирота́, скря́га, сладкоё́жка, сластёна, со́ня, тёзка, тихо́ня, тупи́ца, уби́йца, у́мница, ханжа́, чистю́ля, я́беда.

7.1.1.5. Many masculine nouns denoting members of a profession or trade or people's position may denote female persons if the *past tense verbs* (or verbs in the subjunctive mood) are used in the *feminine gender*: врач пришла́, дире́ктор сказа́ла бы, профе́ссор вы́ступила, etc.

7.1.1.6. The female sex of a living being may sometimes be expressed by adding the word са́мка to the names of animals (са́мка оле́ня, са́мка кита́) or the word же́нщина, де́вушка or стару́ха to the words denoting members of a profession or trade or people's position: агроно́м, молода́я краси́вая же́нщина; инжене́р, де́вушка лет двадцати́ двух; стару́ха-ня́нька.

7.1.2. How to express the male sex of a living being.

7.1.2.1. The male sex of a living being may be expressed by the appropriate *noun* which already has the meaning of the male sex. This meaning may be contained either in the root of the noun concerned (бара́н, оте́ц, сын), or in its suffix (москв**и́ч**, кита́**ец**) or ending (заве́дующ**ий**, ру́сск**ий**).

7.1.2.2. However, when a masculine noun denotes a member of a profession or trade or a person's position, the male sex may be indicated by introducing such words as мужчи́на, стари́к, ю́ноша, ма́льчик. For example: агроно́м, мужчи́на высо́кого ро́ста, etc. If a masculine or feminine noun denotes an animal without specifying its sex, the latter may be indicated by the introduction of the word саме́ц: саме́ц черепа́хи.

7.1.2.3. The *masculine gender* of the adjectives (ordinary and pronominal) and participles which agree with nouns of the common gender (see above, 7.1.1.4) indicates the male sex of the persons denoted by these nouns.

7.1.2.4. The *masculine gender* of the past tense verbs and verbs of the subjunctive mood which agree with nouns denoting members of a profession or trade or people's position makes the meaning "the male sex" more likely, but not certain. Thus, for example, дире́ктор сказа́л or врач попроси́л is more likely to refer to a male person; however, it is not conclusively so (see below, 7.1.3).

7.1.3. How to leave the sex characteristic of a living being unspecified.

If the speaker (or writer) does not want to specify the sex of a living being, he should, firstly, choose a noun whose root, suffix or ending does not include an indication of its sex (see 7.1.1 and 7.1.2). Secondly, he should avoid using adjectives (ordinary or pronominal) and participles and also past tense and subjunctive mood verbs agreeing with the noun chosen. The use of masculine forms agreeing with a masculine noun or feminine forms agreeing with a feminine noun leaves the sex of the being denoted by the noun unexpressed. For example the sex of the living beings in the sentences У нас был хороший директор. Куковала невидимая кукушка. Приплыл огромный кит is not-indicated.

The sex also remains unexpressed in the cases when the noun concerned is used either in the plural (Пришли учителя. Актёры играли прекрасно.) or in the generalised, non-specific, generic meaning (День машиностроителя. Подарок первокласснику.).

7.2. How to express a quantity of objects or persons.

It is obvious that nouns include words which denote objects and phenomena that are uncountable. As a rule, these are nouns denoting aggregates of objects or persons (детвора, листва, финансы, etc.), substances that can be measured but not counted (газ, нефть, сливки, духи, etc.), abstract ideas of qualities and processes (белизна, смех, блеск, хлопоты, дебаты, etc.), and games (преферанс, шахматы, etc.). (See also II C, 1.1 and 1.2.)

7.2.1. How to express the plurality of objects or persons.

7.2.1.1. As a rule, to express the plurality of objects, i. e. not one, but more than one, two, three, four, etc., the *plural* form should be used. For example, the dictionary form denotes one object (дом, дорога, окно, etc.), whereas many such objects are denoted by the plural (дома, дороги, окна, etc.).

7.2.1.2. To express an *indefinite* plurality of objects, the words много, несколько, мало, etc. + the genitive plural may be used: много студентов, несколько домов.

7.2.1.3. To express a *specific* number of objects a phrase consisting of a cardinal numeral and a noun should be used: два студента, двадцать студентов. (For the forms of the numerals and nouns used in such cases, see below, D, 3.)

7.2.1.4. The plurality of countable nouns whose dictionary form is plural can be expressed only with the help of the words несколько, много, мало, nouns of the сотня, тысяча, десяток type, and also the collective numerals двое, трое, четверо, пятеро, шестеро, семеро, восьмеро, девятеро, десятеро, which in the nominative and the accusative identical with the nominative combine with the genitive of a noun: несколько саней, четверо суток, двое брюк, много ворот. In other instances the case forms of the numeral and the noun coincide: от нескольких саней, о двоих брюках, к многим воротам. These nouns are as follows: брюки (брюк), будни (будней), весы (весов), вилы (вил), ворота (ворот), грабли (граблей), гусли (гуслей), девчата (девчат), дети (детей), духи (духов), жабры (жабр), именины (именин), кавычки (кавычек), каникулы (каникул), качели (качелей), клещи (клещей), куранты (курантов), люди (людей), мемуары (мемуаров), мостки (мостков), ножницы (ножниц), ножны (ножен), носилки (носилок), очки (очков), перила (перил), поручни (поручней), похороны (похорон), проводы (проводов), салазки (саля́зок), са́ни (сане́й), се́ни (сене́й), сли́вки (сли́вок), стропи́ла (стропи́л), су́тки (су́ток), счёты (счётов), трусы́ (трусо́в), хло́пья (хло́пьев), часы́ (часо́в), шарова́ры (шарова́р), шо́рты (шорт), штаны́ (штано́в), щипцы́ (щипцо́в), я́сли (я́слей).

7.2.1.5. The plurality of the objects denoted by any of the group of nouns which do not change for number and case, of the ателье́, интервью́, пари́, такси́, type, is indicated—in addition to the use of the relevant lexical markers—by the plural form of the adjectives (ordinary and pronominal) and participles agreeing with them, and also by the plural form of the past tense and subjunctive mood verbs. For example, the sentences Стоя́ли но́вые такси́. Даны́ ва́жные интервью́. В на́шем го́роде откры́ты но́вые телевизио́нные ателье́ convey many objects called такси́, интервью́, ателье́. (See also II C, 2.2.)

7.2.1.6. With some nouns which have the forms of both numbers, the meaning of plurality of objects (and also their aggregation) may be conveyed by means of suffixes; cf. листы́—ли́стья and листва́, учи́тель—учителя́ and учи́тельство, студе́нт—студе́нты and студе́нчество, ребёнок—де́ти and детвора́. However, these formations are not regular and some of them have a low colloquial (popular) stylistic nuance: шофёр—шофёры and шофернл́. Therefore, one may use them only after ascertaining their full meaning and stylistic value in a dictionary.

7.2.1.7. Occasionally the plurality of objects is also conveyed by a singular form, which in such a case stands for the whole class of identical objects or persons: Тури́ст до́лжен люби́ть приро́ду (i. e. not one specific tourist, but any tourist or all the tourists). Здесь растёт сосна́ (i. e. not just one pine-tree, but trees of that species, pine-trees). (See also II C, 1.1.)

Thus, the plurality of objects can be indicated either very imprecisely (with the help of plural endings, the words не́сколько, мно́го, ма́сса, мно́жество, etc.) or quite accurately (два, три, деся́ток, трина́дцать, сто, etc.).

7.2.1.8. In colloquial speech a plurality of objects can be conveyed by means of sentences consisting of only one word—the genitive plural form (pronounced with a special intonation): Цвето́в! Зри́телей! Such sentences are equivalent to the sentences: Как мно́го (ско́лько) здесь цвето́в! Как мно́го (ско́лько) здесь зри́телей! (See also II C, 1.4.)

7.2.1.9. To convey a plurality of objects *approximately*, the word о́коло or приблизи́тельно may be used before the numeral: —Далеко́ ли до дере́вни? —Óколо пяти́ киломе́тров or: Приблизи́тельно пять киломе́тров. (Óколо is followed by the genitive; and приблизи́тельно, by the nominative.)

In Russian an approximate number of objects may be expressed by a change in the usual word order, i. e. by placing the numeral not before the noun as usual, but *after* it: Мы прошли́ киломе́тров пять. Ему́ запла́тят за э́то рубле́й се́мьдесят. Ей бы́ло лет три́дцать пять. (Compare this with the exact indication: пять киломе́тров, се́мьдесят рубле́й, три́дцать пять лет.)

7.2.2. How to express a single object or person.

7.2.2.1. To express a *single* object or person, the singular of a noun should be used: На горе́ стои́т дом. Прие́хала маши́на. На у́лицу вы́шел ма́льчик. Since the singular of a noun does not always have the meaning of singleness (see II C, 1.1), to denote a single object, the word оди́н may be added to the noun, which, depending on the gender of that noun, may take the form оди́н (for the masculine: оди́н дом), одна́ (for the feminine: одна́ дере́вня) or одно́ (for the neuter: одно́ жела́ние).

7.2.2.2. For the nouns which denote objects that can be counted, but whose dictionary form is plural (for a list of the most common of such words, see above, 7.2.1.4), the use of одни́ is the only possibility of indicating a single object: стоя́ли одни́ са́ни, опозда́л на одни́ су́тки, поста́вили одни́ каче́ли.

7.2.2.3. The meaning of singleness of nouns which do not change for number and case can be conveyed by the appropriate gender form of the word оди́н: оди́н атташе́, одна́ ле́ди, одно́ меню́, and also by the singular form of the adjectives (ordinary and pronominal), participles and finite verbs agreeing with them: Э́то кафе́ находи́лось в це́нтре го́рода. Судьёй был назна́чен пена́льти. В углу́ стои́т ста́рое пиани́но. In all these cases single objects are clearly meant, denoted by the appropriate nouns.

When denoting the singleness of an object by means of the appropriate gender forms of the word оди́н, one should bear in mind that оди́н may also have the meaning of "some", "one", "a certain", the idea of indefiniteness reflecting either the speaker's real ignorance of the object spoken about (Подхо́дит ко мне на у́лице оди́н челове́к) or his subjective unwillingness to name that object (Мне сказа́л об э́том оди́н челове́к). In addition, the word оди́н may have the meaning of "only", "exclusively", "nothing but". Thus, for example, the sentence Здесь растёт одна́ сосна́ may be used to convey a single object, a single indefinite object or the fact that in the place concerned there is nothing but that object (in the generalised, collective meaning as an aggregate of identical objects, i. e. "only pine-trees grow here" and there are no other species of trees, such as fir-trees, birches, oaks, etc.).

The fact that the word оди́н is used to denote a single object may be emphasised, as in the following sentences: Здесь растёт одна́ сосна́. Одино́ко стои́т она́, откры́тая со́лнцу и всем ветра́м. Ни де́ревца, ни ку́стика вокру́г неё. (Compare: Здесь растёт одна́ сосна́, и́зредка попада́ется берёза.)

7.2.2.4. In some groups of nouns denoting aggregates of discrete units, one unit of an aggregate can be indicated with the help of either derivational or lexical means. For example: шокола́д — шокола́дка and пли́тка шокола́да, лук — лу́ковица and голо́вка лу́ка, карто́фель, карто́фелина and клу́бень карто́феля. Some nouns can denote both an aggregate of discrete objects and one unit of such an aggregate: морко́вь, свёкла, я́года. With some nouns one unit of an aggregate is denoted by derivational means alone: изю́м — изю́минка, соло́ма — соло́минка, whereas with others it is denoted only by lexical means: капу́ста — коча́н капу́сты, чесно́к — голо́вка чеснока́.

8. How to express a feature or attribute of an object or person by means of noun case and preposition-cum-case forms.

An attribute of an object or person is usually expressed by an *adjective* which agrees with the noun denoting that object or person: высо́-

кий мужчи́на, полоса́тое пла́тье, ба́бушкина я́блоня, телефо́нный разгово́р, окружна́я доро́га, etc. Not infrequently the same meaning can also be expressed with the help of the *case forms of nouns* with or without a preposition.

1. To express the fact that an object or person *belongs* to another object or person, the construction in which the noun denoting the "possessor" takes the *genitive* is used: дом отца́, бе́рег реки́, верши́на горы́, кни́га сестры́, etc. In this case the person who is the possessor may be denoted by a possessive adjective of the type отцо́в (о́тчий, отцо́вский) дом, дя́дина ко́мната, ба́бушкина я́блоня. However, adjectives of this type can be derived from an insignificant number of nouns denoting relatives: оте́ц — отцо́в, па́па — па́пин, ма́ма — ма́мин, дя́дя — дя́дин, тётя — тётин, де́душка — де́душкин, ба́бушка — ба́бушкин, брат — бра́тов, сестра́ — се́стрин.

2. A characteristic of a person or object connected with the presence on his/its surface of other objects is conveyed by the preposition в followed by the *prepositional*: лицо́ в весну́шках, не́бо в звёздах, же́нщина в платке́, стари́к в шине́ли.

3. If a person or object is characterised by his/its possession of another object (or feature, trait, quality or property), then this characteristic is conveyed by the preposition с followed by the *instrumental*: да́ма с соба́чкой, чай с лимо́ном, го́род с миллио́нным населе́нием (с населе́нием в оди́н миллио́н), челове́к со стра́нностями, стари́к с бородо́й. However if, on the contrary, a person or object is characterised by the lack of another object (or feature), then this characteristic is conveyed by the preposition без followed by the *genitive*: челове́к без че́сти, чай без лимо́на, не́бо без звёзд, день без забо́т.

4. A characteristic of a person denoted by the word челове́к, мужчи́на, же́нщина, ма́льчик, де́вочка, ю́ноша or де́вушка may be conveyed by the *genitive* of the phrase "an adjective (numeral) + a noun": (челове́к) большо́го ума́, ре́дких спосо́бностей, удиви́тельной красоты́, большо́го се́рдца, широ́кой души́, весёлого нра́ва, тридцати́ лет. In this case the person is characterised by such words as, for example, ка́чества, спосо́бности, ум, хара́ктер, во́ля, доброта́, му́жество, рост, вес. The same construction can also be used to characterise an object: раство́р высо́кой концентра́ции, существи́тельное сре́днего ро́да, догово́р со́рок восьмо́го го́да.

5. If an object is characterised through the material it consists of, or is made of, this characteristic is conveyed by the preposition из followed by the *genitive* of a noun: сала́т из огурцо́в, буке́т из роз, украше́ния из янтаря́, стена́ из кирпича́.

6. When an object is not made of the material concerned, but only looks as if it were made of it, the preposition под followed by the *accusative* of a noun is used: лю́стра под хруста́ль (i. e. not a crystal chandelier, but one that looks as if it were made of crystal), пальто́ под за́мшу, бу́сы под янта́рь.

7. If a person or object is characterised by his/its size, this характеristic, when compared with another object, is usually conveyed by the

preposition с followed by the *accusative*: отве́рстие с ладо́нь, лицо́ с кулачо́к, ма́льчик-с-па́льчик.

8. When an object is characterised by its size expressed in some conventional units, this characteristic is conveyed by the preposition в followed by the *accusative* of a numeral or noun with a quantitative meaning + the *genitive* singular or plural: кни́га в ты́сячу страни́ц, пре́мия в сто рубле́й, мото́р в сто лошади́ных сил, ла́мпочка в шестьдеся́т ватт, расстоя́ние в два киломе́тра.

9. When a source of information is to be characterised from the point of view of its specific content, either the preposition по followed by the *dative* is used (кни́ги по иску́сству, ле́кции по языкозна́нию, семина́р по фи́зике) or the preposition о (об) followed by the *prepositional* (расска́зы о худо́жниках, све́дения об успева́емости, отчёт о рабо́те, спра́вка об эффекти́вности).

Less frequently (and usually in colloquial speech) the preposition про followed by the *accusative* is used (фильм про любо́вь, расска́з про моряко́в). In all such cases the construction with the preposition о is also possible (see above).

10. While a characteristic of an object which belongs to another object in toto is conveyed by the genitive without a preposition (see above), a characteristic of an object which belongs to another object but exists separately from it is conveyed by the preposition от followed by the *genitive*: ключ от две́ри, пружи́на от часо́в; cf. also но́жка стола́ and но́жка от стола́, ру́чка портфе́ля and ру́чка от портфе́ля, обло́жка кни́ги and обло́жка от кни́ги, etc.

11. Not infrequently an object or person possesses a feature which characterises it/him from the point of view of its/his purpose. In such cases either the construction with the preposition для followed by the *genitive* is used if the characterised object is actually used for a definite purpose (по́лка для книг, пода́рок для бра́та, принадле́жности для бритья́) or the construction with the preposition на followed by the *accusative* if the characterised object is intended for a certain purpose, but in fact this purpose has not yet been achieved (материа́л на костю́м, де́ньги на биле́т). (See also III C, 5.4.)

12. To characterise an object or person by its/his location (дом у доро́ги, дере́вня за реко́й, де́ньги на биле́т) or direction (путь в Москву́, путь на Кавка́з, доро́га к до́му, приве́т из Ленингра́да, приве́т с Украи́ны, грибы́ из-под Калу́ги, уда́р из-за угла́), the same preposition-cum-case constructions are used that convey the place and direction after verbs (see also III C, 5.1).

8.1. How to express the degrees of a quality or property.

A greater degree of a quality or property can be expressed either by the comparative degree of an adjective (see III A, 2.4) or by the construction consisting of бо́лее + the positive degree of the relevant adjective.

A lesser degree of a quality or property is expressed by a similar construction consisting of ме́нее + the positive degree of the relevant adjective.

These constructions are realised in the following regular patterns: бо́лее + an adjective + чем; ме́нее + an adjective + чем: Брат бо́лее высо́кий, чем сестра́. Фильм ме́нее интере́сный, чем спекта́кль. The meaning of a greater degree of a quality conveyed by the comparative degree may be realised in these constructions: Брат вы́ше, чем сестра́.Спекта́кль интере́снее, чем фильм, and also in constructions without чем, but with the genitive form of the noun which possesses the lesser degree of the quality substituted for the nominative form: Брат вы́ше сестры́. Спекта́кль интере́снее фи́льма.

The superlative degree, which expresses the greatest degree of a quality or property, also has two forms: a synthetic (suffixal) form: велича́йший, добре́йший, and an analytical one, built with the help of the pronoun са́мый: са́мый краси́вый, са́мый высо́кий, са́мый о́пытный.

The suffixal superlative degree may be used to convey not only the fact that a person or object possesses a higher degree of the quality concerned than any other person or object, but also the fact that a person or object simply possesses a high degree of this quality.

The degree of a quality greater than the norm can also be expressed by means of the adverbs о́чень, весьма́, исключи́тельно, чрезвыча́йно, невообрази́мо, etc.: о́чень плохо́й, весьма́ стра́нный, чрезвыча́йно весёлый.

The degree of a quality lesser than the norm can be expressed by means of the adverbs немно́го, не́сколько, слегка́, чуть-чу́ть: немно́го стра́нный, слегка́ уста́лый, чуть-чу́ть гру́стный.

With some adjectives the degree of a quality greater than the norm can be expressed by the suffixes **-ущ-/-ющ-** and **-енн-**: худю́щий, толсте́нный, the prefixes **пре-**: преми́лый, предо́брый, and **раз- (рас-)**: разлюбе́зный, распрекра́сный, and also by the repetition of an adjective, of the чи́стый-чи́стый (or чи́стый-пречи́стый) type. All such derivatives occur only in colloquial speech. A lesser degree of a quality can be expressed by means of the suffix **-оват-**: скуднова́тый, глупова́тый, краснова́тый.

The actual existence of such suffixal derivatives must be ascertained in a dictionary.

9. How to express in Russian the meanings expressed in other languages by grammatical means.

In the preceding paragraphs we discussed the meanings which are expressed in Russian by the grammatical means most of which have equivalents in other languages. However, there are a number of meanings expressed in other languages by grammatical means which are lacking in Russian. Among them are (1) the idea of the definiteness or indefiniteness of an object; (2) characterisation of an action as taking place at a certain moment as distinct from an action taking place habitually; and (3) characterisation of actions as preceding a certain moment of time or another action. These meanings are expressed in Russian either with the help of lexical means or are not expressed formally at all.

9.1. How to express the definiteness or indefiniteness of an object or person.

In many languages the meaning of the definiteness or indefiniteness of an object is conveyed by articles. There are no articles in Russian; however, this meaning can be conveyed by lexical means.

9.1.1. To convey an unfamiliar, indefinite object or person, i. e. to express the meaning corresponding to that conveyed by the *indefinite article*, the word какóй-то or нéкий in the appropriate gender, number and case is added to the noun denoting this object or person: Какóй-то студéнт пришёл сдавáть экзáмен. The utmost degree of the indefiniteness of an object may be expressed by means of the pronominal words ктó-то, чтó-то, ктó-либо, чтó-либо, ктó-нибудь, чтó-нибудь, кое-ктó, кое-чтó: Пусть ктó-нибудь (any one out of many) отвéтит на мой вопрóс. Я чтó-то (something very indefinite) слы́шал об э́том.

9.1.2. To convey a definite, specific, familiar object or person, i. e. to express the meaning corresponding to that conveyed by the *definite article*, the word э́тот, тот сáмый, извéстный or вышеупомя́нутый in the appropriate gender, number and case is added to the noun denoting this object or person: Э́тот человéк посовéтовал нам так поступи́ть. В рабóте мы руковóдствовались вышеупомя́нутыми решéниями.

9.1.3. A text may not contain a formal indication as to whether the object concerned is definite or indefinite. In such a case the reader infers this from a broader context. To avoid a possible misunderstanding, it is desirable to use various qualifiers to characterise each object as distinct from the other similar objects (such as possessive pronouns, the contrastive use of the pronouns э́тот and тот, and other means). In this case the information contained in such a Russian text will be more precise than in a similar text in another language, in which the article would be the only qualifier.

9.2. How to express the contrast between an action performed at a specific moment and an action performed habitually.

In a number of languages actions taking place at a specific moment and actions taking place habitually are conveyed by different grammatical forms. Such forms do not exist in Russian. Therefore, Russian sentences of the type Он кýрит. Онá покупáла я́годы на ры́нке. Мы ходи́ли в теáтр are, strictly speaking, ambiguous. They may express either an action taking place at a definite, specific moment (cf. Сейчáс он стои́т в коридóре и кýрит. Лéтом онá покупáла я́годы на ры́нке. В прóшлом годý мы ходи́ли в теáтр.) or an action taking place habitually (cf. Он кýрит, поэ́тому у негó больны́е лёгкие. Обы́чно онá покупáла я́годы на ры́нке, но сегóдня онá не ходи́ла на ры́нок. Мы чáсто ходи́ли в теáтр, поэ́тому нам здесь нé было скýчно.).

9.2.1. To show that the action concerned took place *only at a specific moment*, various lexical markers denoting a limited space of time should be used, of the type однáжды, оди́н раз, вчерá, сию́ минýту, в настоя́щий момéнт, в прóшлую суббóту, etc. Lexical markers of the type с утрá до вéчера, с девяти́ до шести́, с мáя по октя́брь, etc. do not remove the ambiguity, since their presence can indicate both a single occurrence of an action within the length of time specified and its regular (daily, yearly) occurrence.

If such words and phrases as до́лго, продолжи́тельное вре́мя, (весь) век, (весь) год, (всю) неде́лю, (всё) у́тро, (весь) ве́чер, etc. are chosen to indicate the limited duration of an action, then one should use either an imperfective verb or a perfective verb with the prefix **про-**, which has the meaning of an action limited in time: про́жил год, прорабо́тал неде́лю, прогуля́л весь день, проспа́л всё у́тро.

9.2.2. To emphasise the fact that an action has a *habitual* character, not contained within any strict time limits, one can use such words and phrases as без конца́, всё (он всё чита́л и чита́л) (with the meaning of a continuing process), ежедне́вно, ежеча́сно, ежемину́тно, ежеме́сячно, до́лго-до́лго, несконча́емо, etc., вечера́ми, часа́ми, дня́ми, неде́лями, су́тками, месяца́ми, etc., ка́ждый ве́чер, ка́ждый день, etc., по вечера́м, по утра́м, etc., ритми́чно, регуля́рно, периоди́чески, системати́чески, etc. Only *imperfective* verbs can combine with such markers. In addition to imperfective verbs, the words всегда́, иногда́, обы́чно, ре́дко, и́зредка, ча́сто can also combine with finite perfective verb forms, which in this case, however, do not acquire the meaning of a habitual, repeated action: иногда́ ска́жет что́-нибудь смешно́е, ре́дко посмо́трит на меня́. (See also III C, 5.2.2.4.)

Not infrequently a sentence does not contain a formal expression of a direct indication of what action—concrete or habitual—is implied. Then the speaker or writer must show in the general context whether it is a concrete fact or some habitual, repeated situation that is implied.

9.3. How to express the sequence of actions preceding or following the moment of speaking.

In a number of languages actions occurring at different times, either preceding the moment of speaking or following it, are denoted by means of various grammatical forms. In Russian there are no grammatical means distinguishing the past and the before-past, and the future and the before-future.

To emphasise the fact that one of the actions preceding the moment of speaking occurred before the other(s), the words (or phrases) снача́ла (сперва́, пре́жде) — пото́м (по́сле, зате́м), пре́жде чем, до того́ как (по́сле того́ как) are used: Снача́ла поду́мал, пото́м сказа́л. Пре́жде чем сказа́л, поду́мал. До того́ как сказа́л, поду́мал. The same markers can also be used to show that one of the actions following the moment of speaking will take place after the other(s): Сперва́ поду́мает, зате́м ска́жет. По́сле того́ как поду́мает, ска́жет. До того́ как ска́жет, поду́мает.

Not infrequently the sequence of the actions preceding or following the moment of speaking is not indicated lexically, but is shown by the order of the verbs themselves: the verb denoting the action occurring earlier in absolute time takes the first place, followed by the verbs denoting the actions occurring later in absolute time: поду́мал и сказа́л (first he thought and then said), поду́мает и ска́жет (first he will think and then say).

D. WHAT FORMAL RULES SHOULD BE FOLLOWED WHEN BUILDING A SENTENCE

When formulating one's thought in Russian, one should not merely place the units that express one's meaning side by side. One should also take into account the rules that determine the purely formal organisation of phrases and sentences in Russian.

1. What the form of a verb should be, depending on the grammatical features of the word which denotes the object characterised by the verb.

If a sentence includes a past tense indicative mood verb form or a subjunctive mood verb form, then this form takes *the same number*—and in the singular *the same gender*—as the noun (or pronoun) which denotes the object or person characterised by that form: Ле́то пришло́. Он чита́л. Она́ чита́ла. Е́сли бы наступи́ла зима́! Де́ти гуля́ли. Мы наде́ялись.

If a sentence includes a present or future tense indicative mood verb form, then this form takes *the same person and number* as the object or person which it characterises and which is expressed by a personal pronoun: Я жду. Ты молчи́шь. Она́ отдыха́ет. Мы рабо́таем. Они́ зна́ют, and the same *number* as the object or person which it characterises and which is expressed by a noun: Лес шуми́т. Снега́ та́ют.

When "the characterised object or person" is a phrase consisting of a numeral and a noun, the finite verb form should be used in the plural in accordance with the actual number of the persons: пришли́ де́сять челове́к, два ора́тора заяви́ли.

If "the characterised object or person" is a group of more than one person (of the брат с сестро́й, я и О́ля type), the finite verb form should be used in the plural: Вошли́ дед с ма́терью. Я и сестра́ счита́ем. Ты и сестра́ ду́маете. Брат и сестра́ счита́ют.

2.1. What the form of the adjectives and participles which qualify nouns should be.

Long-form adjectives and participles take *the same gender, number and case* as the singular nouns they qualify and the same *number* and *case* as the plural nouns they qualify: у но́вого стро́ящегося зда́ния, об э́тих но́вых стро́ящихся зда́ниях.

If a long-form adjective or participle qualifies a phrase consisting of a cardinal numeral in the nominative or the accusative identical with the nominative and a noun, then in the case of a *masculine* or *neuter* noun it takes the *genitive* plural: четы́ре ста́рых до́ма, сто неожи́данных вопро́сов, три кра́йних окна́, and in the case of a *feminine* noun either the *nominative* or the *genitive*: три молоды́е же́нщины and три молоды́х же́нщины, четы́ре золоты́х и три сере́бряные меда́ли. However, if the numeral (and the noun) are in any other case form, then the usual agreement between the adjectives and participles and the nouns which they qualify takes place: о четырёх стро́ящихся но́вых дома́х, к трём сере́бряным меда́лям, etc.

If a long-form adjective qualifies simultaneously a number of words connected by means of conjunctions, of the сад и огород, день да ночь type, or by means of prepositions, of the отец с матерью type, then the adjective takes the plural: маленькие сад и огород, у моих отца с матерью.

Pronominal nouns with the meaning of indefiniteness, of the кто-то (masculine), что-нибудь (neuter) or некто (masculine) type, are qualified by long-form adjectives and participles in the same way as ordinary nouns of the respective genders are: кто-то высокий, что-то чёрное. Other pronominal nouns (personal, reflexive, negative), which combine with adjectives extremely rarely, also require that the adjective should take the form determined by the gender of the pronominal noun concerned.

2.2. What the form of the words один, два, оба and полтора should be in combination with a noun.

When combined with a noun, один, like an adjective, takes the same gender, number and case as this noun: один дом, одна лошадь, одно поле, одни сани.

If the numerals два, оба and полтора combine with masculine or neuter nouns and are used in the nominative (or the accusative identical with the nominative), they should take the forms два, оба, полтора (часа, окна). If they combine with feminine nouns, they should take the forms две, обе, полторы (минуты, тетради).

In the other cases the stem of the numeral оба is обо- with the appropriate endings, and the stem of the numeral обе is обе- with the appropriate endings: об обоих братьях, but об обеих сёстрах. (see also 3).

2.3. How to determine the gender of a noun from its dictionary form.

A speaker or a writer may have some difficulty in inferring the gender of a noun whose dictionary form he knows. To resolve this difficulty, he need not refer to the dictionary every time: the gender of a noun can often be determined by the appearance of its dictionary form.

2.3.1. If the dictionary form of a noun ends in **-а** or **-я**, this noun belongs to the *feminine* gender. Exceptions to this rule are: (1) nouns denoting male persons: юноша, дедушка, Вася, etc. (They belong to the masculine gender.); (2) nouns denoting people of either sex: невежа, сирота, соня, etc. (They belong either to the common, or the masculine, or the feminine gender.) (See III C, 7.1.1.4.); (3) indeclinable nouns: антраша, Золя, etc. (They may belong to any gender, including feminine.); (4) nouns with the augmentative suffix **-ина**, usually occurring in colloquial speech: домина, холодина, etc. (They belong either to the masculine or the feminine gender.)

2.3.2. If the dictionary form of a noun ends in a *consonant*, this noun belongs to the *masculine* gender. Exceptions to this rule are some nouns, either unchangeable or borrowed from other languages, and compound abbreviated words: мадáм, ГЭС. (They belong to the feminine gender.)

2.3.3. If the dictionary form of a noun ends in **-o** or **-e**, this noun belongs to the *neuter* gender. Exceptions to this rule are: (1) unchangeable nouns, either borrowed from other languages or compound abbreviated: кóфе, ронó, НÁТО; (2) nouns with the diminutive suffix **-ишк(о)**: городи́шко, заводи́шко, etc. (They may belong either to the masculine or to the neuter gender.)

2.3.4. If the dictionary form of a noun ends in **-ь**, the gender of such a noun can be ascertained only from a dictionary.

3. What the form of a noun should be in combination with a numeral.

If the numeral полторá (полторы́), два (две), óба (óбе), три or четы́ре is in the nominative (or the accusative identical with the nominative), then the noun which combines with it is used in the *genitive singular*: полторá рубля́, две подру́ги, óба герóя, три урóка. The same rule applies to the compound numerals whose last element is два, три, четы́ре, of the type двáдцать три, сéмьдесят два, двéсти сóрок четы́ре.

If the preceding numerals are not in the nominative (or the accusative identical with the nominative), but in some other case, then the nouns connected with them are used in the plural and the cases of the numeral and the noun coincide: от двух друзéй, на трёх домáх, к полу́тора страни́цам.

If nouns combine with any of the other numerals except those mentioned above, whether cardinal or collective (see I, 3), and if these numerals are in the nominative (or the accusative identical with the nominative), then these nouns are used in the *genitive plural*: пять домóв, семь часóв, сóрок разбóйников. In all the other cases the nouns are also used in the plural and the cases of the numerals and the nouns coincide: к пяти́ часáм, о восьми́ прия́телях, с двумястáми студéнтами.

The collective numerals двóе, трóе, чéтверо, etc. are used only with nouns denoting male persons: двóе друзéй, трóе студéнтов; however, два дру́га and три студéнта are also possible.

4. What the form of an adjective or participle characterising an object should be.

In sentences of the Ребёнок послу́шный. Ребёнок послу́шен type the adjective (or participle) takes the same gender and number as the noun which denotes the object characterised by this adjective (or participle): Э́та кóмната твоя́. Э́ти игру́шки óбщие. Решéние при́нято. Хорóши́ лéтние вечерá.

In such cases the participle usually occurs in the short form, while the use of the short or long form of the adjective depends on a number of circumstances.

If an adjective has only the long or the short form, then in sentences of this type the form which the adjective has is used.

However, if an adjective has both the short and the long form, then in sentences of this type either form may be used without affecting the meaning: Дорóга длúнная and Дорóга длиннá; Обéд вкýсный and Обéд вкýсен.

Only the *long* form is generally used when the adjective occurs together with a finite notional or semi-auxiliary verb: Дéти вы́глядели довóльными.

Only the *short* form of the adjectives благодáрен, вы́нужден, вúден, виновáт, готóв, достóин, довóлен, жив, знакóм, намéрен, обя́зан, пóлон, похóж, прав, рáвен, соглáсен, сыт, цел is used to denote a quality which is not permanent, but exists only at a certain time: Ребёнок не виновáт. Вы прáвы. Я сыт.

Only the *short* form is also used when the adjective is extended by other words (a noun with or without a preposition or an infinitive): Град опáсен для посéвов. Он спосóбен так поступúть, or by clauses: Я счáстлив, что вúжу вас. Он довóлен, что вы емý позвонúли.

Only the *short* forms of some adjectives (длúнный, ширóкий, корóткий, ýзкий, etc.) are used when the quality they convey characterises an object in such a way that it is shown to be unusable: тýфли узкú, костю́м ширóк, брю́ки длинны́. The use of the long form in such cases would have simply described the object concerned without any reference to its usability: тýфли ýзкие, костю́м ширóкий, брю́ки длúнные.

Only the *short* form is also used when the object or state which it characterises is expressed by: (1) an infinitive or verbal noun: Курéние врéдно. Курúть врéдно; (2) the pronoun то, э́то, что, вот что, однó, другóе or то и другóе, or the adjective остальнóе, послéднее, пéрвое or вторóе: Вот что вáжно. Другóе — существéнно. Послéднее не тóчно; (3) a noun with an attribute of the type такóй, какóй, вся́кий, кáждый, любóй, подóбный, аналогúчный, настоя́щий, úстинный, пóдлинный or такóго рóда, такóго тúпа: Настоя́щий талáнт — рéдок. Дискýссии такóго рóда бесполéзны.

5. What case forms should be used after prepositions.

In a sentence the case forms of nouns are subordinated to other nouns, verbs, numerals and adjectives, and express definite relations between the performer and the experiencer or modifiers (see III C, 4 and III C, 5). However, not infrequently a case form is determined only by the preposition which it follows. Below is a list giving the cases of nouns and pronouns required by some prepositions.

без — *Gen.*
благодаря́ — *Dat.*
близ — *Gen.*
в — *Acc., Prep.*
в борьбé за — *Acc.*
в вúде — *Gen.*
во врéмя — *Gen.*
вдалú от — *Gen.*

в дéле — *Gen.*
в дýхе — *Gen.*
в завúсимости от — *Gen.*
в заключéние — *Gen.*
в знак — *Gen.*
во избежáние — *Gen.*
в кáчестве — *Gen.*

в колúчестве — *Gen.*
в кругý — *Gen.*
в лицé — *Gen.*
в мéру — *Gen.*
в направлéнии к — *Dat.*
в направлéнии на — *Acc.*

в нача́ле — *Gen.*
в о́бласти — *Gen.*
в отли́чие от — *Gen.*
в отноше́нии — *Gen.*
в отноше́нии к — *Dat.*
в продолже́ние — *Gen.*
в противове́с — *Dat.*
в ра́мках — *Gen.*
в результа́те — *Gen.*
в све́те — *Gen.*
в связи́ с — *Instr.*
в си́лу — *Gen.*
в слу́чае — *Gen.*
в смы́сле — *Gen.*
в соотве́тствии с — *Instr.*
в сравне́нии с — *Instr.*
в сто́рону от — *Gen.*
в тече́ние — *Gen.*
в хо́де — *Gen.*
в це́лях — *Gen.*
в честь — *Gen.*
до — *Gen.*
для — *Gen.*
за — *Acc., Instr.*
за исключе́нием — *Gen.*
за счёт — *Gen.*
задо́лго до — *Gen.*
из — *Gen.*
изнутри́ — *Gen.*
из-за — *Gen.*
из-под — *Gen.*
исключа́я — *Gen., Acc.*
исходя́ из — *Gen.*
к — *Dat.*
каса́тельно — *Gen.*
кро́ме — *Gen.*

круго́м — *Gen.*
ме́жду — *Instr., Gen.*
ми́мо — *Gen.*
на — *Acc., Prep.*
на предме́т — *Gen.*
на протяже́нии — *Gen.*
на пути́ — *Gen.*
навстре́чу — *Dat.*
над — *Instr.*
на́искось — *Gen.*
накану́не — *Gen.*
напереко́р — *Dat.*
наподо́бие — *Gen.*
напро́тив — *Gen.*
наравне́ с — *Instr.*
наряду́ с — *Instr.*
начина́я с — *Gen.*
не взира́я на — *Acc.*
не говоря́ о — *Prep.*
не счита́я — *Gen.*
о — *Acc., Prep.*
одновре́менно с — *Instr.*
от — *Gen.*
относи́тельно — *Gen.*
по — *Dat., Acc., Prep.*
по вопро́су о — *Prep.*
по ли́нии — *Gen.*
по ме́ре — *Gen.*
по отноше́нию к — *Dat.*
по по́воду — *Gen.*
по пути́ к — *Dat.*
по причи́не — *Gen.*
по слу́чаю — *Gen.*
по сравне́нию с — *Instr.*
по ча́сти — *Gen.*
пове́рх — *Gen.*
под — *Acc., Instr.*

по́дле — *Gen.*
подо́бно — *Dat.*
позади́ — *Gen.*
помимо — *Gen.*
посре́дством — *Gen.*
поперёк — *Gen.*
по́сле — *Gen.*
посреди́ — *Gen.*
посреди́не — *Gen.*
пре́жде — *Gen.*
про́тив — *Gen.*
при — *Prep.*
примени́тельно к — *Dat.*
про — *Acc.*
путём — *Gen.*
ра́ди — *Gen.*
с — *Gen., Acc., Instr.*
сбо́ку — *Gen.*
све́рху — *Gen.*
свы́ше — *Gen.*
сза́ди — *Gen.*
сквозь — *Acc.*
сле́дом за — *Instr.*
смотря́ по — *Dat.*
сни́зу — *Gen.*
со стороны́ — *Gen.*
согла́сно — *Dat.*
согла́сно с — *Instr.*
сообра́зно с — *Instr.*
соотве́тственно — *Dat.*
соотве́тственно с — *Instr.*
соразме́рно с — *Instr.*
спустя́ — *Acc.*
су́дя по — *Dat.*
че́рез — *Acc.*
у — *Gen.*

E. HOW TO ASK A QUESTION

Quite often a speaker does not intend to give his listener(s) information, but, on the contrary, wants to receive information from him (them). The nature of the required information may be of two kinds.

First, the speaker may need only an *affirmation* or *negation* of his idea of a situation, i. e. the answer да or нет. In such cases he has only to pronounce practically any sentence built on the patterns described in Part III C with an interrogative intonation. In writing he should put a question mark (?) instead of a full stop (.) at the end of such a sentence.

If an interrogative sentence includes a word containing information in which the questioner is interested, this word is singled out by intonation in speaking: *Отéц*—в садý? (The questioner wants to get a confirmation of the fact that it is his father who is in the garden and not somebody else.) or Отéц—*в садý*? (The questioner wants to get a confirmation of the fact that his father is precisely in the garden and not somewhere else.) It is impossible to specify questions in this way in writing. However, questions of this type may be strengthened by the particle ли, usually placed immediately after the word which the questioner singles out by intonation in speaking, since he considers it to be particularly important: Брáту ли э́то нýжно? (The questioner wants to know whether it is his brother or someone else who needs it.) or Брáту э́то ли нýжно? (The questioner wants to know whether his brother needs precisely this object and not something else.) or Брáту э́то нýжно ли? (The questioner wants to know whether his brother really needs this.) It should be mentioned that the particle ли often introduces an additional nuance of doubt or uncertainty. The same nuance of distrust, uncertainty, doubt or supposition is introduced into a question by the particles рáзве and неужéли: Рáзве я говори́л вам об э́том? Неужéли мóжно éхать? As a rule, the particles рáзве and неужéли stand at the beginning of a sentence.

Second, the questioner may require various *new information*. This information may relate to the performer and his characteristics, the action or state and its characteristics, and various circumstances. To build interrogative sentences, statements should be used as the basis and their intonation changed and various interrogative words introduced into them (at the beginning of the sentence) in accordance with the character of the information required: кто, что, какóй, какóв, чей, котóрый, скóлько, как, где, кудá, откýда, когдá, почемý, отчегó, зачéм, нéсколько: Кто идёт сюдá? Кудá уéхал цирк? Что он дéлает? Зачéм ты э́то написáл?, etc. In such interrogative sentences the word order of the statements is usually retained, but the pronoun in the nominative invariably follows the interrogative word and the noun in the nominative stands in third place (i.e. after the verb): Кудá он éдет? Кудá éдет отéц?

Questions whose meaning is the most general are those which the questioner asks when he wants to get an explanation of the nature of an object, action or state: Что это такое? Кто он такой? Answers to such questions are specific. Questions built on the pattern "Что такое or Что значит + a noun in the nominative or an infinitive" (Что такое жизнь? Что значит любить?) admit of more abstract answers, or they may be simply rhetorical questions not intended to elicit an answer.

In conversation questions are frequently asked about those words of a conversation partner which the questioner did not understand and which he repeats in questions of the Что значит..? type. For example: Я приеду в августе. — Что значит в августе?

PART IV
HOW TO PRONOUNCE WHAT IS WRITTEN CORRECTLY

Often a student of Russian has not only to understand what is written (see Parts I and II), but also correctly to read what is written, i.e. to transform written language into spoken language. Detailed information on the pronunciation of the Russian sounds, sound combinations and words can be found in numerous works on Russian phonetics.[1] Here we shall give, first, some rules for "transforming" letters into sounds, and, second, some rules for determining shifts of stress in specific grammatical word forms in comparison with their dictionary forms.

What **sounds** are represented by the **letters** of the Russian alphabet.

The letters **а, о, у, э, е, и, ы, ё, ю, я**[2] represent **vowel** sounds (for some peculiarities of the sounds represented by the letters **е, ё, ю** and **я**, see below).

The letters **б, в, г, д, ж, з, й, к, л, м, н, п, р, с, т, ф, х, ц, ч, ш, щ** represent **consonant** sounds.

The letter **ь** before a vowel represents the same sound as the letter **й**, and before a consonant and at the end of a word it does not represent any sound at all, indicating only the softness (or palatalisation; see below) of the preceding consonant.

The letter **ъ** occurs only before a vowel and represents the same sound as the letter **й** (see below).

1. How to Pronounce Consonants

1.1. How to pronounce consonants at the end of a word and before other consonants.

The consonants **б, в, г, д, ж, з,** when either at the end of a word, or before **к, п, с, т, ф, х, ц, ч, ш, щ,** or before **ь** (which either follows these consonants or is itself the last letter in the word), should be pronounced as [п], [ф], [к], [т], [ш], [с], respectively: слаб[п], прочита́в[ф], снег[к], го́род[т], свеж[ш], моро́з[с], го́лубь[п'], кровь[ф'], медве́дь[т'], режь[ш'], грязь[с'], ры́бка[п], всё[ф], подписа́ть[т], ре́жьте[ш'], ле́зьте[с']. This rule also operates at the juncture of the final consonant of a preposition and the initial consonant of a noun, pronoun, adjective or numeral: в[ф] саду́, пе́ред[т] па́рком, из[с] са́да.

---

[1] See, for example, Орфоэпический словарь современного русского языка. М., 1983; Н.А.Любимова. Обучение русскому произношению. М. 1982; Е. А. Брызгунова. Звуки и интонация русской речи. М., 1983.

[2] Letters are represented as **a, б**, etc., and the corresponding sounds as [а], [б], etc.

The consonants к, п, с, т, ш, immediately preceding б, г, д, ж, з or separated from them by ь, should be pronounced as [г], [б], [з], [д], [ж], respectively: вокза́л [г], сде́лал [з], про́сьба [з'], о́тзыв [д].

This rule also operates at the junctures of the final consonant of a preposition and the initial consonant of a noun, pronoun, adjective or numeral: с[з] Зи́ной, от[д] до́ма, к[г] до́му.

г preceding к and ч should be pronounced as [х]: легко́ [х], мя́гче [х].

In the words что and что́бы and also in a few words where ч precedes н, it is pronounced as [ш]: моло́чный [ш], коне́чно [ш], ску́чно [ш]; however: со́лнечный [чн], да́чный [чн], ручно́й [чн], etc.

In the following combinations the letters т and д are not pronounced: стн: че́стный [сн], здн: по́здно [зн], стл: счастли́вый [сл], рдц: се́рдце [рц], рдч: сердчи́шко [рч], нтск: гига́нтский [нск], стск: маркси́стский [сск].

The letter л in the word со́лнце is not pronounced.

The letter н is pronounced soft if it precedes ч or щ: же́нщина [н'], ко́нчен [н'].

-ться and -тся at the end of verb forms are pronounced as [цца].

-тс- and -дс- preceding a consonant should be pronounced as [ц]: бра́тский [ц], заводско́й [ц].

-тц- and -дц- should be pronounced as a long [цц]: отца́ [цц], два́дцать [цц].

-сш- and -зш- are pronounced as a long [шш]: сшил [шш], ни́зший [шш]. This rule also operates at the junctures of the final consonants с and з of a preposition and the initial consonant ш of a noun or numeral: с ша́пкой [шш], без ша́пки [шш].

-тч- and -дч- are pronounced as a long [чч] both inside words and at the junctures of a prefix and the root: отчита́ть [чч], под черёмухой [чч].

-зж- is pronounced as a long [жж]: разжéчь. This rule also operates when these consonants come together at the juncture of a preposition and a noun or adjective: без жи́зни [жж].

-сч- and -зч- should be pronounced as [шч] or as a soft long [ш'ш']: сча́стье [ш'ш'], гру́зчик [ш'ш']. This rule also operates at the juncture of the final consonant с or з of a preposition and the initial consonant ч of a noun, adjective or numeral: с че́стью [ш'ш'], без че́тверти [ш'ш'].

1.2. How to pronounce consonants before ь.

If ь follows the letters б, в, д, з, л, м, н, п, р, с, т, ф (or stands at the end of a word, or before consonants, or before a vowel), then the consonants represented by these letters should be pronounced *soft*, i.e. their articulation should be accompanied by the raising of the middle part of the tongue to a great height. (While doing this, one should bear in mind the change in the quality of the relevant consonants; see 1.1): го́лубь [п'], червь [ф'], ся́дьте [т'], лезь [с'], фильм [л'], во́семь [м'], встань [н'], цепь [п'], ла́герь [р'], бро́сьте [с'], ждать [т'].

If ь follows the letters ж, ш, ч, щ, it does not affect the pronunciation of the sounds represented by these letters.

1.3. How to pronounce consonants before vowels.

If the consonants **б, в, г, д, з, к, л, м, н, п, р, с, т, ф, х** precede the vowels **е, ё, и, ю, я**, these consonants should be pronounced like the corresponding *soft* sounds, i.e. their articulation should be accompanied by the raising of the middle part of the tongue to a great height: бе́лый [б'], весёлый [в'], беги́ [г'], дя́дя [д'], зима́ [з'], кино́ [к'], ле́то [л'], мечта́ [м'], коню́ [н'], пять [п'], река́ [р'], се́рый [с'], тётя [т'], Фёдор [ф'], стихи́ [х'].

If the above consonants precede **а, о, у, ы, э**, their articulation is unchanged and they remain *hard*.

The articulation of the consonants **ж, ц, ч, ш, щ** is not affected by the vowel they precede, **ж, ш, ц** always remaining *hard*, and **ч** and **щ** always remaining *soft*.

The letter **г** in the endings **-ого/-его** of adjectives and all the pronouns, numerals and nouns declined like adjectives should be pronounced as [в].

2. How to Pronounce Vowels

2.1. How to pronounce the vowels represented by the letters **а, у, ы, и** and **э**.

In any position in a word the vowels represented by the letters **а, у, ы, и** and **э** should be pronounced in the same way as the respective sounds are pronounced in an isolated position. However, they should be articulated less energetically if they are not stressed.

After **ж, ш, ц** the letter **и** should be pronounced as [ы]: жизнь [жызн'], мы́ши [мы́шы], ци́фра [цы́фра].

2.2. How to pronounce the vowel represented by the letter **о**.

When stressed, the vowel represented by the letter **о** is pronounced in the same way as in an isolated position. If it is unstressed, it is pronounced as a faint [а]: голова́ [галава́].

2.3. How to pronounce the vowel represented by the letter **ё**.

The vowel represented by the letter **ё** occurs only in a stressed position. (It should be noted that in most books this vowel is represented by the letter **е**.) If this vowel occurs at the beginning of a word, after a vowel or after **ь** or **ъ**, it should be pronounced as a combination of the consonant represented by the letter **й** and the vowel [о]: ёлка [йо́лка], моё [майо́].

However, if the letter **ё** occurs after a consonant, it affects this consonant in the way described in 1.3.

2.4. How to pronounce the vowel represented by the letter **е**.

If the letter **е** is in a stressed position at the beginning of a word, or after a vowel, or after **ь** or **ъ**, it should be pronounced as a combination of a consonant represented by the letter **й** and the vowel [э]: е́сли [йэ́сл'и], вое́нный [вайэ́нный], подъе́хали [падйэ́хали].

If the letter **е** is in an unstressed position at the beginning of a word or after a vowel, it should be pronounced as a combination of the consonant represented by the letter **й** and the vowel [и]: Егóр [йигóр], моемý [майимý].

However, if the letter **e** occurs after a consonant, it affects this consonant in the way described in 1.3.

In a stressed position following **ж, ш, ц** the letter **e** is pronounced as [э], and in an unstressed position as [ы]: желéзо [жыл'э́за]. After the other consonants it is pronounced as [и]: селó [с'илó].

2.5. How to pronounce the vowel represented by the letter **я**.

If the letter **я** is in a stressed position at the beginning of a word, or after a vowel, or after **ь** or **ъ**, it should be pronounced as a combination of the consonant represented by the letter **й** and the vowel [а]: я́сный [йа́сный], ма́як [майа́к].

If the letter **я** is in an unstressed position at the beginning of a word or after a vowel (but not at the end of a word), it should be pronounced as a combination of the consonant represented by the letter **й** and the vowel [и]: янва́рь [йинва́р'], маяки́ [майики́].

However, if the letter **я** occurs after a consonant, it affects this consonant in the way described in 1.3.

In this case the letter **я** in a stressed position is pronounced as [а], and in an unstressed position as [и]: мя́со [м'а́са], мяснóй [м'иснóй].

At the very end of a word **я** is never pronounced as [и] or [йи], but only as [йа] (after a vowel) or [а] (after a consonant): а́рмия [а́рм'ийа], земля́ [з'имл'а́], моя́ [майа́], Кóля [кóл'а].

2.6. How to pronounce the vowel represented by the letter **ю**.

If the letter **ю** occurs at the beginning of a word, or after a vowel, or after **ь** or **ъ**, it should be pronounced as a combination of the consonant represented by the letter **й** and the vowel [у]: ю́ность [йу́нас'т'], юри́ст [йур'и́ст], твою́ [твайу́].

If the letter **ю** follows a consonant, it affects it in the way described in 1.3. The quality of the vowel sound represented by the letter **ю** does not depend on whether it is stressed or unstressed: юг [йук], югосла́в [йугасла́ф], мою́ [майу́].

3. How to Determine the Position of the Stress in a Word[1]

Practically any notional word (as a sequence of letters between two consecutive intervals) has one of its syllables under stress. On the other hand, syntactic words—prepositions and particles—are usually unstressed and in pronunciation merge with the notional words they precede or follow: на хлеб [нахл'э́п], под Москвóй [падмасквóй], чита́л бы [чита́лбы], скажи́ же [скажы́жы]; prepositions merging with the word that follows, and particles, with the word that precedes them.

---

[1] For details on stress, see Н.А.Федя́нина. Ударение в современном русском языке. М., 1982.

Stress may fall on *any syllable* in a word. When a word occurs in a text in its dictionary form, the position of the stress is easily established with the help of a dictionary. However, in the process of declension or conjugation the position of the stress in a word may change. Besides, in some preposition-cum-case forms the stress infrequently shifts either to the preposition or the particle не: на́ пол, не́ был, but на полу́, не знал.

3.1. How the position of the stress may shift in most nouns.

Five main types of stress (with respect to its position) are distinguished in nouns.

1. The position of the stress remains *unchanged* (it falls either on the stem or on the ending) in all the forms of nouns, except only those cases when the ending is a zero sound (it may be either in the nominative and the accusative singular which is identical with the nominative, or in the genitive and the accusative plural which is identical with the genitive), in which case the stress inevitably falls on the noun stem. Thus, for example, the stress is fixed on the stem in the nouns спор and ка́рта, and it is fixed on the ending in the noun стол (except the nominative and the accusative singular): стола́, столу́, столо́м, etc.

2. In the *singular* the stress falls on the *stem*, and in the *plural* on the *ending*. Thus, for example, the position of the stress is fixed in the nouns мо́ре (мо́ря, мо́рю..., but моря́, море́й...) and сад (са́да, са́ду..., but сады́, садо́в, сада́м...).

3. In the *singular* the stress falls on the *ending*, and in the *plural* on the *stem*. Thus, for example, the position of the stress is fixed in the nouns лицо́ (лица́, лицу́..., but ли́ца, лиц, ли́цам...) and лист (листа́, листу́, but ли́стья, ли́стьев, ли́стьям...). (The stress on the stem in the nominative and the accusative singular in the word лист is forced, since in these forms it cannot fall on the ending owing to the latter's absence.)

4. In the singular and the nominative plural the stress falls on the *stem*, and in all the other plural forms on the *ending*. Thus, for example, the position of the stress is fixed in the nouns зуб (зу́ба, зу́бу, зуб, зу́бом, зу́бе; зу́бы, зубо́в, зу́бы, зуба́м, зуба́ми, зуба́х) and вещь (ве́щи, ве́щи, вещь, ве́щью; ве́щи, веще́й, веща́м, ве́щи, веща́ми, веща́х).

5. The stress falls on the *ending* in all the forms except the nominative plural, in which it falls on the *stem*. Thus, for example, the stress is fixed in the nouns губа́ (губы́, губе́, губу́, губо́й, губе́; гу́бы, губ, губа́м, гу́бы, губа́ми, губа́х) and конь (коня́, коню́, коня́, конём, коне́; ко́ни, коне́й, коня́м, коне́й, коня́ми, коня́х). (The stress on the stem in the nominative singular of the word конь and in the genitive plural of the word губ is forced, since in these forms it cannot fall on the ending owing to the latter's absence.)

The following rules apply equally to the nouns of all the five types:

When the stress is to fall on the stem, then, if the dictionary form is stem-stressed, it usually falls on the same syllable of the stem in the other forms too. If in the dictionary form the stem is unstressed, then in words belonging to the 5th type the stress falls on the initial syllable of the stem: голова́ — *nom. pl.* го́ловы, and in words belonging to the other types it falls on the last syllable of the stem provided this syllable does not include a vowel alternating with zero sound: величина́ — *nom. pl.* величи́ны. However, if in this case the last stem syllable includes a vowel alternating with zero sound, the stress falls on the penultimate syllable: судьба́ — *nom. pl.* су́дьбы, *gen. pl.* су́деб.

In disyllabic stressed endings the stress falls on the first syllable of the ending: дома́ми.

If the stress is to fall on the ending which is actually absent (i.e. the word ends in ø, ь or й), then it falls on the last stem syllable: се́рдце — сердца́ — серде́ц.

It must be borne in mind that the dictionary form of a noun does not enable one to determine the type of stress shift to which this noun belongs. Besides, the dictionary form of many nouns does not have an ending, and, therefore, the stress falls on the stem (стол). This may give rise to misinformation about the true type of stress shift in the other word forms (стола́, стола́м, стола́ми, etc.). Monolingual Russian dictionaries usually indicate the position of the stress in nouns in their dictionary form, the genitive singular and (if the position of the stress shifts) the nominative or genitive plural. This information is usually sufficient to draw a conclusion about which of the 5 types of stress shift the noun concerned belongs to. Knowing the type of stress shift, one can easily determine the position of the stress in any specific noun form.

For example, let us assume that one wants to determine the position of the stress in the form домами. The dictionary form is дом. The dictionary gives this information: **-a**, *pl.* дома́, **-о́в**. So in the singular the stress falls on the stem; and in all the forms of the plural, on the ending. Consequently, the word belongs to Type 2. In the form дома́ми the stress falls on the ending. Since the ending is disyllabic, it falls on the first syllable of the ending: дома́ми.

3.2. How the position of the stress may shift in adjectives and in nouns declined like adjectives.

In **long-form** adjectives and nouns declined like adjectives the stress is invariably *fixed*: it falls either on the stem or on the ending. The dictionary form always enables one to determine whether the stress is fixed on the *stem* (in such a case the dictionary form ends in an unstressed **-ий** or **-ый**, and in the case of feminine and neuter nouns in **-ая/-яя** or **-ое/-ее**, as in the words си́ний, до́брый, вожа́тый, столо́вая, моро́женое) or on the *ending* (in such a case the dictionary form ends in a stressed **-о́й**, and in the case of feminine and neuter nouns in **-а́я/-я́я** or **-о́е/-е́е**, as in the words большо́й, густо́й, портно́й, запята́я, жарко́е).

The position of the stress in **short-form** adjectives is not predetermined by its position in the corresponding long-form adjectives. Three types of the distribution of stress in feminine, neuter and plural short-form adjectives may be distinguished. (Masculine short-form adjectives, which have no endings, are invariably stressed on the *stem*.)

1. The stress invariably falls on the *stem* (удо́бный — удо́бна, удо́бно, удо́бны).
2. The stress invariably falls on the *ending* (смешно́й — смешна́, смешно́, смешны́).
3. In feminine forms the stress falls on the *ending*, and in neuter and plural forms on the *stem* (гро́мкий — громка́, гро́мко, гро́мки).

In the stem of the masculine short form the stress falls on the vowel alternating with zero if the stress in the short form is distributed in accordance with Type 2: смешо́н. In all the other cases the vowel alternating with zero is unstressed in the masculine short form.

3.3. How the position of the stress shifts in pronouns.

There are three types of stress shift in the pronouns.

1. The stress invariably falls on the *stem*. The pronouns э́тот, наш, ваш, кой, нико́й belong to this type.
2. The stress invariably falls on the *ending* (with the exception of the cases where there is no ending and the stress of necessity falls on the stem). The pronouns тот, оди́н, сей, весь, мой, твой, свой, чей, ниче́й belong to this type.
3. The pronoun сам belongs to the type identical with Type 5 of nouns: the stress always falls on the *ending* (with the exception of the nonsyllabic endings), barring the nominative and the accusative plural identical with the nominative, in which it falls on the *stem*.

If pronominal words are stressed on the disyllabic ending **-ого/-его** or **-ому/-ему**, the stress falls on the last syllable: моего́, самому́. In all the other cases the general rule of stressing the first syllable of a disyllabic ending applies (see 3.1).

The pronouns я, ты, он, она́, оно́, кто, что, никто́, ничто́, себя́ are invariably stressed on the last syllable (except the forms мно́ю, то́бою, собо́ю, е́ю, не́ю). The pronouns не́кого and не́чего are invariably stressed on не; when they are "disrupted" by a preposition, they constitute a phonetic entity all the same and bear one stress, although they are spelt as separate words: не́ у кого, не́ для чего, не́ за кем.

3.4. How the position of the stress shifts in the derivation of finite verb forms.

Since verbs have two stems relatively independent of each other— an infinitive stem and a present tense stem—with forms derived from them, the types of stress shift are distinguished separately for each of the two systems of forms.

In the **past** tense forms, derived from the infinitive stem, three main types of stress shift are distinguished.

1. The stress invariably falls on the *stem*: де́лать — де́лал, де́лала, де́лало, де́лали.
2. The stress invariably falls on the *ending* (with the exception of nonsyllabic endings and also of **-ся**, which is usually unstressed): бере́чь — берёг, берегла́, берегло́, берегли́.
3. In the feminine forms the stress falls on the *ending*, and in the

other forms on the *stem*: сорва́ть — сорва́л, сорвала́, сорва́ло, сорва́ли.

The same rules also determine the position of the stress in the subjunctive mood forms.

In the **present/future** tense forms also three types of stress shift are distinguished.

1. The stress invariably falls on the *stem*: ве́рю, ве́ришь, ве́рит, ве́рим, ве́рите, ве́рят, верь, ве́рьте.
2. The stress invariably falls on the *ending* (with the exception of nonsyllabic endings and also of **-ся**, which is usually unstressed): беру́, берёшь, берёт, берём, берёте, беру́т, бери́, бери́те.
3. In the 1st person singular and the imperative the stress falls on the *ending*, and in all the other forms on the *stem*: пишу́, пи́шешь, пи́шет, пи́шем, пи́шете, пи́шут, пиши́, пиши́те.

An exception is the verb хоте́ть, all the plural forms of which are stressed on the ending: хочу́, хо́чешь, хо́чет, хоти́м, хоти́те, хотя́т.

The statement that the stress should fall on the *stem* means that it falls on the same syllable, counting from the beginning, as in the dictionary form (the infinitive). However, if the stem of the form concerned has fewer syllables than the infinitive, then the stress falls on the final stem syllable: рисова́ть — рису́ю.

The statement that the stress should fall on the *ending* which is disyllabic means that it falls on the first syllable of such an ending: идёте, учи́тесь. If the stress is to fall on the ending which is either a zero or an element containing no vowel, if falls on the final *stem* syllable: стою́ — стой, бере́чь — берегла́ — берёг. This rule usually holds good when the ending is followed by the marker **-те, -ся** or **-тесь**: these markers are invariably unstressed.

Practically all variants of combinations of types of stress shift are encountered in past and present tense forms. Therefore, to determine the type in accordance with which the stress shifts in past and present tense forms, one should refer to monolingual Russian dictionaries. A. A. Zaliznyak's *Грамматический словарь русского языка* indicates the type of stress shift for each verb both in the past and future tense forms. Monolingual Russian dictionaries usually indicate the positions of the stress in the dictionary form of verbs, in their 1st person singular present tense, and in their 2nd person singular present tense if these positions differ. Besides, the position of the stress in the past tense forms is indicated if it is different from the position of the stress in the infinitive. As a rule, this information is sufficient to determine the type of the stress shift to which the present tense verb forms belong and the type of the stress shift to which the past tense verb forms belong. Knowing the type of stress shift, it is easy to determine the position of the stress in any specific finite verb form. For example, one wants to determine the position of the stress in the form ле́чат. This form belongs to the present tense. Its dictionary form is лечи́ть. The dictionary gives лечу́, ле́чишь. So in the 1st person singular (and the imperative) the stress falls on the ending, and in the other present tense forms on the stem. Consequently, it follows Type 3. In the form ле́чат the stress falls on the stem.

Dictionaries also reflect the few discrepancies between the position of the stress in the dictionary form (the infinitive) and its position in the past tense forms: заня́ть — за́нял, заняла́, за́няло, за́няли or запере́ть — за́пер, заперла́, за́перло, за́перли.

3.5 How the position of the stress shifts in the derivation of participles and verbal adverbs.

1. In the forms ending in -ущ(ий) and -ющ(ий) of **active present** participles the stress falls on the same syllable as in the 3rd person plural present tense: пишу́ — пи́шут — пи́шущий, несу́ — несу́т — несу́щий; and in the forms ending in -ащ(ий) and -ящ(ий), on the same syllable as in the 1st person singular present tense: держу́ — де́ржат — держа́щий. However, there are a few verbs in which the stress falls on the syllable just to the left of the one on which it should fall in accordance with the rule: люблю́, but лю́бящий, лечу́(сь), but ле́чащий(ся), i. e. the stress falls on the same syllable as in the 3rd person plural.

2. In **active past** participles the position of the stress usually coincides with that of the masculine past tense forms: чита́л — чита́вший. Exceptions are a number of verbs in which the position of the stress in the infinitive is different from its position in the past tense. In the active past participles of these verbs the stress falls on the same syllable as in the infinitive: заня́ть — за́нял — заня́вший.

3. In the forms ending in -ем(ый) and -ом(ый) of **passive present** participles the stress falls on the same syllable as in the 1st person plural present tense: ведём — ведо́мый, чита́ем — чита́емый. Passive present participles ending in -им(ый) are stressed on the same syllable as the 1st person singular present tense: хвалю́ — хвали́мый, люблю́ — люби́мый.

In short-form participles the position of the stress remains the same as in their long-form counterparts.

4. As a rule, in long-form **passive past** participles the stress falls on the same syllable as in masculine past tense forms: разби́л — разби́тый, чи́стил — чи́щенный, ви́дел — ви́денный. However, there are many exceptions to this rule. In passive past participles derived from verbs whose infinitive ends in -ать/-ять (except those whose 1st person singular present tense ends in -ну or -му) the stress falls on the syllable just to the left of the one on which it falls in the infinitive, provided the infinitive is not monosyllabic and is stressed on the last syllable: написа́ть — напи́санный, прочита́ть — прочи́танный. If the last two restrictions do not apply, the stress in passive past participles falls on the same syllable as in the infinitive: ткать — тка́нный, ма́зать — ма́занный.

In passive past participles derived from verbs whose infinitive ends in -ить the stress falls on the same syllable as in the 3rd person singular future tense: принесёт — принесённый, and in passive past participles derived from verbs whose infinitive ends in -еть it falls on the syllable just left of the one on which it falls in the infinitive, provided the infinitive is not monosyllabic and is stressed on the last syllable (вертéть — вéрченный), and on the same syllable as in the infinitive if these restrictions do not apply: обессúлеть — обессúленный.

In passive past participles derived from verbs whose infinitive ends in **-зти́/-зть, -сти́/-сть** or **-чь** the stress falls on the same syllable (from the beginning) as in the feminine past tense forms: расплести́ — расплела́ — расплетённый, сбере́чь — сберегла́ — сбережённый, постри́чь — постри́гла — постри́женный.

In passive past participles derived from verbs whose infinitive ends in **-нуть, -олоть** or **-ороть** the stress falls on the syllable just to the left of the one on which it falls in the infinitive, provided the infinitive is not monosyllabic and is stressed on the last syllable: моло́ть — мо́лотый. If the latter restriction does not apply (i. e. if the infinitive is not stressed on the last syllable), the participles are stressed on the same syllable as the infinitive: сти́снуть — сти́снутый.

5. In the derivation of **short-form** passive participles the following shift of the stress takes place:

The short forms of participles ending in an unstressed **-анн(ый), -янн(ый)** or **-енн(ый)** retain the stress on the same syllable as their long-form counterparts: прочи́танный — прочи́тан, прочи́тана, прочи́тано, прочи́таны; разба́вленный — разба́влен, разба́влена, разба́влено, разба́влены.

In the short forms of participles ending in **-ённ(ый)** the stress shifts to the ending, with the obvious exception of masculine forms, which have no ending: удивлённый — удивлён, удивлена́, удивлено́, удивлены́.

In the short forms of participles ending in **-тый** the position of the stress depends on the type of stress shift in the past tense forms of the relevant verb. If in these forms the stress is fixed on the stem, then in the short forms of the passive past participles the stress also invariably falls on the stem: приши́ть — приши́л, приши́ла, приши́ло, приши́ли and приши́т, приши́та, приши́то, приши́ты. However, if in the past tense forms the stress falls on the ending in the feminine forms and on the stem in the other forms, then in the passive short-form past participles the stress is distributed in the same way: снять — снял, сняла́, сня́ло, сня́ли; снят, снята́, сня́то, сня́ты.

3.6. The cases in which the stress shifts from a noun or numeral to the preposition.

The stress shifts from a noun or numeral to the preposition only when the noun or pronoun is not followed by any qualifiers or modifiers.

Such a shift of the stress from nouns usually occurs when these nouns are preceded by the prepositions за, на and по, but not in just any of their meanings.

The stress is usually shifted from the noun to the preposition за when the latter has the following meanings: "on the other side of", "behind" (заложи́ть за́ спину, за́ щеку, за́ ухо, за́ голову), "the point to which a force is applied" (держа́ть за́ руку, за́ нос, за́ плечи), "during", "in the course of" (вы́полнить за́ день, за́ год, за́ ночь, however: за неде́лю, за ме́сяц, за кварта́л, за полуго́дие) and "beforehand" (прие́хать за́ день, за́ год до сро́ка, however: за мину́ту, за час, за неде́лю, за ме́сяц).

The stress is usually shifted from the noun to the preposition на when the latter has the following meanings: "in the direction of", "downwards" (упа́сть на́ пол, на́ руку, на́ спину), "the point of contact with a support" (встать на́ руки, на́ ноги, на́ голову), "calculated for a certain period" (запасти́сь на́ зиму, на́ год, на́ ночь, на́ день, however: на ме́сяц, на ле́то, на о́сень, на дека́ду) and "an indication of the extent of a difference" (ста́рше на́ год, на́ день, however: на ме́сяц, на век).

The stress is usually shifted from the noun to the preposition по when the latter means "along a surface", "within some limits" (идти́ по́ полю, по́ лесу, по́ двору, по́ снегу, however: по ча́ще, по доро́ге, etc.).

Besides, such a shift of stress occurs in a number of set phrases of the type бок о́ бок ("side by side"), зуб на́ зуб не попада́ет ("one's teeth are chattering"), как бог на́ душу поло́жит("anyhow"), на́ дом ("home"), за́ городом ("in the country"), до́ смерти ("extremely", "very much"), по́д гору ("downhill"), etc.

The stress is usually shifted from a numeral to the preposition when the numeral concerned is a simple one and the unit of measurement is not stated: получи́ли по́ два, раздели́ть на́ три, засчита́ть за́ сто.

PART V
HOW TO WRITE DOWN WHAT ONE HEARS CORRECTLY

Not infrequently a student of Russian has to write down what other people say. In other words, his task often consists in rendering somebody's speech in writing. Or he may need to express in writing what he himself wants to say. He may find a detailed exposition of the principles and rules of Russian spelling and also of the distinctive features of Russian handwriting in numerous monographs and reference books on this subject.[1] Here we will describe only the main methods of dividing a spoken text into separate words and the main principles of recording sounds and their combinations by means of letters. In a certain sense the task of Part V is the "opposite" of that of Part IV: in the latter the discussion proceeded "from letters to sounds", whereas here it will proceed "from sounds to letters".

1. What is written as one word, what as two words, and what is hyphenated.

To write down a spoken sentence, it is necessary first of all to divide it into the word forms of which it consists. Obviously, this can be done only if the sentence is understood correctly. It must be borne in mind that in writing every word (including syntactic words, prepositions and some particles) is separated by an interval from the other words. This principle, which is quite clear in theory, is rather difficult to put into practice, since the difference between an individual word and the notional part of a word, a compound word or a phrase is not always clear. The most difficult problem is that of the spelling of some adverbs and words consisting of two or more roots, which are sometimes spelt as one word and sometimes as two words. In this case one should refer to Russian spelling and monolingual dictionaries. The most comprehensive dictionary containing words whose spelling—as one word or two—proves to be a stumbling block is «Слитно или раздельно?» (compiled by B. Z. Bukchina, L. P. Kalakutskaya and L. K. Cheltsova).

There are these general rules of spelling words as one word or two:
The particle не and a *verb* are invariably spelt as two words, with very few exceptions when the verb is not used without не (нездоро́вится, неймётся, etc.). One should not think, however, that any verb at the beginning of which one hears не actually has the particle не before it: не may be part of a root (не́житься) or quite frequently part of

---

[1] See, for example, Орфографический словарь русского языка (any edition published after 1956) and М. В. Па́нов. Занимательная орфография. М., 1984, etc.

the verb prefix **недо-** (недолюбливать, недосчитаться). In all such cases **не** and the verb are, of course, spelt as one word.

He and a *participle* are spelt as two words if the participle has qualifiers, and as one word if it has no such qualifiers: нераспустившийся цветок — не распустившийся из-за холода цветок.

He and a *verbal adverb* are invariably spelt as two words.

The particle **не** and a *noun* or *adjective* are usually spelt as two words when a person, object or quality is negated. He and a noun or adjective are spelt as one word when **не** helps to create a new word: несчастье, неспециалист.

As a rule, **не** and a *pronoun* are spelt as one word, with the exception of the cases when there is a preposition between **не** and the pronoun: некто and не к кому, нечто and не во что.

The *particle* **ни** and a noun, adjective or verb are generally spelt as two words. However, **ни** and a pronoun are spelt as one word, with the exception of the cases when there is a preposition between **ни** and the pronoun: никто and ни у кого, ничто and ни за что.

The particles **-то, -либо, -нибудь, -таки, -ка**, usually following their head-word with which they form a phonetic entity, are joined to it by a hyphen: кто-то, какой-либо, что-нибудь, скажи-ка. The particle **кое-**, usually preceding its head-word with which it forms a phonetic entity, is joined to it by a hyphen, too; the prefixes **по-** and **в-(во-)** in adverbs of the type по-мужски, по-новому, в-третьих, во-первых are also joined to the adverbs by a hyphen.

The particles **ли, же, бы** and prepositions and the nouns, adjectives or numerals they are connected with are invariably spelt as two words.

Numerals (both those denoting a quantity and those denoting the sequence of objects in counting) can be represented either by numbers or by letters. In the latter case, one should bear in mind that only the numerals from 1 to 20, the numerals denoting tens and hundreds, and also the words тысяча, миллион and миллиард are spelt as one word.

2. How to carry words from one line to the next.

When it is necessary to carry part of a word from one line to the next, the following rules for the division of words should be observed. To carry a part of a word from one line to the next, this word must be divided into syllables: only the part before or after the syllable boundary can be carried over: го-род, руч-ка. When there are variant syllable boundaries, that boundary should be preferred which coincides with the division of the word into the prefix, the root and the suffix: под-прыг-нуть, рас-сто-я-ние. Syllables consisting of one letter must not be left on a line or carried over to the next, therefore no part of some words may be carried over to the next line: она, моя, Азия.

3. When to use capital letters.

1. Capital letters are generally used at the beginning of a sentence, i. e. at the beginning of a text and after a full stop (.), an exclamation mark (!) and a question mark (?).

2. Capital letters are used at the beginning of people's Christian (first) names, patronymics and surnames (family names) (Михаи́л Васи́льевич Ломоно́сов) and the names of countries (А́нглия, Югосла́вия), cities, towns, villages (Москва́, Севасто́поль, Звени́город, Вельями́ново), streets (Арба́т, Сре́тенка), by-streets (Неопали́мовский, Староконю́шенный), squares (пло́щадь Иску́сств), avenues (Ломоно́совский, Не́вский), and motorways and roads (Щёлковское, Моско́вское). When the preceding topographical names consist of two words, both the words are generally spelt with a capital letter: Больша́я Пирого́вская у́лица, Си́вцев Вра́жек, Ясная Поля́на, Бе́лая Це́рковь.

3. The names of various organisations which consist of a number of words generally have a capital letter only at the beginning of the first word: Моско́вский госуда́рственный университе́т, Музе́й наро́дного тво́рчества. However, if such names are abbreviations composed of only the first letters of the words making up the full name, these abbreviations consist of capital letters alone: Большо́й драмати́ческий теа́тр — БДТ, Моско́вский Худо́жественный академи́ческий теа́тр — МХАТ.

4. What letters represent stressed vowel sounds at the beginning of a word and after vowels and consonants, with the exception of [ж], [ш], [ч], [щ].

If a *stressed* vowel is heard after a *soft consonant*, except [ч] or [щ], this vowel should be represented by **я** if [a] is heard (пять), by **ё** if [o] is heard (лён), by **ю** if [y] is heard (трюм), by **e** if [э] is heard (нет), and by **и** if [и] is heard (тип).

If a stressed vowel is heard after the sound usually represented by **й**, then the sound [йа] is generally represented by **я**, [йу] by **ю**, [йо] by **ё**, and [йэ] by **e**.

However, if the stressed vowel [a], [o], [y] or [э] is heard at the beginning of a word or after a *hard* consonant (except [ж], [ш], [ц]) or another vowel, it is represented by the letter **a, o, y** or **э**, respectively.

5. What letters represent unstressed vowel sounds after the soft consonants, with the exception of [ч] and [щ].

If an *unstressed* [y] is heard after a *soft* consonant (except [ч] or [щ]), **ю** should be written. If something like [и] is heard after a soft consonant (except [ч] or [щ]), this sound may be represented either by **и**, or by **e**, or by **я**: [зимо́й] зимо́й, [лисно́й] лесно́й, [мисно́й] мясно́й. The use of any of these three letters is determined by the following general principle. In an unstressed position vowel sounds are represented by *the same letters* by which they are represented in the same root, prefix or suffix when these parts of the word are *stressed*. Зимо́й is spelt with an **и** because, when stressed, [и] is heard in the root of this word: [зи́мний]. Лесно́й is spelt with an **e** because, when stressed, [е] is heard in the root of this word: [ле́с]. Мясно́й is spelt with an **я** because, when stressed, [a] is heard in the root of this word: [м'а́со].

If after a *soft* consonant a stressed [o] is heard, then in an unstressed position it should be represented by **e**. For example, if [с'истра́] is heard, it should be spelt as сестра́, because in the nominative plural [с'о́стры] is heard.

The preceding general principle mostly determines the spelling of unstressed vowels after a soft consonant (with the exception of [ч], [щ]); however, there are two types of deviation from this general principle. First, some roots (and prefixes and suffixes) are never stressed (бегемо́т, чита́тель). Second, the spelling of a word may be at variance with what is written in the stressed position (блеск, but блиста́ть, and yet: блесте́ть; подня́ть, but поднима́ть, and yet: по́днял; счёт, but счита́ть).

Thus, in practice to decide what letter should be written in the position of an unstressed vowel following a consonant, one should first of all determine in what part of the word (the root, prefix, suffix or ending) this unstressed vowel is. Then a word must be found which would include the same element (a root, prefix, suffix or ending), but in a stressed position. In some cases, first, such a word may not exist; second, one may not always be able to find the necessary word owing to one's insufficient knowledge of Russian; and, finally, third, the stressed vowel does not always determine the letter to be written to represent the unstressed vowel with one hundred per cent accuracy. Therefore, to make sure, one will quite frequently have to refer to a dictionary.

The dictionary may be dispensed with only when deciding what vowel letter should be written in endings. In this case dictionaries usually do not provide the necessary information. So the information on the types of declensions and conjugations contained in grammars will prove helpful.

6. What letters represent unstressed vowel sounds after a hard consonant (with the exception of [ж], [ш], [ц]) at the beginning of a word or after a vowel.

If an *unstressed* [у], [ы] or [э] is heard after a *hard* consonant (except [ж], [ш], [ц]) at the beginning of a word or after a vowel, it is represented by the letter **у, ы,** or **э**, respectively. However, if [а] or a sound similar to [а] is heard after a hard consonant, at the beginning of a word or after a vowel, this sound may be represented either by **а** or **о**: [падн'а́т'] — подня́ть, [като́к] — като́к. The use of the one letter or the other is fully determined by the general rule described in detail in 5.

7. What letters represent vowel sounds after the consonants [ж], [ш], [ч], [щ], [ц].

Three of the so-called sibilants—[ж], [ш] and [ц]—are hard and two—[ч] and [щ]—are soft. The softness of a sibilant is not indicated by any letters. A sibilant (either hard or soft) can be followed only by the letter **а, у, о, и** or **е**, practically never by **ю, я** or **э**, rarely by **ё**, and never by **ы** (with the exception of some groups of words, in which **ы** is written after **ц**). If a *stressed* [а] is heard after a sibilant, then **а** is written; if [у] is heard, **у** is written; if [е] is heard, **е** is written; and if [и] is heard, **и** is written. An exception is the position after **ц** for the sound [и], which may be represented either by **и** or by **ы**. One can decide whether one should write **и** or **ы** after **ц** in the root of a word only after consulting a dictionary; however, only **-ци-** is spelt in the suffixes, and only **-цы** in the endings.

If a stressed [o] is heard after a sibilant, then more often than not **ё** is written in roots, although **o** is also possible (this can be determined only with the help of a dictionary), and in suffixes and endings only **o** is written: ножо́м, огурцо́в, лужо́к, галчо́нок.

If in an *unstressed position* [y] is heard after a sibilant, then **y** is written. If in an unstressed position [a] is heard after a sibilant, then more often than not **a** is written, and much less frequently **o**. To make a decision, one should use the rule described in detail in 5, bearing in mind, however, the possible deviations from it. In accordance with this rule **a** should generally be written in roots, because there are practically no words in which **o** should be spelt that can be confirmed by placing the relevant part of the word under stress. For example, when one hears [шаги́], one should write it down as шаги́, because of шаг; when one hears [шакала́т], one should write шокола́д; however, it is impossible to place this root in a position where **o** would be stressed.

If [и] or [ы] is heard after a sibilant, then either **и** or **e** should be written after **ж** and **ш**, either **и, e** or **a** after **ч** and **щ**, and either **и, ы** or **e** after **ц**.

For the unstressed vowels following **ж, ш, ч** or **щ** in a root, one should use the rule described in 5. When one hears [жыво́й], one should write живо́й, because of жив (**ы** is never written after **ж**); when one hears [шырст'ино́й], one should write шерстяно́й, because of шерсть; when one hears [вы́чис'т'ит'], one should write вы́чистить, because of чи́стый; when one hears [щика́], one should write щека́, because of щёчка; when one hears [чисы́], one should write часы́, because of час, etc.

The use of **и** or **ы** after **ц** in unstressed roots can be determined only with the help of a dictionary. (For the spelling of **цы** and **ци** in suffixes and endings, see above.) The use of the letter **e** or **и/ы** after **ц** is also determined in accordance with the rule described in 5.

Unstressed vowels after a sibilant in the endings are represented in accordance with the rules for the types of declension and conjugation described in this grammar. It is useless to refer to dictionaries in this case.

8. How to represent voiceless and voiced consonants.

If voiceless or voiced consonants are pronounced before a vowel or before the consonant [р], [л], [м], [н], [й] or [в], they are represented by the same letters.

If a voiceless consonant is heard at the end of a word or before a voiceless consonant (including at the juncture of a prefix and a root), one should not immediately write down the letter representing the relevant voiceless consonant. At first one should determine whether this voiceless consonant is in the root, prefix, suffix or the ending. Then one should place this root, prefix or suffix in such a position that the consonant concerned should precede a vowel or [р], [л], [м], [н], [в] or [й] and write down the letter representing the consonant that will be heard in that position. For example, when one hears [го́рат], one should try to place the root in a position before a vowel or [р], [м], [л], [н], [в] or [й]: [гарадо́к], [гарада́]. So one should write го́род. When one hears [патки́нут'], one should first of all single out the prefix and then place it before a vowel or [р], [л], [м], [н], [в] or [й]: [падруби́т']. So one should write подки́нуть. There are cases where, for various reasons, the desired position is impossible. Then one should turn to a dictionary for the spelling of the prefixes, roots and suffixes concerned. The spelling of consonants in the endings **-ть** (of the infinitive) and **-ешь** or **-ишь** (of the 2nd person present/future tense of verbs) conforms to their pronunciation. The markers **-вш-** of participles and **-в** and **-вши** of verbal adverbs are spelt with **в**, contrary to their pronunciation.

If a voiced consonant is heard before another voiced consonant, then before writing it down, one should act in the same way as when one hears a voiceless consonant at the end of a word or before a voiceless consonant. When one hears [адбро́с'ит'], one should find a word in which this prefix precedes a vowel or [р], [л], [м], [н], [в] or [й]: [атру-б'и́т']. So [адбро́с'ит'] should be spelt отбро́сить. When such a procedure is impossible, one should turn to a dictionary, which will give such spellings as вокза́л, анекдо́т, где, зда́ние, здоро́вье, etc.

Exceptions to the rules described in this section is the spelling of the prefixes **из-, воз-, раз-** and **без-**, which are spelt in accordance with their pronunciation: [з] represented by the letter **з**, and [с] by the letter **с**: разде́ться, расписа́ться.

9. How to represent the long sounds [цц], [чч], [шш], [жж], the soft [ш'ш'] and some consonant clusters.

If the sound [ц] is heard in the middle of a word between vowels, it may be represented either by the letter **ц** or by a combination of two letters. Especially often this is a combination of the letters **т** and **с**, the former letter being the final one of the verb ending, and the latter the initial letter of the element **-ся**. In an infinitive the soft mark (**ь**) is written between **т** and **с**: нача́ли ката́ться, реши́л боро́ться. No **ь** is written in finite verb forms: ката́ются, бо́рется. These spellings confirm once again the general principle, described in 5 and 8, in accordance with which each constituent part of a word must be spelt uniformly, irrespective of its pronunciation.

The long sound [цц] is usually pronounced either at the juncture of a prefix terminating in **т** or **д** (of the **от-, под-, над-**, etc. type) and a root beginning with **ц** or at the juncture of a root ending in **т** or **д** and a suffix beginning with **ц**. It is easy to understand that in accordance with the general principle of spelling each constituent part of a word must be spelt uniformly, in this case either **тц** or **дц** should be written. In such cases, too, one should check one's surmise with a dictionary. A long [цц] may also be heard at the juncture of a preposition and a noun, which, as is known, are always written as two words: от ци́рка.

A long [чч] is invariably represented by the letter combination **тч** or дч. As a rule, the boundary separating the constituent parts of a word lies between these two letters. One should place the first constituent part (a prefix or a root) in such a position that its final consonant should precede a vowel or [р], [л], [н], [м], [в] or [й] and write down the letter representing this consonant. For example, when one hears [паччи́стит'], one should place the prefix под- before р: [падры́т']. So [паччи́стит'] should be spelt подчи́стить.

A long [чч] may also be heard at the juncture of a preposition terminating in т or д and a noun or numeral beginning with ч, which, as is known, are written as two words: под часа́ми.

The long sound [шш] is usually represented by the letter combination сш or, less frequently, зш. The boundary between the constituent parts of a word—a prefix and a root—often lies between these two letters. In this position all the prefixes are spelt with с: расшуме́ться, сшить. At the juncture of a root and a suffix the final root consonant is determined in the same way as in the pronunciation of the long [чч] (see above). A long [чч] may also be heard at the juncture of the preposition с or a preposition terminating in з (of the из, без type) and a noun or numeral beginning with ш, which, as is known, are invariably written as two words: без шу́ма.

The long sound [жж] is usually represented by the letter combination зж or сж. The boundary between the constituent parts of a word—a prefix and a root—often lies between these letters. In this position the prefix с- is written as с, and the prefixes terminating in -з (of the из-, без-, etc. type) are written with з: сжать, изжи́ть. A long [жж] may also be heard at the juncture of the preposition с or a preposition terminating in з (of the из, без, etc. type) and a noun beginning with ж, which, as is known, are written as two words: без жены́.

The use of letters for some words with a long [жж] (either hard or soft) is determined by individual rules. Here belong the spellings дожди́, до́ждик, дро́жжи, во́жжи and a number of others.

The long soft sound [ш'ш'] or the sound combination [шч] may be represented by the letter щ: щи, щит, щипа́ть, мощь, etc. However, not infrequently these sounds characterise the boundary between two constituent parts of a word. If they occur at the juncture of a prefix and a root, they may represent the prefix с- or the end of a prefix terminating in з (of the из-, без-, etc. type) and the beginning of a root with the initial ч. In such a case one should always write сч. However, one should consult a dictionary for confirmation. If a long soft [ш'ш'] is heard at the juncture of a root and a suffix, it may represent a combination of a suffix whose beginning is written with ч and the end of a root written with с, з or ж. To decide which letter should be written at the end of the root, one should place this root before a vowel or [р], [л], [н], [м], [в] or [й]. For example, when one hears [муш' ш' и́на], one should distinguish the suffix -чин(а) and the root муж- (because of му́жа, мужи́к). So one should write мужчи́на.

To generalise all the preceding rules, we must once again remind the student that each time he hears a cluster of consonants, he should ask himself whether there is a boundary between the constituent parts of the word; this being the case, he should make sure whether no consonant is missing in the cluster (this may be due to the position of a consonant before another consonant and not before a vowel). For example, when he hears [ме́сный], it is important to see that -н- is a suffix and that the root of this word is the same as in the word ме́сто. So, in accordance with the general principle of Russian spelling, which requires that the constituent parts of words must be spelt uniformly, irrespective of their pronunciation, [ме́сный] should be spelt ме́стный. Exactly in the same way these words should be spelt: счастли́вый, although т in it is not pronounced, because there is the word сча́стье; звёздный, although д in it is not pronounced, because there is the word звезда́; со́лнце, although л is not pronounced, because there is the word со́лнечный; etc.

10. How to indicate the softness of a consonant.

The letters б, в, д, з, л, м, н, п, р, с, т, ф may represent both hard and soft sounds, i.e. б represents both [б] and [б']. The consonant sounds [г], [к] and [х] can be soft practically only when they precede [и] and [е]; in all the other cases they are invariably hard; [ж], [ц] and [ш] are invariably hard, whereas [ч], [щ] and [й] are invariably soft.

The softness of the consonants belonging to the first group may be indicated in different ways. *Before a vowel* their softness is indicated by means of the vowels и, е, ю, я and ё, which designate not only the softness of a consonant, but also a certain vowel sound which follows it.

At the end of words the softness of a consonant is indicated by means of the letter ь.

In the middle of a word before a consonant the softness of л is practically always indicated by means of ь. The softness of other consonants within roots and at the juncture of a root and a suffix is indicated either by means of ь (про́сьба, ре́дька) or not at all. The latter is the case with the consonants б, м, в, п, ф preceding any other consonant, with the consonants с and з preceding т and д, respectively (посте́ль, здесь), with н preceding ч and щ (ко́нчик, го́нщик), and with some others. However, to avoid mistakes when indicating the softness of a consonant preceding another consonant, one is advised to consult a dictionary.

11. How to indicate the sound [й].

Before a vowel (at the beginning of a word or after a vowel) the sound [й], not infrequently indicated by the letter й, is usually represented by the letters е, ю, я and ё, which render not only [й], but also a certain vowel that follows (е́сли, ю́бка, я́корь, ёлочка). In the middle of a word *after a consonant and before a vowel* [й] is usually represented by ъ at the juncture of a prefix and a root: объявле́ние [аб'йавл'е́н'ийе], съезд [с'йэст], and by ь in all the other positions in a word: льют [л'йут], певу́нья [п'эву́н'йа], соловьи́ [салав'йи́]. The numerous exceptions to the preceding rules make it imperative to consult a dictionary to check the spelling of ь and ъ within roots and the spelling of the vowels that follow.

12. When to write ь after ж, ш, ч, щ.

After **ж, ш, ч** and **щ** at the end of a word **ь** is written in the nominative (and the accusative identical with the nominative) of *feminine* nouns: рожь, мышь, дичь, вещь. In the other cases of feminine nouns and in all the cases of nouns *that are not feminine no* **ь** *is written* after **ж, ш, ч** or **щ**: нож, туч.

After **ж, ш, ч** and **щ**, the letter **ь** is written in the *imperative* of verbs: режь, услы́шь. The presence of **-те** or **-ся** does not affect this: ма́жьте, ма́жься. Besides, **ь** is written after **ч** in the infinitive (and also before **-ся**): бере́чь, мочь, стри́чься, and after **ш** in the 2nd person singular present/future tense: зна́ешь, ви́дишь.

13. How to spell adjectival endings in the genitive singular masculine and neuter.

In the genitive singular the endings of masculine and neuter adjectives are pronounced with the sound [в], but are spelt with the letter **г**: до́брого, хоро́шего, второ́го. The same rule holds good in the case of nouns declined like adjectives: вожа́того, пиро́жного.

Игорь Григорьевич
Милославский

КРАТКАЯ
ПРАКТИЧЕСКАЯ ГРАММАТИКА
РУССКОГО ЯЗЫКА

Зав. редакцией *Н. П. Спирина*
Редактор *И. Н. Малахова*
Редактор английского текста *В. А. Гапаков*
Младшие редакторы *М. А. Тарасова, И. И. Шкуропат*
Художественный редактор *Н. И. Терехов*
Технический редактор *В. Ф. Козлова*
Корректор *Г. Н. Кузьмина*

ИБ № 6089

Сдано в набор 10.12.87. Подписано в печать 22.07.88. Формат 60 × 90^1/$_{16}$. Бумага офсетная № 1. Гарнитура таймс. Печать офсетная. Усл. печ. л. 15,5. Усл. кр.-отт. 31,25. Уч.-изд. л. 17,92. Тираж 15 000 экз. Заказ № 1385. Цена 1 р. 10 к.

Издательство «Русский язык» В/О «Совэкспорткнига» Государственного комитета СССР по делам издательств, полиграфии и книжной торговли. 103012 Москва, Старопанский пер., д.1/5.

Можайский полиграфкомбинат В/О «Совэкспорткнига» Государственного комитета СССР по делам издательств, полиграфии и книжной торговли. 143200 Можайск, ул. Мира, 93.

В 1989 ГОДУ В ИЗДАТЕЛЬСТВЕ «РУССКИЙ ЯЗЫК» ВЫЙДЕТ В СВЕТ

ХАЛИЗЕВА В. С., БЕЛЯКОВА Н. Н., ВОРОБЬЕВА Г. Ф. СБОРНИК УПРАЖНЕНИЙ ПО СИНТАКСИСУ РУССКОГО ЯЗЫКА (С КОММЕНТАРИЯМИ). ПРОСТОЕ ПРЕДЛОЖЕНИЕ: Учебное пособие (для говорящих на английском языке) — 6-е изд., перераб.

Учебное пособие предназначено для взрослых, изучающих русский язык за рубежом самостоятельно или под руководством преподавателя и имеющих начальную языковую подготовку.

Основное внимание в пособии уделяется трудным вопросам синтаксиса простого предложения: согласованию и управлению, употреблению наклонения, вида и времени глагола в зависимости от словосочетаний и т. п. В сборник включены задания лексико-синтаксического характера. Многие упражнения снабжены комментарием. Продвинутый этап обучения.

ХАЛИЗЕВА В. С., БЕЛЯКОВА Н. Н., ВОРОБЬЕВА Г. Ф. СБОРНИК УПРАЖНЕНИЙ ПО СИНТАКСИСУ РУССКОГО ЯЗЫКА (С КОММЕНТАРИЯМИ). СЛОЖНОЕ ПРЕДЛОЖЕНИЕ: Учебное пособие (для говорящих на английском языке) — 6-е изд., перераб.

Учебное пособие предназначено для взрослых, изучающих русский язык за рубежом самостоятельно или под руководством преподавателя и имеющих начальную языковую подготовку.

Основное внимание в пособии уделяется трудным вопросам синтаксиса сложного предложения: употреблению союзов и союзных слов, соподчиненности предложений и т. п. В сборник включены упражнения лексико-синтаксического характера. Многие упражнения снабжены комментарием. Продвинутый этап обучения.

В 1989 ГОДУ В ИЗДАТЕЛЬСТВЕ «РУССКИЙ ЯЗЫК» ВЫЙДЕТ В СВЕТ

ЛОПАТИН В. В., МИЛОСЛАВСКИЙ И. Г., ШЕЛЯКИН М. А. СОВРЕМЕННЫЙ РУССКИЙ ЯЗЫК. ТЕОРЕТИЧЕСКИЙ КУРС. СЛОВООБРАЗОВАНИЕ. МОРФОЛОГИЯ. (Под ред. Иванова В. В.)

Учебник предназначен для студентов отделений и факультетов, готовящих преподавателей русского языка как иностранного.

В учебнике освещены основные особенности морфемики, словообразовательного и морфологического строя современного русского языка, функционирование основных видов морфем.

**В 1989 ГОДУ
В ИЗДАТЕЛЬСТВЕ «РУССКИЙ ЯЗЫК»
ВЫЙДЕТ В СВЕТ**

АКИШИНА А. А., БАРАНОВСКАЯ С. А. РУССКАЯ ФОНЕТИКА.— 2-е изд., испр.

В пособии рассматриваются основные вопросы общей фонетики, анатомо-физиологические основы образования звуков речи, излагаются принципы классификации гласных и согласных. Центральное место занимает описание артикуляции русских звуков. Особенности звукового строя русского языка освещаются в системе данных общей фонетики.

Предназначается для преподавателей русского языка как иностранного, аспирантов и студентов-филологов.